용자비

DRAGON HUNTER

4

DRAGON HUNTER

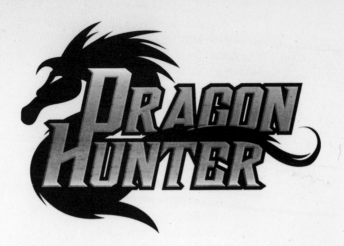

Translator - Hye-Young Im
English Adaptation - J. Torres
Copy Editors - Bryce P. Coleman, Carol Fox
Retouch and Lettering - Deron Bennett
Cover Layout - Patrick Hook
Editor - Rob Tokar

Managing Editor - Jill Freshney
Production Coordinator - Antonio DePietro
Production Managers - Jennifer Miller, Mutsumi Miyazaki
Art Director - Matt Alford
Editorial Director - Jeremy Ross
VP of Production - Ron Klamert
President & C.O.O. - John Parker
Publisher & C.E.O. - Stuart Levy

Email: editor@TOKYOPOP.com
Come visit us online at www.TOKYOPOP.com

A  Manga

TOKYOPOP Inc.
5900 Wilshire Blvd. Suite 2000
Los Angeles, CA 90036

Dragon Hunter Vol. 4

Dragon Hunter © 2000 by Hong Seock Seo
All rights reserved. First published in Korea in 2000 by SEOUL CULTURAL PUBLISHERS Inc., Seoul.
English translation rights arranged by SEOUL CULTURAL PUBLISHERS Inc.

English text copyright ©2004 TOKYOPOP Inc.

ISBN: 1-59182-434-6
First TOKYOPOP printing: January 2004

10 9 8 7 6 5 4 3 2 1
Printed in the USA

Dragon Hunter

Volume 4

By

Hong Seock Seo

With

Studio Redstone

TOKYOPOP®

Los Angeles • Tokyo • London

WHO'S WHO IN DRAGON HUNTER

SEUR-CHONG

There's only one thing Seur-Chong loves more than hunting dragons, and that's getting paid for doing it. He's infected with the Dragon's Curse, a condition which gives him incredible strength and stamina, but is slowly killing him. Despite his greedy nature, he has a heart almost as big as his enormous sword.

As far back as he can remember, Seur-Chong was part of the gang of assassins known as the Yong-Chun. He doesn't recall when he started working for them or why...only that life was forfeit if he didn't. The closest thing Seur-Chong had to a father figure was his master, the Captain of the Fight Instructors. Seur-Chong's master also mentored Kok-Jung, despite worries about the young man's innate brutality. Seur-Chong and Kok-Jung were like brothers...until the master defected from the Yong-Chun.

Unfortunately, quitting the Yong-Chun is considered betrayal and betrayal is punishable by death. The Yong-Chun offered the Captain of the Fight Instructors' job as a reward for whomever killed him. Seur-Chong could never kill his own master...but Kok-Jung had no such qualms. That day, Seur-Chong decided to leave the Yong-Chun and, soon after, the politically troubled country splintered into many new kingdoms. Many members of the Yong-Chun were absorbed into the Chunjoo, a group that has already tried to kill Seur-Chong and his associates.

In the context of this book, Mi-Ru-Me is Seur-Chong's title and means "The best of all dragon hunters." In Korean, Mi-Ru (mee-roo) is an old word for dragon and "me" (meh) means mountain peak. Together, the two terms mean "best" or "highest".

MYUNG-HO:

A rare male shaman born with exceptional gifts (most shaman are female), Myung-Ho can cast spells that confuse or control the minds of most dragons. Myung-Ho lost his right eye during a dragon hunt that went awry. In an uncharacteristic moment of sympathy, Seur-Chong helped Myung-Ho in his moment of need and the two young men became business partners.

Recently, during a particularly difficult dragon hunt, Seur-Chong and Myung-Ho were betrayed by the Chunjoo, a mysterious and powerful dragon-hunting gang that doesn't tolerate competition. The Chunjoo planned to kill Myung-Ho and, with him, the control spell Myung-Ho was casting. With the spell gone, Seur-Chong would have been no match for the dragon. In the ensuing melee, Myung-Ho was mortally wounded.

Seeing only one way to save Myung-Ho's life, Seur-Chong gave his dying friend a drink of dragon's blood. The young shaman's strength was restored, but now Myung-Ho must endure the dreaded dragon's curse: power that will eventually cost him his life. Myung-Ho has already manifested an incredible "second sight"...seen through a monstrous third eye in the middle of his forehead!

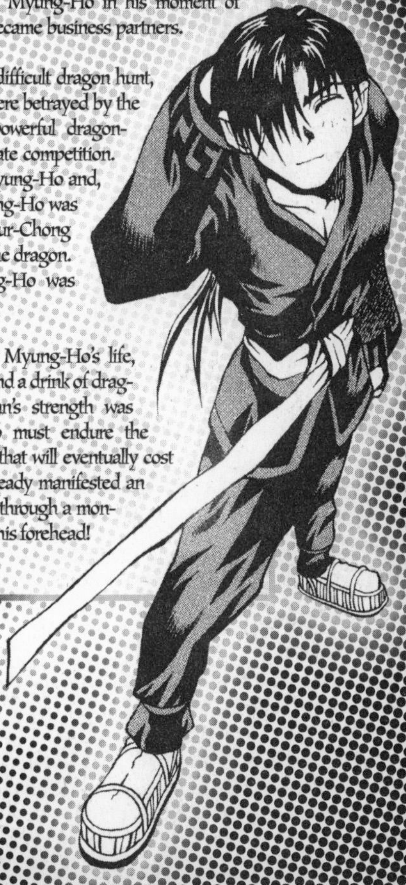

MONG-YEUN:

A Shaman with a soft spot for dragons, she was in So-Chun's service until she stole a dragon from her master. Now she's joined with Seur-Chong and Myung-Ho, but she finds the mercenary lifestyle not to her liking.

ARANSEUR:

Myung-Ho's little sister, Aranseur is a swindler and petty thief. Her brother cares a great deal for her, but lost touch with her for a long time. Aranseur doesn't like Seur-Chong and thinks he uses her brother for his own selfish gains.

SO-CHUN:

A powerful shaman priestess, she's also the feudal lord of the Kaya Province.

THE GENERAL / DAECHANG-NIM:

Leader of the Invisible Shadow Killer Clan of the Chunjoo. Like Seur-Chong, he has the Dragon's Curse. It's rumored that he once fought the Dragon King himself. (NOTE: Daechang means "leader" or "boss" and "Nim" is an honorific term comparable to "sama" in Japanese (which is the more honorific form of "san".)

RU-AHN:

The general's right-hand-woman. Ru-ahn's weapon of choice is The Five Hand Spear, a glove with five long retractable claws. Ru-ahn is responsible for mortally wounding Myung-Ho.

CHUNJOO:

A shadowy clan of professional dragon hunters originally from Bal-Hae. Over the years, their numbers grew as they forced independent Dragon Hunters to join them...or die. Now, the clan is huge and powerful and still just as determined to wipe out their competition as they are to kill dragons.

INVISIBLE SHADOW KILLER CLAN OF THE CHUNJOO:

Assassins for the Chunjoo, charged with killing rival dragon hunters.

KOK-JUNG / TAE-RANG

A former colleague of Seur-Chong, whom Seur-Chong holds responsible for killing their master. Kok-Jung tries to go by the name Tae-Rang to avoid having people laugh at his given name (which means "worry" in Korean.)

THE YONG-CHUN GANG

A Dragon Hunting organization to which Seur-Chong and Kok-Jung once belonged. When Seur-Chong decided to leave the Yong-Chun, Kok-Jung declared Seur-Chong his enemy. On Seur-Chong's last hunt with the Yong-Chun, Seur-Chong met Myung-Ho and Myung-Ho lost his left eye.

SUN-HWA

A female shaman who lives in the Shi-La region.

JOJANG

The leader of the Japanese force that is after the Man-Pa-Shin-Juck.

MOON-MU

A beloved king of Shi-La, Moon-Mu was so upset by war and piracy in his land that he was determined to continue fighting it even after his death. Moon-Mu's final wish was to have his ashes cast upon the East Sea so he could become a guardian dragon for his country and bring peace to Shi-La. It is believed that Moon-Mu did, in fact, become the guardian dragon of Shi-La.

MAN-PA-SHIN-JUCK

A national treasure of Shin-La, this legendary magic flute is rumored to have come from a dragon that lived on a turtle-shaped island in the East Sea. Its name means "Tame the waves and bring peace into this world" and it is kept in a special vault called the Chun-Jon-Go in the city of Wal-Sung. The shamans who take care of the guardian dragon of Shi-La also protect the magic flute.

KING SHIN-MOON

Successor to Moon-Mu, Shin-Moon erected the Gam-Eun-Sa temple facing the East Sea in honor of Moon-Mu.

THE STORY THUS FAR

...

SEUR-CHONG IS AN ELITE (AND CASH-OBSESSED) DRAGON HUNTER WHO, DUE TO AN INVOLUNTARY INFUSION OF DRAGON'S BLOOD, POSSESSES INCREDIBLE STRENGTH AND DURABILITY...ALONG WITH A SUBSTANTIALLY SHORTENED LIFESPAN. SEUR-CHONG'S PARTNER, MYUNG-HO, IS A SHAMAN WHO CAN USE MAGIC TO CONTROL DRAGONS--AND THUS MAKE THEM EASIER TO KILL.

ALWAYS SEEKING WAYS TO EARN MORE MONEY, THE DUO ACCEPTED AN ASSIGNMENT FROM THE RULERS OF THE KAYA PROVINCE TO DESTROY A WATER DRAGON. THIS ALREADY DIFFICULT TASK WAS MADE EVEN HARDER BY INTERFERENCE FROM THE CHUNJOO, A MYSTERIOUS AND POWERFUL DRAGON-HUNTING GANG THAT DOESN'T TOLERATE COMPETITION. IN THE ENSUING MELEE, MYUNG-HO WAS MORTALLY WOUNDED.

IN RETALIATION, A VENGEFUL SEUR-CHONG VISITED THE LOCAL CHUNJOO HEADQUARTERS AND SINGLE-HANDEDLY WIPED OUT EVERYONE THERE. SEEING ONLY ONE WAY TO SAVE MYUNG-HO'S LIFE, SEUR-CHONG GAVE HIS DYING FRIEND A DRINK OF DRAGON'S BLOOD. THE YOUNG SHAMAN'S STRENGTH WAS RESTORED, BUT NOW MYUNG-HO MUST ENDURE THE DREADED DRAGON'S CURSE: POWER THAT WILL EVENTUALLY COST HIM HIS LIFE. MYUNG-HO HAS ALREADY MANIFESTED AN INCREDIBLE "SECOND SIGHT"...SEEN THROUGH A MONSTROUS THIRD EYE IN THE MIDDLE OF HIS FOREHEAD!

AFTER NARROWLY DEFEATING AN ASSASSIN FROM THE INVISIBLE SHADOW KILLER CLAN OF THE CHUNJOO, SEUR-CHONG AND COMPANY LEFT THE KAYA PROVINCE FOR SHI-LA. THEIR QUEST: TO END THE DRAGON'S CURSE ON THE TWO MEN BY SLAYING THE DRAGON GOD. OF COURSE, NOBODY GETS TO THE DRAGON GOD WITHOUT FIRST DEALING WITH THE DRAGON GOD'S GUARDIAN...AND THE DRAGON GOD'S GUARDIAN HAS NEVER BEEN DEFEATED.

AS THEY NEARED SHI-LA, THE DRAGON HUNTING DUO WERE SIDETRACKED BY A DESPERATE WOMAN NAMED SUN-HWA. SHE, TOO, IS A SHAMAN, AND SHE'S IN POSSESSION OF THE MAN-PA-SHIN-JUCK, A POWERFUL AND LEGENDARY MAGIC FLUTE. PURSUED BY A SINISTER GROUP OF JAPANESE NINJAS WHO WANT THE FLUTE FOR THEMSELVES, SUN-HWA BEGGED SEUR-CHONG FOR HELP BEFORE PASSING OUT.

TRUE TO FORM, SEUR-CHONG CLAIMED THE MAN-PA-SHIN-JUCK FOR HIMSELF AND TOOK OUT MOST OF THE NINJAS IN HIS EFFORT TO KEEP IT. AS THE LEADER OF THE NINJAS THREATENED SEUR-CHONG'S LIFE, THE RECKLESS DRAGON HUNTER DECIDED TO TEST THE LEGEND OF THE FLUTE'S INCREDIBLE POWER...BY PLAYING IT HIMSELF!

DRAGON HUNTER

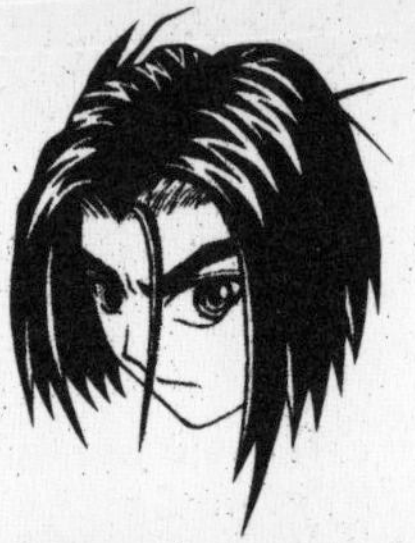

ABOUT DRAGON HUNTER, PART 4

I've said it before and I'll say it again: the country called "Korea" in this comic book is a fictional place! *Dragon Hunter* is not intended to be a history lesson. Sure, some of the characters are real people from Korea's past, and some of the places really do appear on the map. Or, at least, they might have a long, long time ago. But make no mistake about it--this story is complete fantasy. I'm making the whole thing up.

If any of you don't believe me, I'd like to point out one small detail: *Dragon Hunter* has dragons in it! Get it? That's fantasy. I created the characters and I make them fight those mystical beasts known as dragons, all in a world of my own design.

I know what you're thinking. "If everything in the story is made up, why set the whole thing in Korea?" The answer is simple. I love Korean history. But I never intended the saga of *Dragon Hunter* to be restricted by the real history of my country.

In the previous volume, I told you that *Dragon Hunter* will eventually feature western-style dragons in addition to Korean-style dragons. Think of our journey through dragon lore as you would any other type of travel. First, you visit nearby places. Later, you move on to unfamiliar, foreign settings. That's why it would be weird if I threw in western dragons early in the story. Be patient. I'm saving them--they'll appear at just the right time, when we're all ready for them. Don't touch that dial! Or at least, keep buying the *Dragon Hunter* books. You'll see all sorts of dragons before we're done.

For now, enjoy this installment, based on the legend of the magic flute, the Man-Pa-Shin-Juck!

Hong Seock Seo

MAN-PA-SHIN-JUCK: THE MAGIC FLUTE

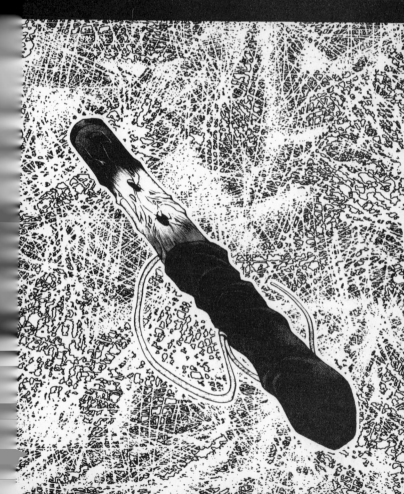

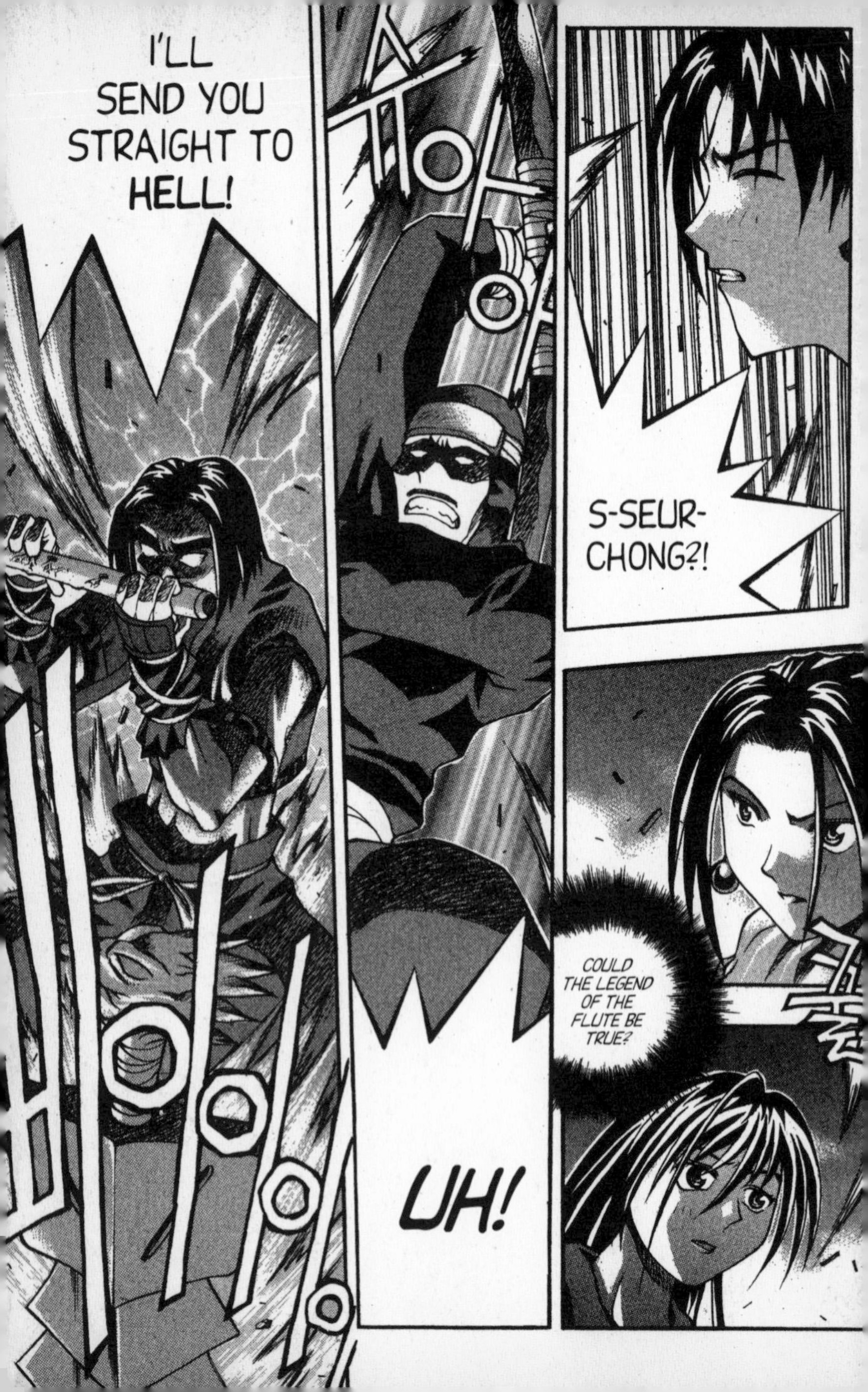
I'LL SEND YOU STRAIGHT TO HELL!
UH!
S-SEUR-CHONG?!
COULD THE LEGEND OF THE FLUTE BE TRUE?

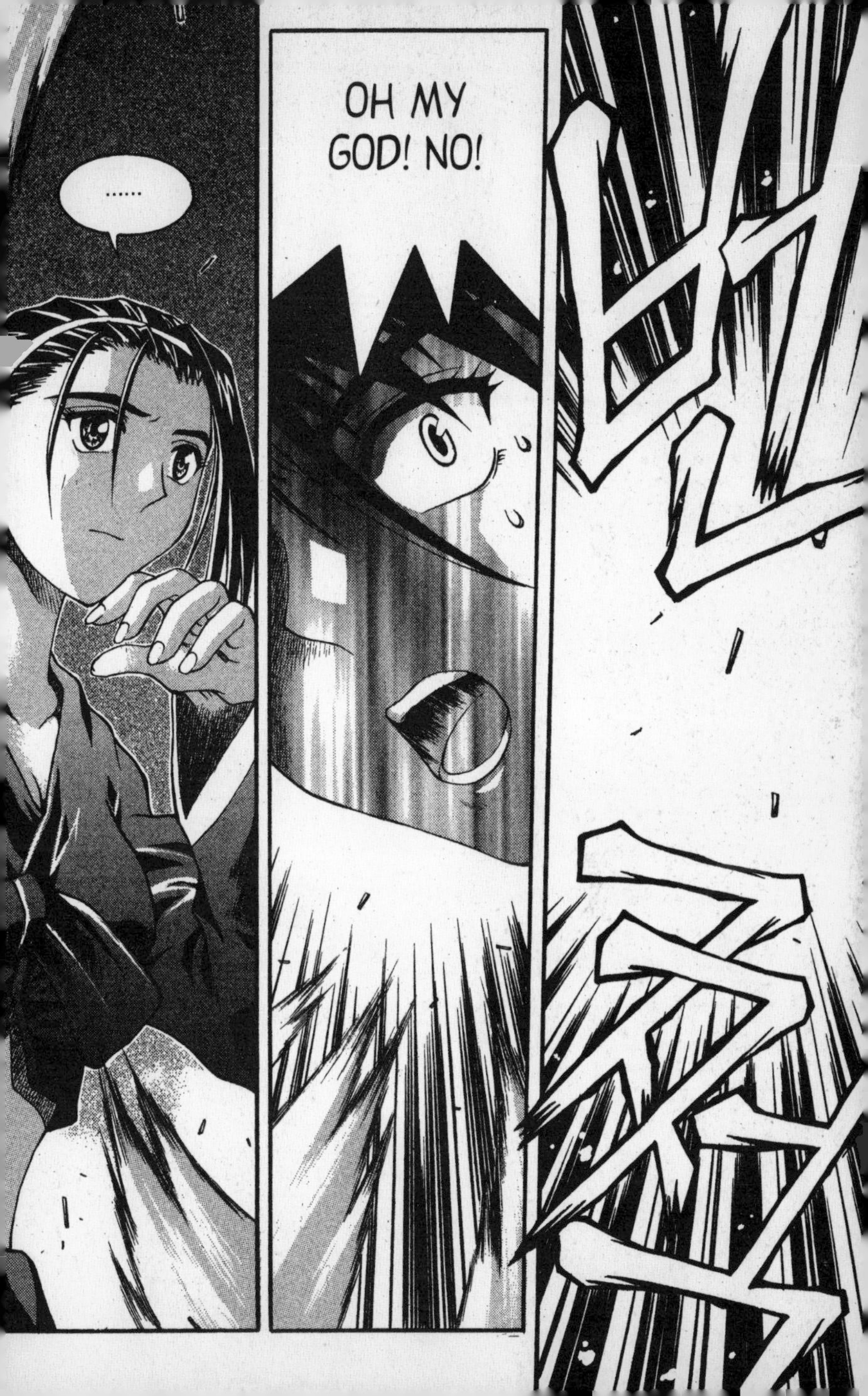
......
OH MY GOD! NO!

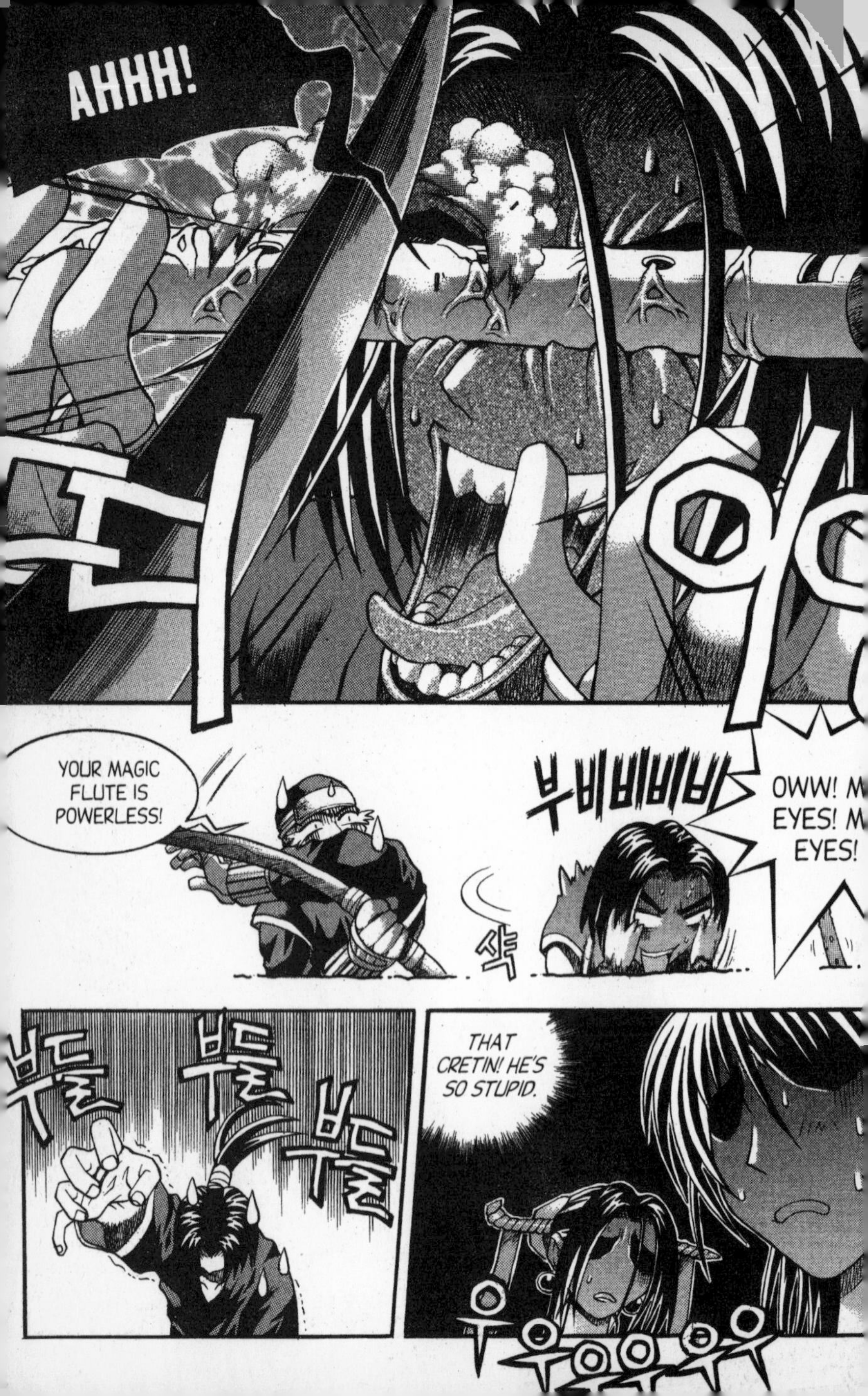
AHHH!
YOUR MAGIC FLUTE IS POWERLESS!
부비비비비
OWW! M EYES! M EYES!
샥
부들 부들 부들
THAT CRETIN! HE'S SO STUPID.

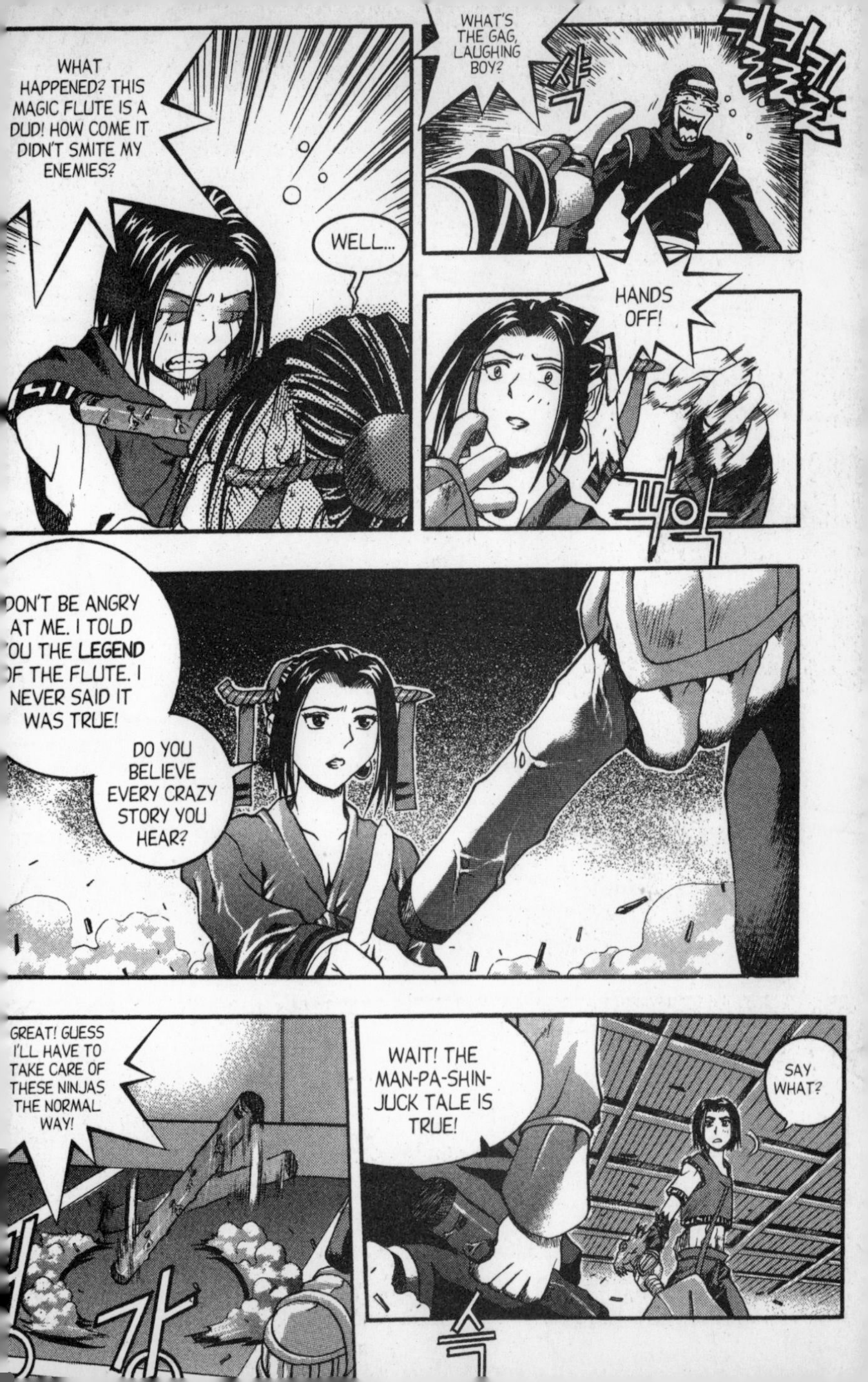
WHAT HAPPENED? THIS MAGIC FLUTE IS A DUD! HOW COME IT DIDN'T SMITE MY ENEMIES?
WELL...
WHAT'S THE GAG, LAUGHING BOY?
HANDS OFF!
DON'T BE ANGRY AT ME. I TOLD YOU THE **LEGEND** OF THE FLUTE. I NEVER SAID IT WAS TRUE!
DO YOU BELIEVE EVERY CRAZY STORY YOU HEAR?
GREAT! GUESS I'LL HAVE TO TAKE CARE OF THESE NINJAS THE NORMAL WAY!
WAIT! THE MAN-PA-SHIN-JUCK TALE IS TRUE!
SAY WHAT?

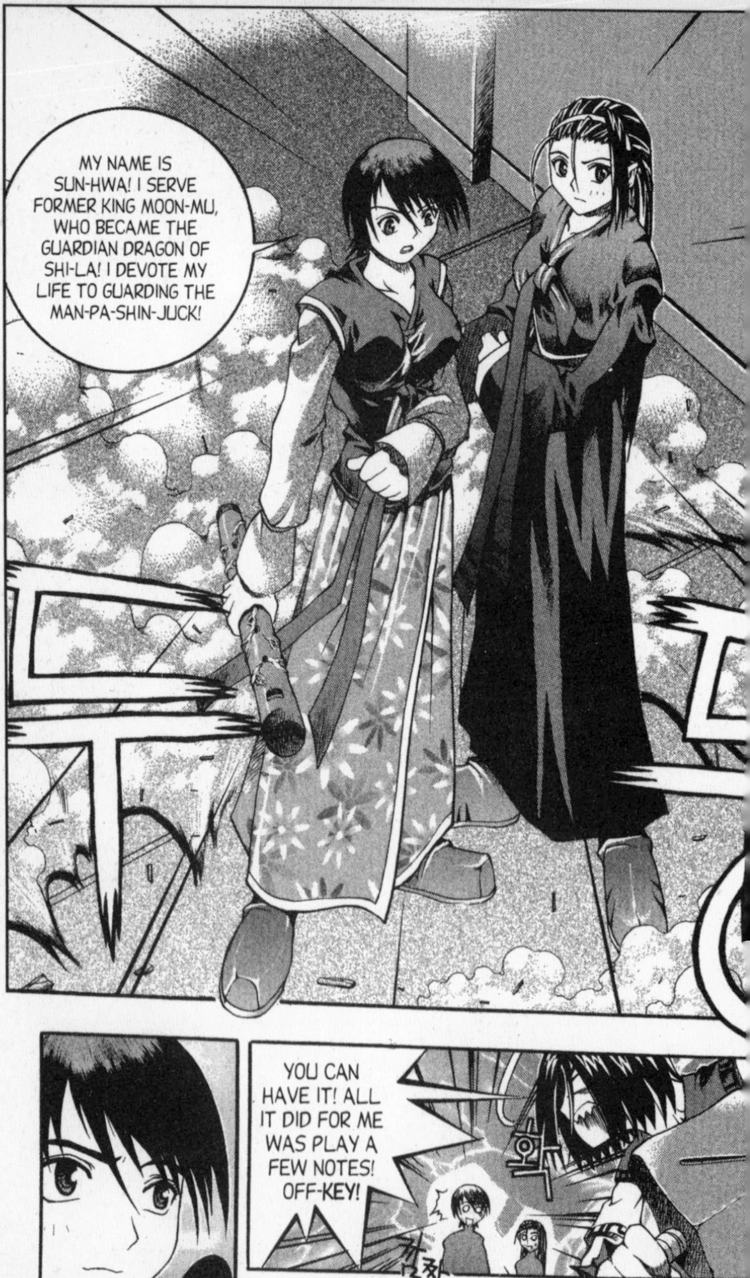
MY NAME IS SUN-HWA! I SERVE FORMER KING MOON-MU, WHO BECAME THE GUARDIAN DRAGON OF SHI-LA! I DEVOTE MY LIFE TO GUARDING THE MAN-PA-SHIN-JUCK!
SIGH
YOU CAN HAVE IT! ALL IT DID FOR ME WAS PLAY A FEW NOTES! OFF-KEY!

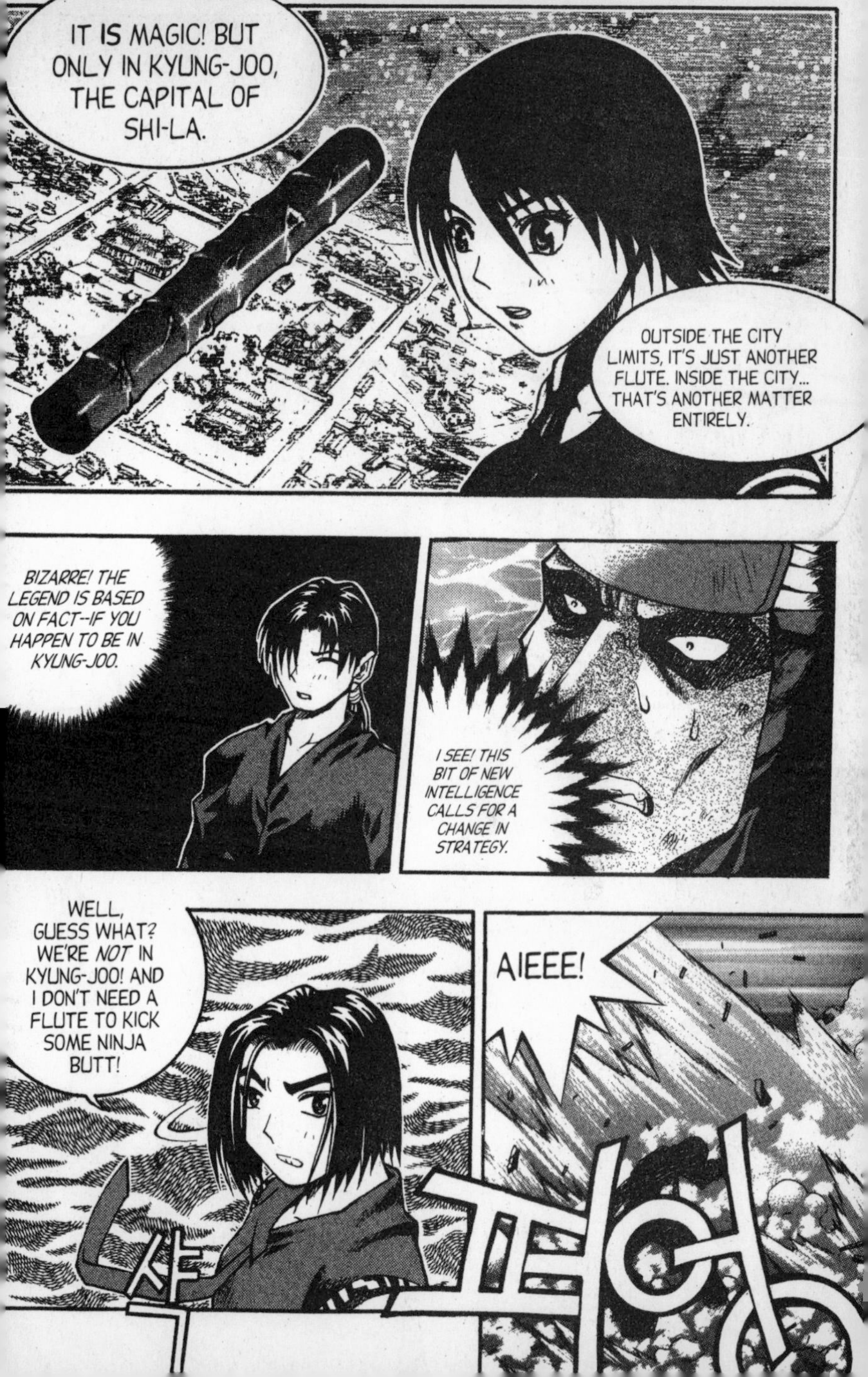
IT IS MAGIC! BUT ONLY IN KYUNG-JOO, THE CAPITAL OF SHI-LA.
OUTSIDE THE CITY LIMITS, IT'S JUST ANOTHER FLUTE. INSIDE THE CITY... THAT'S ANOTHER MATTER ENTIRELY.
BIZARRE! THE LEGEND IS BASED ON FACT--IF YOU HAPPEN TO BE IN KYUNG-JOO.
I SEE! THIS BIT OF NEW INTELLIGENCE CALLS FOR A CHANGE IN STRATEGY.
WELL, GUESS WHAT? WE'RE NOT IN KYUNG-JOO! AND I DON'T NEED A FLUTE TO KICK SOME NINJA BUTT!
AIEEE!

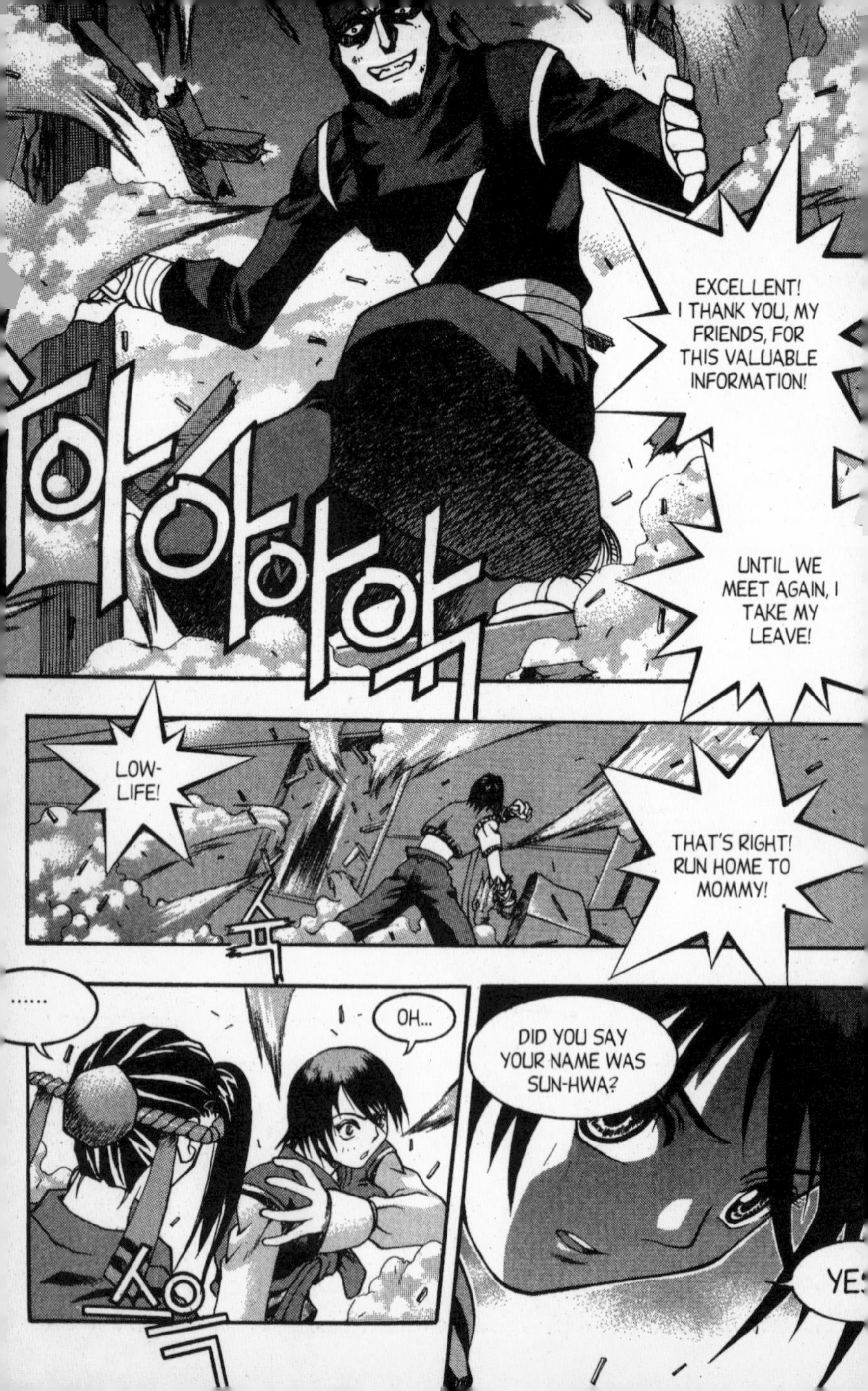

EXCELLENT! I THANK YOU, MY FRIENDS, FOR THIS VALUABLE INFORMATION!
UNTIL WE MEET AGAIN, I TAKE MY LEAVE!
LOW-LIFE!
THAT'S RIGHT! RUN HOME TO MOMMY!
......
OH...
DID YOU SAY YOUR NAME WAS SUN-HWA?
YE

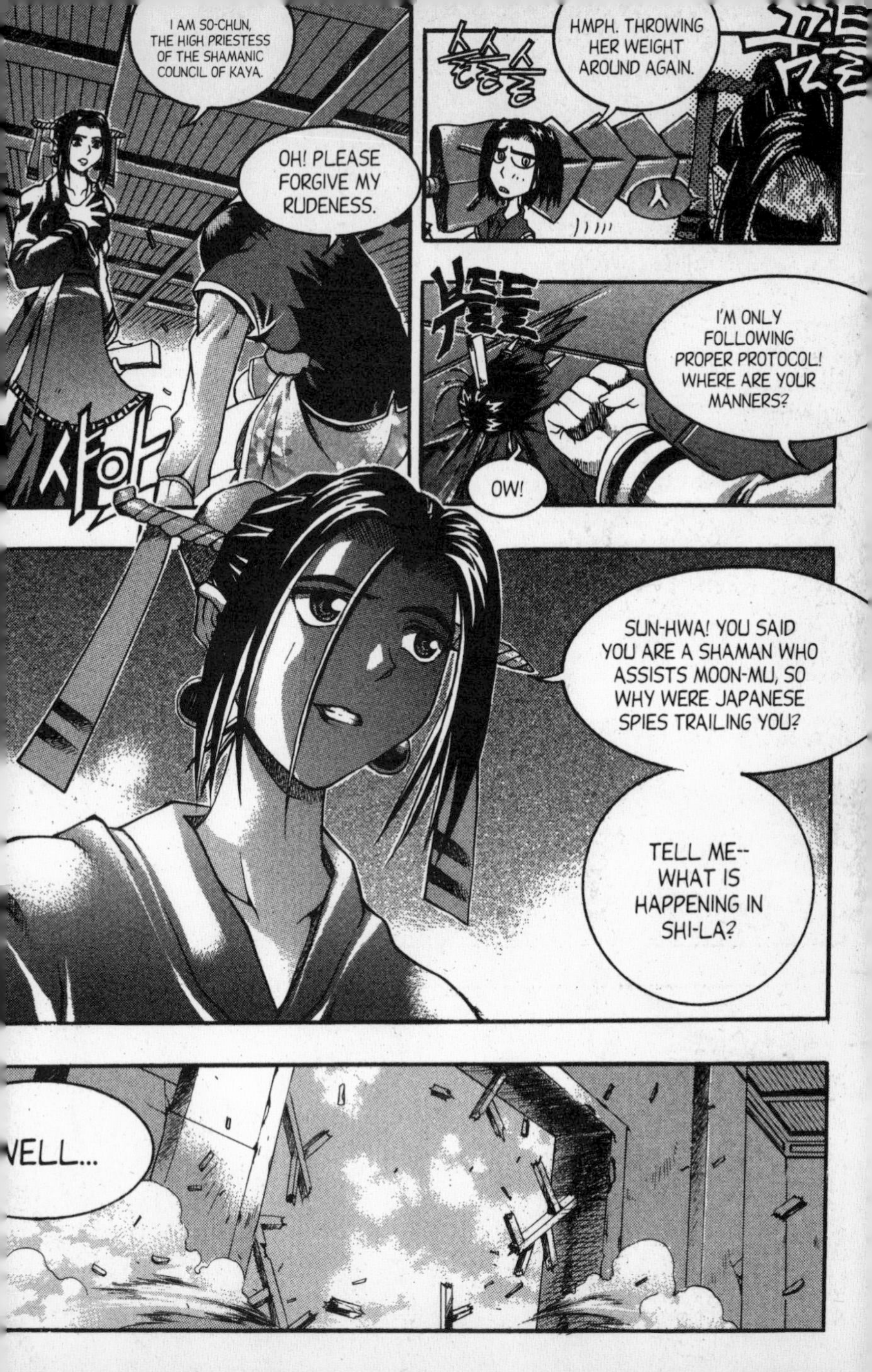
I AM SO-CHUN, THE HIGH PRIESTESS OF THE SHAMANIC COUNCIL OF KAYA.
OH! PLEASE FORGIVE MY RUDENESS.
HMPH. THROWING HER WEIGHT AROUND AGAIN.
I'M ONLY FOLLOWING PROPER PROTOCOL! WHERE ARE YOUR MANNERS?
OW!
SUN-HWA! YOU SAID YOU ARE A SHAMAN WHO ASSISTS MOON-MU, SO WHY WERE JAPANESE SPIES TRAILING YOU?
TELL ME--WHAT IS HAPPENING IN SHI-LA?
WELL...

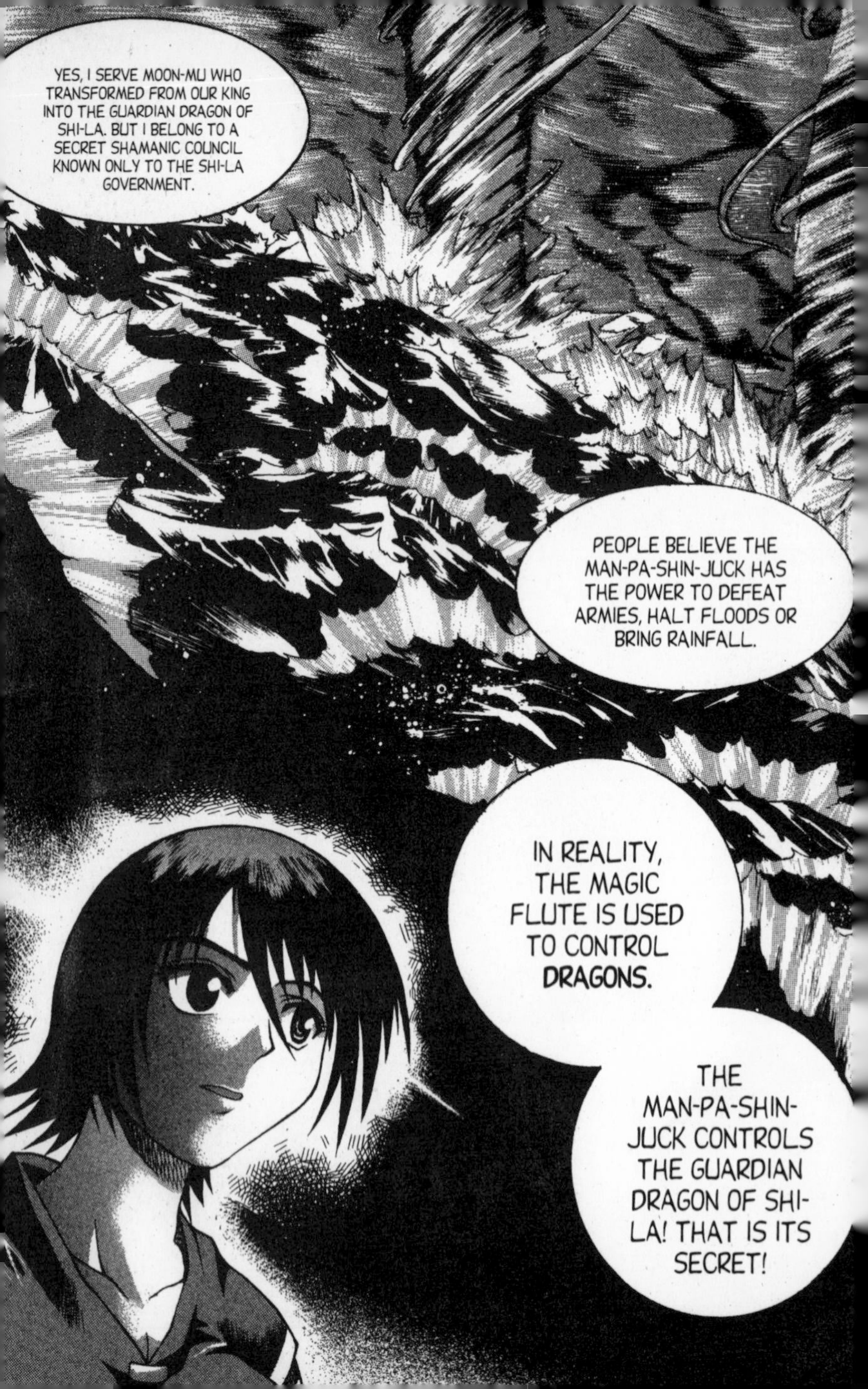
YES, I SERVE MOON-MU WHO TRANSFORMED FROM OUR KING INTO THE GUARDIAN DRAGON OF SHI-LA. BUT I BELONG TO A SECRET SHAMANIC COUNCIL KNOWN ONLY TO THE SHI-LA GOVERNMENT.
PEOPLE BELIEVE THE MAN-PA-SHIN-JUCK HAS THE POWER TO DEFEAT ARMIES, HALT FLOODS OR BRING RAINFALL.
IN REALITY, THE MAGIC FLUTE IS USED TO CONTROL **DRAGONS.**
THE MAN-PA-SHIN-JUCK CONTROLS THE GUARDIAN DRAGON OF SHI-LA! THAT IS ITS SECRET!

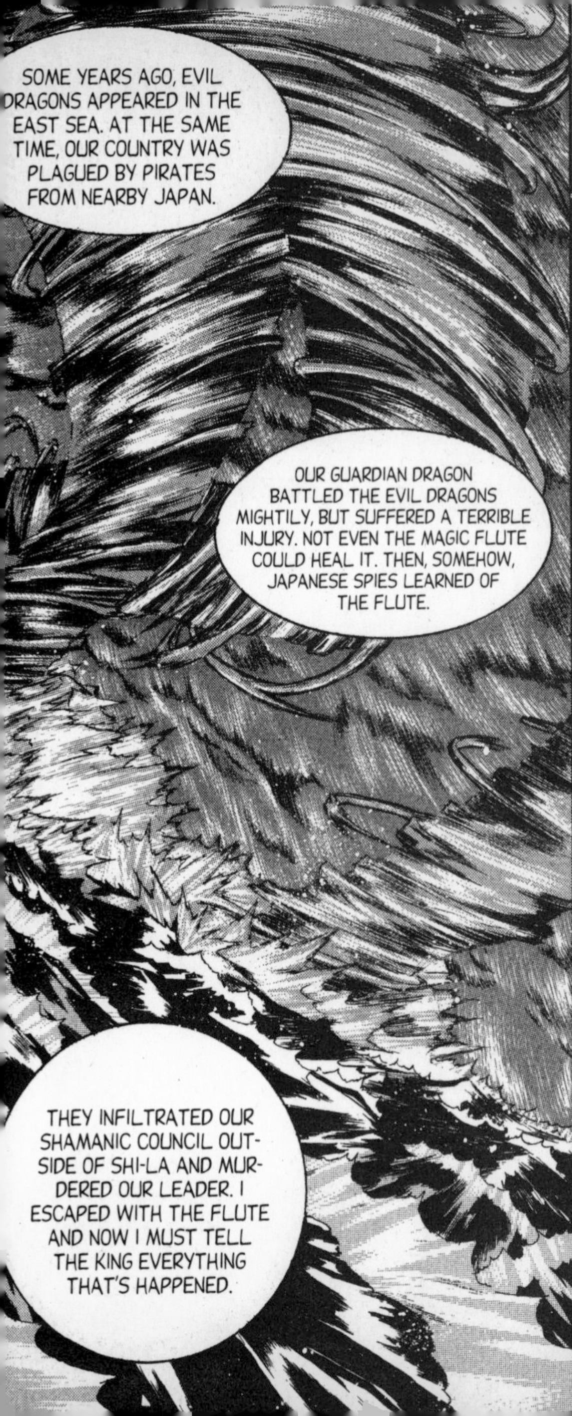
SOME YEARS AGO, EVIL DRAGONS APPEARED IN THE EAST SEA. AT THE SAME TIME, OUR COUNTRY WAS PLAGUED BY PIRATES FROM NEARBY JAPAN.
OUR GUARDIAN DRAGON BATTLED THE EVIL DRAGONS MIGHTILY, BUT SUFFERED A TERRIBLE INJURY. NOT EVEN THE MAGIC FLUTE COULD HEAL IT. THEN, SOMEHOW, JAPANESE SPIES LEARNED OF THE FLUTE.
THEY INFILTRATED OUR SHAMANIC COUNCIL OUTSIDE OF SHI-LA AND MURDERED OUR LEADER. I ESCAPED WITH THE FLUTE AND NOW I MUST TELL THE KING EVERYTHING THAT'S HAPPENED.

Dragon Hunter's Encyclopedia

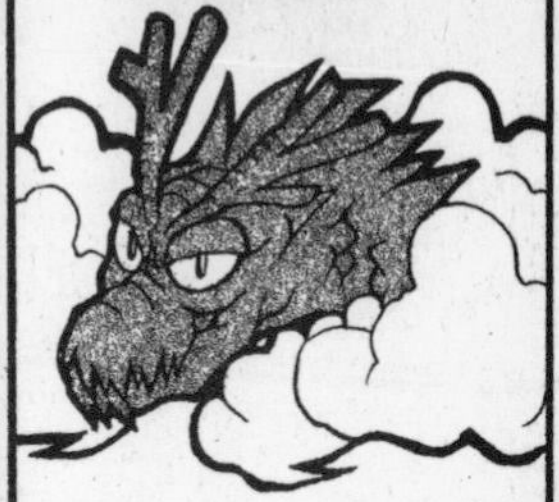

About Imogi, Part 3

Imogi come in many breeds, but they can be divided into four categories: Shin, Woo-Ryong (or Ee), Hong-Ye and Kil-Jo

Shin originated in ancient China. They have antlers and dark black scales. Below the waist, their scales point upwards towards the face, and scales above the waist grow in the opposite direction. Shin dragons have the psychic power to project mirages, a very useful ability when hunting for food. The Shin's favorite dish is sparrow, so people who live near a Shin dragon's nest are well advised to leave sparrow off their dinner menus. Shin is considered a very rare species of dragon. A Shin egg results from a snake mating with a pheasant. Clouds will form around the egg, and lightning is drawn to it. When an egg is struck by lightning, it is driven deep underground, where it hardens into a rock. After 200-300 years, this rock emerges from the depths of the Earth. Once the rock is bathed in moonlight, a Shin hatches, fully grown. Because of this complicated process, the Shin is often looked upon as a full-fledged dragon, rather than an Imogi. Stick with Dragon Hunter, and you'll see Shin dragons soon. Next time, I will tell you a bit about Woo-Ryong (Ee). See you then!

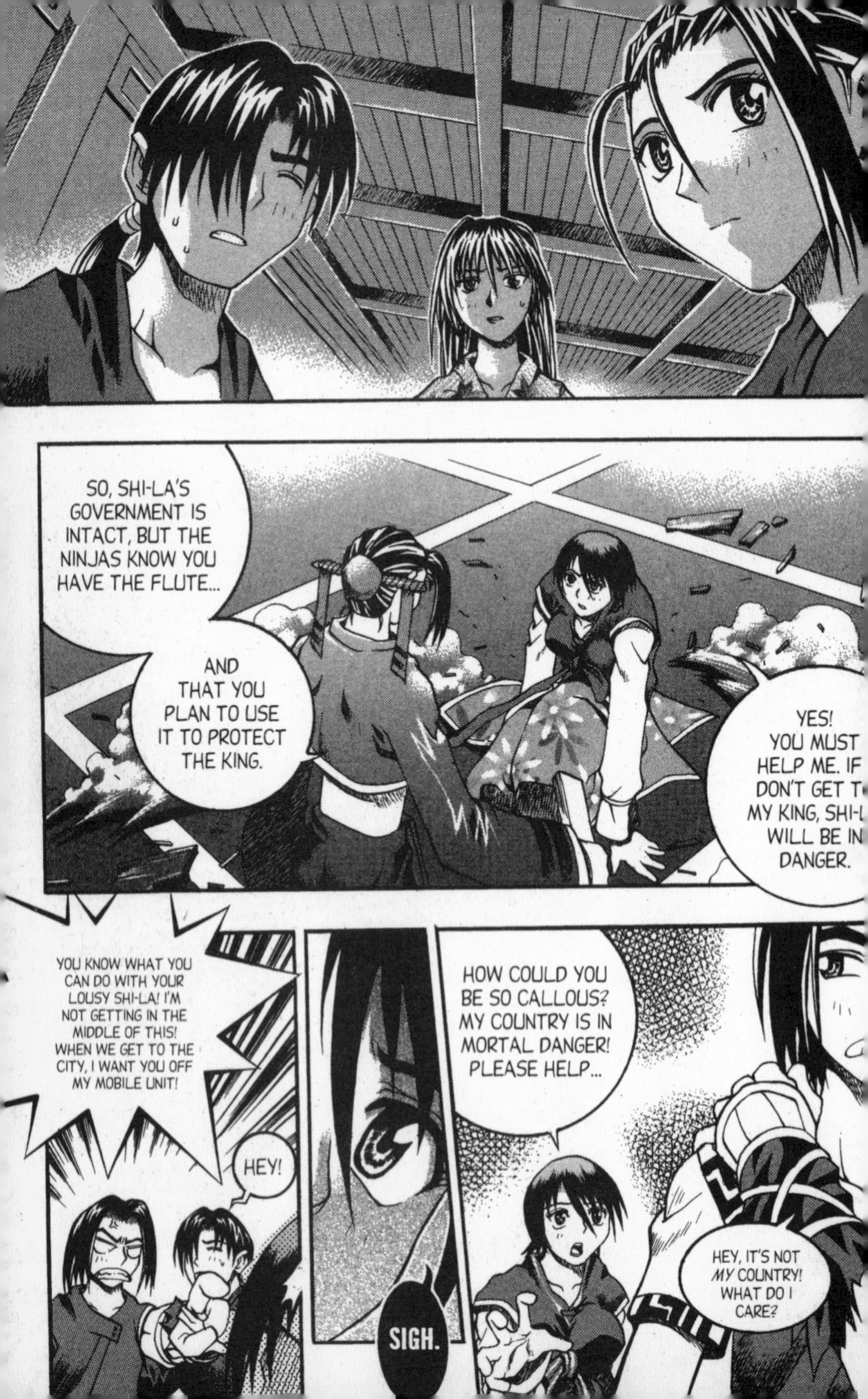
SO, SHI-LA'S GOVERNMENT IS INTACT, BUT THE NINJAS KNOW YOU HAVE THE FLUTE...
AND THAT YOU PLAN TO USE IT TO PROTECT THE KING.
YES! YOU MUST HELP ME. IF DON'T GET T MY KING, SHI-L WILL BE IN DANGER.
YOU KNOW WHAT YOU CAN DO WITH YOUR LOUSY SHI-LA! I'M NOT GETTING IN THE MIDDLE OF THIS! WHEN WE GET TO THE CITY, I WANT YOU OFF MY MOBILE UNIT!
HEY!
SIGH.
HOW COULD YOU BE SO CALLOUS? MY COUNTRY IS IN MORTAL DANGER! PLEASE HELP...
HEY, IT'S NOT *MY* COUNTRY! WHAT DO I CARE?

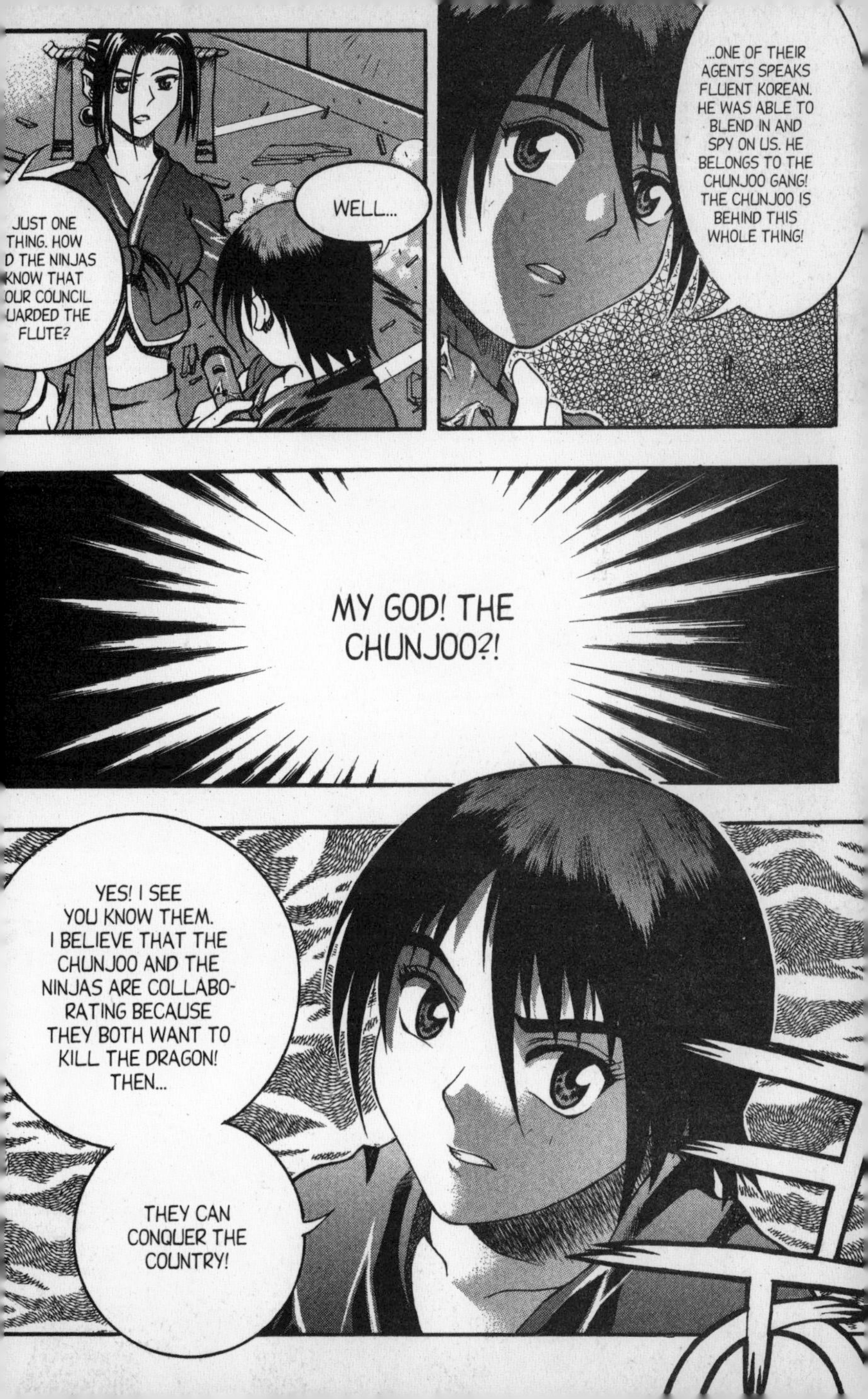
JUST ONE THING. HOW D THE NINJAS KNOW THAT OUR COUNCIL UARDED THE FLUTE?
WELL...
...ONE OF THEIR AGENTS SPEAKS FLUENT KOREAN. HE WAS ABLE TO BLEND IN AND SPY ON US. HE BELONGS TO THE CHUNJOO GANG! THE CHUNJOO IS BEHIND THIS WHOLE THING!
MY GOD! THE CHUNJOO?!
YES! I SEE YOU KNOW THEM. I BELIEVE THAT THE CHUNJOO AND THE NINJAS ARE COLLABO-RATING BECAUSE THEY BOTH WANT TO KILL THE DRAGON! THEN...
THEY CAN CONQUER THE COUNTRY!

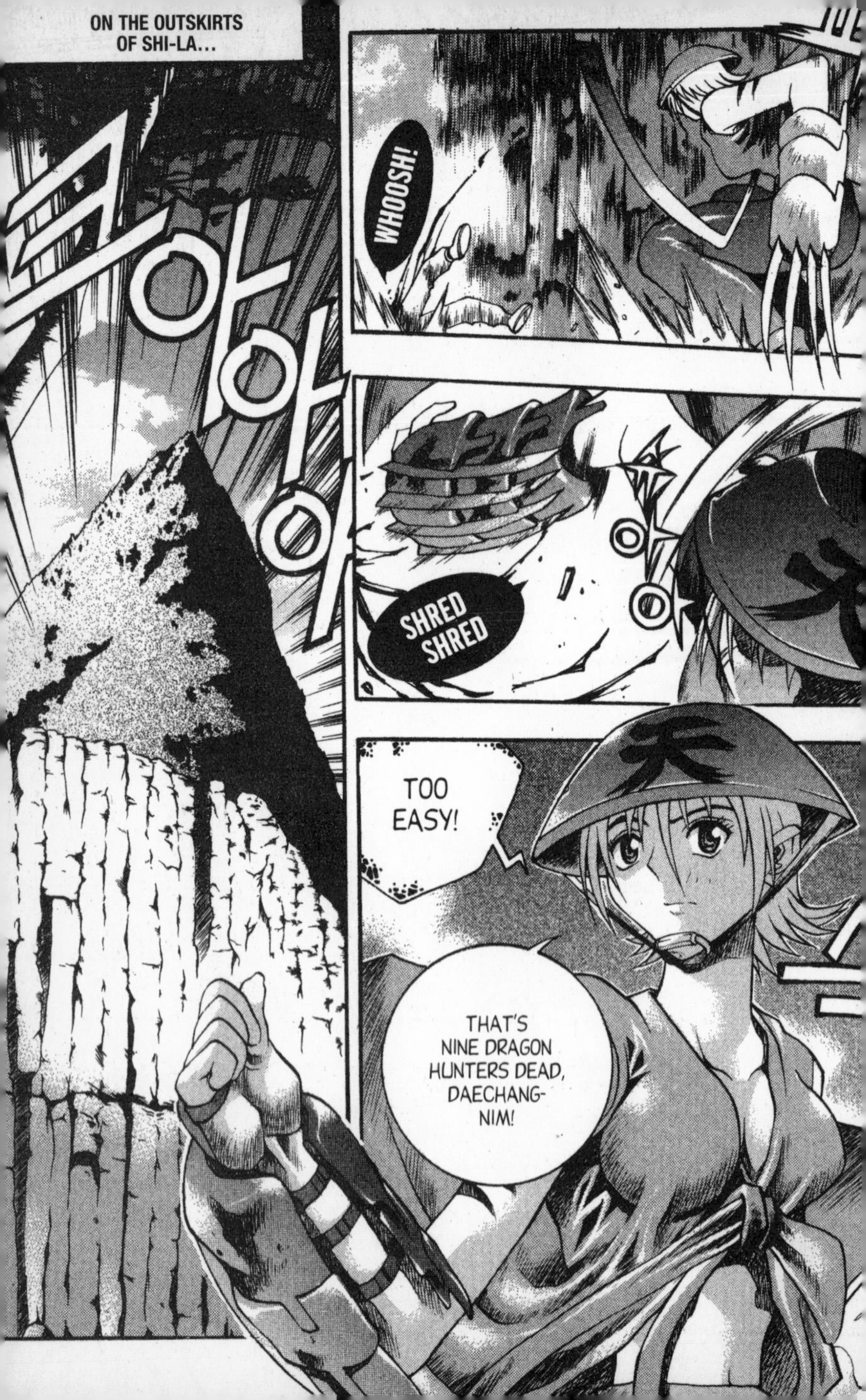
ON THE OUTSKIRTS OF SHI-LA...
WHOOSH!
SHRED SHRED
TOO EASY!
THAT'S NINE DRAGON HUNTERS DEAD, DAECHANG-NIM!

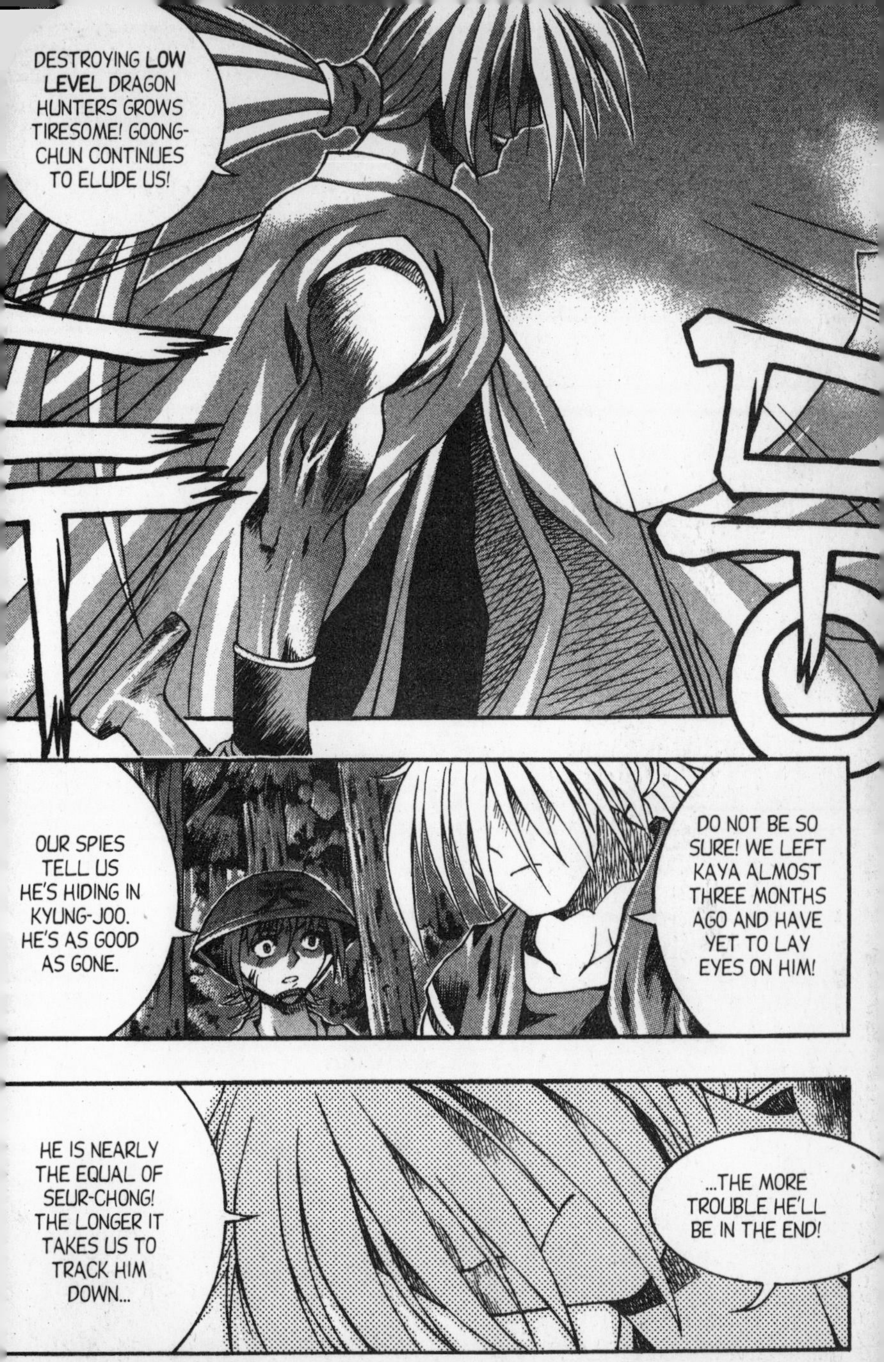
DESTROYING LOW LEVEL DRAGON HUNTERS GROWS TIRESOME! GOONG-CHUN CONTINUES TO ELUDE US!
OUR SPIES TELL US HE'S HIDING IN KYUNG-JOO. HE'S AS GOOD AS GONE.
DO NOT BE SO SURE! WE LEFT KAYA ALMOST THREE MONTHS AGO AND HAVE YET TO LAY EYES ON HIM!
HE IS NEARLY THE EQUAL OF SEUR-CHONG! THE LONGER IT TAKES US TO TRACK HIM DOWN...
...THE MORE TROUBLE HE'LL BE IN THE END!

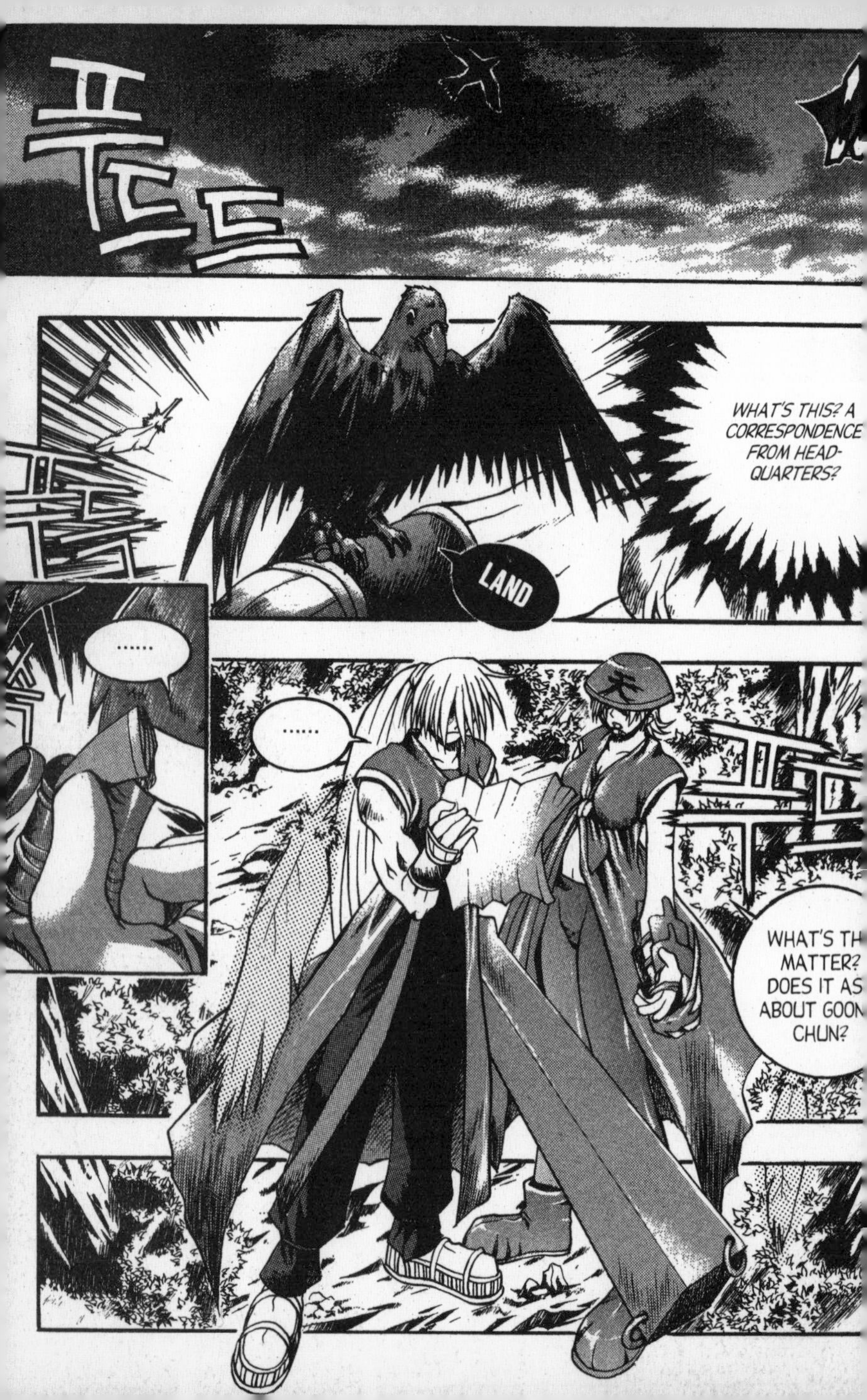

WHAT'S THIS? A CORRESPONDENCE FROM HEAD-QUARTERS?
LAND
......
......
WHAT'S TH MATTER? DOES IT AS ABOUT GOON CHUN?

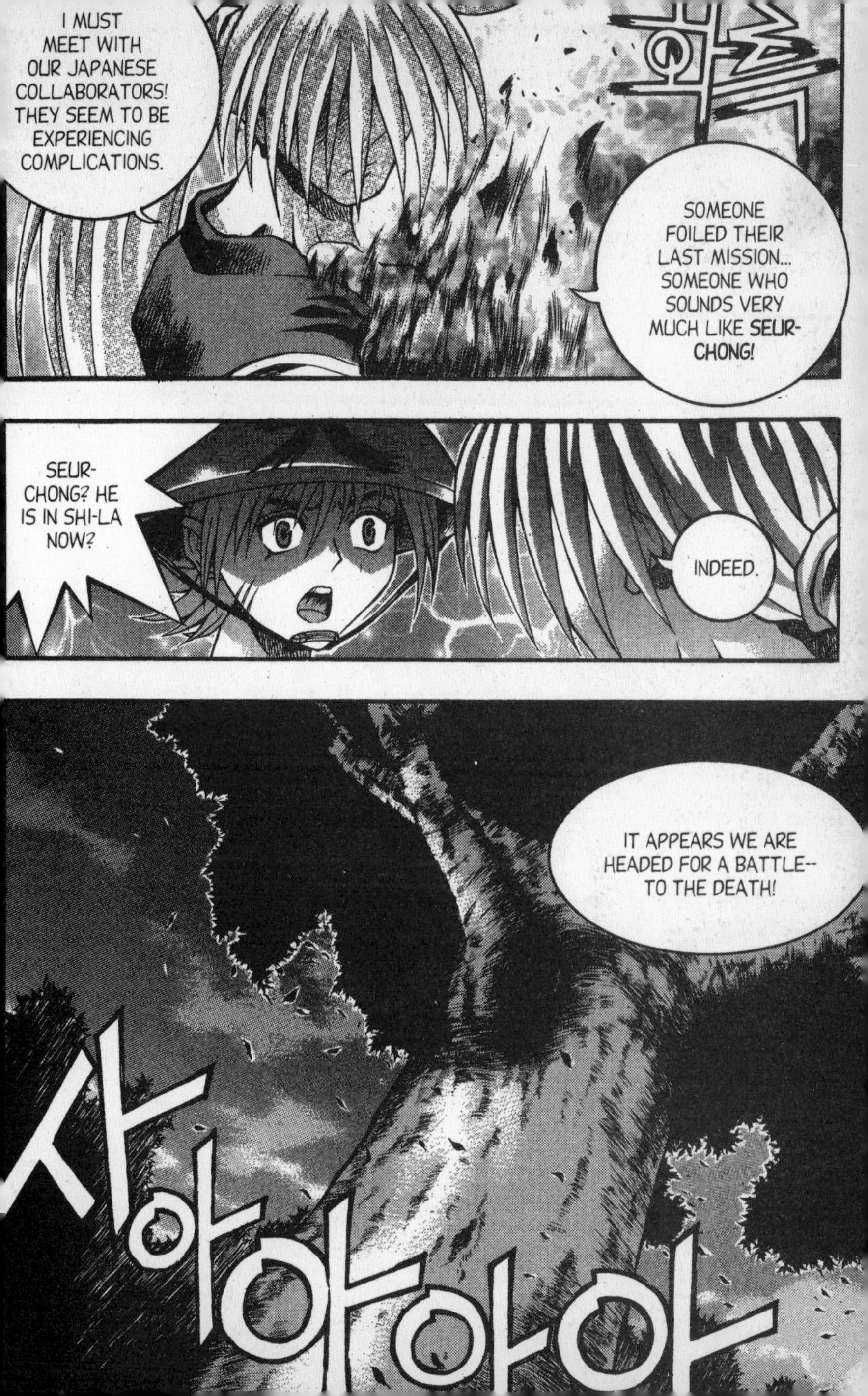
I MUST MEET WITH OUR JAPANESE COLLABORATORS! THEY SEEM TO BE EXPERIENCING COMPLICATIONS.
SOMEONE FOILED THEIR LAST MISSION... SOMEONE WHO SOUNDS VERY MUCH LIKE **SEUR-CHONG!**
SEUR-CHONG? HE IS IN SHI-LA NOW?
INDEED.
IT APPEARS WE ARE HEADED FOR A BATTLE--TO THE DEATH!

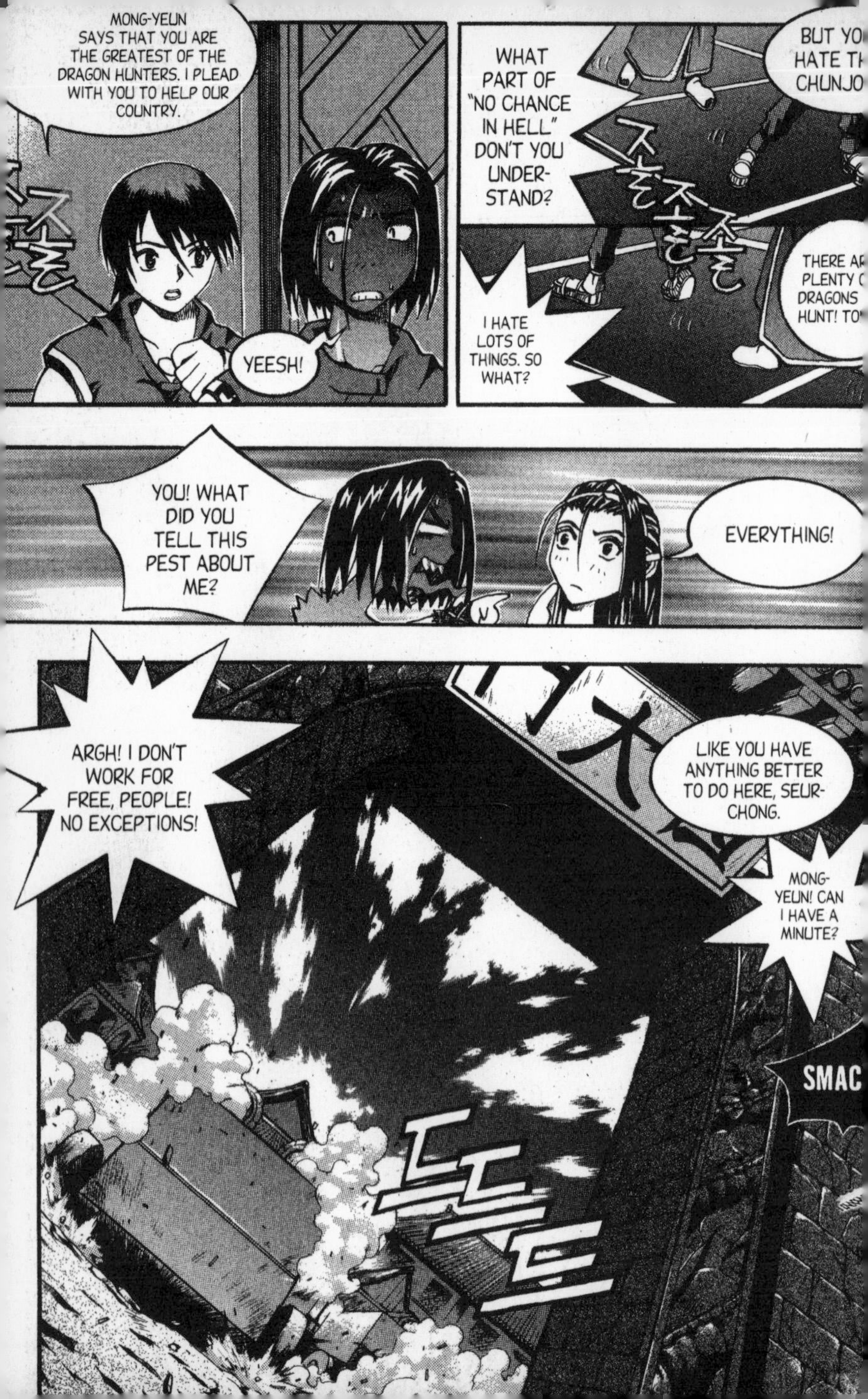
MONG-YEUN SAYS THAT YOU ARE THE GREATEST OF THE DRAGON HUNTERS. I PLEAD WITH YOU TO HELP OUR COUNTRY.
YEESH!
WHAT PART OF "NO CHANCE IN HELL" DON'T YOU UNDER-STAND?
I HATE LOTS OF THINGS. SO WHAT?
YOU! WHAT DID YOU TELL THIS PEST ABOUT ME?
EVERYTHING!
ARGH! I DON'T WORK FOR FREE, PEOPLE! NO EXCEPTIONS!
LIKE YOU HAVE ANYTHING BETTER TO DO HERE, SEUR-CHONG.
MONG-YEUN! CAN I HAVE A MINUTE?

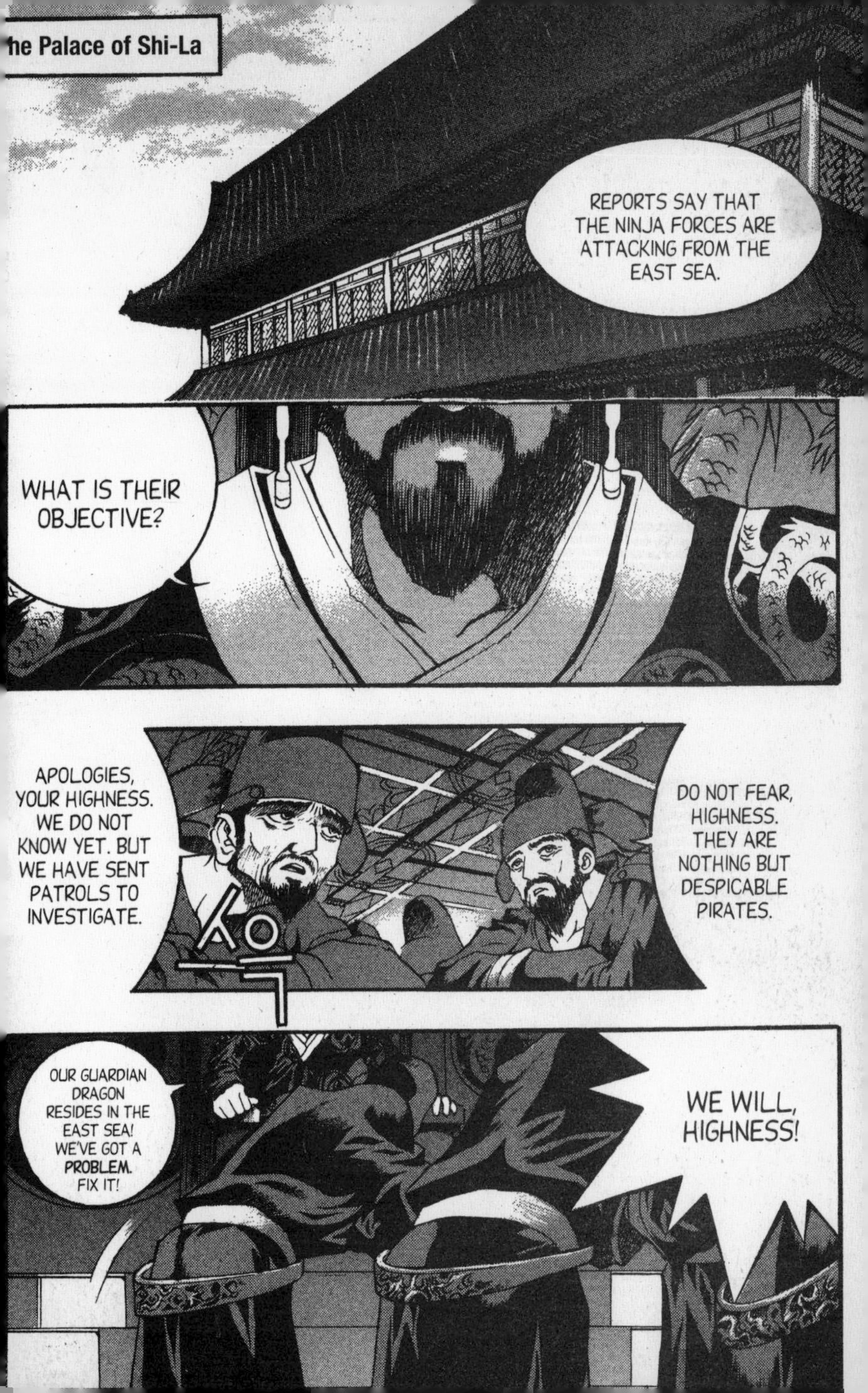
he Palace of Shi-La
REPORTS SAY THAT THE NINJA FORCES ARE ATTACKING FROM THE EAST SEA.
WHAT IS THEIR OBJECTIVE?
APOLOGIES, YOUR HIGHNESS. WE DO NOT KNOW YET. BUT WE HAVE SENT PATROLS TO INVESTIGATE.
DO NOT FEAR, HIGHNESS. THEY ARE NOTHING BUT DESPICABLE PIRATES.
OUR GUARDIAN DRAGON RESIDES IN THE EAST SEA! WE'VE GOT A **PROBLEM.** FIX IT!
WE WILL, HIGHNESS!

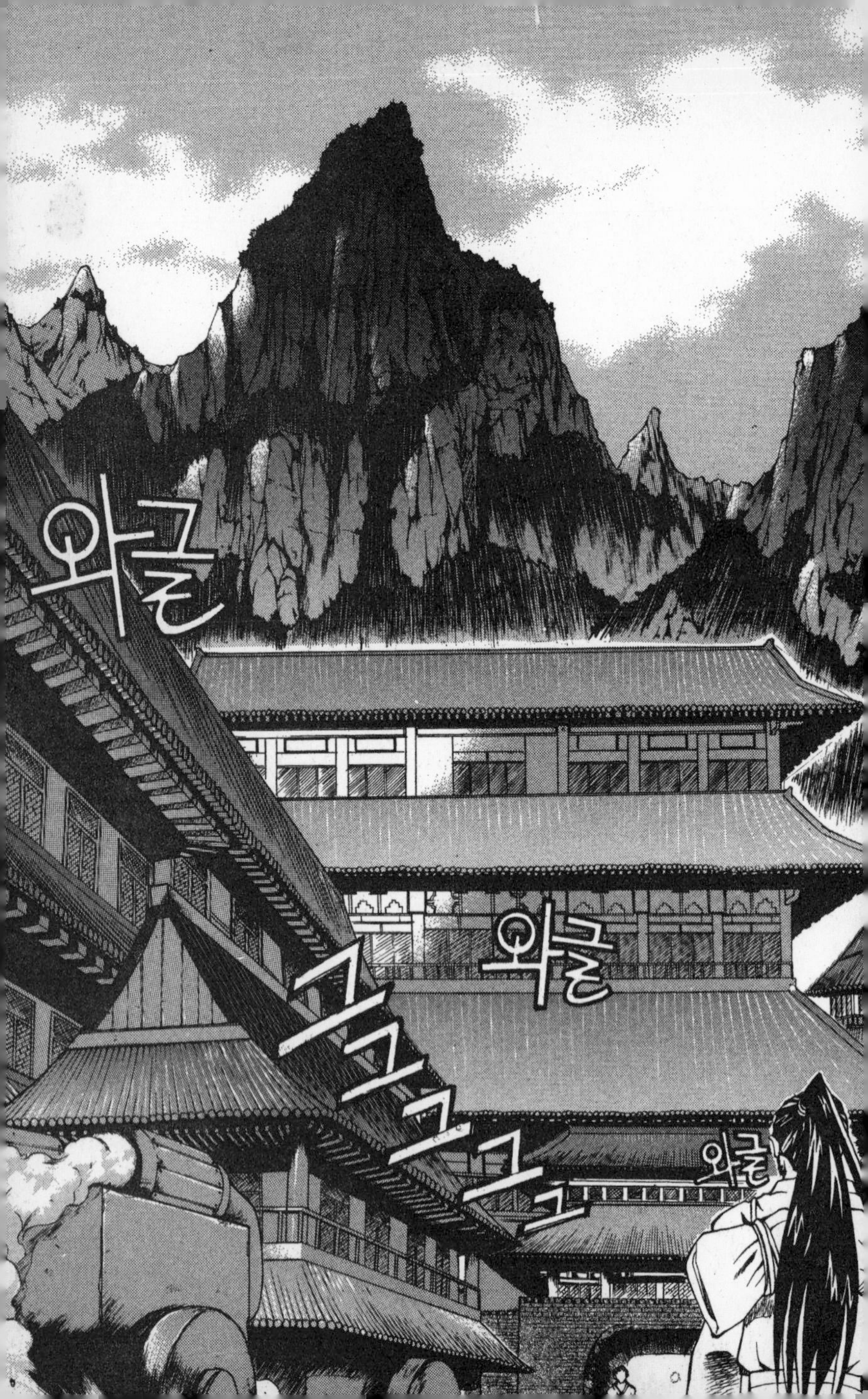
와글
와글
그그그그그
와글

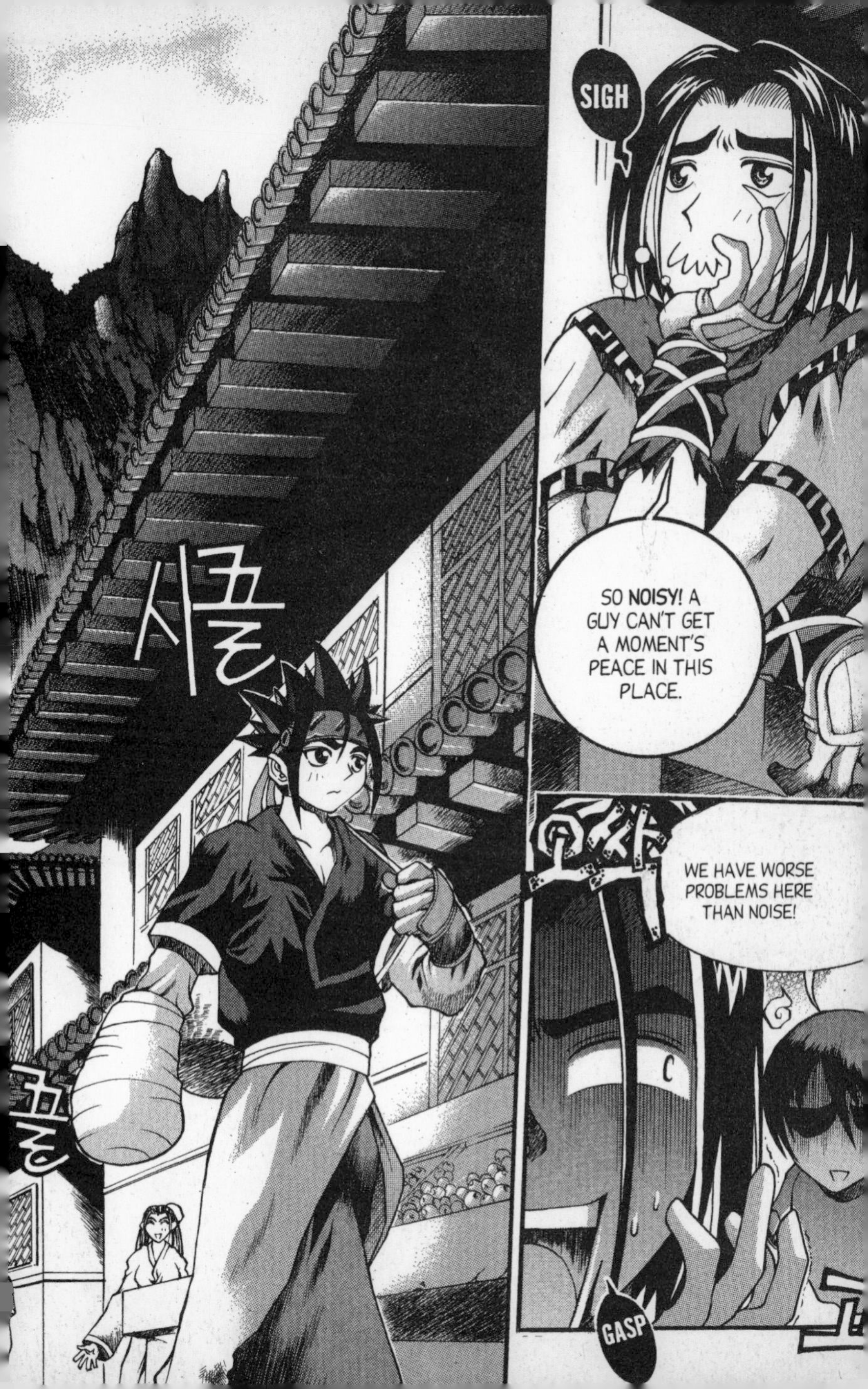
시끌
시끌
SIGH
SO NOISY! A GUY CAN'T GET A MOMENT'S PEACE IN THIS PLACE.
WE HAVE WORSE PROBLEMS HERE THAN NOISE!
GASP

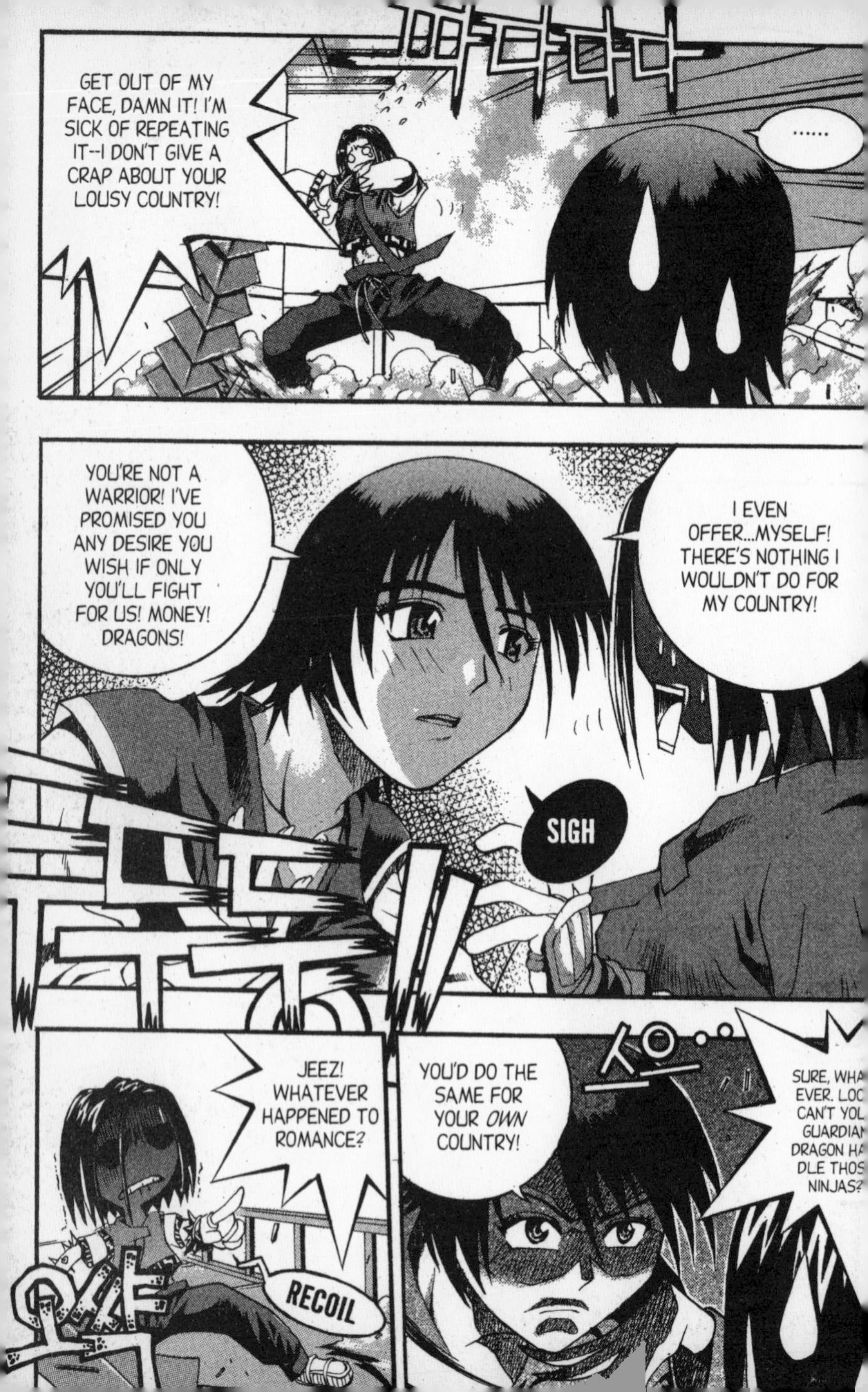
GET OUT OF MY FACE, DAMN IT! I'M SICK OF REPEATING IT--I DON'T GIVE A CRAP ABOUT YOUR LOUSY COUNTRY!
......
YOU'RE NOT A WARRIOR! I'VE PROMISED YOU ANY DESIRE YOU WISH IF ONLY YOU'LL FIGHT FOR US! MONEY! DRAGONS!
I EVEN OFFER...MYSELF! THERE'S NOTHING I WOULDN'T DO FOR MY COUNTRY!
SIGH
JEEZ! WHATEVER HAPPENED TO ROMANCE?
RECOIL
YOU'D DO THE SAME FOR YOUR *OWN* COUNTRY!
SURE, WHA EVER. LOC CAN'T YOL GUARDIAN DRAGON HA DLE THOS NINJAS?

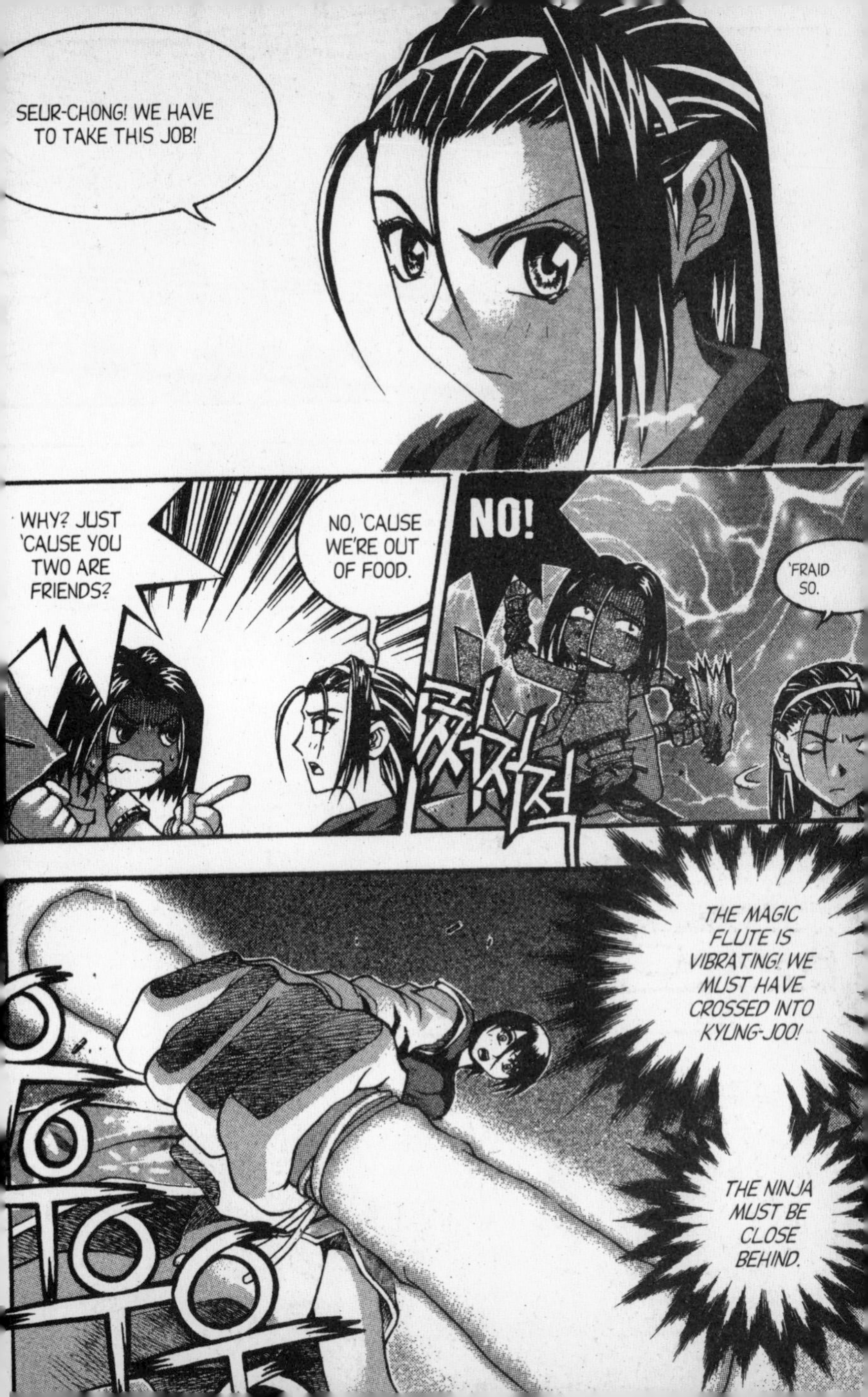
SEUR-CHONG! WE HAVE TO TAKE THIS JOB!
WHY? JUST 'CAUSE YOU TWO ARE FRIENDS?
NO, 'CAUSE WE'RE OUT OF FOOD.
NO!
'FRAID SO.
THE MAGIC FLUTE IS VIBRATING! WE MUST HAVE CROSSED INTO KYUNG-JOO!
THE NINJA MUST BE CLOSE BEHIND.

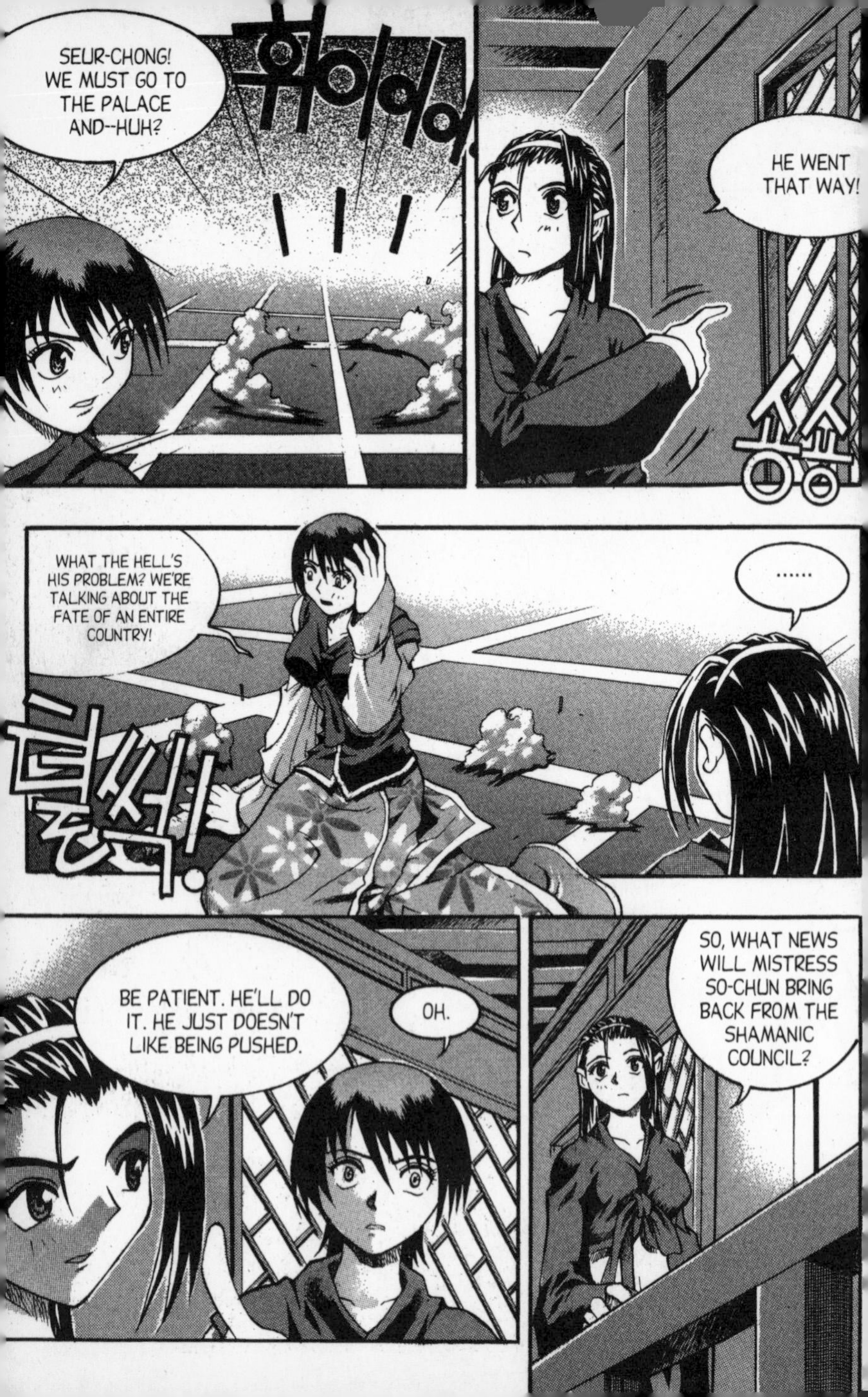
SEUR-CHONG! WE MUST GO TO THE PALACE AND--HUH?
HE WENT THAT WAY!
WHAT THE HELL'S HIS PROBLEM? WE'RE TALKING ABOUT THE FATE OF AN ENTIRE COUNTRY!
......
BE PATIENT. HE'LL DO IT. HE JUST DOESN'T LIKE BEING PUSHED.
OH.
SO, WHAT NEWS WILL MISTRESS SO-CHUN BRING BACK FROM THE SHAMANIC COUNCIL?

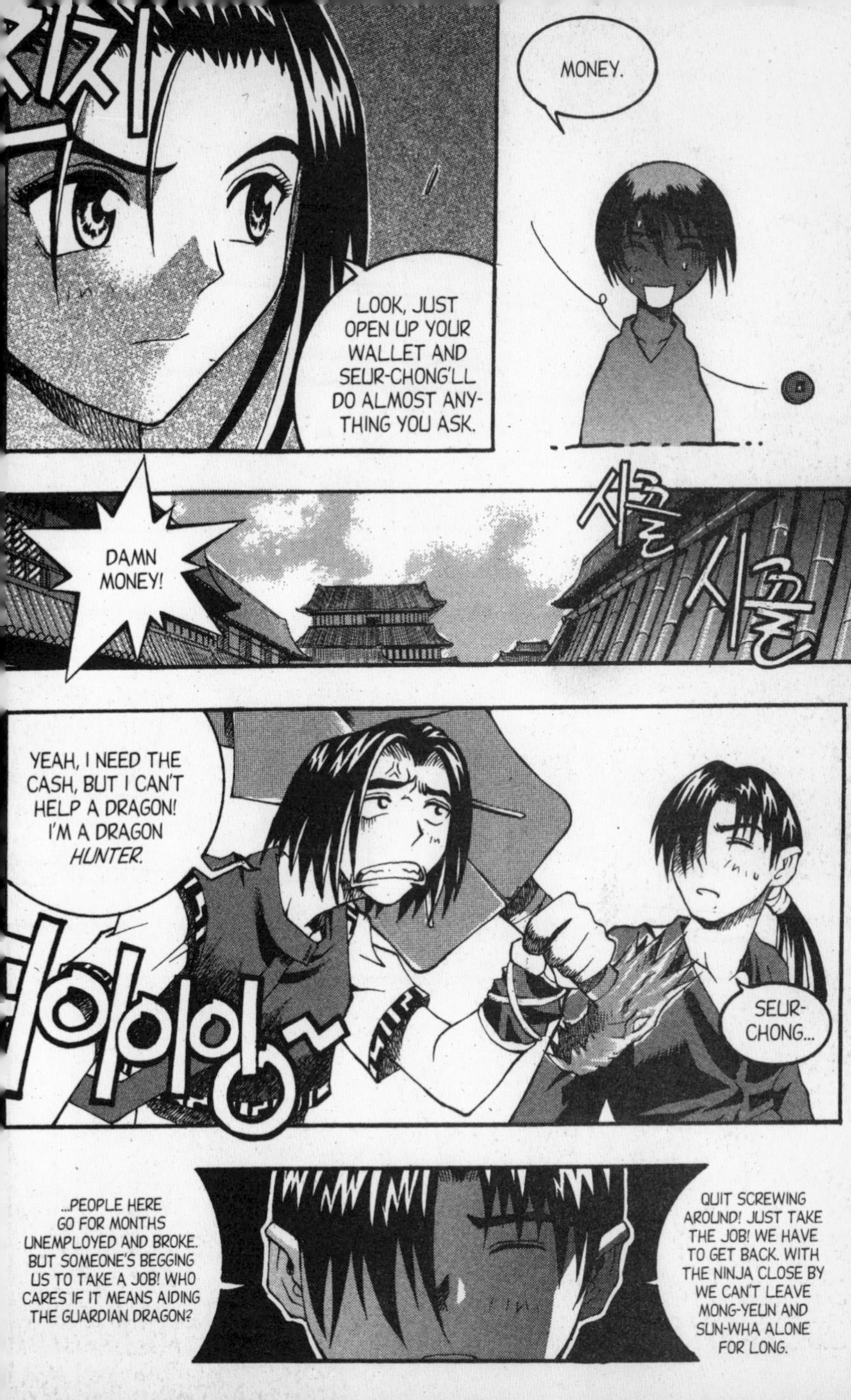

LOOK, JUST OPEN UP YOUR WALLET AND SEUR-CHONG'LL DO ALMOST ANY-THING YOU ASK.
MONEY.
DAMN MONEY!
시끌 시끌
YEAH, I NEED THE CASH, BUT I CAN'T HELP A DRAGON! I'M A DRAGON *HUNTER*.
SEUR-CHONG...
...PEOPLE HERE GO FOR MONTHS UNEMPLOYED AND BROKE. BUT SOMEONE'S BEGGING US TO TAKE A JOB! WHO CARES IF IT MEANS AIDING THE GUARDIAN DRAGON?
QUIT SCREWING AROUND! JUST TAKE THE JOB! WE HAVE TO GET BACK. WITH THE NINJA CLOSE BY WE CAN'T LEAVE MONG-YEUN AND SUN-WHA ALONE FOR LONG.

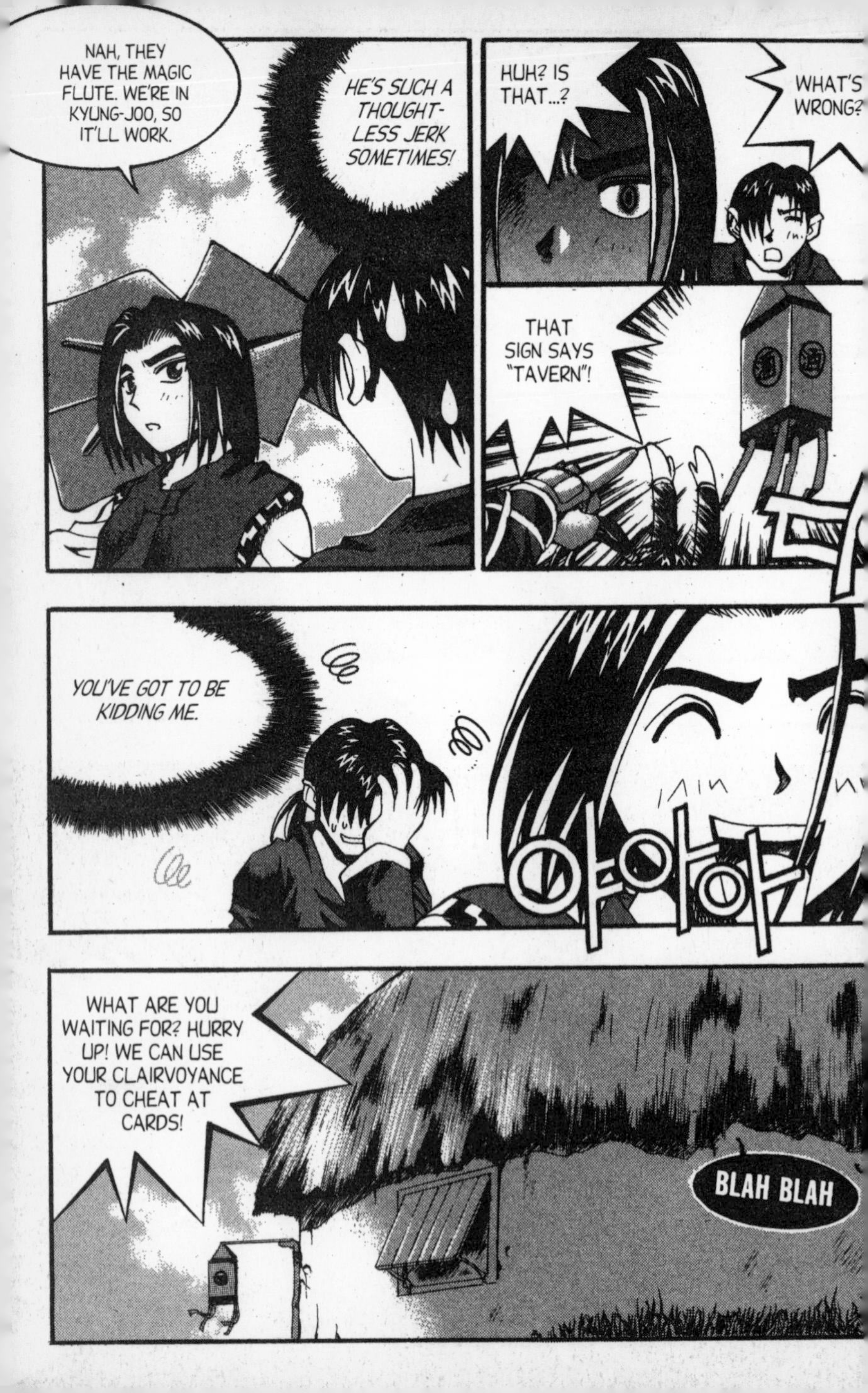
NAH, THEY HAVE THE MAGIC FLUTE. WE'RE IN KYUNG-JOO, SO IT'LL WORK.
HE'S SUCH A THOUGHT-LESS JERK SOMETIMES!
HUH? IS THAT...?
WHAT'S WRONG?
THAT SIGN SAYS "TAVERN"!
YOU'VE GOT TO BE KIDDING ME.
WHAT ARE YOU WAITING FOR? HURRY UP! WE CAN USE YOUR CLAIRVOYANCE TO CHEAT AT CARDS!
BLAH BLAH

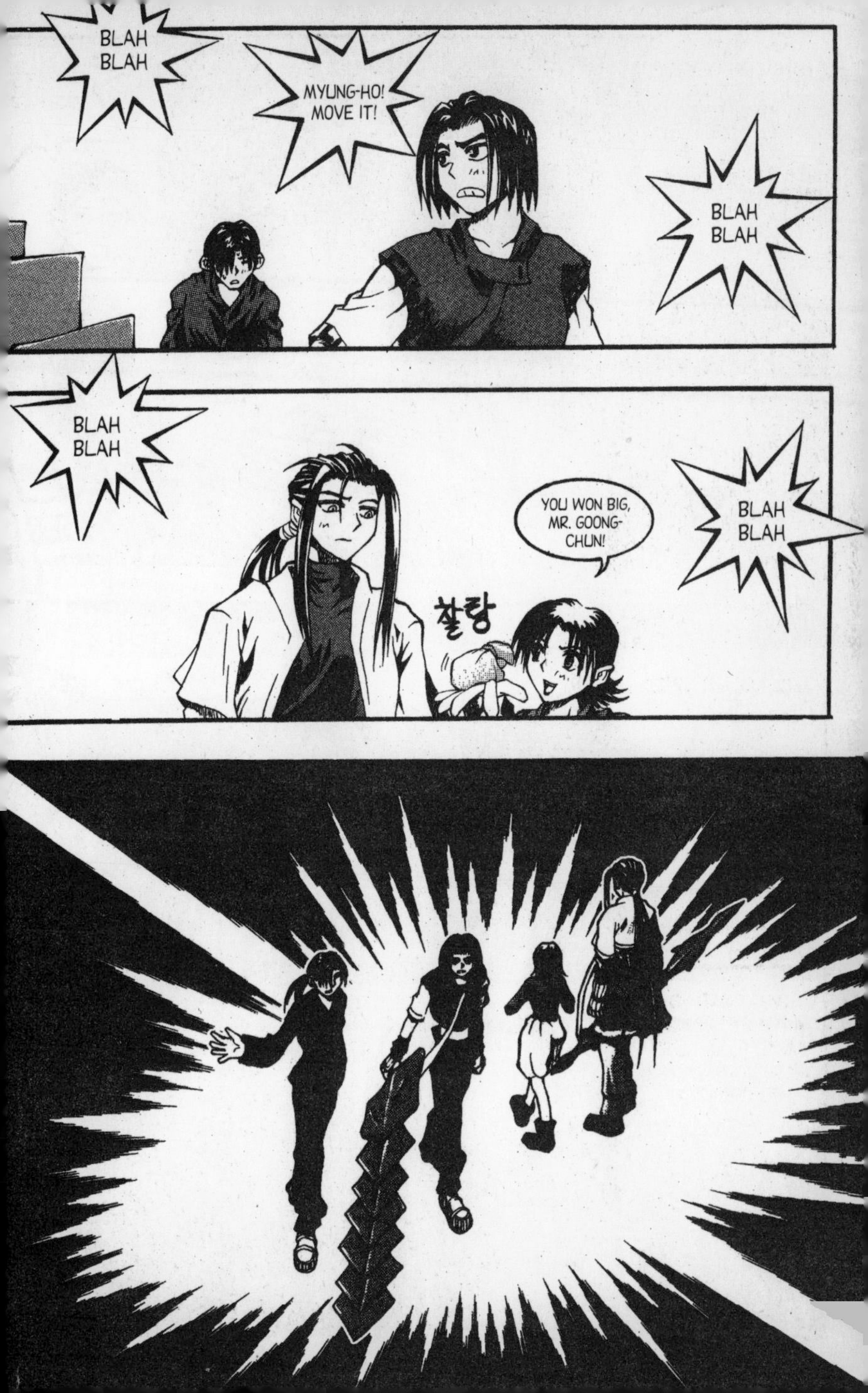
BLAH BLAH
MYUNG-HO! MOVE IT!
BLAH BLAH
BLAH BLAH
YOU WON BIG, MR. GOONG-CHUN!
BLAH BLAH
찰랑

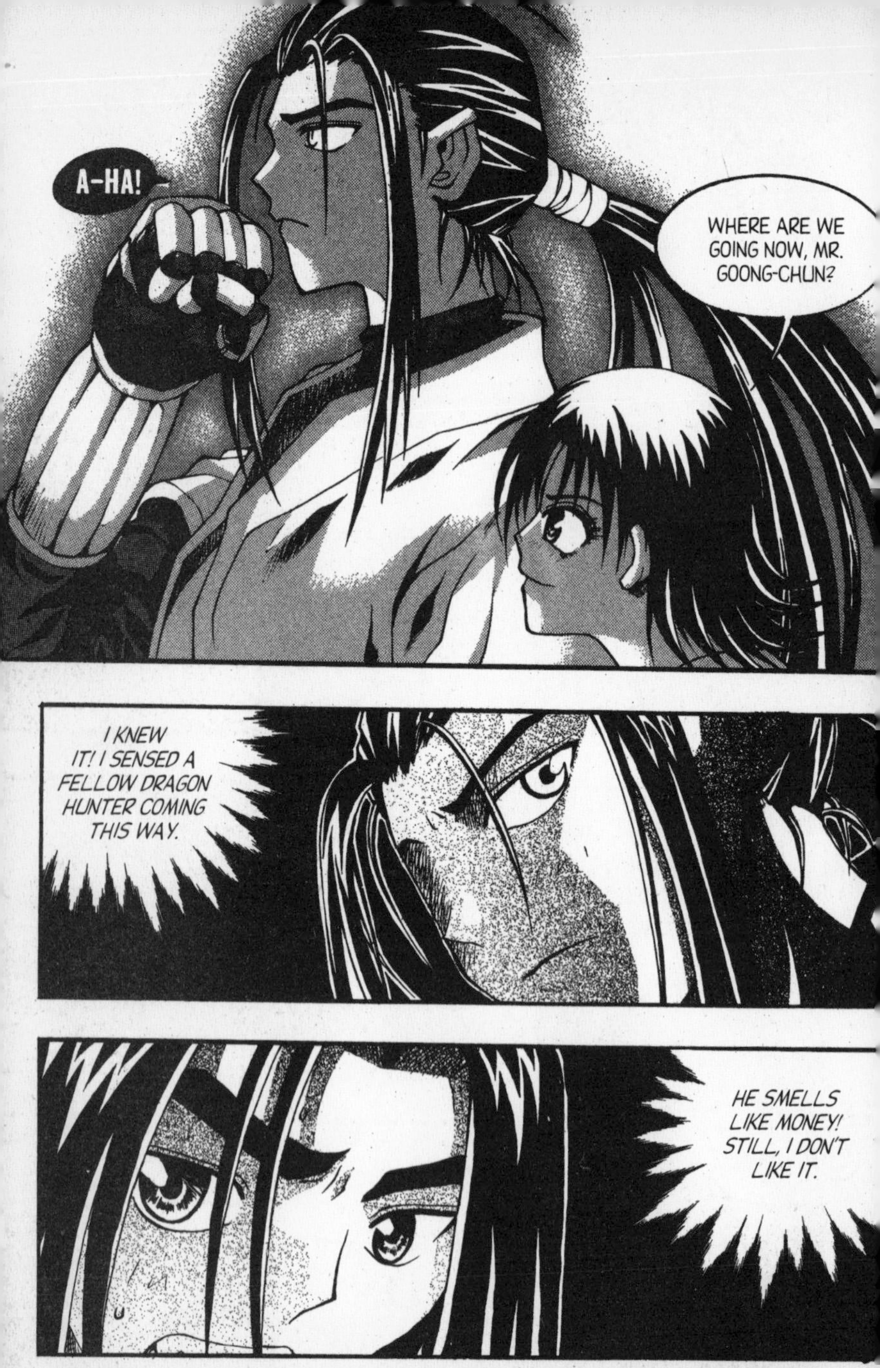
A-HA!
WHERE ARE WE GOING NOW, MR. GOONG-CHUN?
I KNEW IT! I SENSED A FELLOW DRAGON HUNTER COMING THIS WAY.
HE SMELLS LIKE MONEY! STILL, I DON'T LIKE IT.

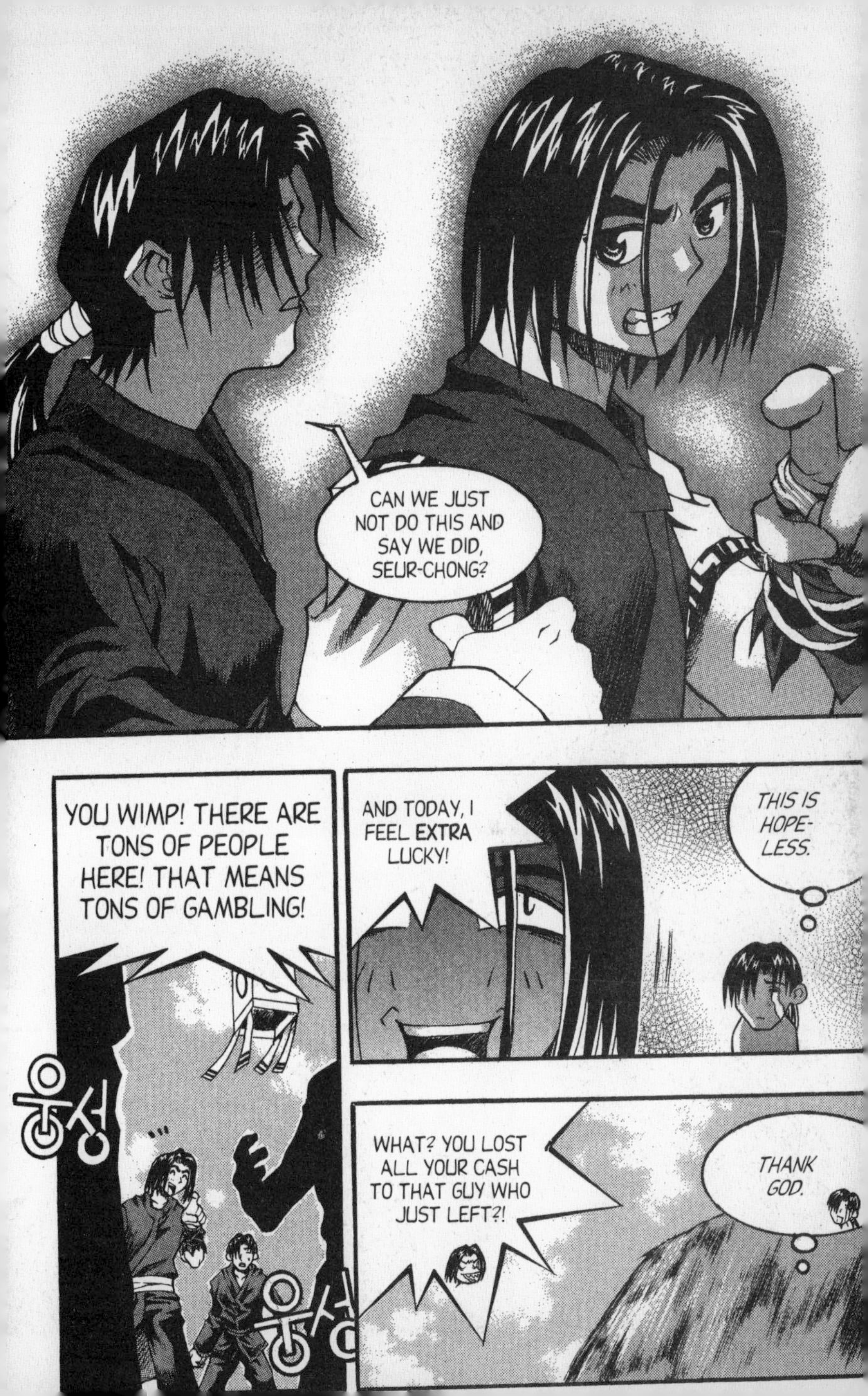
CAN WE JUST NOT DO THIS AND SAY WE DID, SEUR-CHONG?
YOU WIMP! THERE ARE TONS OF PEOPLE HERE! THAT MEANS TONS OF GAMBLING!
웅성
...
웅성
AND TODAY, I FEEL **EXTRA** LUCKY!
THIS IS HOPE-LESS.
WHAT? YOU LOST ALL YOUR CASH TO THAT GUY WHO JUST LEFT?!
THANK GOD.

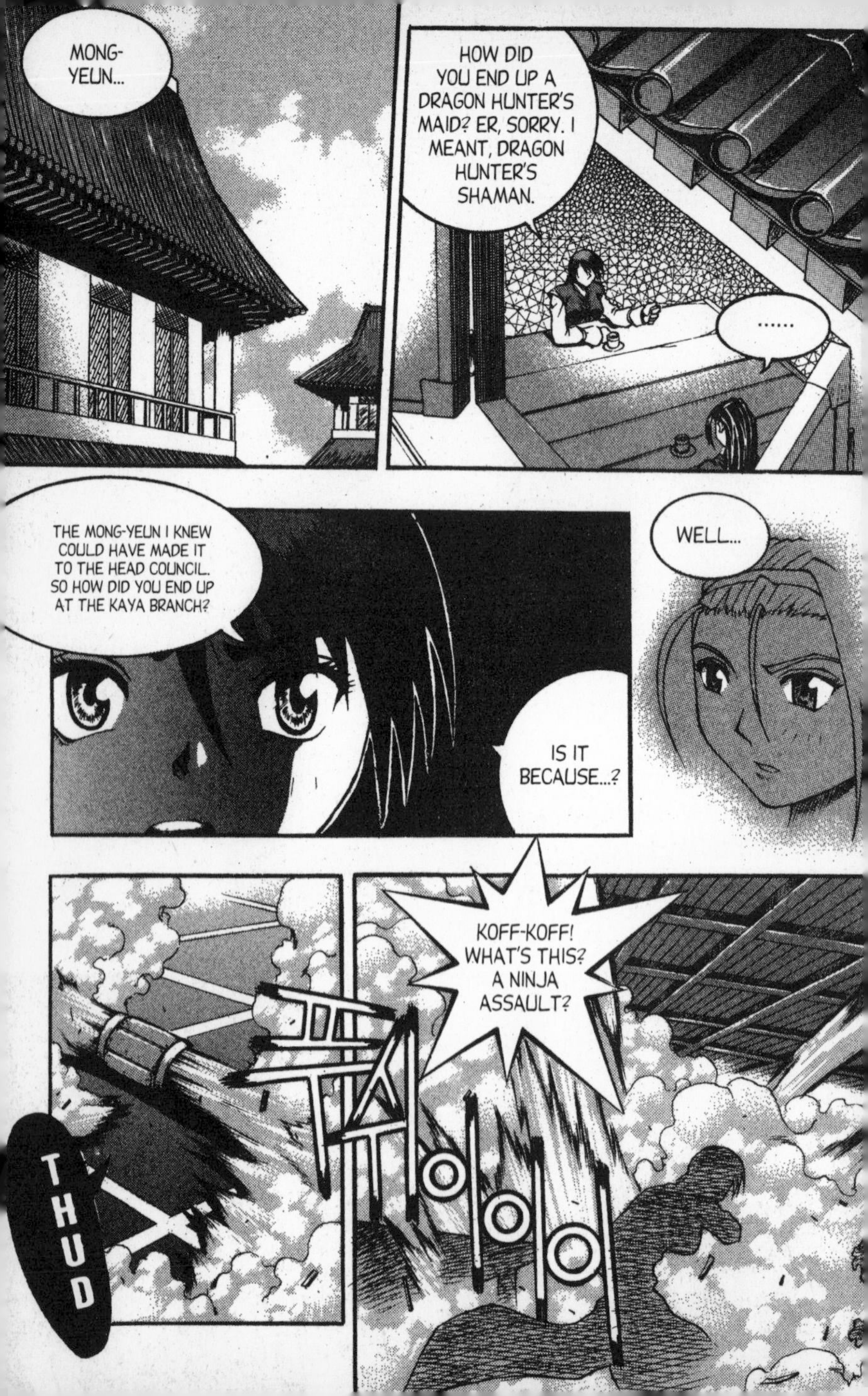
MONG-YEUN...
HOW DID YOU END UP A DRAGON HUNTER'S MAID? ER, SORRY. I MEANT, DRAGON HUNTER'S SHAMAN.
......
THE MONG-YEUN I KNEW COULD HAVE MADE IT TO THE HEAD COUNCIL. SO HOW DID YOU END UP AT THE KAYA BRANCH?
IS IT BECAUSE...?
WELL...
THUD
KOFF-KOFF! WHAT'S THIS? A NINJA ASSAULT?

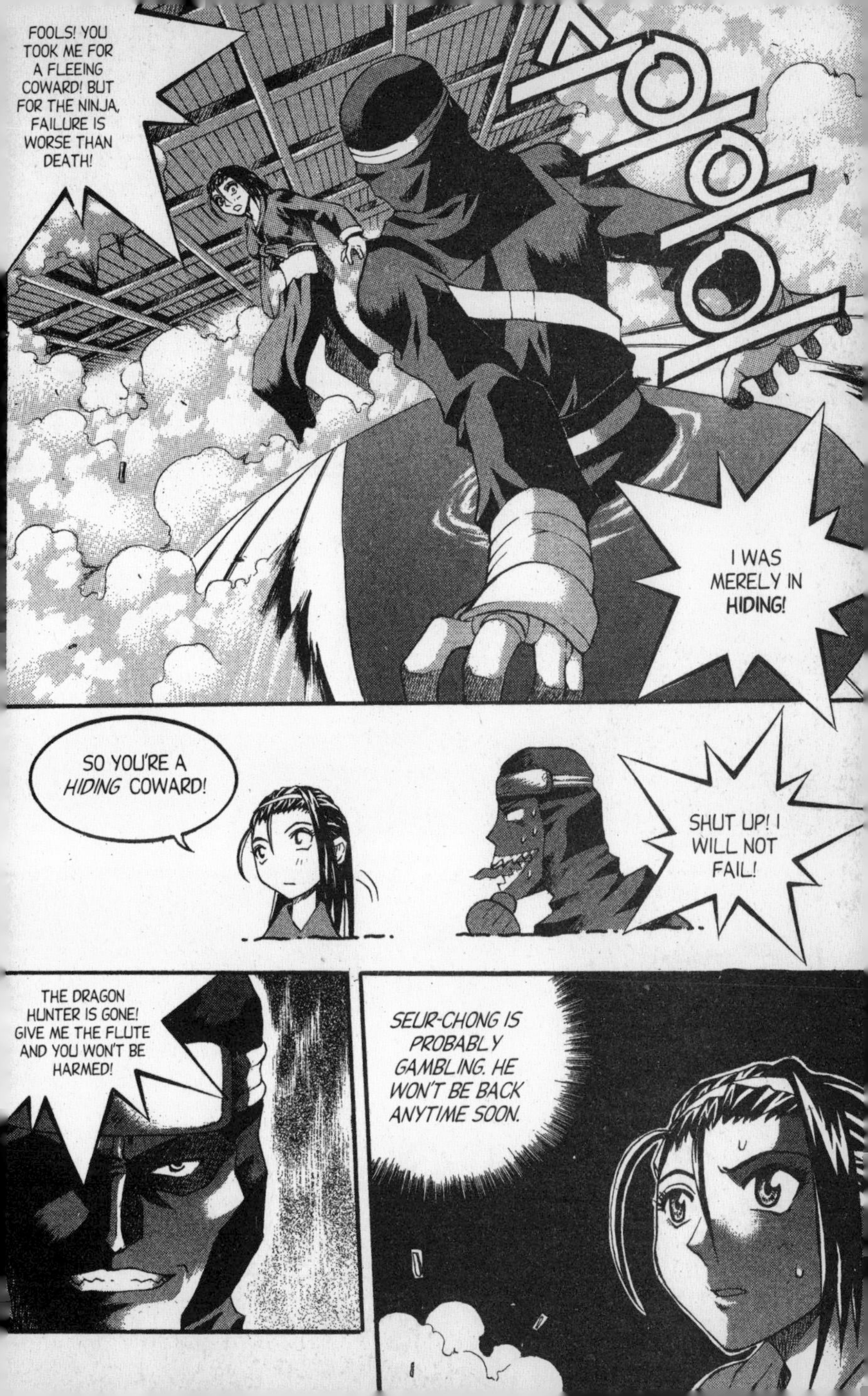
FOOLS! YOU TOOK ME FOR A FLEEING COWARD! BUT FOR THE NINJA, FAILURE IS WORSE THAN DEATH!
I WAS MERELY IN HIDING!
SO YOU'RE A *HIDING* COWARD!
SHUT UP! I WILL NOT FAIL!
THE DRAGON HUNTER IS GONE! GIVE ME THE FLUTE AND YOU WON'T BE HARMED!
SEUR-CHONG IS PROBABLY GAMBLING. HE WON'T BE BACK ANYTIME SOON.

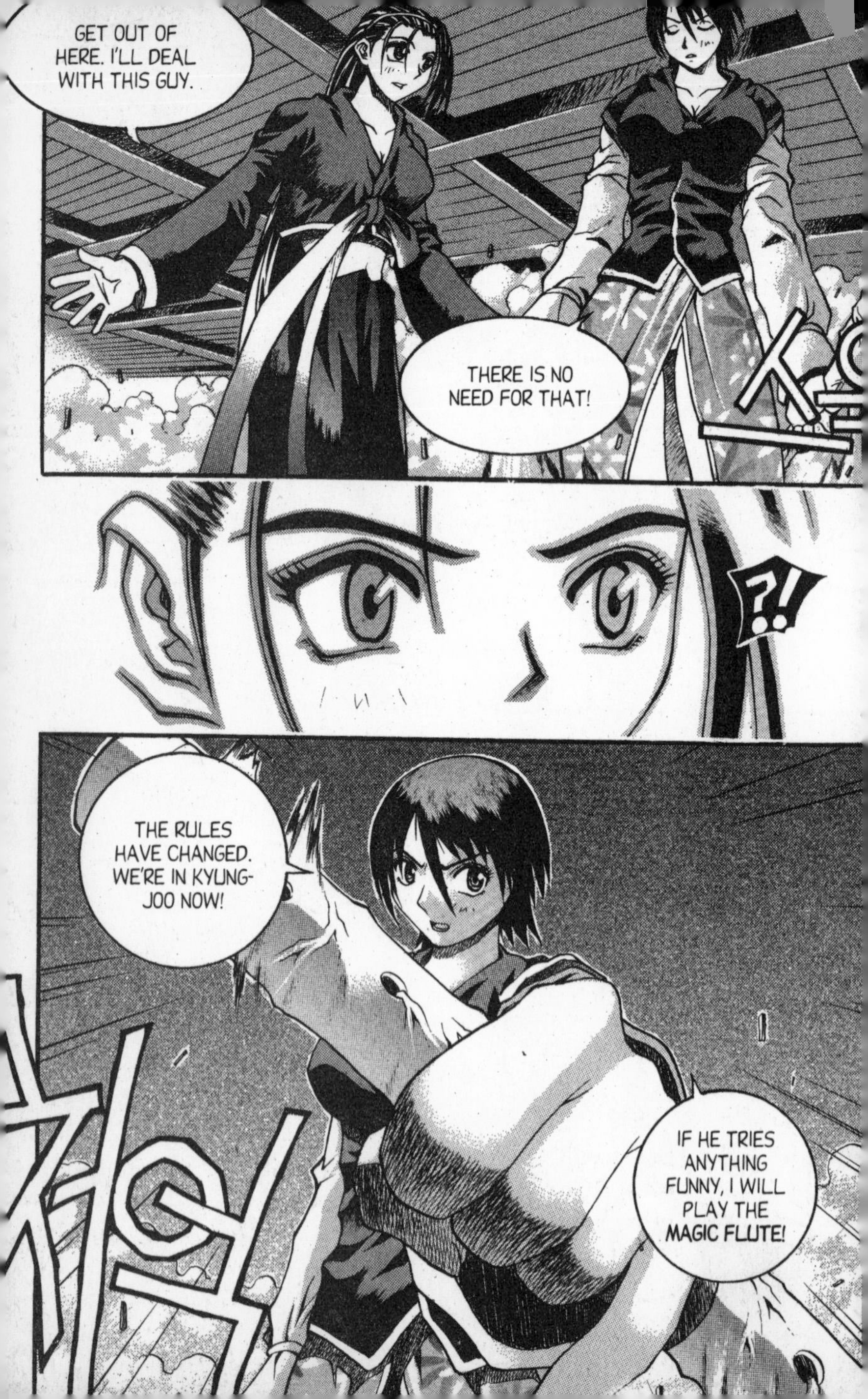
GET OUT OF HERE. I'LL DEAL WITH THIS GUY.
THERE IS NO NEED FOR THAT!
?!
THE RULES HAVE CHANGED. WE'RE IN KYUNG-JOO NOW!
IF HE TRIES ANYTHING FUNNY, I WILL PLAY THE MAGIC FLUTE!

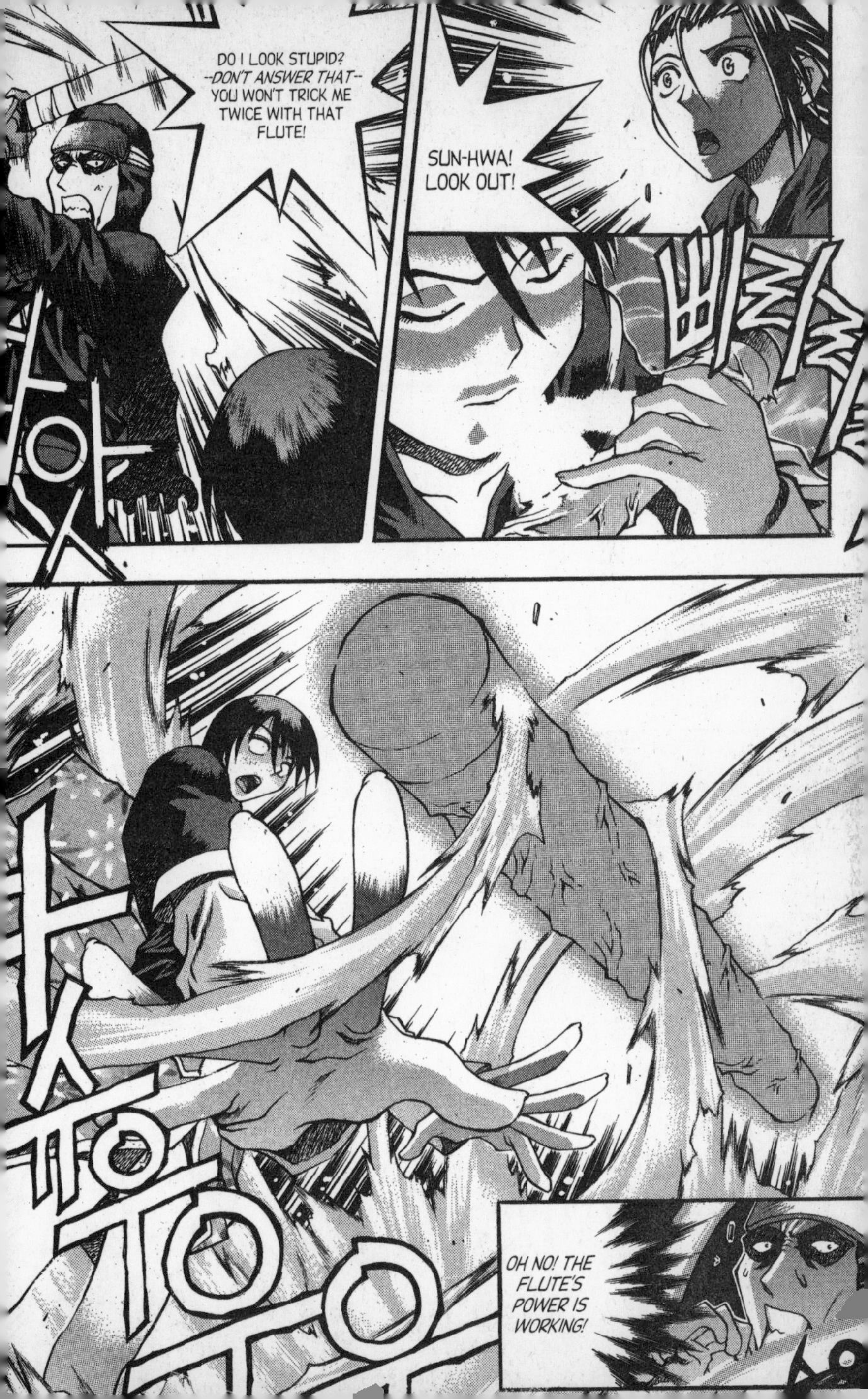
DO I LOOK STUPID? *--DON'T ANSWER THAT--* YOU WON'T TRICK ME TWICE WITH THAT FLUTE!
SUN-HWA! LOOK OUT!
OH NO! THE FLUTE'S POWER IS WORKING!

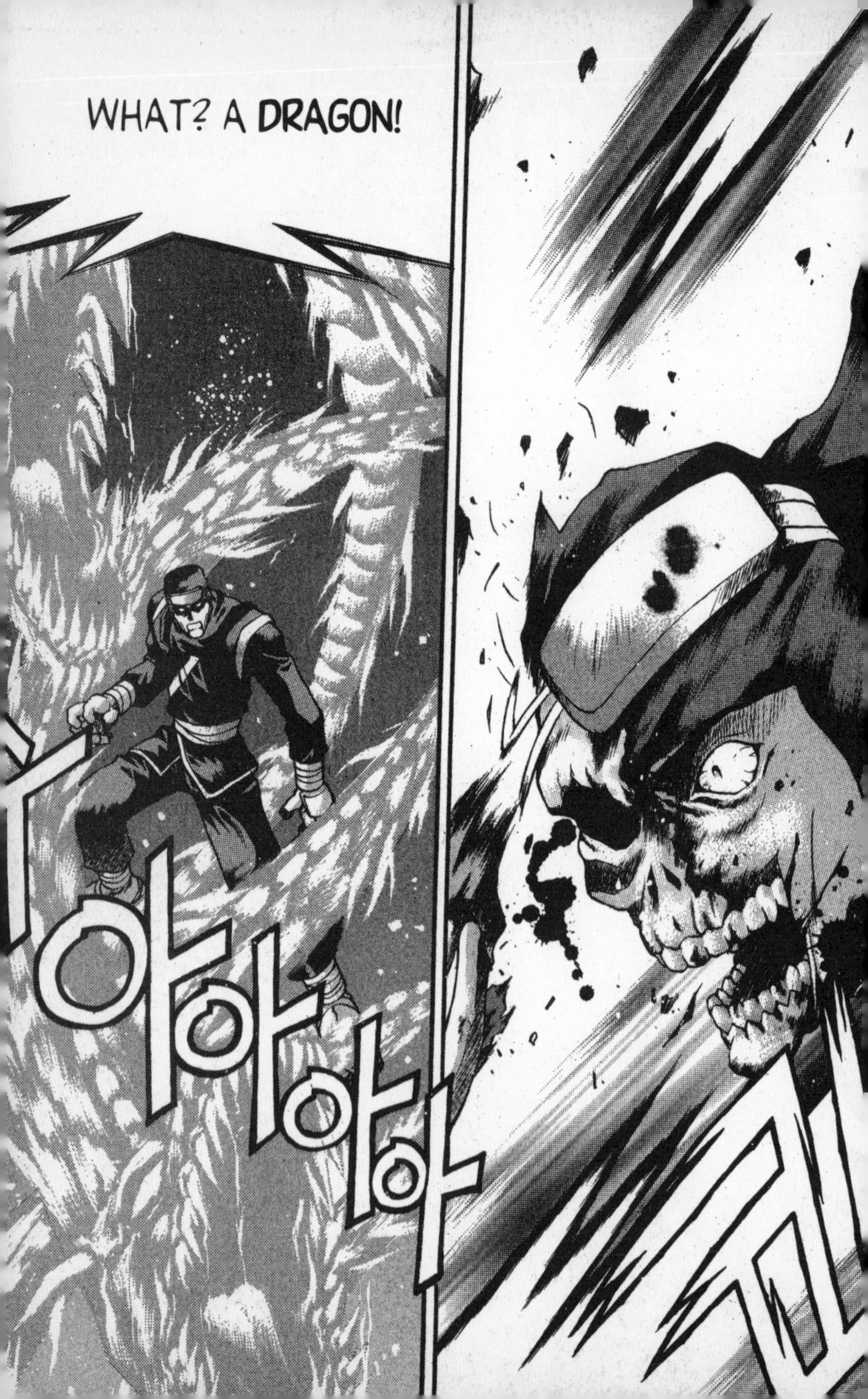
WHAT? A DRAGON!

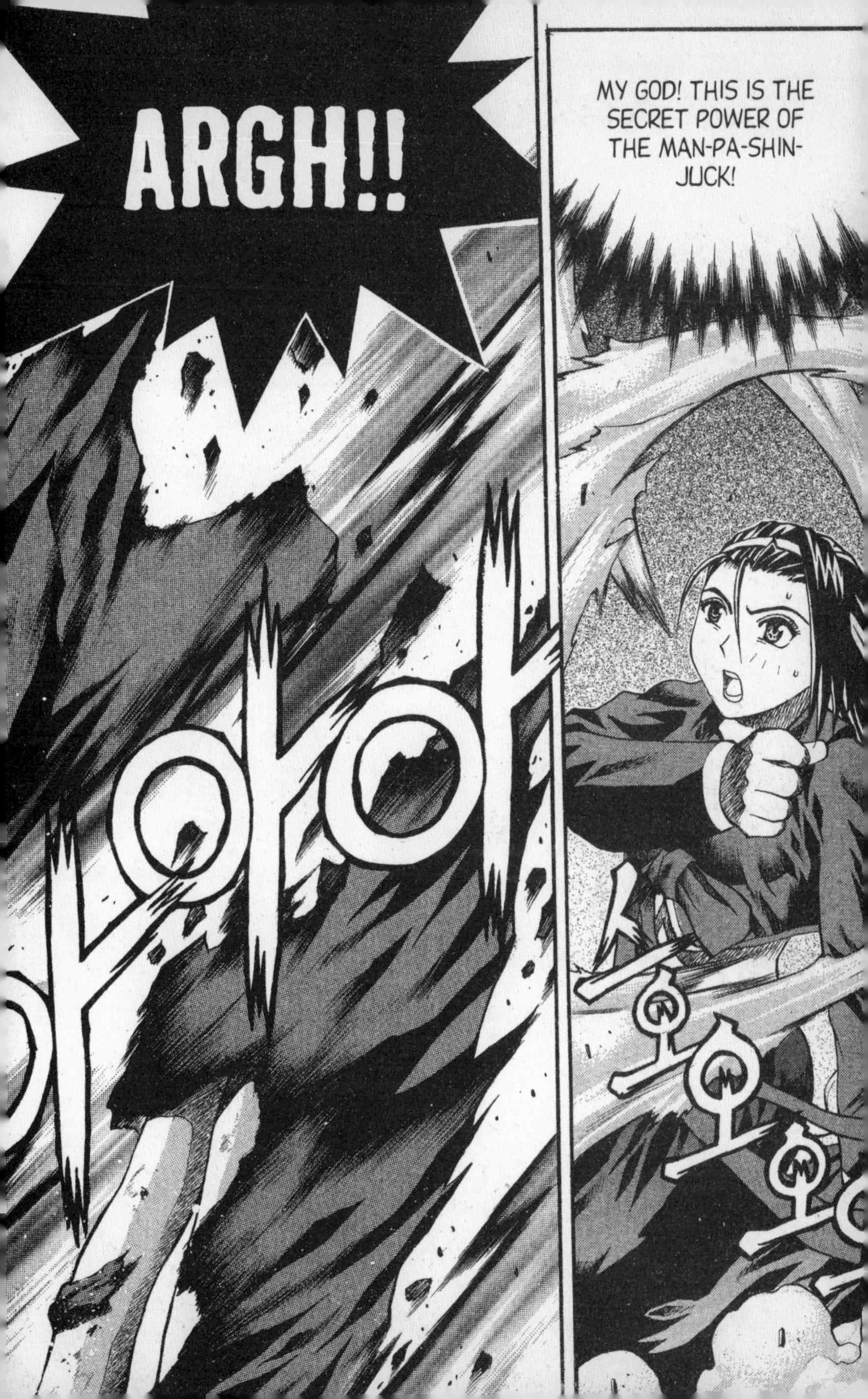
ARGH!!
MY GOD! THIS IS THE SECRET POWER OF THE MAN-PA-SHIN-JUCK!

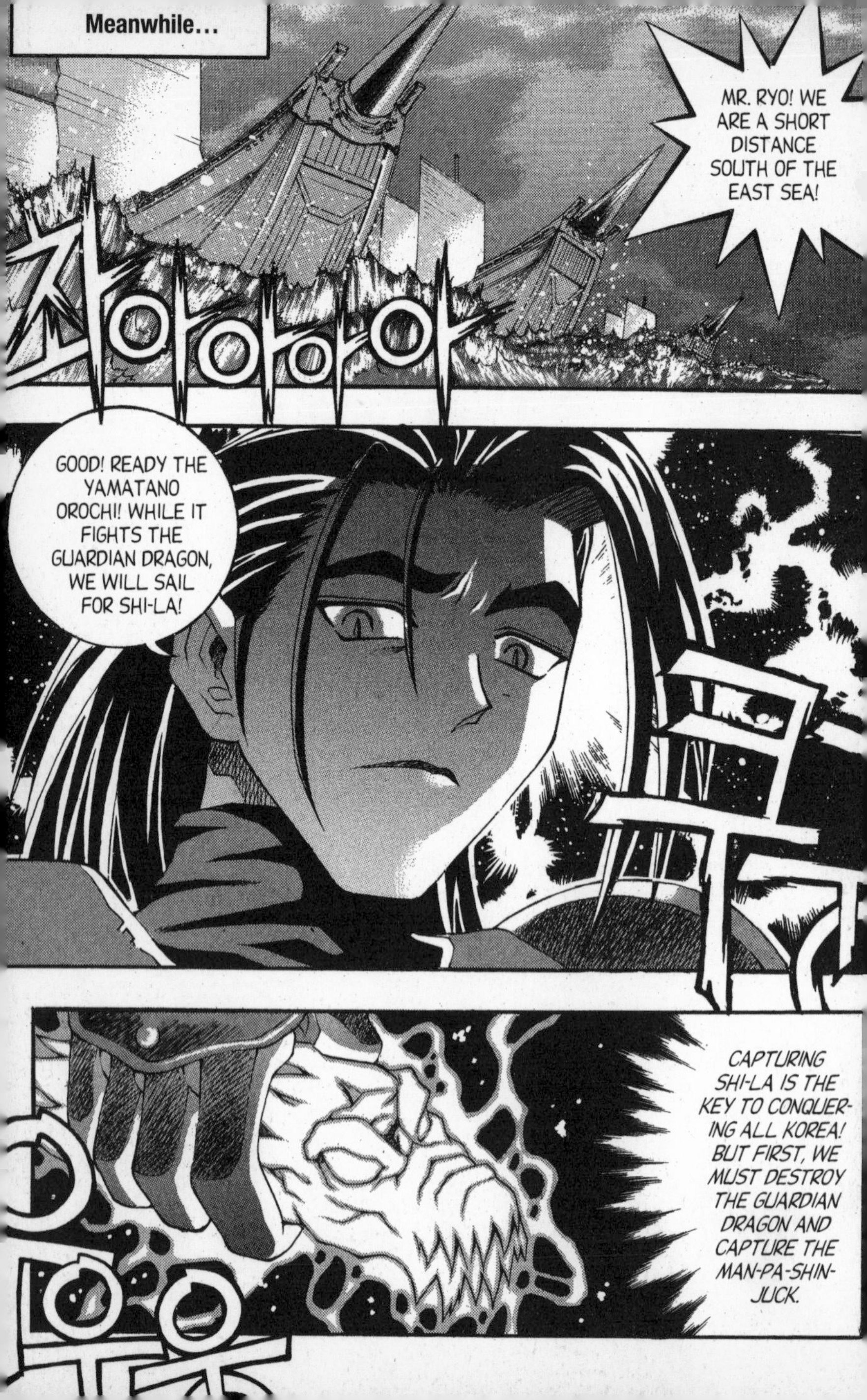
Meanwhile...
MR. RYO! WE ARE A SHORT DISTANCE SOUTH OF THE EAST SEA!
GOOD! READY THE YAMATANO OROCHI! WHILE IT FIGHTS THE GUARDIAN DRAGON, WE WILL SAIL FOR SHI-LA!
CAPTURING SHI-LA IS THE KEY TO CONQUERING ALL KOREA! BUT FIRST, WE MUST DESTROY THE GUARDIAN DRAGON AND CAPTURE THE MAN-PA-SHIN-JUCK.

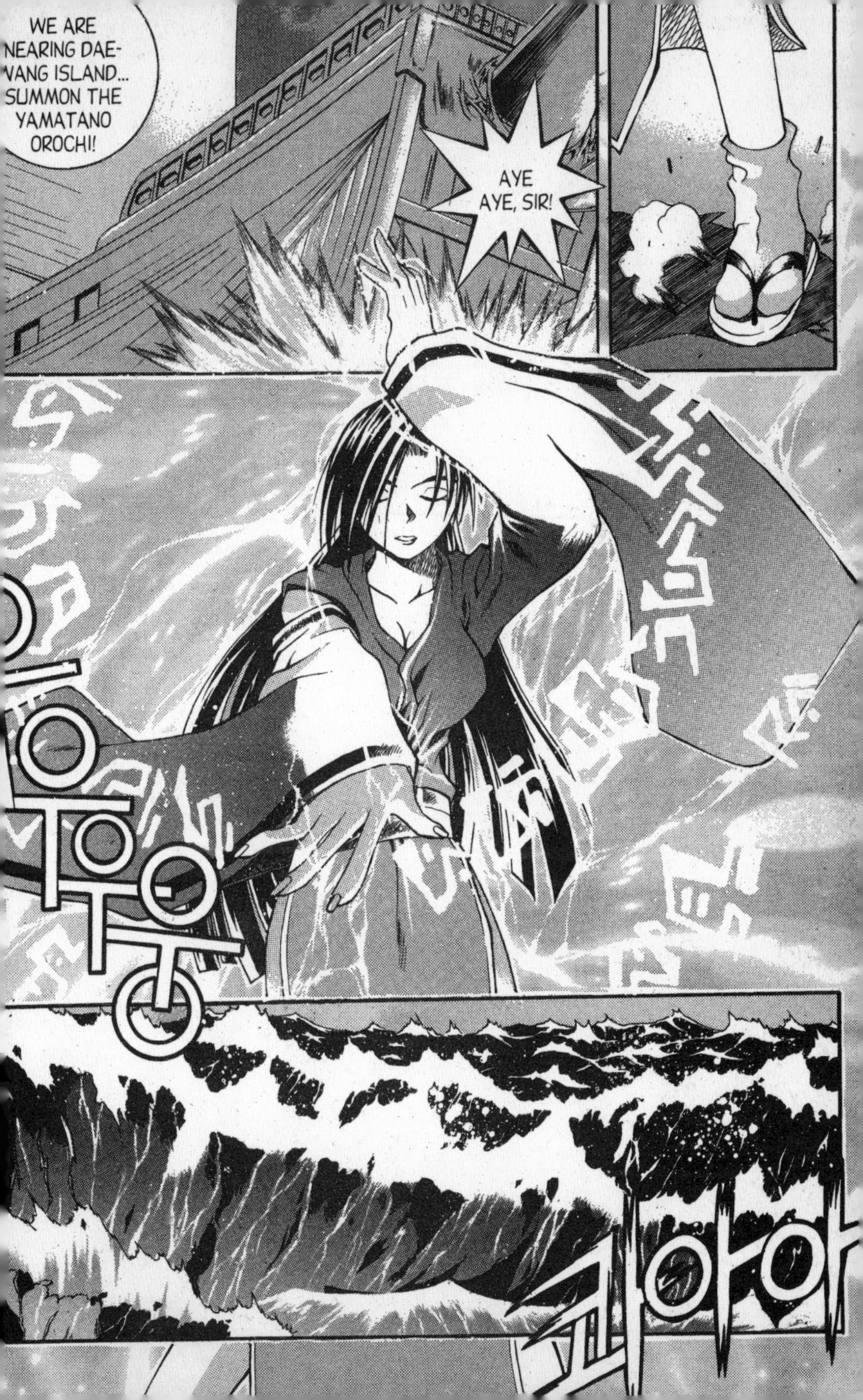
WE ARE NEARING DAE-VANG ISLAND... SUMMON THE YAMATANO OROCHI!
AYE AYE, SIR!

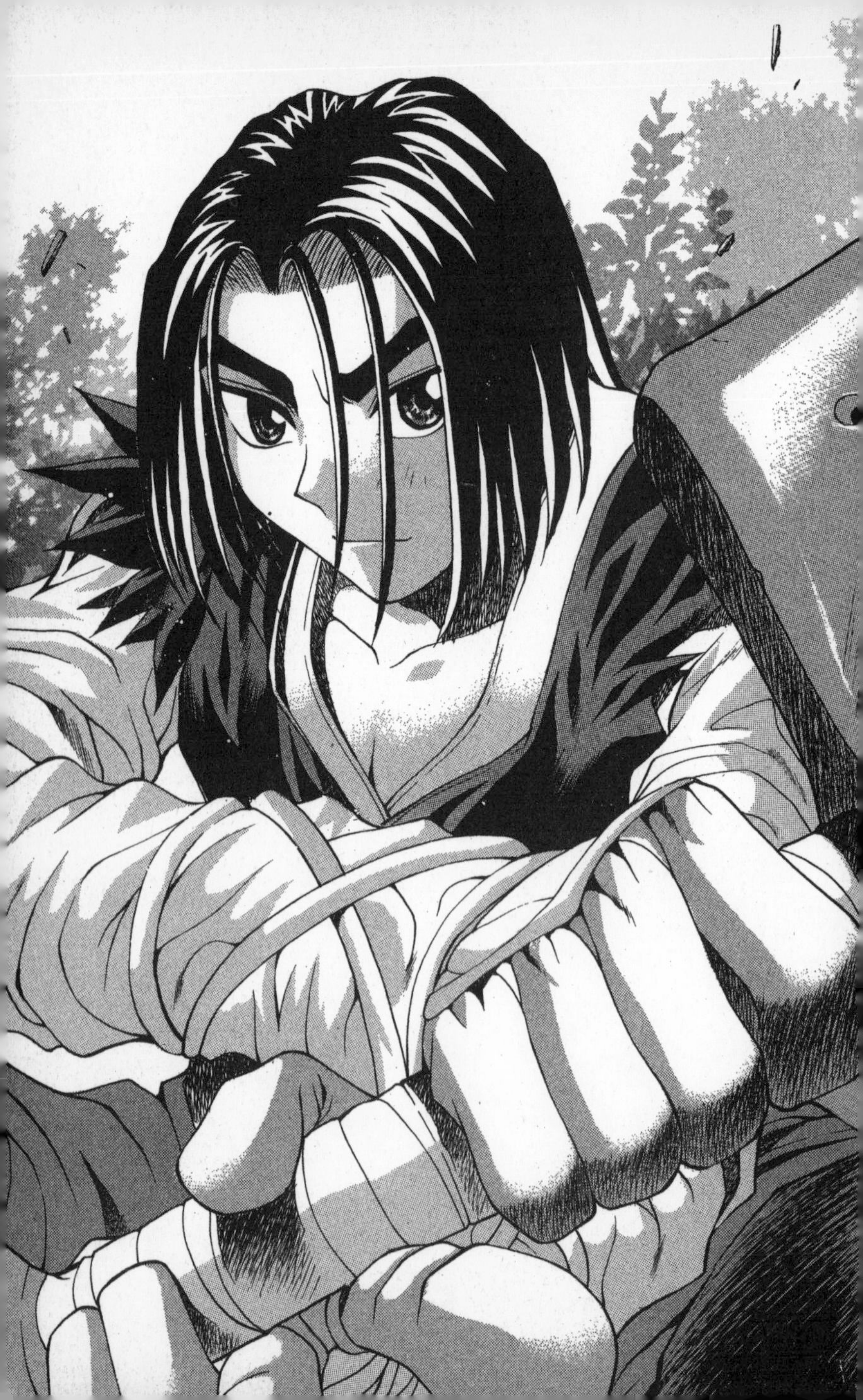

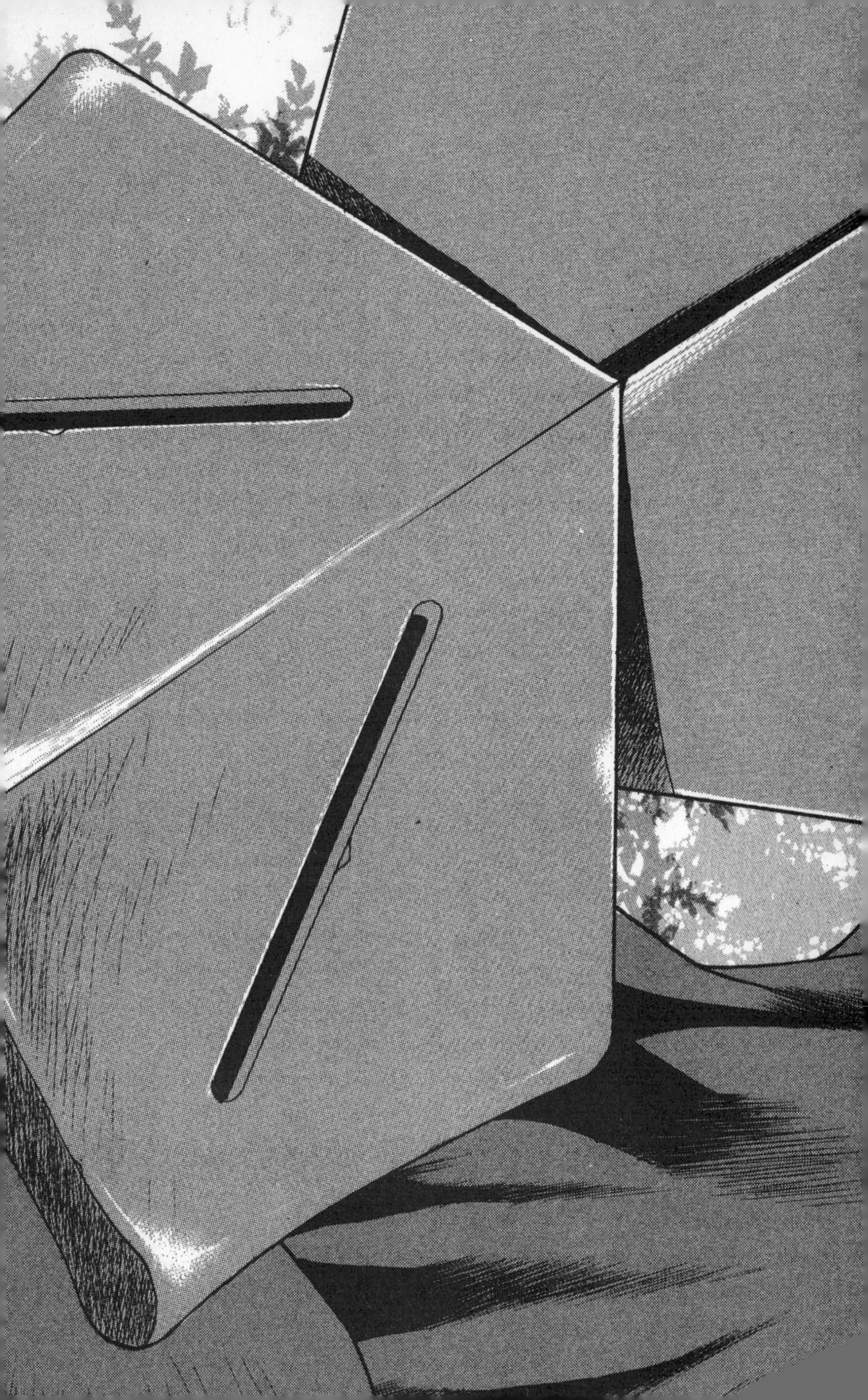

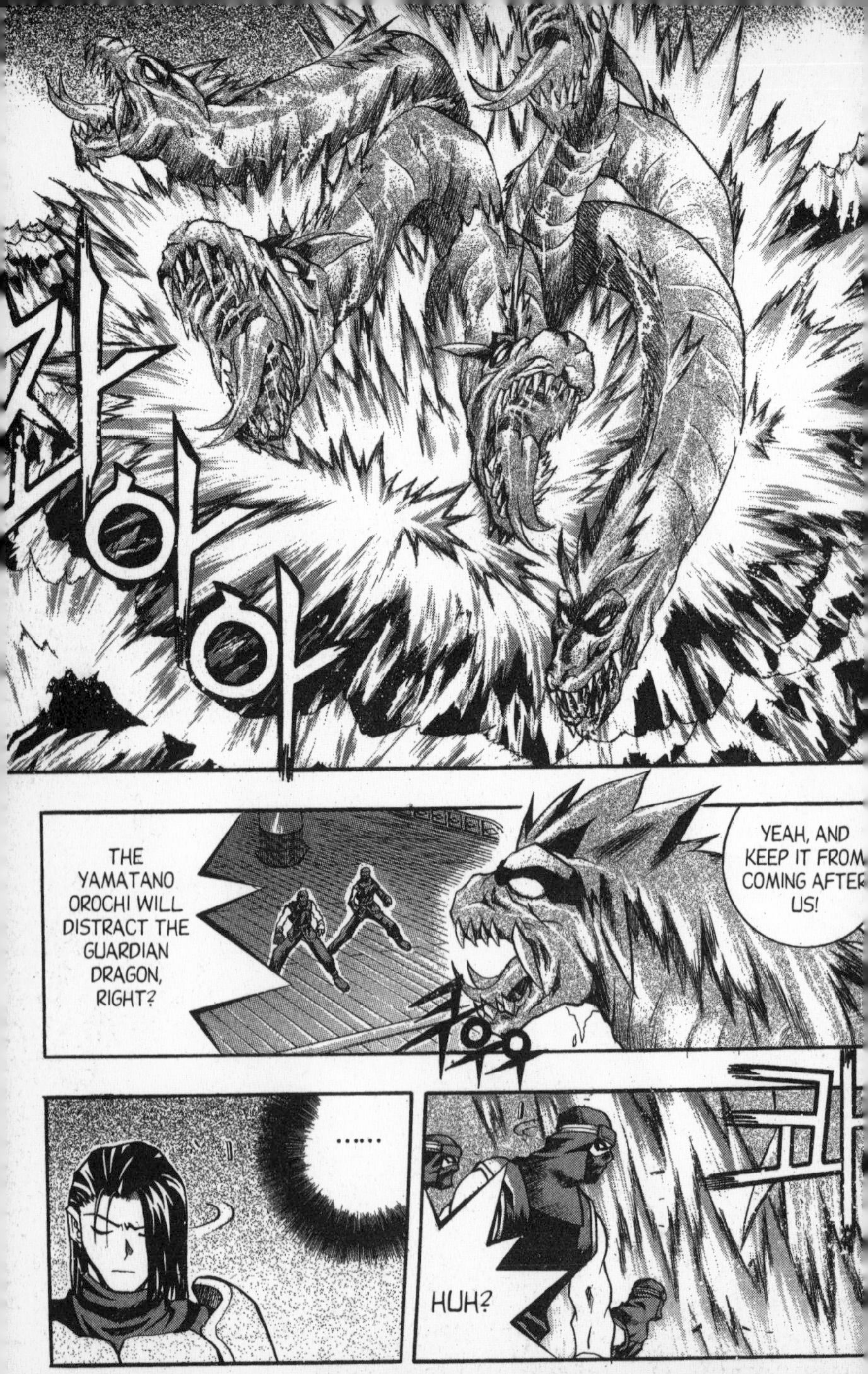
THE YAMATANO OROCHI WILL DISTRACT THE GUARDIAN DRAGON, RIGHT?
YEAH, AND KEEP IT FROM COMING AFTER US!
......
HUH?

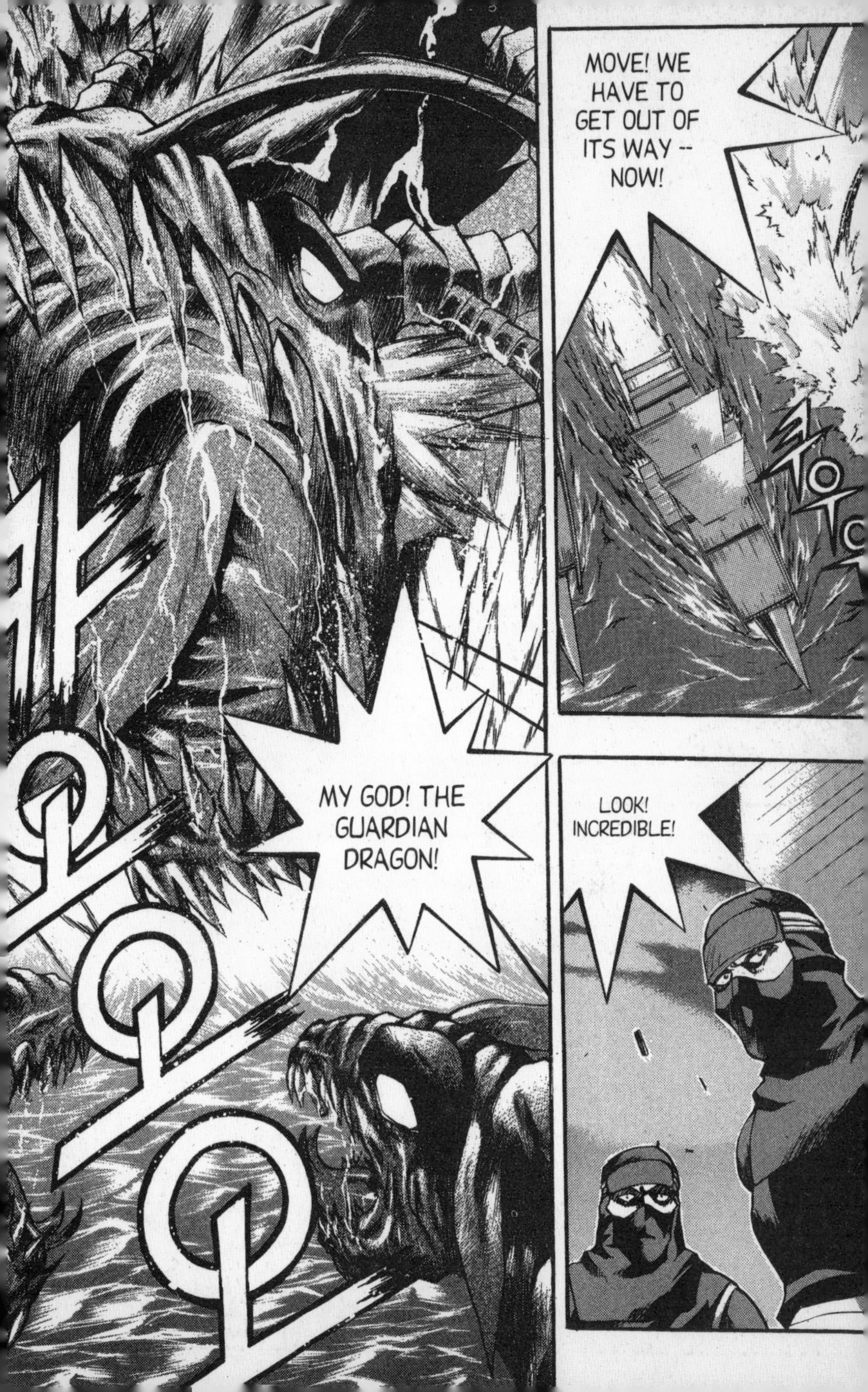
MY GOD! THE GUARDIAN DRAGON!
MOVE! WE HAVE TO GET OUT OF ITS WAY -- NOW!
LOOK! INCREDIBLE!

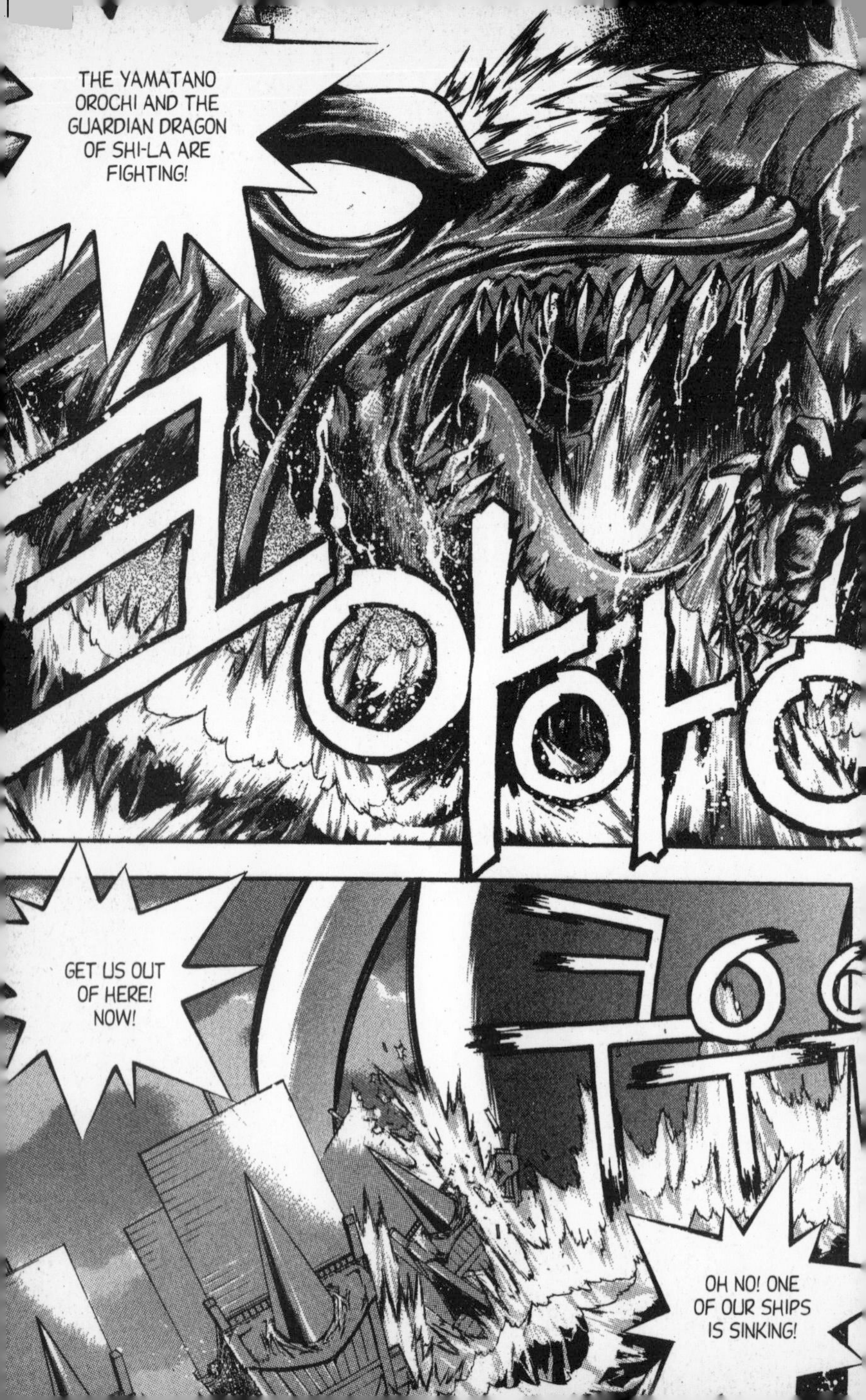
THE YAMATANO OROCHI AND THE GUARDIAN DRAGON OF SHI-LA ARE FIGHTING!
GET US OUT OF HERE! NOW!
OH NO! ONE OF OUR SHIPS IS SINKING!

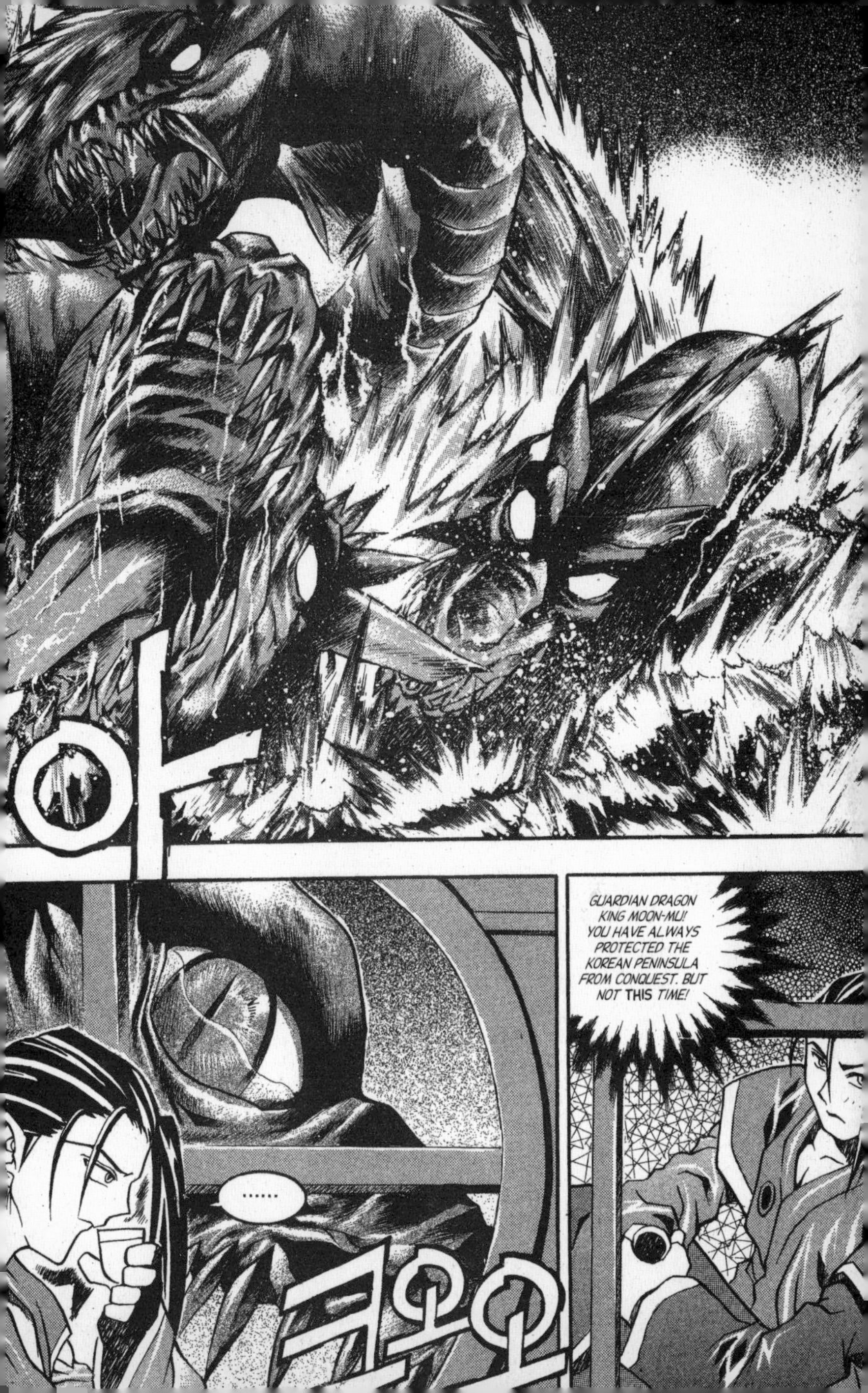
......
GUARDIAN DRAGON KING MOON-MU! YOU HAVE ALWAYS PROTECTED THE KOREAN PENINSULA FROM CONQUEST. BUT NOT THIS TIME!

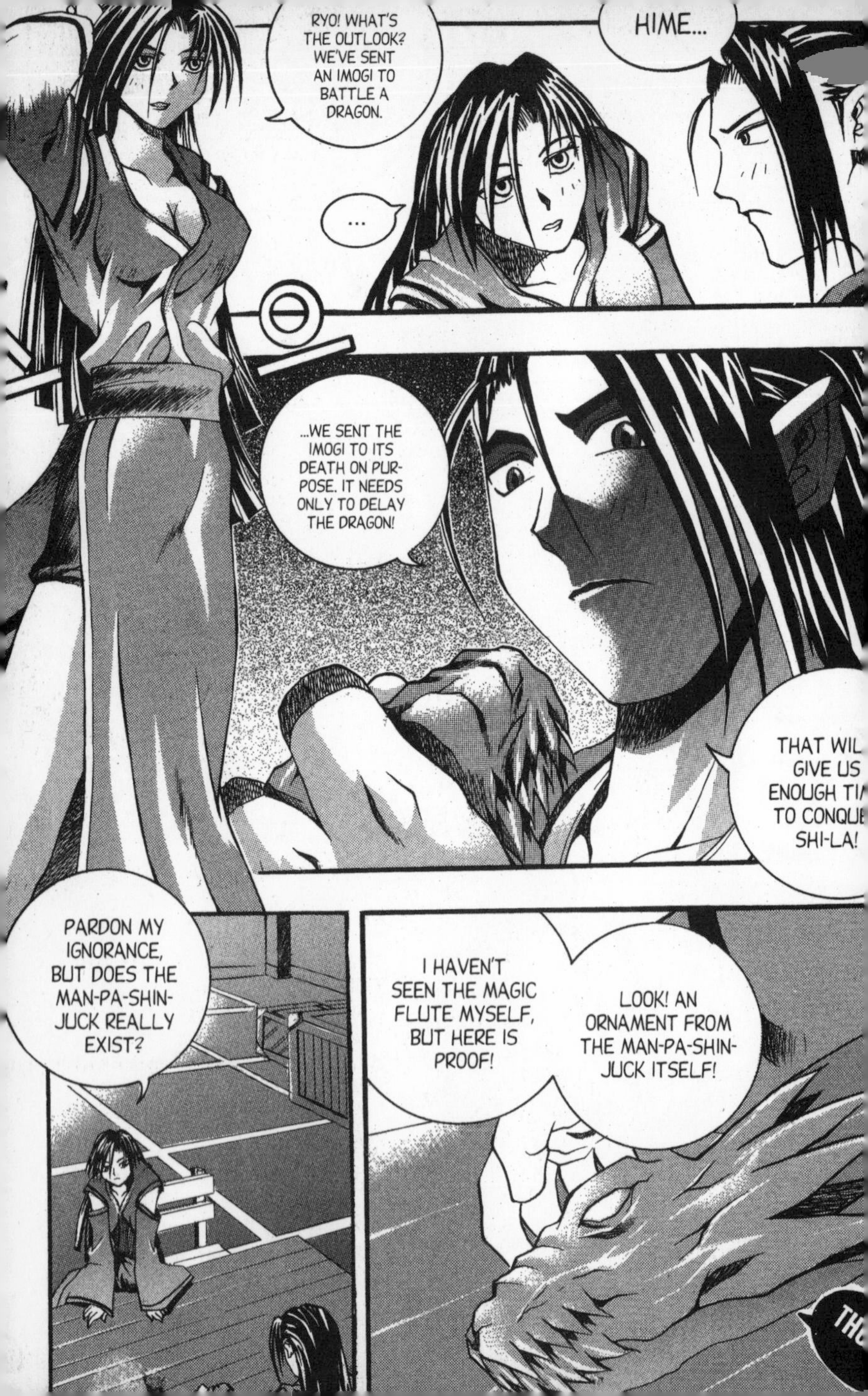
RYO! WHAT'S THE OUTLOOK? WE'VE SENT AN IMOGI TO BATTLE A DRAGON.
HIME...
...
...WE SENT THE IMOGI TO ITS DEATH ON PURPOSE. IT NEEDS ONLY TO DELAY THE DRAGON!
PARDON MY IGNORANCE, BUT DOES THE MAN-PA-SHIN-JUCK REALLY EXIST?
I HAVEN'T SEEN THE MAGIC FLUTE MYSELF, BUT HERE IS PROOF!
LOOK! AN ORNAMENT FROM THE MAN-PA-SHIN-JUCK ITSELF!

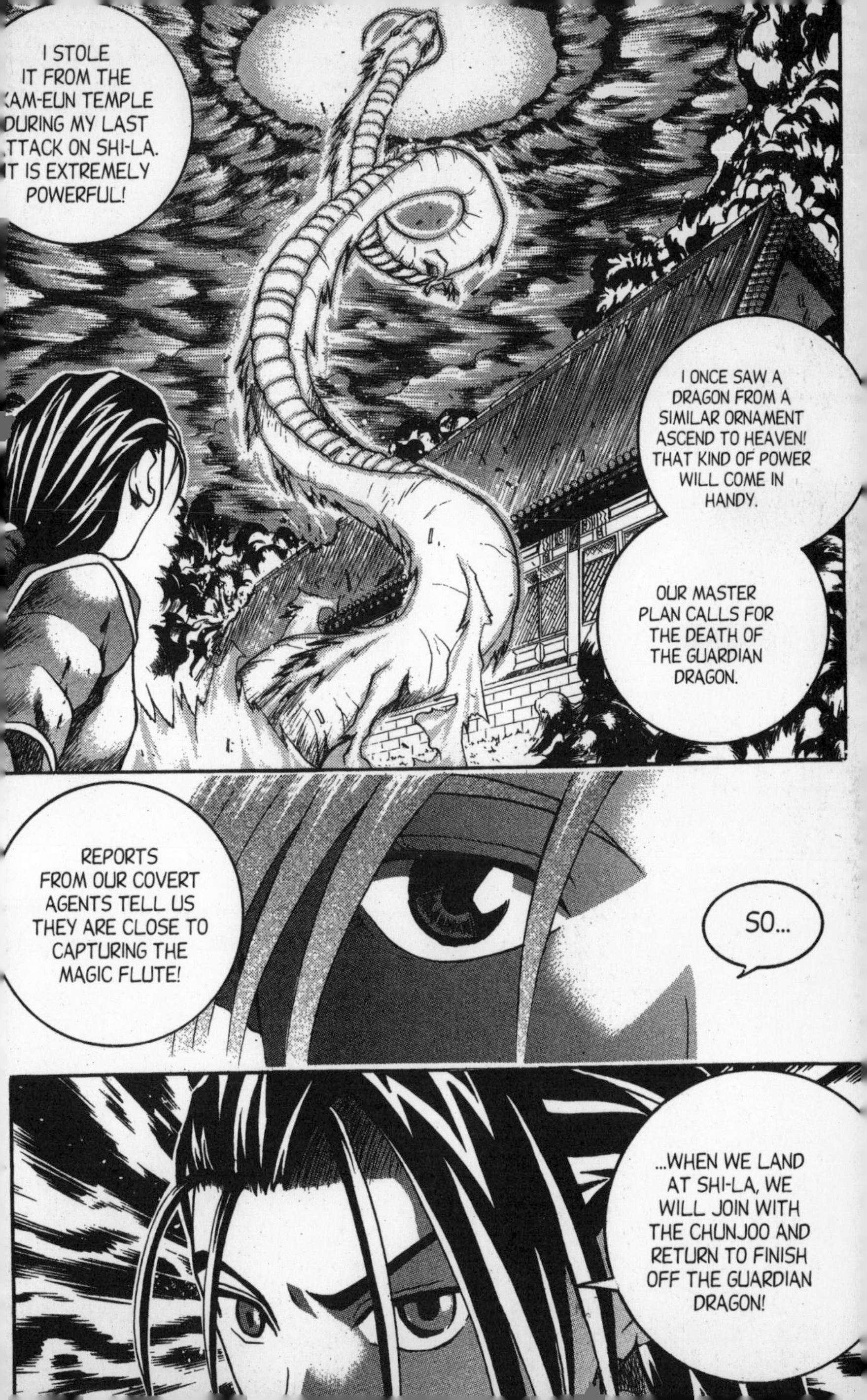

I STOLE IT FROM THE KAM-EUN TEMPLE DURING MY LAST ATTACK ON SHI-LA. IT IS EXTREMELY POWERFUL!
I ONCE SAW A DRAGON FROM A SIMILAR ORNAMENT ASCEND TO HEAVEN! THAT KIND OF POWER WILL COME IN HANDY.
OUR MASTER PLAN CALLS FOR THE DEATH OF THE GUARDIAN DRAGON.
REPORTS FROM OUR COVERT AGENTS TELL US THEY ARE CLOSE TO CAPTURING THE MAGIC FLUTE!
SO...
...WHEN WE LAND AT SHI-LA, WE WILL JOIN WITH THE CHUNJOO AND RETURN TO FINISH OFF THE GUARDIAN DRAGON!

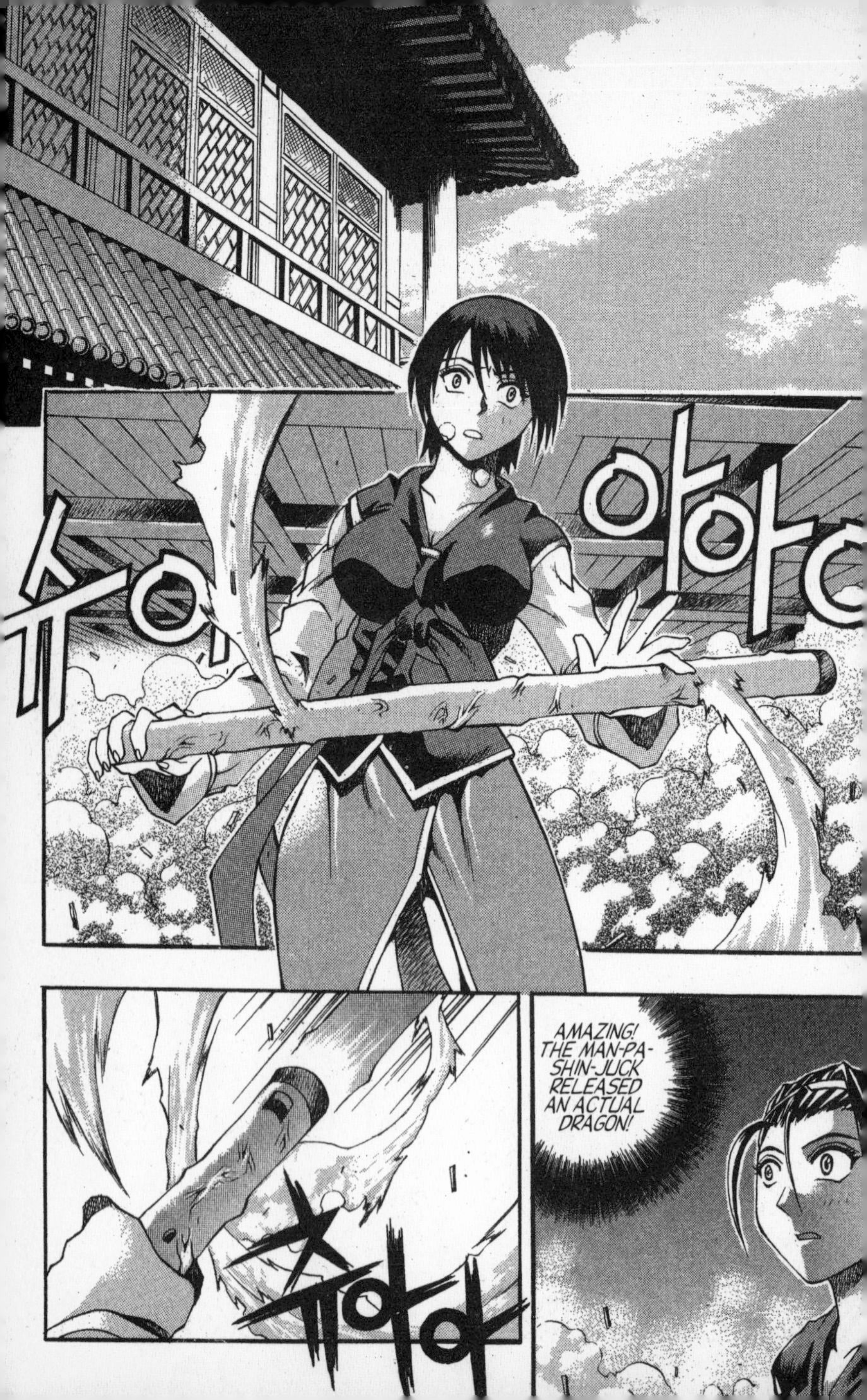
AMAZING! THE MAN-PA-SHIN-JUCK RELEASED AN ACTUAL DRAGON!

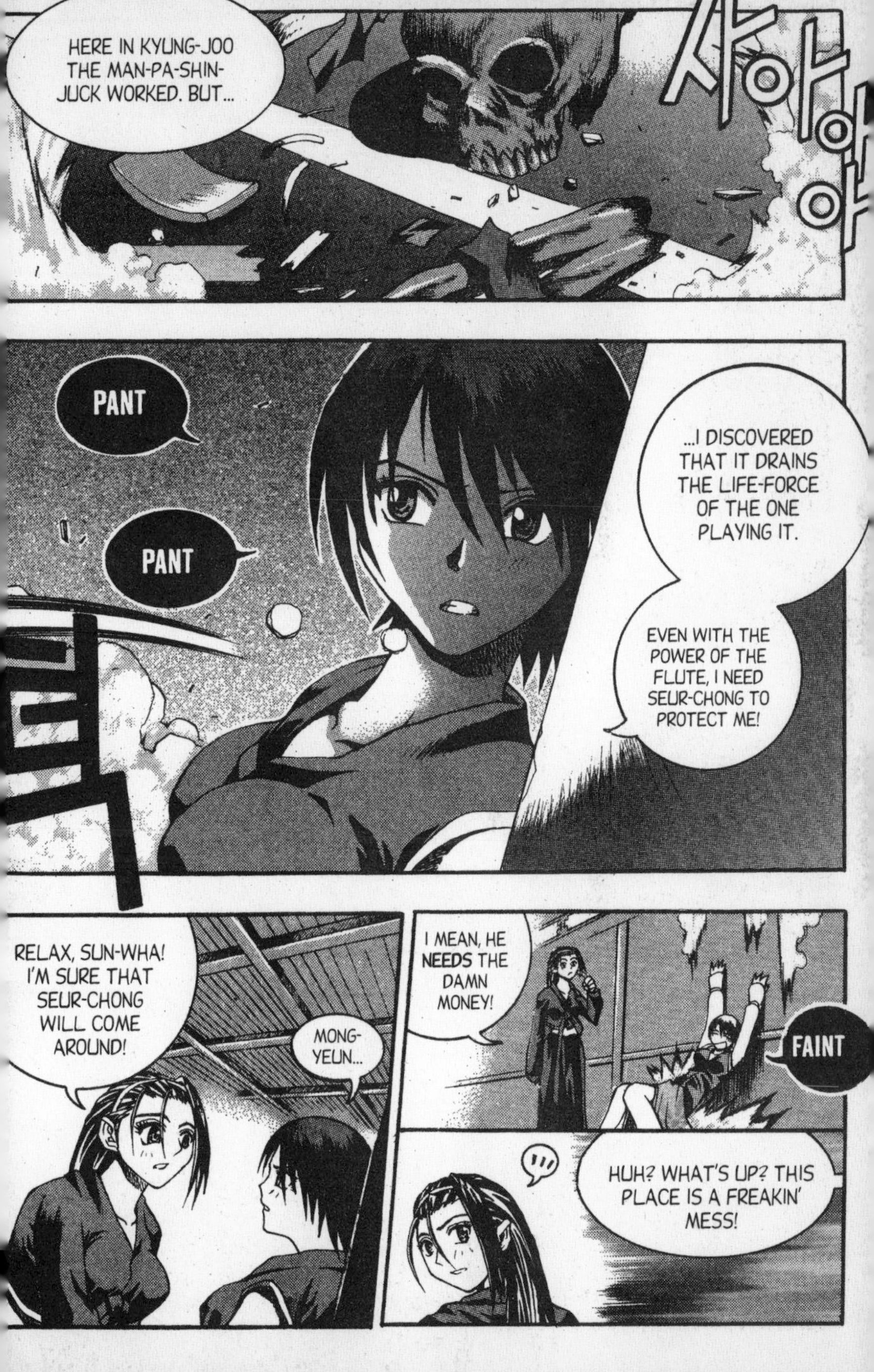

HERE IN KYUNG-JOO THE MAN-PA-SHIN-JUCK WORKED. BUT...
샤아아아
PANT
PANT
...I DISCOVERED THAT IT DRAINS THE LIFE-FORCE OF THE ONE PLAYING IT.
EVEN WITH THE POWER OF THE FLUTE, I NEED SEUR-CHONG TO PROTECT ME!
RELAX, SUN-WHA! I'M SURE THAT SEUR-CHONG WILL COME AROUND!
MONG-YEUN...
I MEAN, HE **NEEDS** THE DAMN MONEY!
FAINT
HUH? WHAT'S UP? THIS PLACE IS A FREAKIN' MESS!

DID THAT NINJA COME BACK? I HOPE YOU KICKED HIS BUTT.

MONG-YEUN? ARE YOU OKAY? DID HE HURT YOU?

NO.

SEE, SEUR-CHONG! THEY COULD HAVE BEEN KILLED!

WEL THEY WE WERE T

I SEE! YOU WASTED HIM WITH THE MAGIC FLUTE? HAH! THAT'S CLASSIC! NOW I UNDER-STAND WHY THEY WANT THE FLUTE SO BADLY.

......

DO YOU NOW COMPREHEND THAT THIS THREAT AFFECTS NOT ONLY SHI-LA BUT THE ENTIRE KOREAN PENINSULA?

STAND

YEAH, I GET IT. AND I STILL DON'T GIVE A DAMN. I CARE ABOUT MONEY AND HUNTING DRAGONS THAT'S IT.

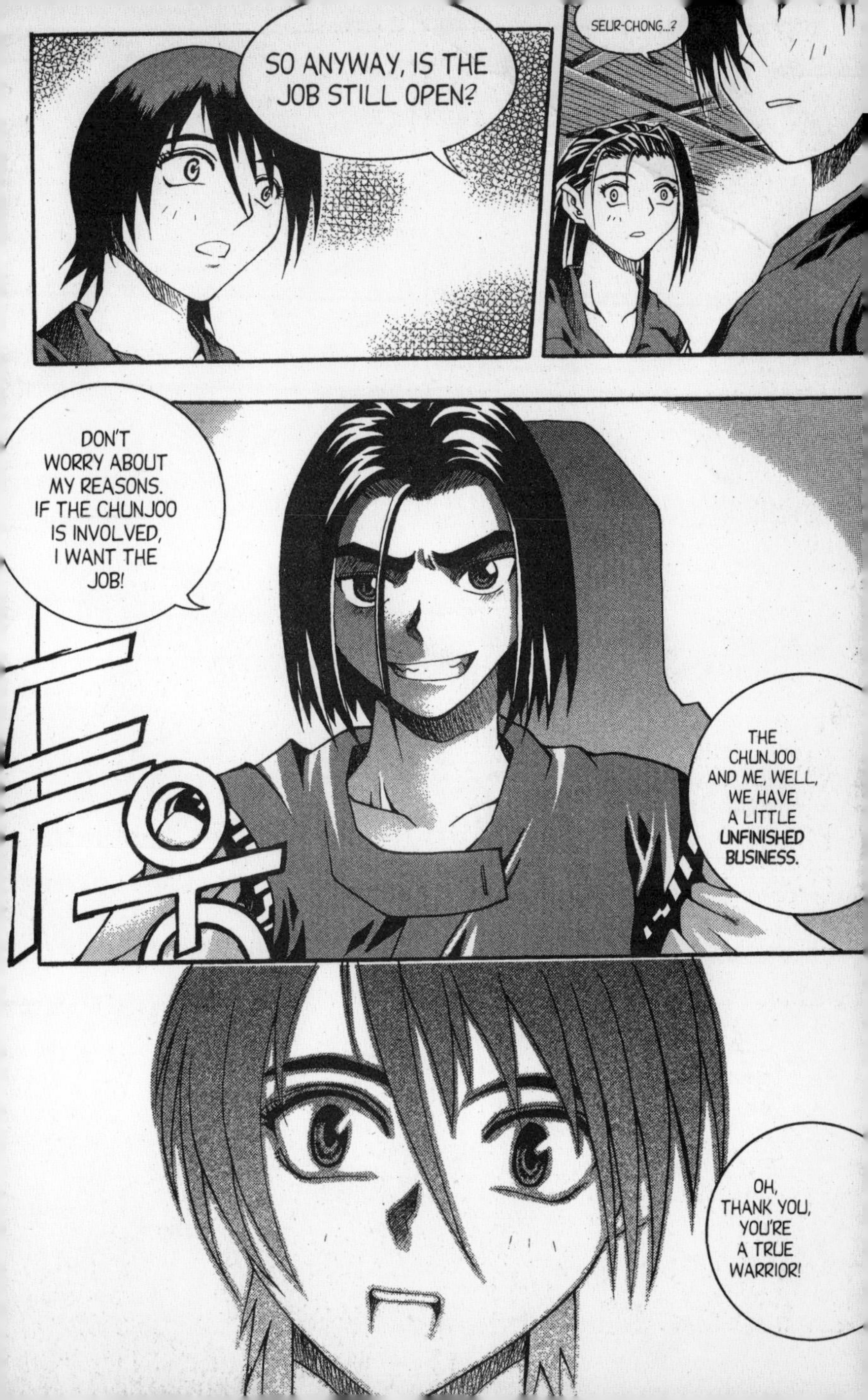
SO ANYWAY, IS THE JOB STILL OPEN?
SEUR-CHONG...?
DON'T WORRY ABOUT MY REASONS. IF THE CHUNJOO IS INVOLVED, I WANT THE JOB!
THE CHUNJOO AND ME, WELL, WE HAVE A LITTLE **UNFINISHED BUSINESS.**
OH, THANK YOU, YOU'RE A TRUE WARRIOR!

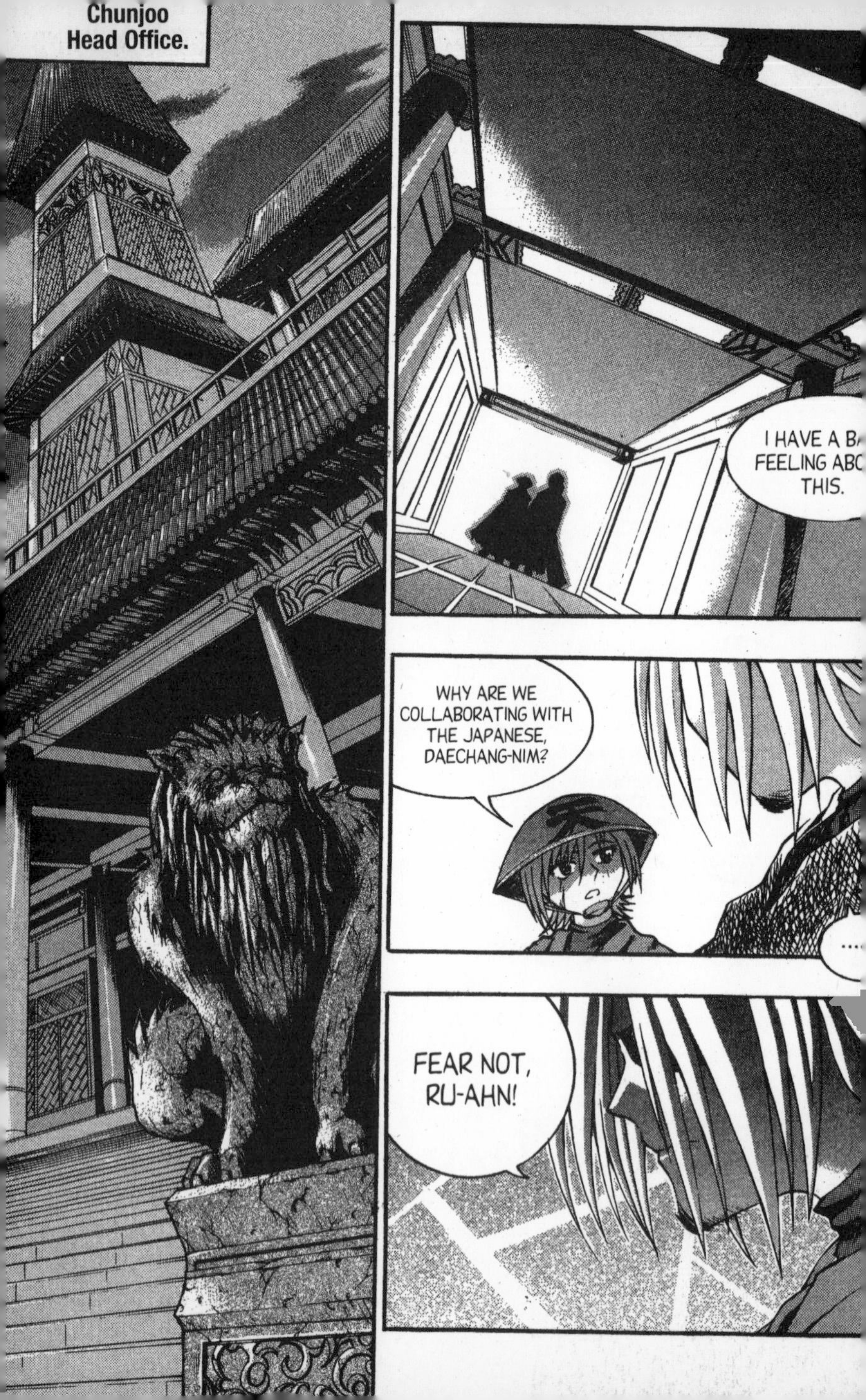
Chunjoo Head Office.
I HAVE A B FEELING ABO THIS.
WHY ARE WE COLLABORATING WITH THE JAPANESE, DAECHANG-NIM?
....
FEAR NOT, RU-AHN!

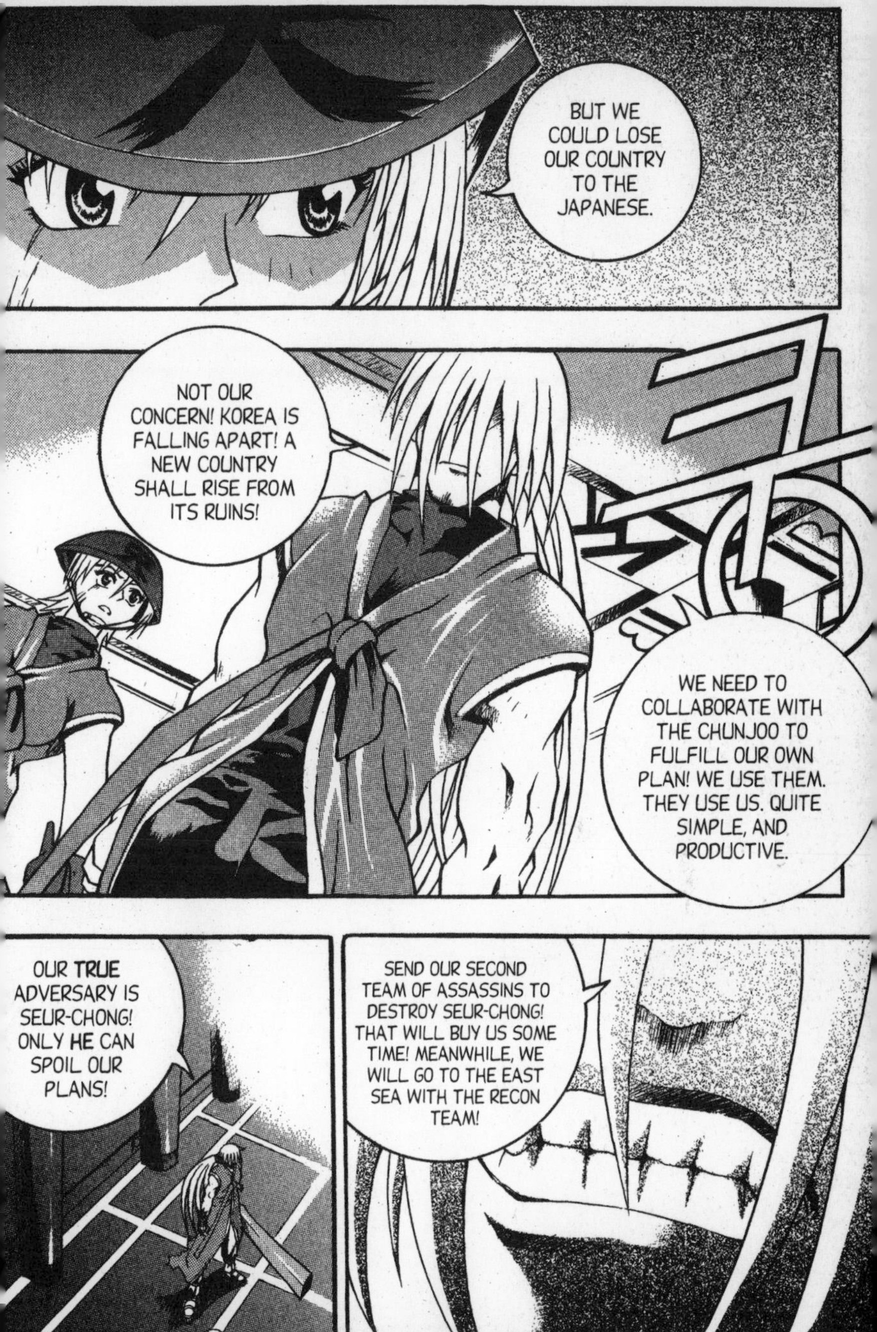
BUT WE COULD LOSE OUR COUNTRY TO THE JAPANESE.
NOT OUR CONCERN! KOREA IS FALLING APART! A NEW COUNTRY SHALL RISE FROM ITS RUINS!
WE NEED TO COLLABORATE WITH THE CHUNJOO TO FULFILL OUR OWN PLAN! WE USE THEM. THEY USE US. QUITE SIMPLE, AND PRODUCTIVE.
OUR **TRUE** ADVERSARY IS SEUR-CHONG! ONLY **HE** CAN SPOIL OUR PLANS!
SEND OUR SECOND TEAM OF ASSASSINS TO DESTROY SEUR-CHONG! THAT WILL BUY US SOME TIME! MEANWHILE, WE WILL GO TO THE EAST SEA WITH THE RECON TEAM!

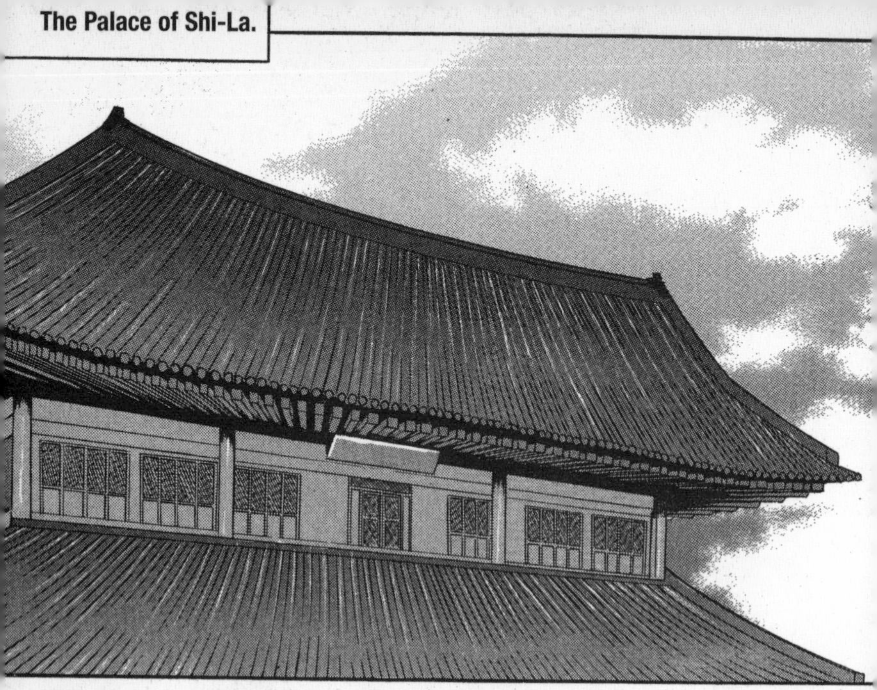
The Palace of Shi-La.

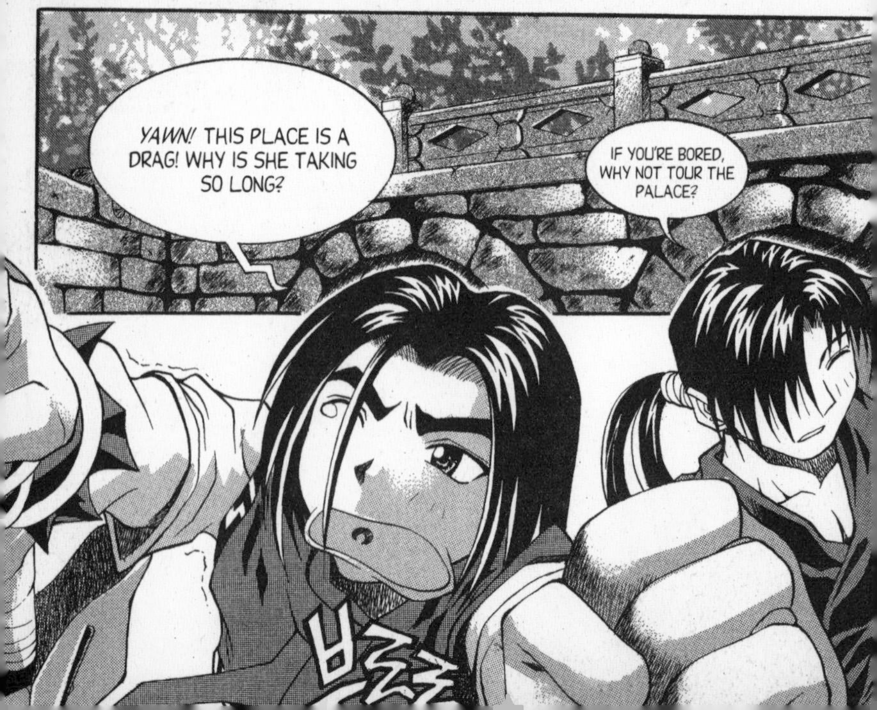
YAWN! THIS PLACE IS A DRAG! WHY IS SHE TAKING SO LONG?
IF YOU'RE BORED, WHY NOT TOUR THE PALACE?

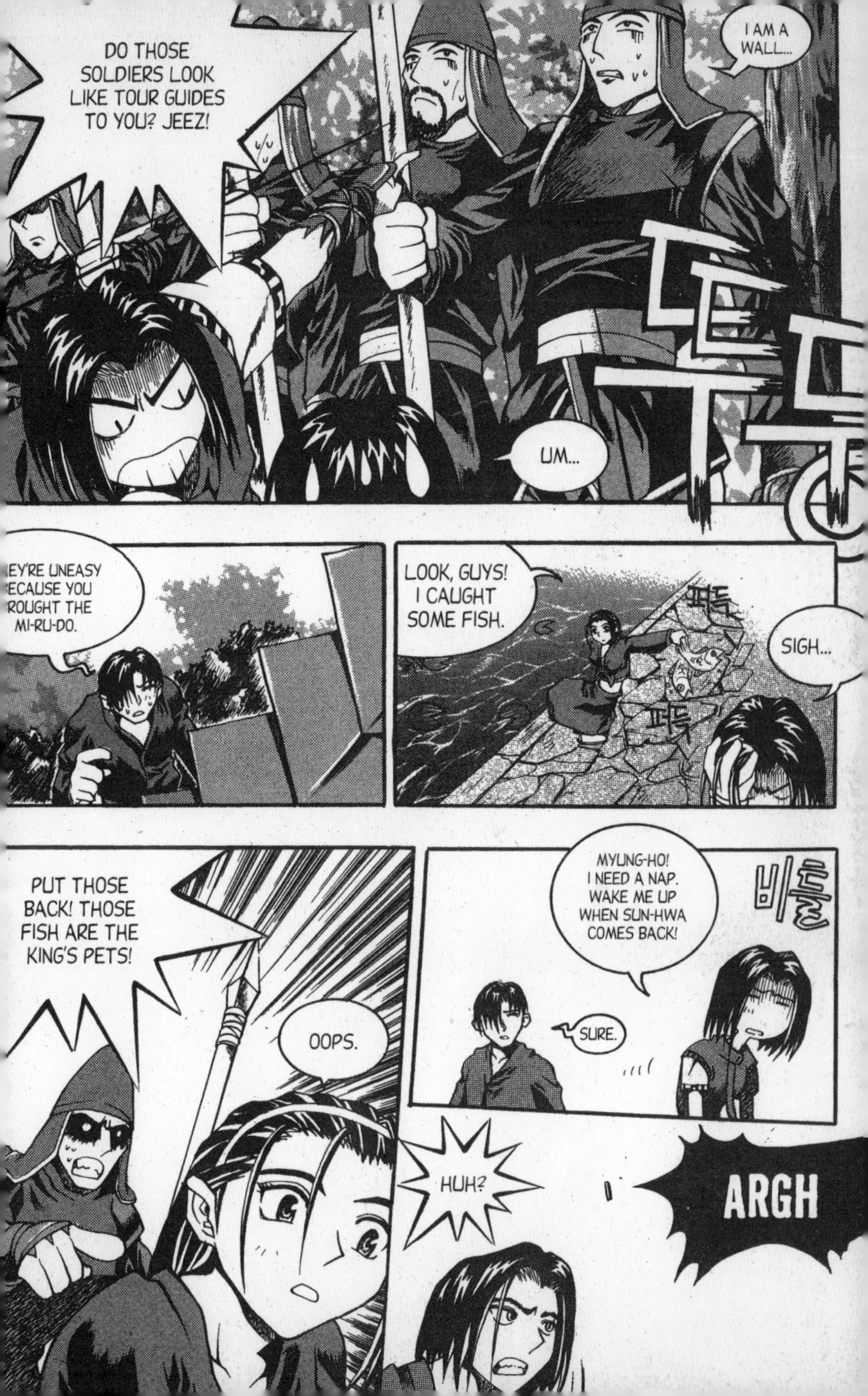
DO THOSE SOLDIERS LOOK LIKE TOUR GUIDES TO YOU? JEEZ!
I AM A WALL...
UM...
EY'RE UNEASY ECAUSE YOU ROUGHT THE MI-RU-DO.
LOOK, GUYS! I CAUGHT SOME FISH.
SIGH...
PUT THOSE BACK! THOSE FISH ARE THE KING'S PETS!
OOPS.
MYUNG-HO! I NEED A NAP. WAKE ME UP WHEN SUN-HWA COMES BACK!
비틀
SURE.
HUH?
ARGH

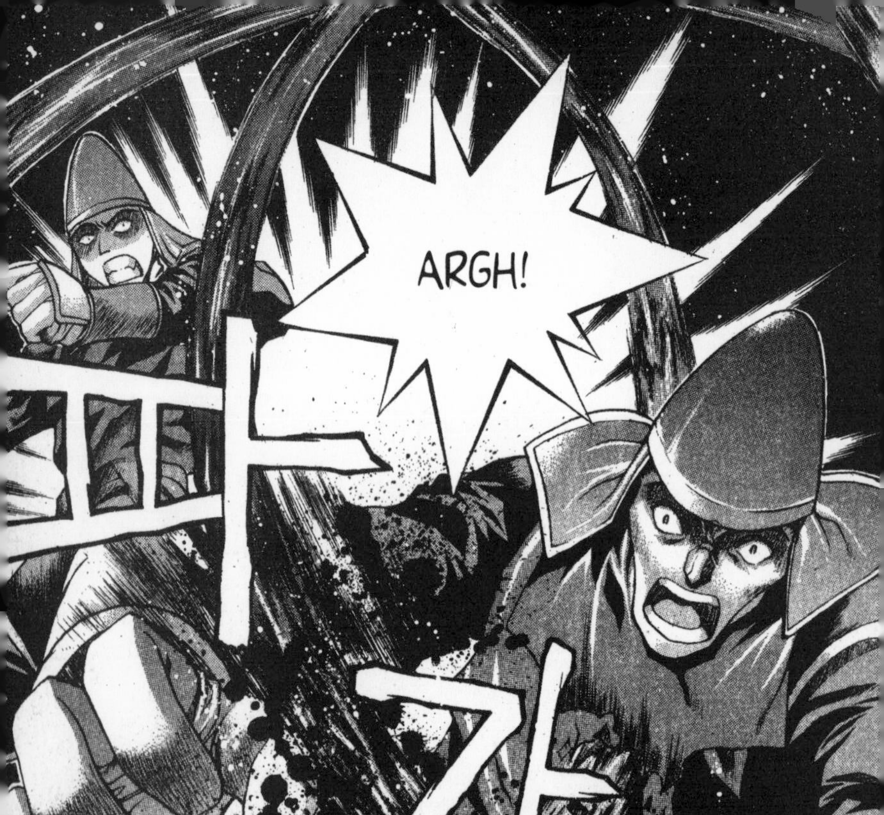
ARGH!
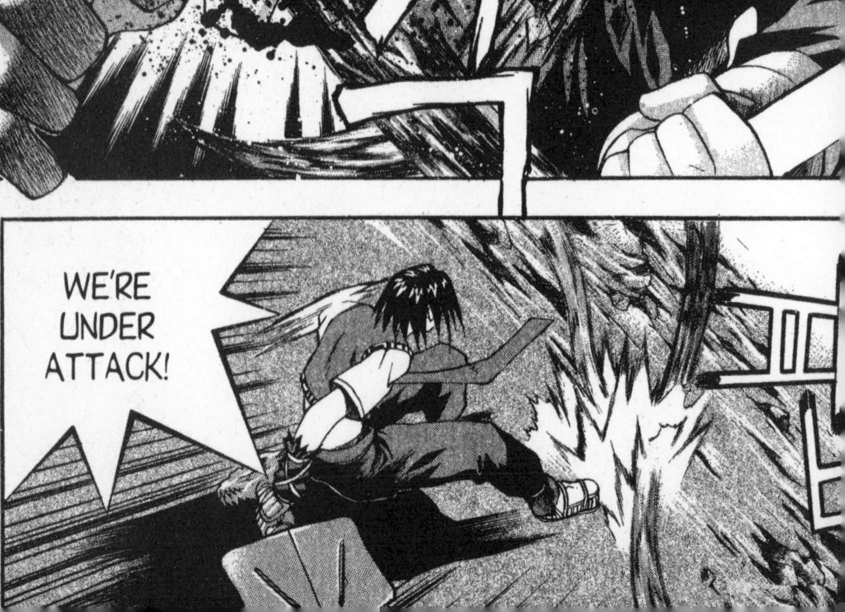
WE'RE UNDER ATTACK!

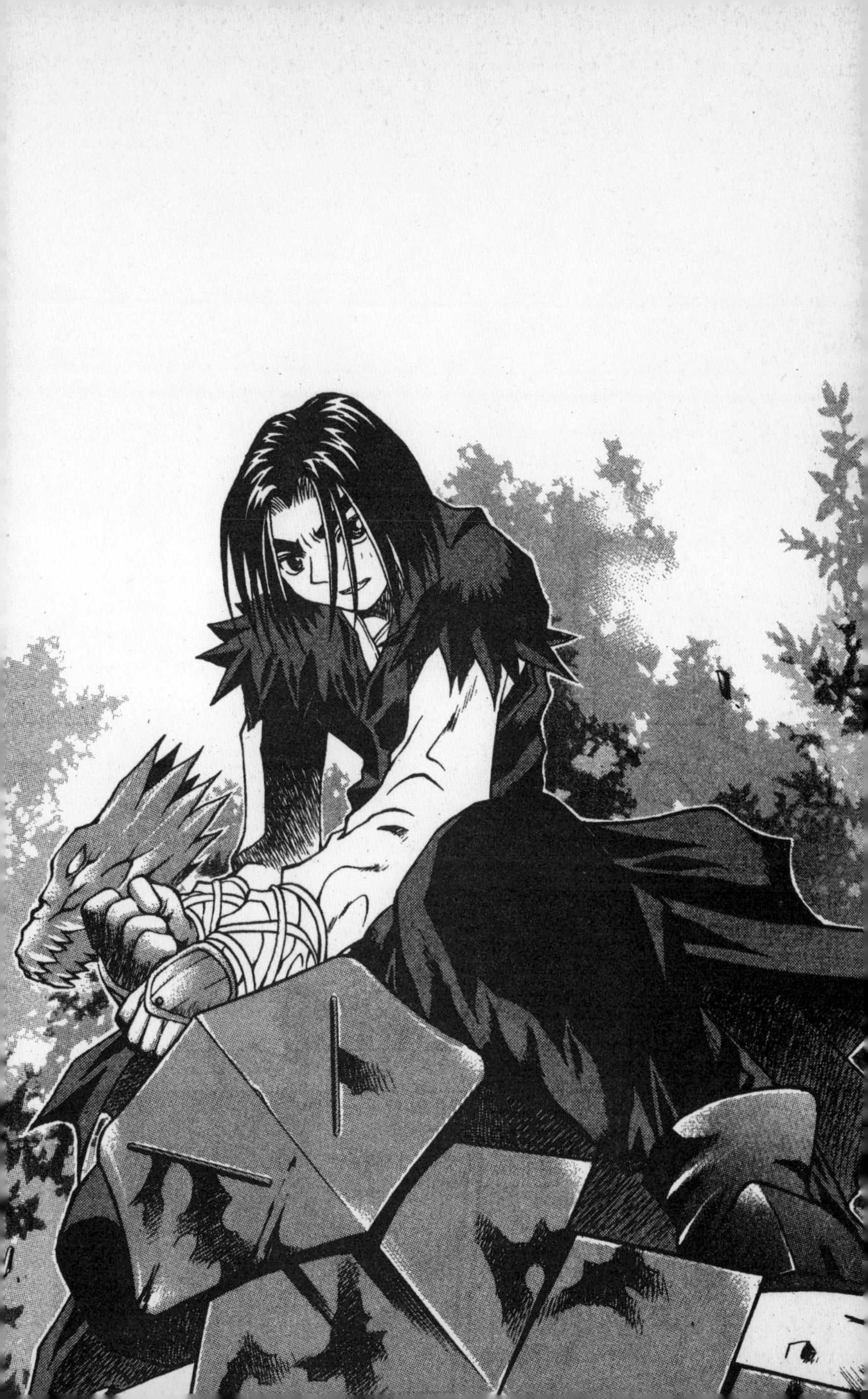

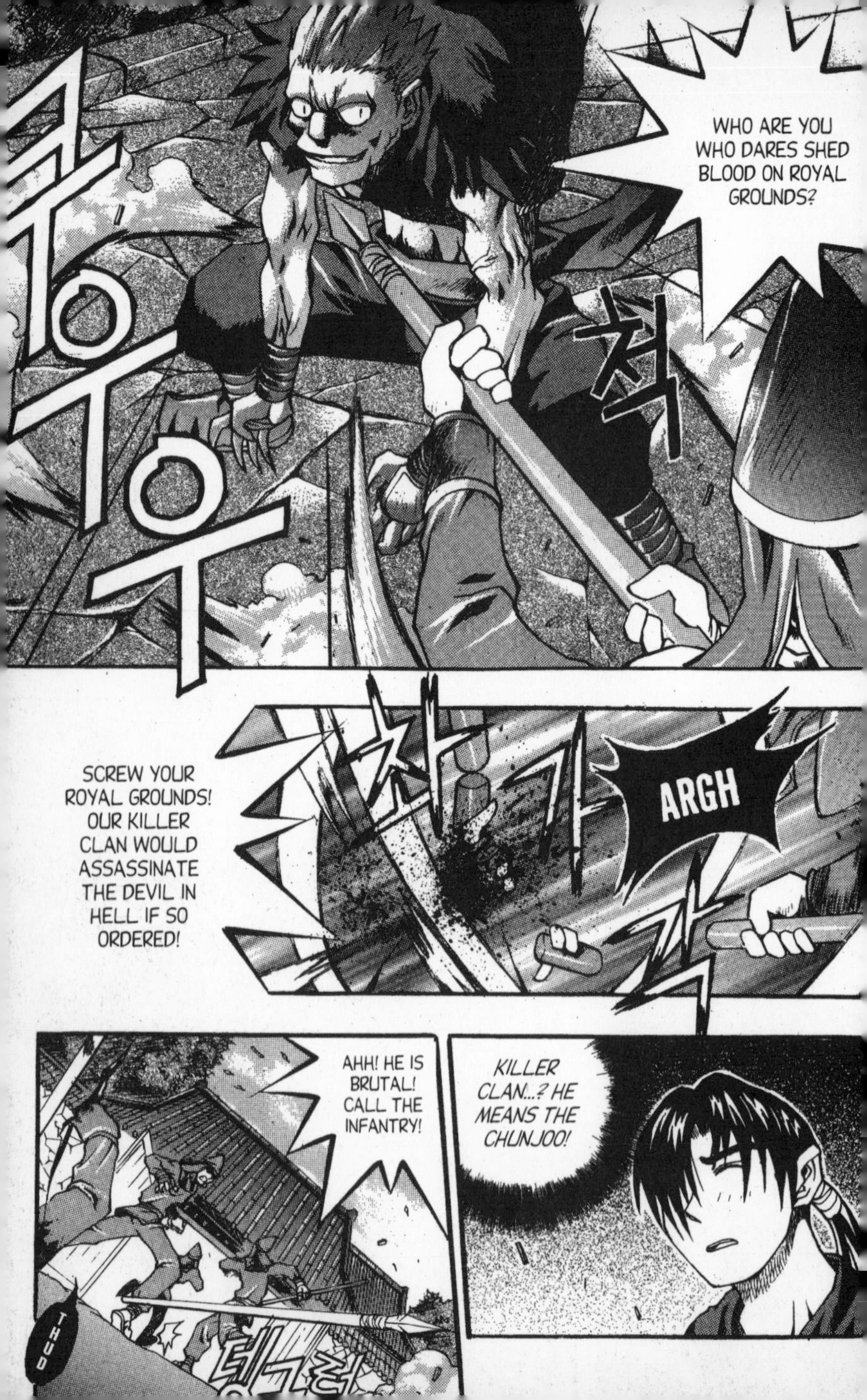
WHO ARE YOU WHO DARES SHED BLOOD ON ROYAL GROUNDS?
SCREW YOUR ROYAL GROUNDS! OUR KILLER CLAN WOULD ASSASSINATE THE DEVIL IN HELL IF SO ORDERED!
ARGH
AHH! HE IS BRUTAL! CALL THE INFANTRY!
THUD
KILLER CLAN...? HE MEANS THE CHUNJOO!

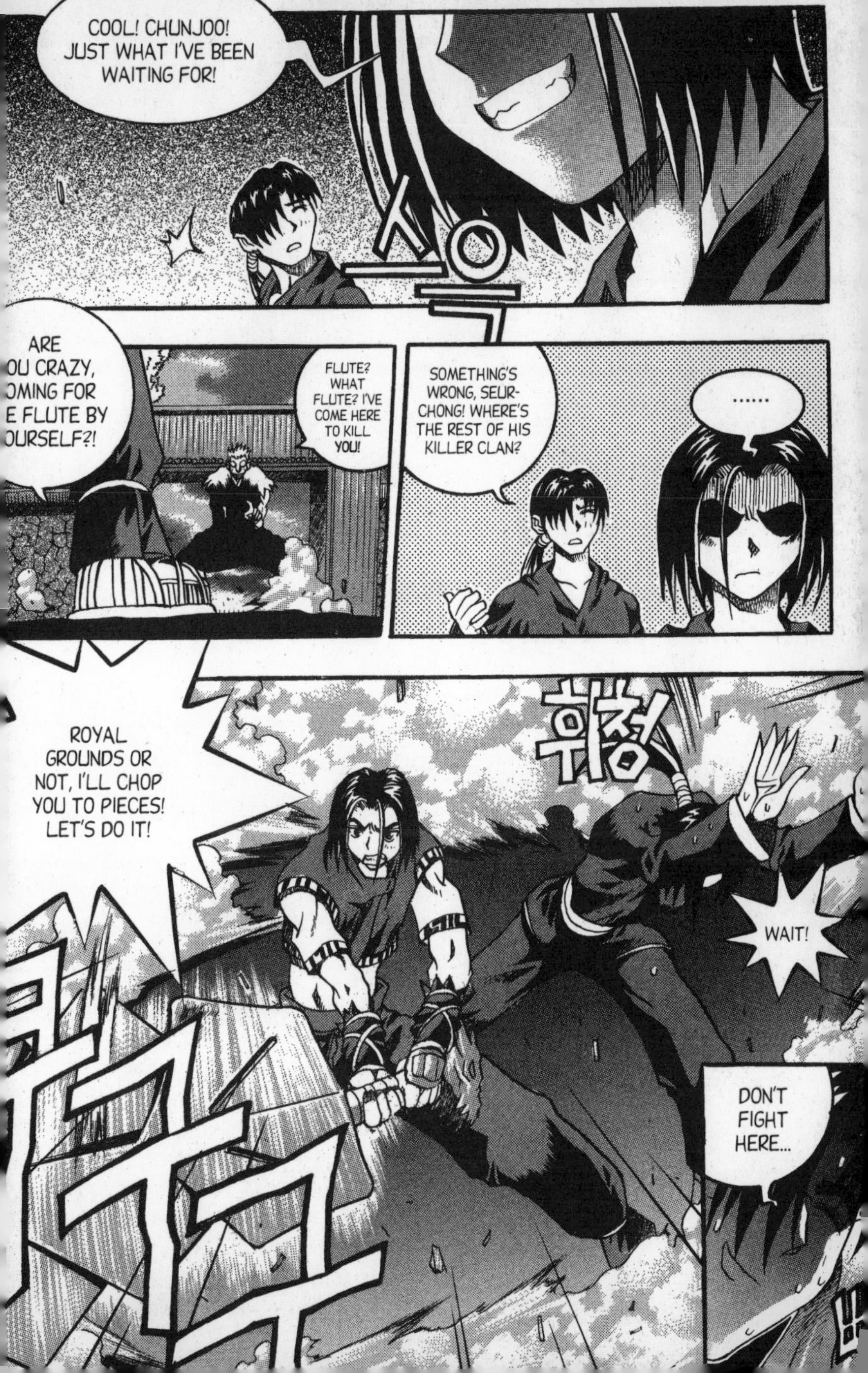
COOL! CHUNJOO! JUST WHAT I'VE BEEN WAITING FOR!
ARE
OU CRAZY,
OMING FOR
E FLUTE BY
OURSELF?!
FLUTE? WHAT FLUTE? I'VE COME HERE TO KILL YOU!
SOMETHING'S WRONG, SEUR-CHONG! WHERE'S THE REST OF HIS KILLER CLAN?
......
ROYAL GROUNDS OR NOT, I'LL CHOP YOU TO PIECES! LET'S DO IT!
WAIT!
DON'T FIGHT HERE...

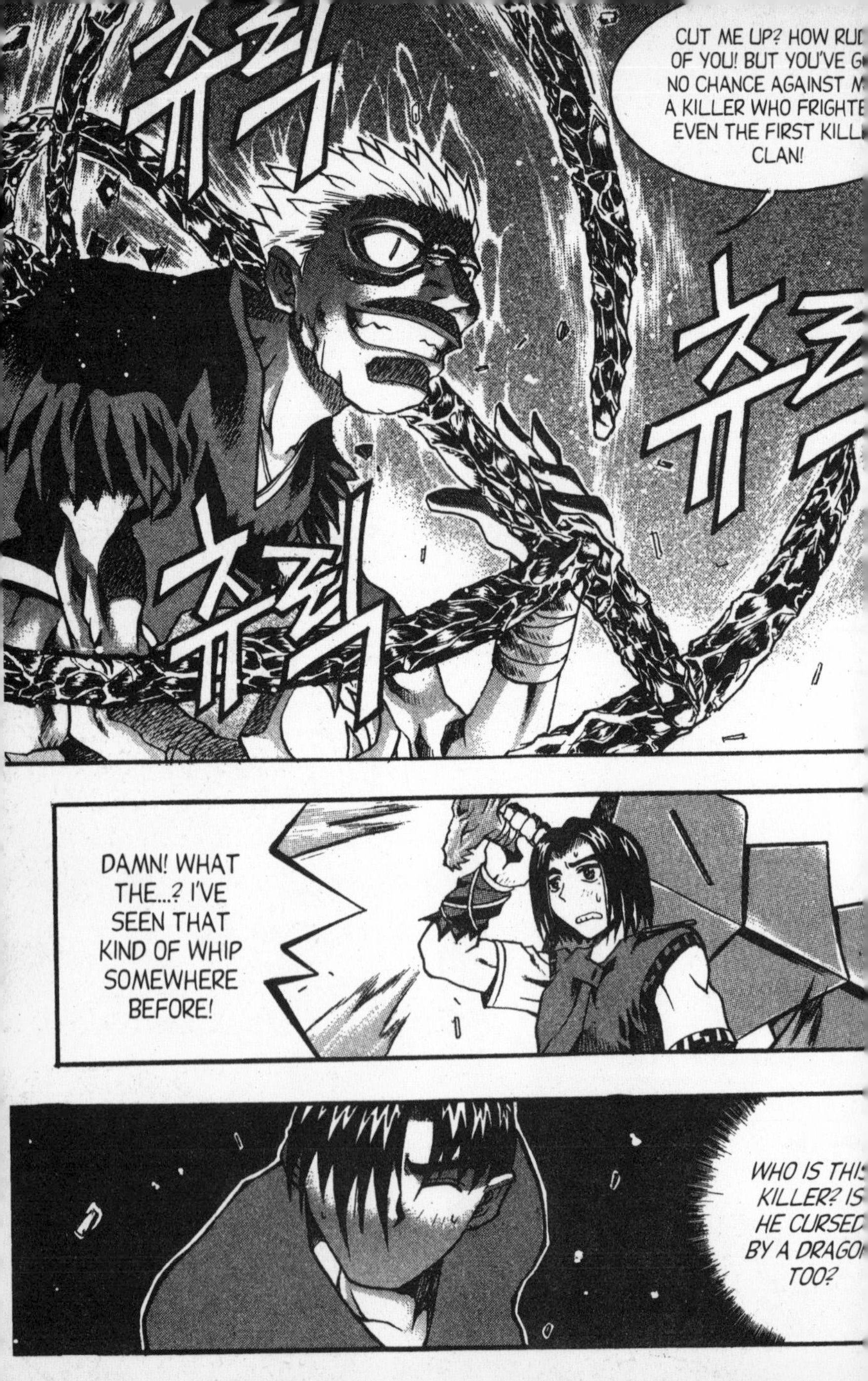
CUT ME UP? HOW RUD
OF YOU! BUT YOU'VE G
NO CHANCE AGAINST M
A KILLER WHO FRIGHTE
EVEN THE FIRST KILL
CLAN!
DAMN! WHAT THE...? I'VE SEEN THAT KIND OF WHIP SOMEWHERE BEFORE!
WHO IS THI
KILLER? IS
HE CURSED
BY A DRAGO
TOO?

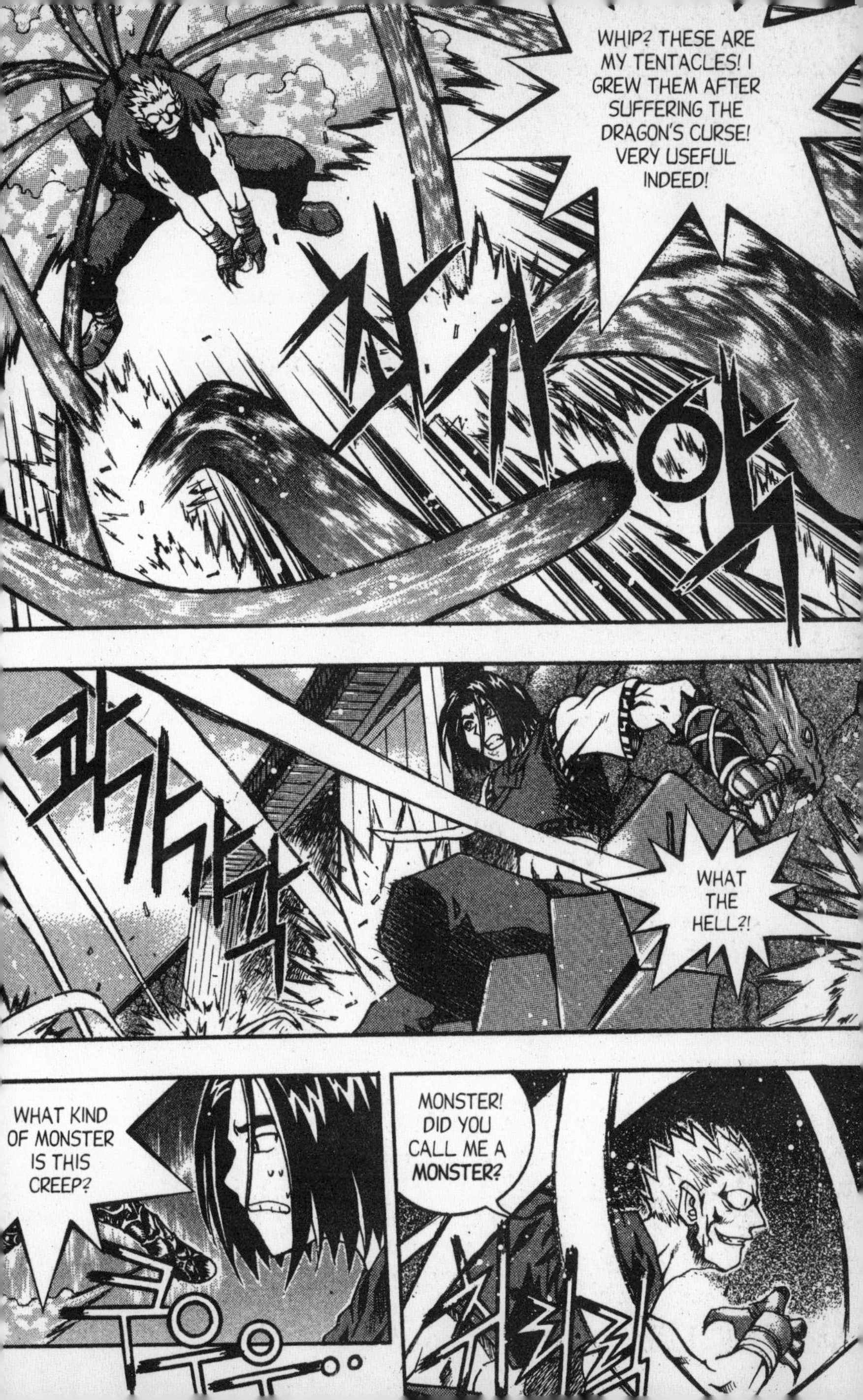
WHIP? THESE ARE MY TENTACLES! I GREW THEM AFTER SUFFERING THE DRAGON'S CURSE! VERY USEFUL INDEED!
WHAT THE HELL?!
WHAT KIND OF MONSTER IS THIS CREEP?
MONSTER! DID YOU CALL ME A MONSTER?

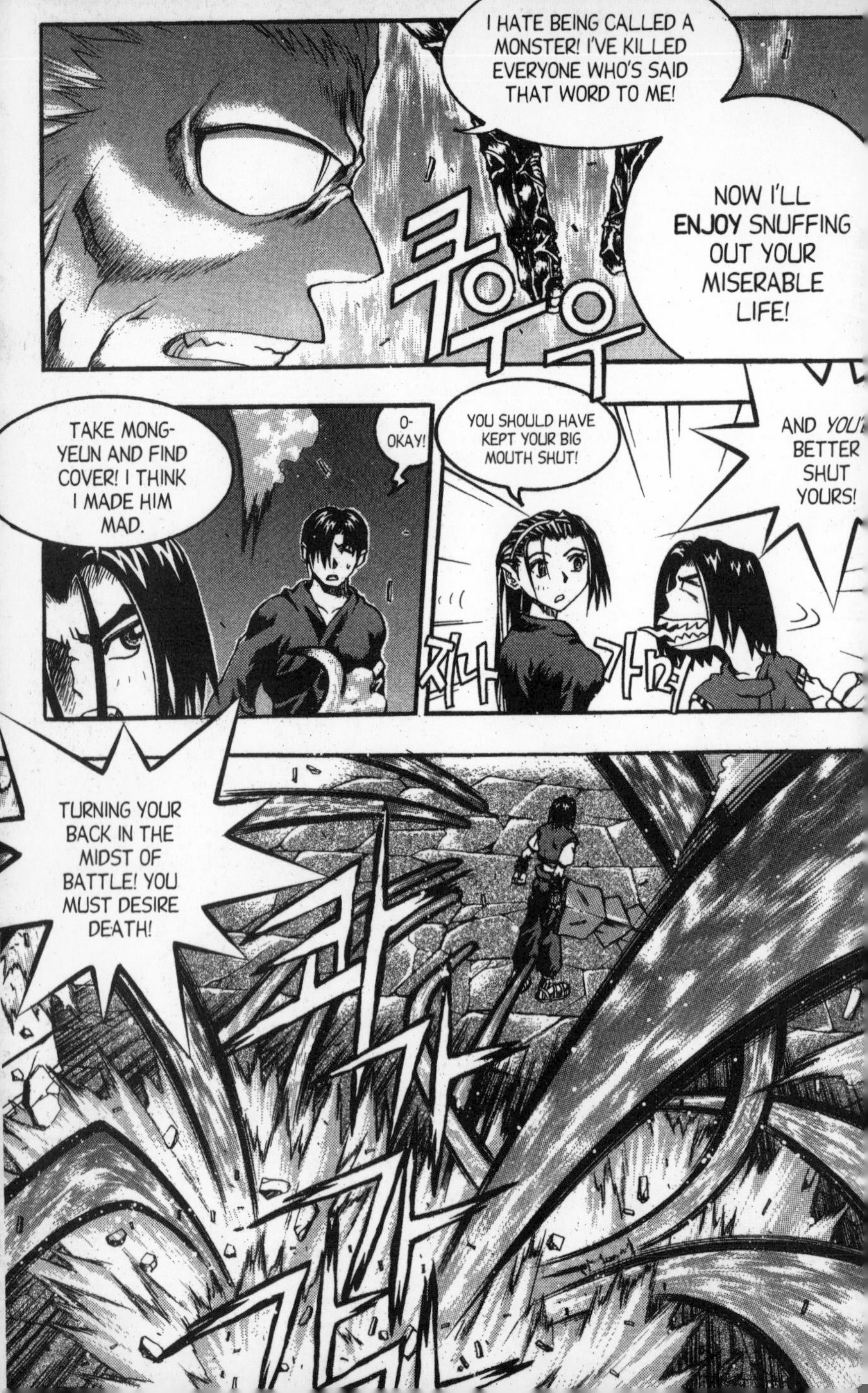
I HATE BEING CALLED A MONSTER! I'VE KILLED EVERYONE WHO'S SAID THAT WORD TO ME!
NOW I'LL **ENJOY** SNUFFING OUT YOUR MISERABLE LIFE!
TAKE MONG-YEUN AND FIND COVER! I THINK I MADE HIM MAD.
O-OKAY!
YOU SHOULD HAVE KEPT YOUR BIG MOUTH SHUT!
AND *YOU'* BETTER SHUT YOURS!
TURNING YOUR BACK IN THE MIDST OF BATTLE! YOU MUST DESIRE DEATH!

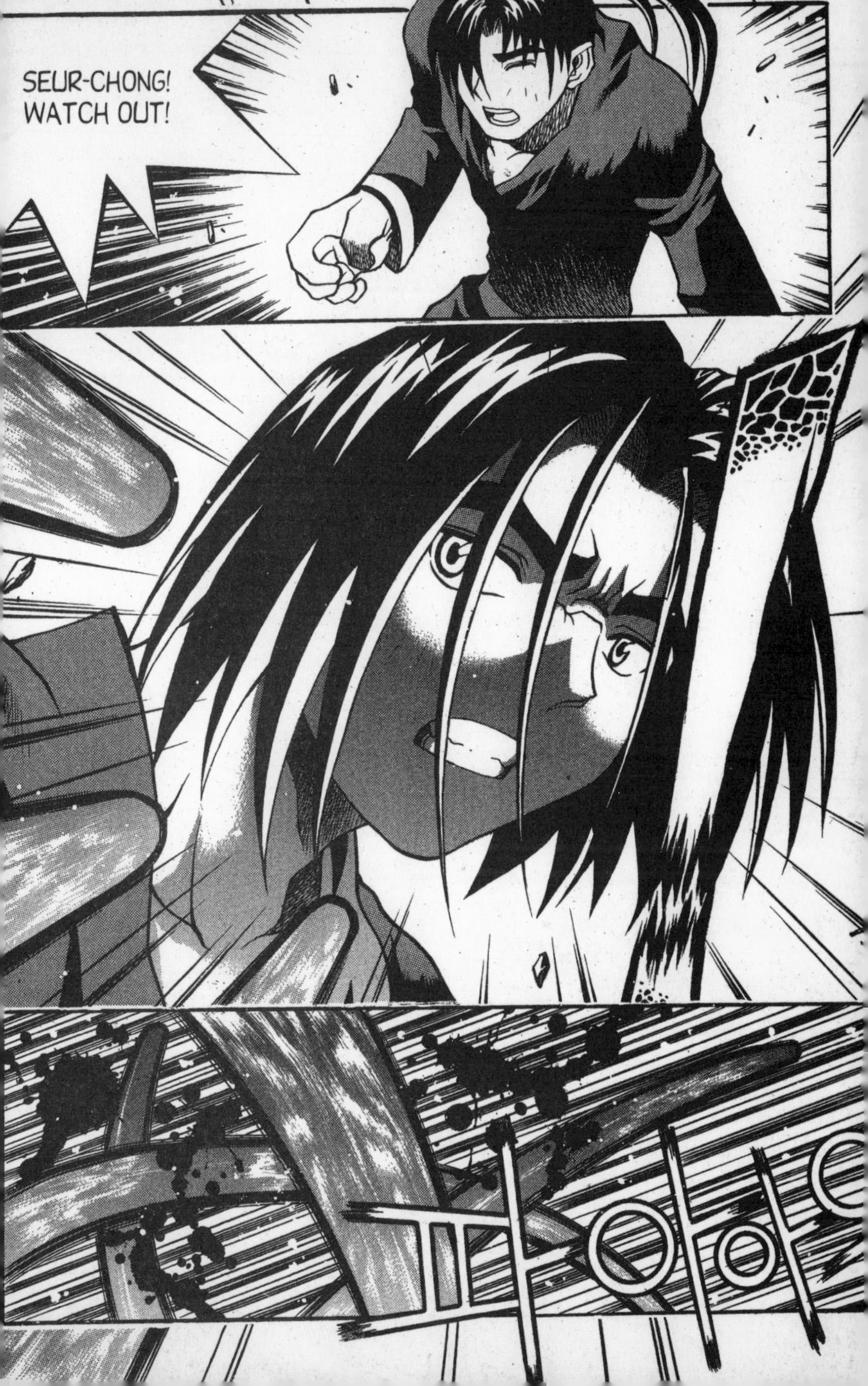
SEUR-CHONG! WATCH OUT!

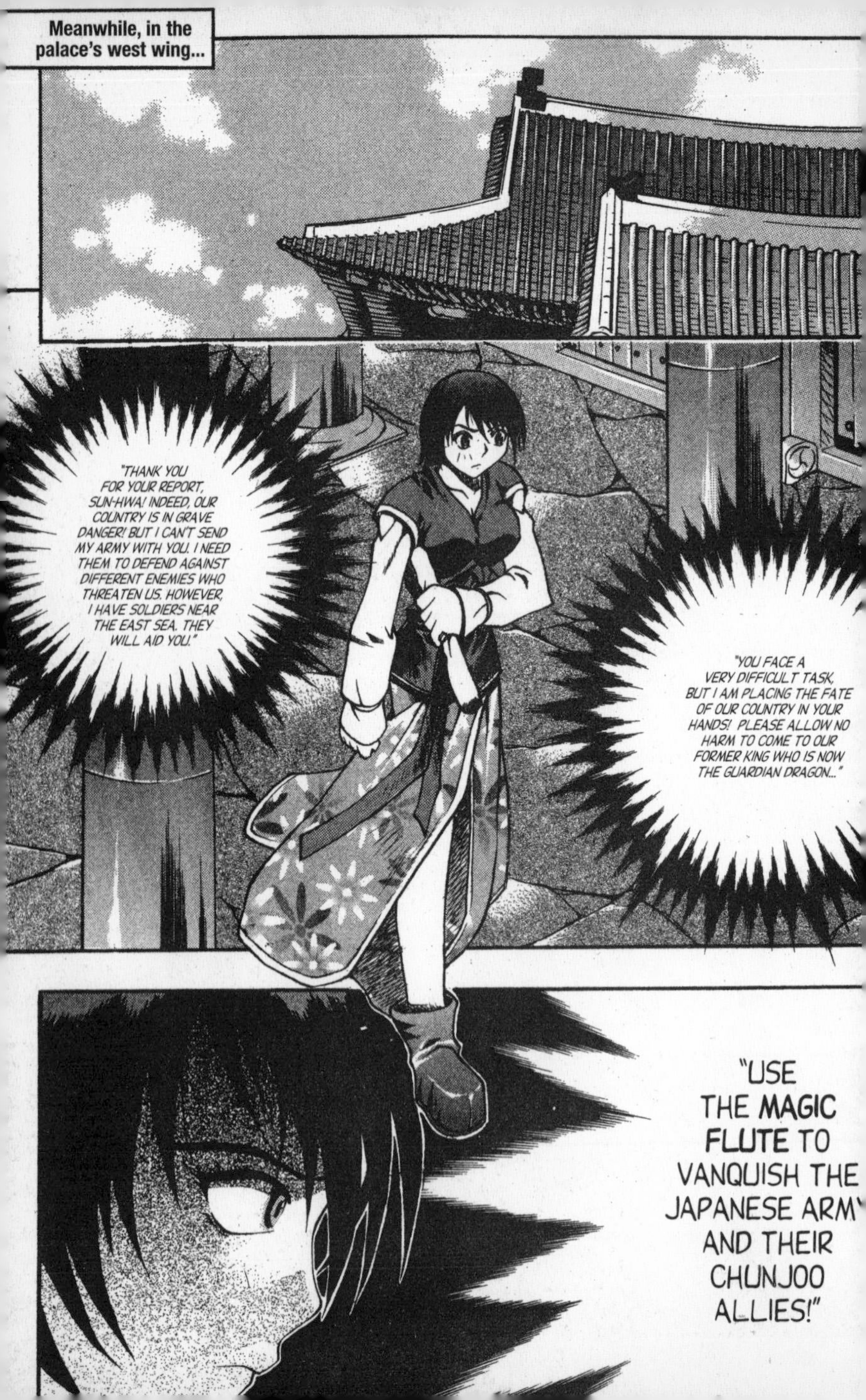
Meanwhile, in the palace's west wing...
"THANK YOU FOR YOUR REPORT, SUN-HWA! INDEED, OUR COUNTRY IS IN GRAVE DANGER! BUT I CAN'T SEND MY ARMY WITH YOU. I NEED THEM TO DEFEND AGAINST DIFFERENT ENEMIES WHO THREATEN US. HOWEVER, I HAVE SOLDIERS NEAR THE EAST SEA. THEY WILL AID YOU."
"YOU FACE A VERY DIFFICULT TASK, BUT I AM PLACING THE FATE OF OUR COUNTRY IN YOUR HANDS! PLEASE ALLOW NO HARM TO COME TO OUR FORMER KING WHO IS NOW THE GUARDIAN DRAGON..."
"USE THE MAGIC FLUTE TO VANQUISH THE JAPANESE ARMY AND THEIR CHUNJOO ALLIES!"

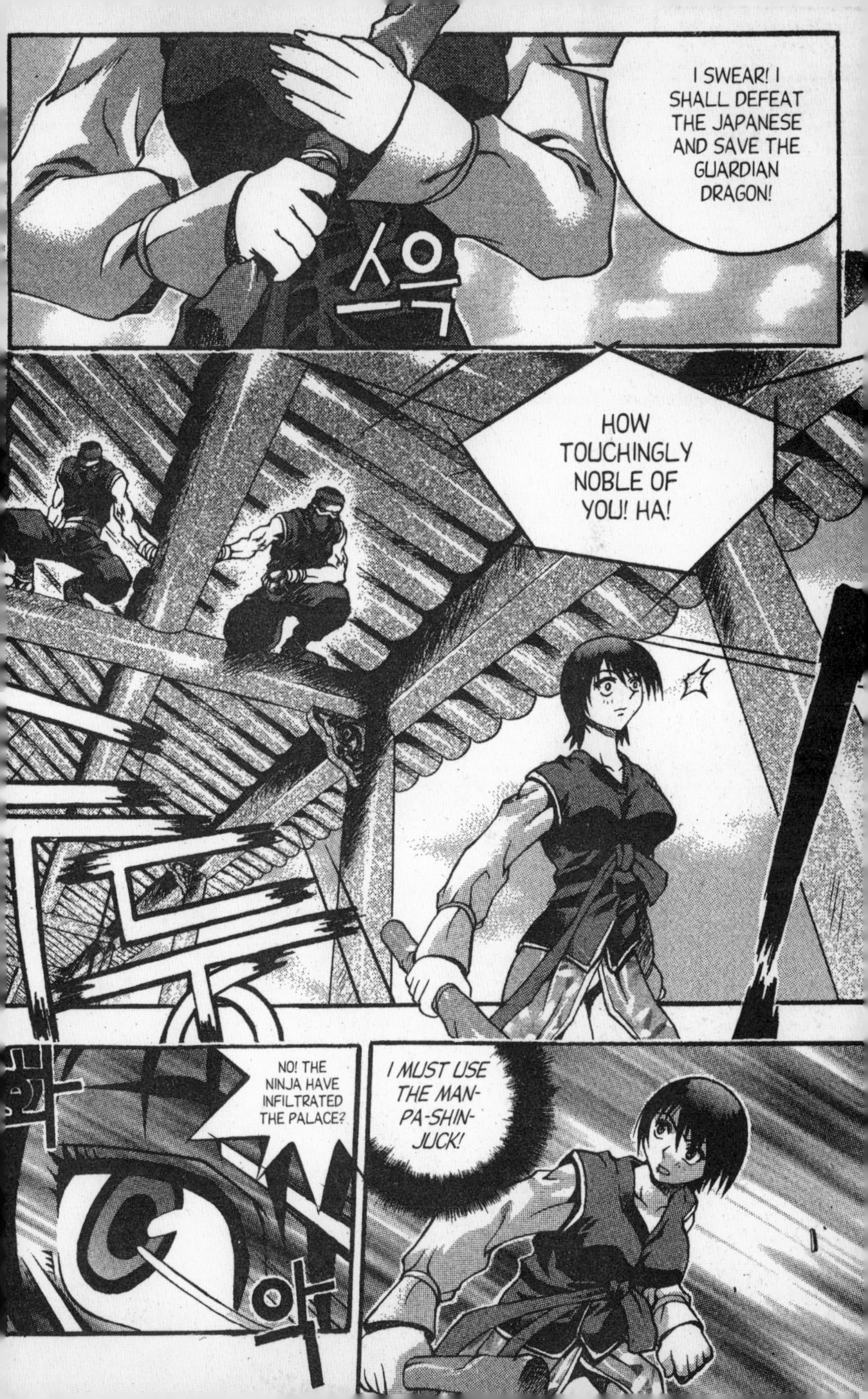
I SWEAR! I SHALL DEFEAT THE JAPANESE AND SAVE THE GUARDIAN DRAGON!
HOW TOUCHINGLY NOBLE OF YOU! HA!
NO! THE NINJA HAVE INFILTRATED THE PALACE?
I MUST USE THE MAN-PA-SHIN-JUCK!

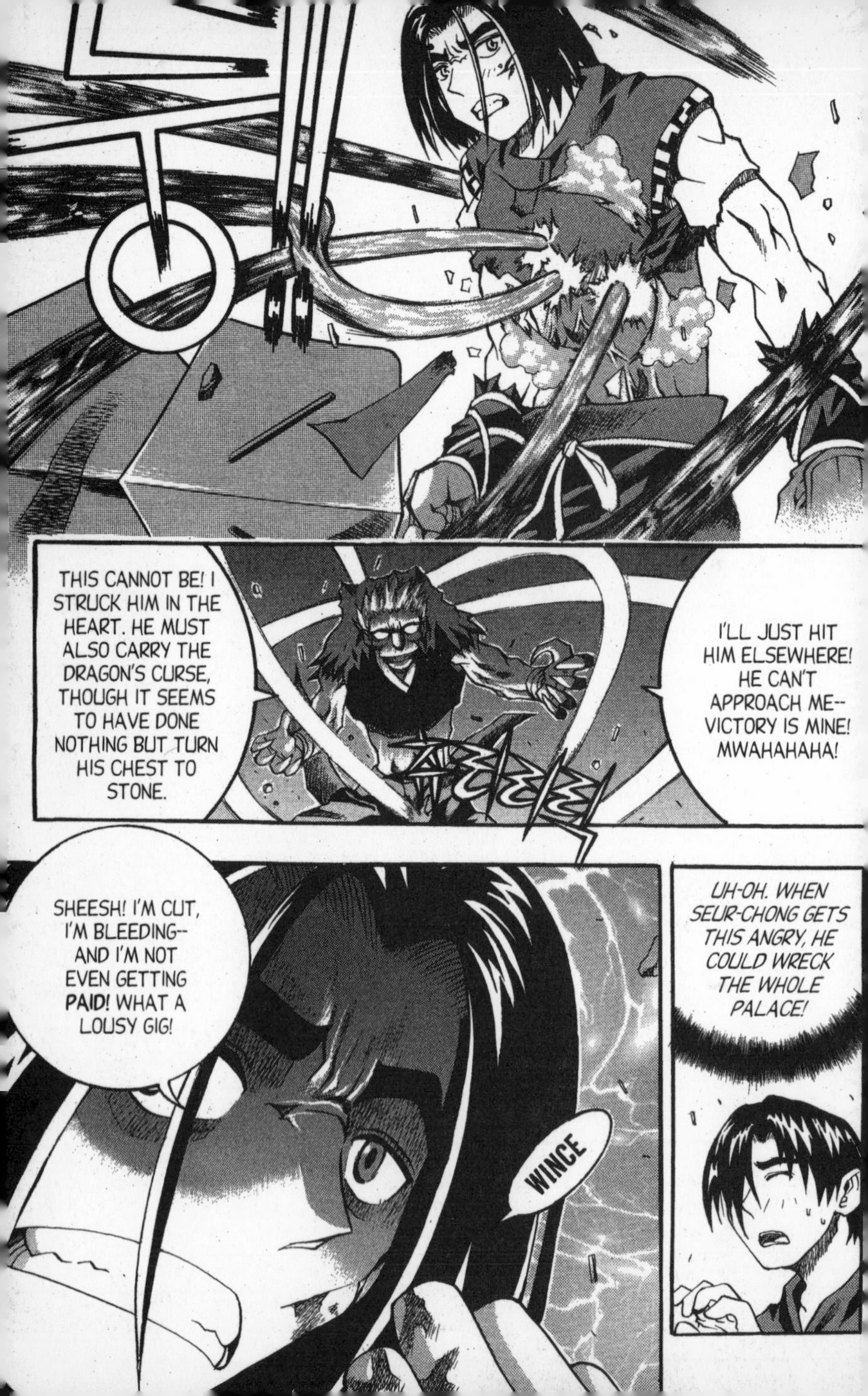
THIS CANNOT BE! I STRUCK HIM IN THE HEART. HE MUST ALSO CARRY THE DRAGON'S CURSE, THOUGH IT SEEMS TO HAVE DONE NOTHING BUT TURN HIS CHEST TO STONE.
I'LL JUST HIT HIM ELSEWHERE! HE CAN'T APPROACH ME-- VICTORY IS MINE! MWAHAHAHA!
SHEESH! I'M CUT, I'M BLEEDING-- AND I'M NOT EVEN GETTING **PAID!** WHAT A LOUSY GIG!
WINCE
UH-OH. WHEN SEUR-CHONG GETS THIS ANGRY, HE COULD WRECK THE WHOLE PALACE!

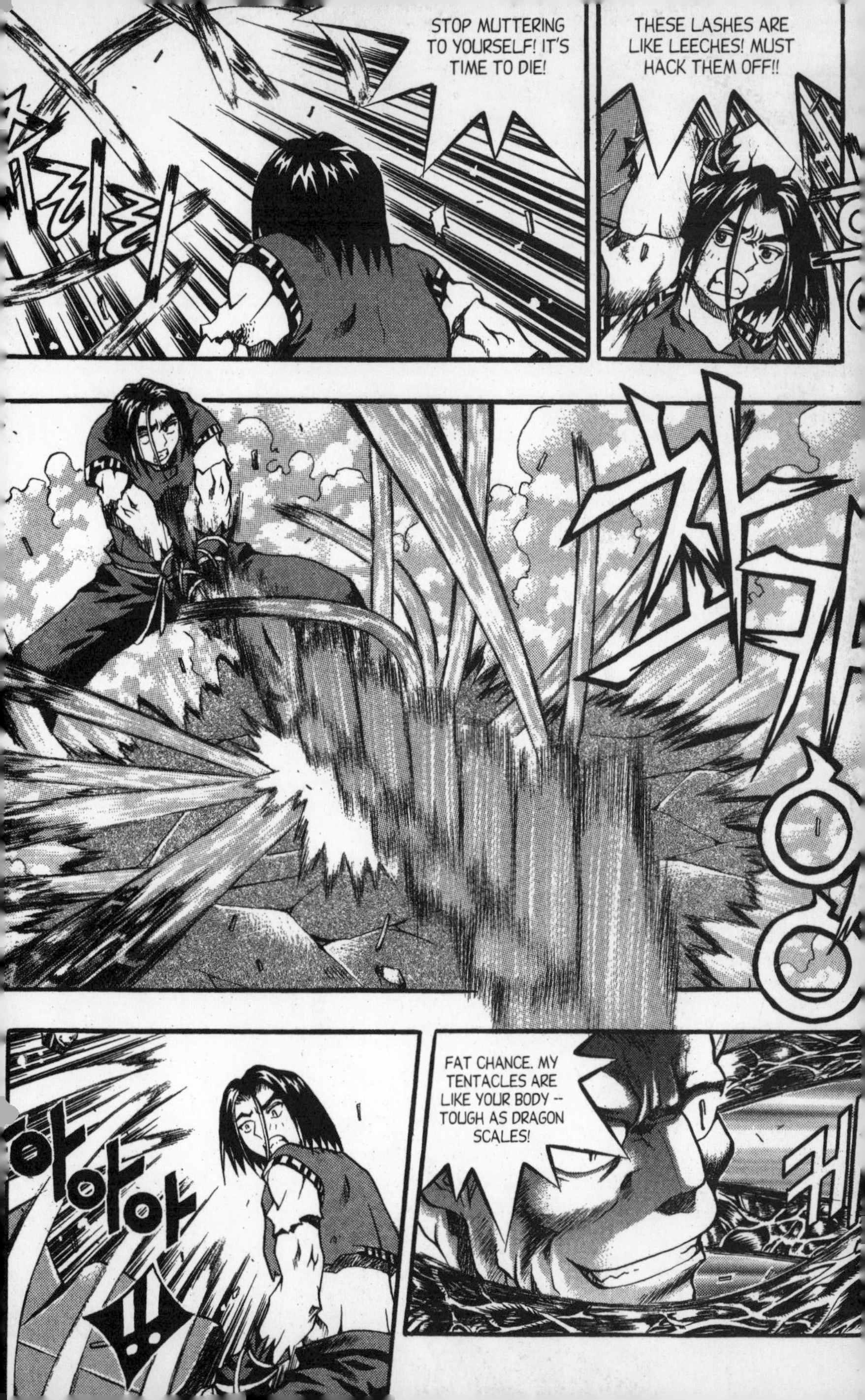
STOP MUTTERING TO YOURSELF! IT'S TIME TO DIE!
THESE LASHES ARE LIKE LEECHES! MUST HACK THEM OFF!!
!!
FAT CHANCE. MY TENTACLES ARE LIKE YOUR BODY -- TOUGH AS DRAGON SCALES!

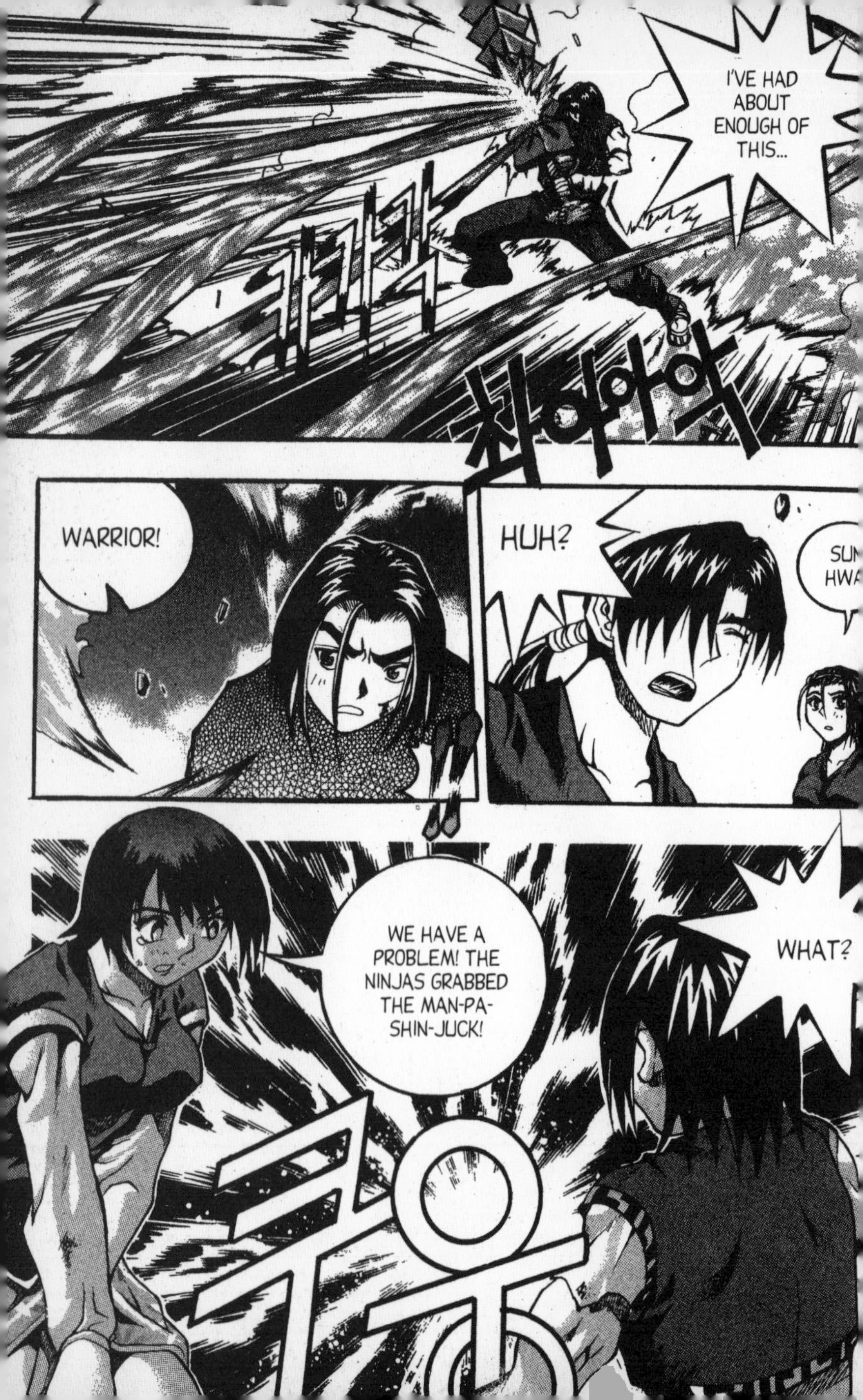
I'VE HAD ABOUT ENOUGH OF THIS...
WARRIOR!
HUH?
WE HAVE A PROBLEM! THE NINJAS GRABBED THE MAN-PA-SHIN-JUCK!
WHAT?

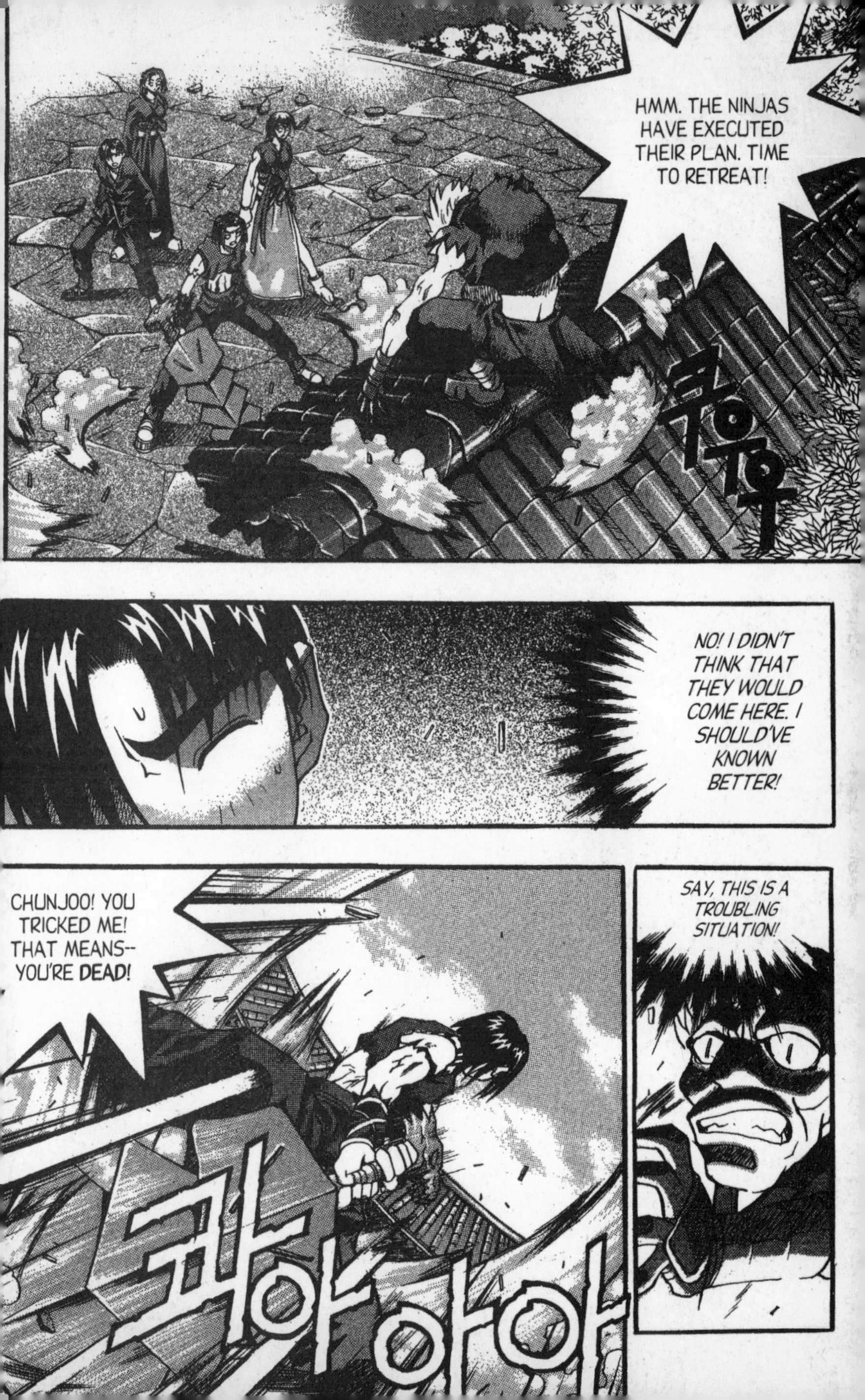
HMM. THE NINJAS HAVE EXECUTED THEIR PLAN. TIME TO RETREAT!
NO! I DIDN'T THINK THAT THEY WOULD COME HERE. I SHOULD'VE KNOWN BETTER!
CHUNJOO! YOU TRICKED ME! THAT MEANS-- YOU'RE **DEAD**!
SAY, THIS IS A TROUBLING SITUATION!

MI-RU DRAGON DECAPITATION STRIKE!

SEUR-CHONG! STOP! YOU'LL DESTROY THE WHOLE PALACE!

IMPOSSIBLE! HE SEVERED SEVERAL OF MY TENTACLES! HE IS INDEED A GREAT WARRIOR. PERHAPS I SHOULD NOT HAVE RAISED HIS IRE. NONETHELESS, I SHALL EXTRACT MY REVENGE!

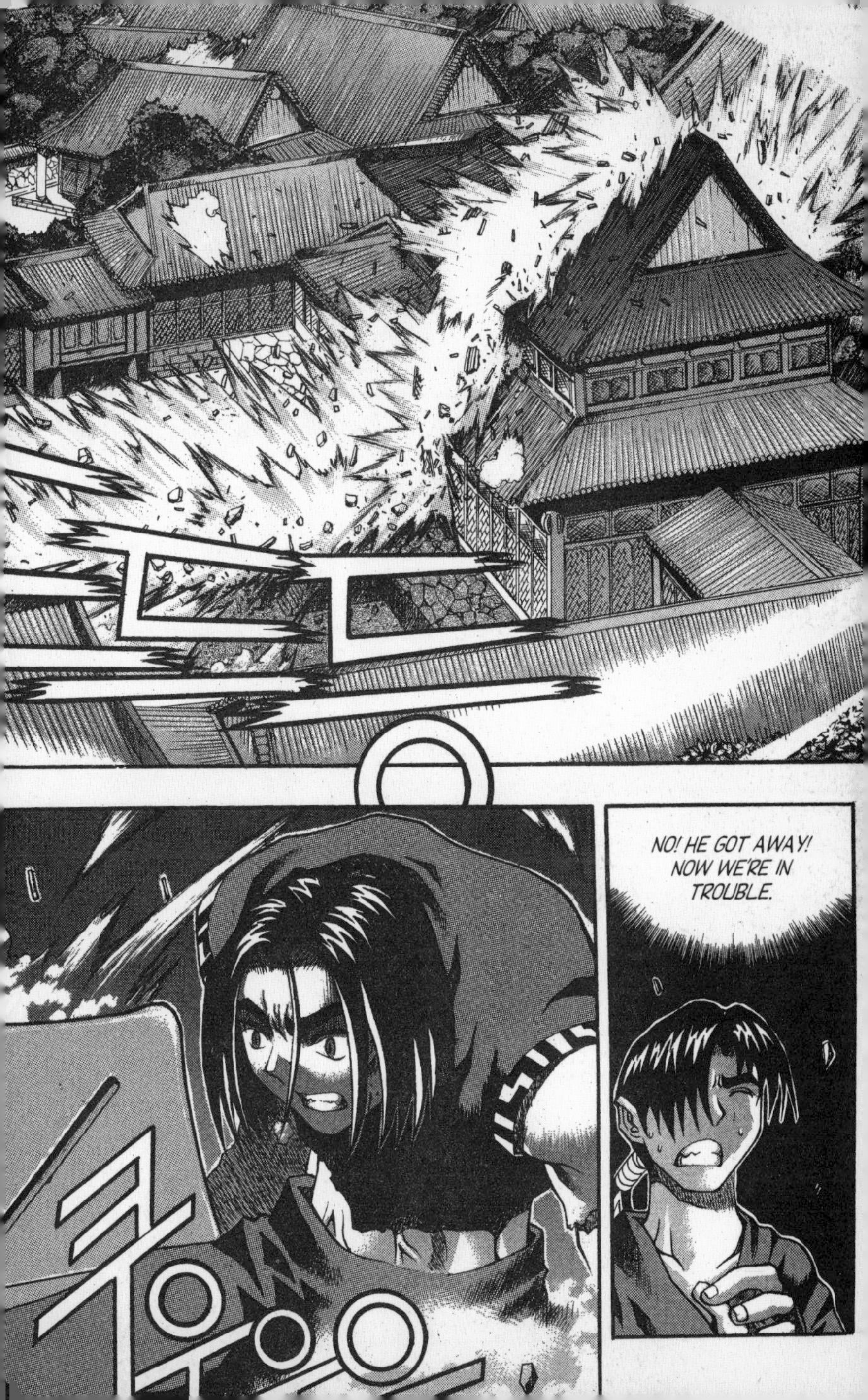
NO! HE GOT AWAY! NOW WE'RE IN TROUBLE.

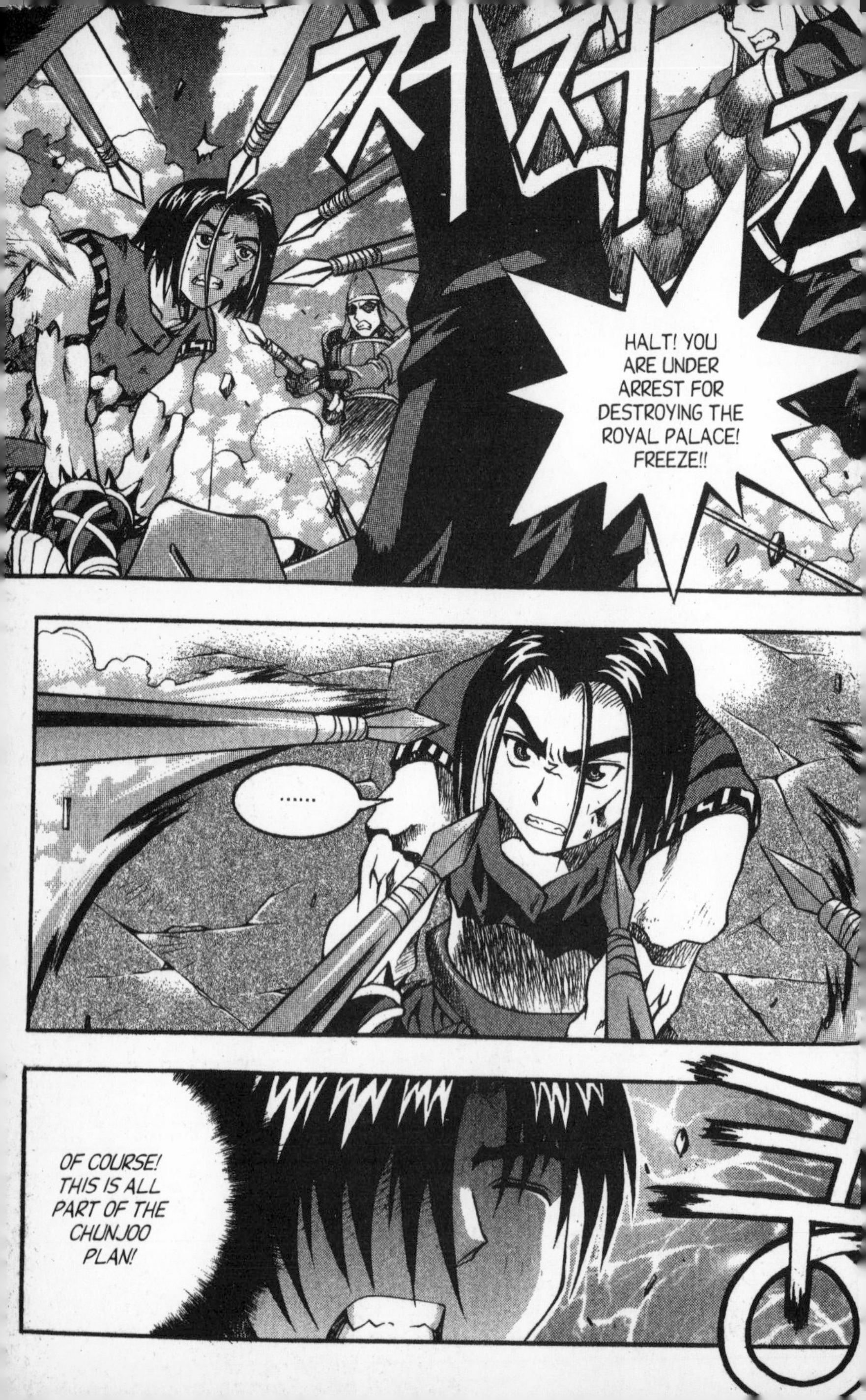
HALT! YOU ARE UNDER ARREST FOR DESTROYING THE ROYAL PALACE! FREEZE!!
......
OF COURSE! THIS IS ALL PART OF THE CHUNJOO PLAN!

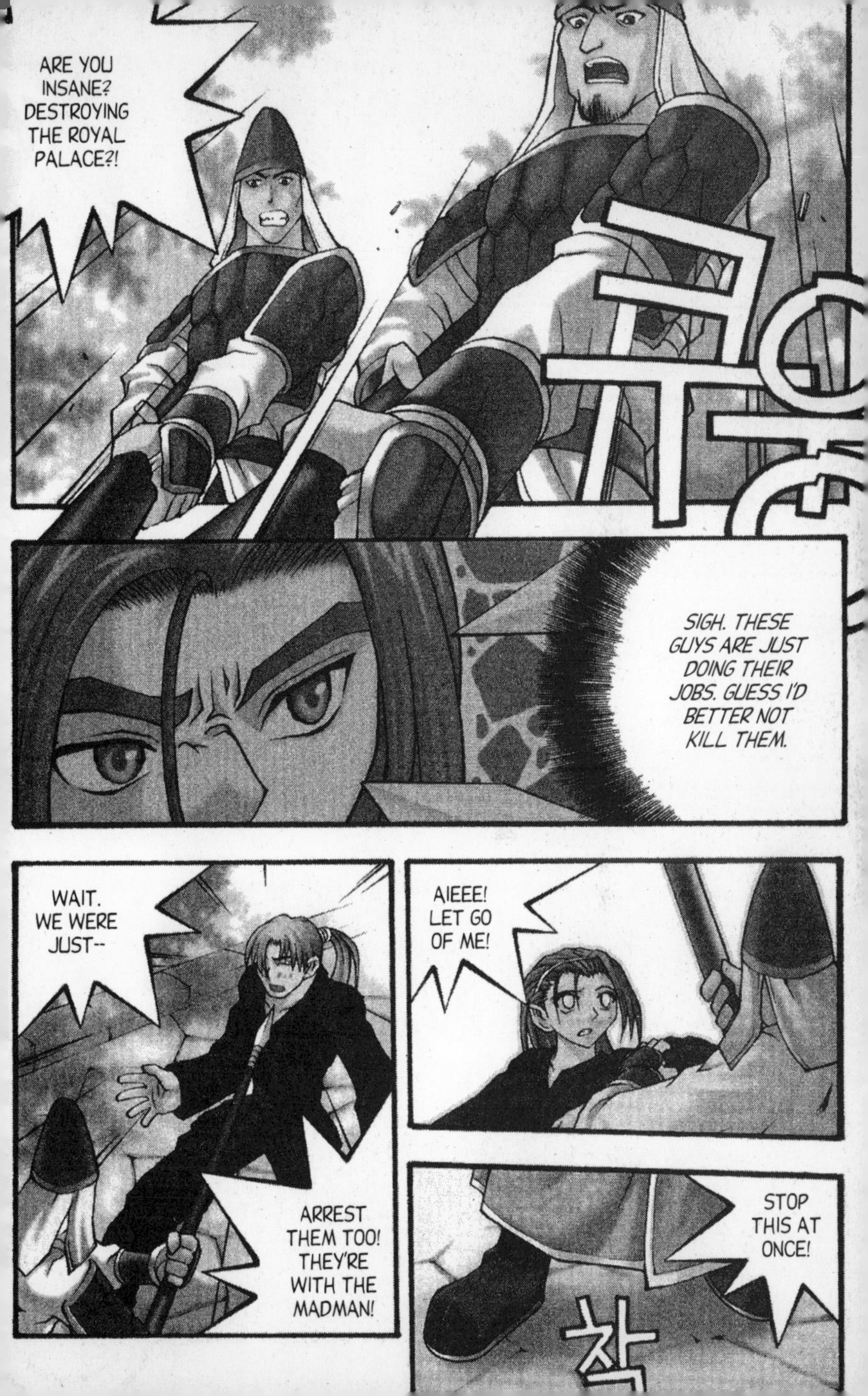
ARE YOU INSANE? DESTROYING THE ROYAL PALACE?!
SIGH. THESE GUYS ARE JUST DOING THEIR JOBS. GUESS I'D BETTER NOT KILL THEM.
WAIT. WE WERE JUST--
ARREST THEM TOO! THEY'RE WITH THE MADMAN!
AIEEE! LET GO OF ME!
STOP THIS AT ONCE!
착

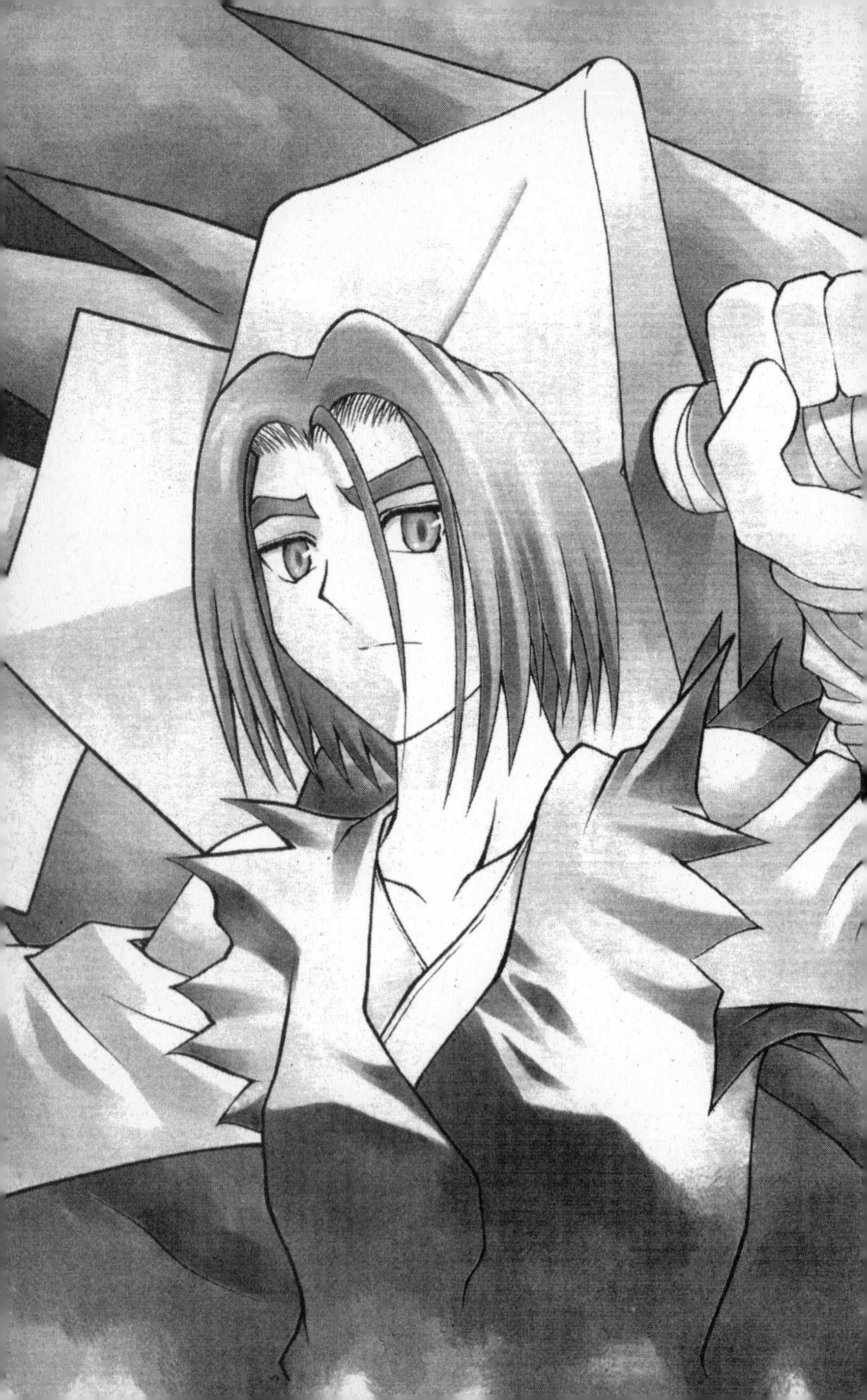

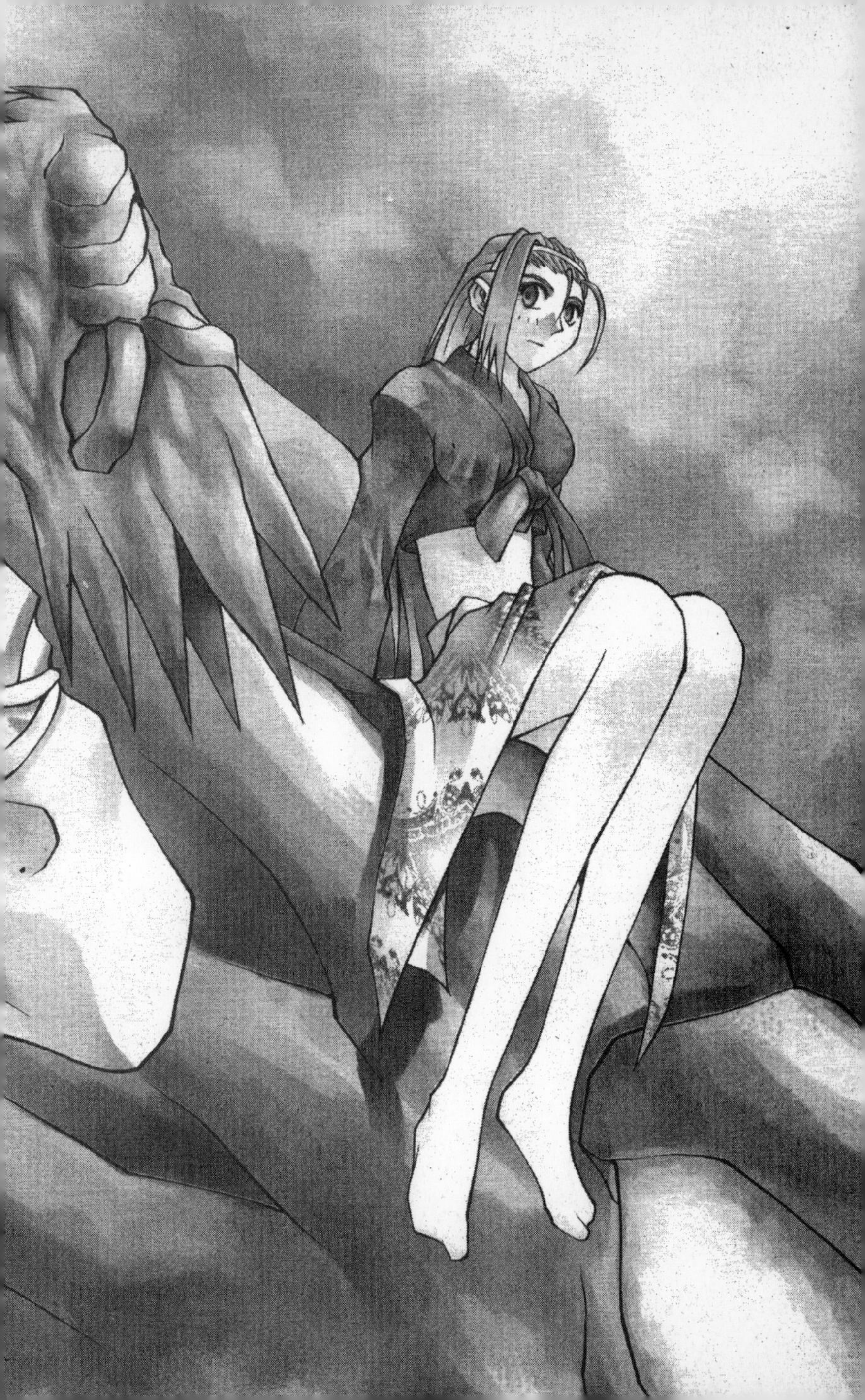

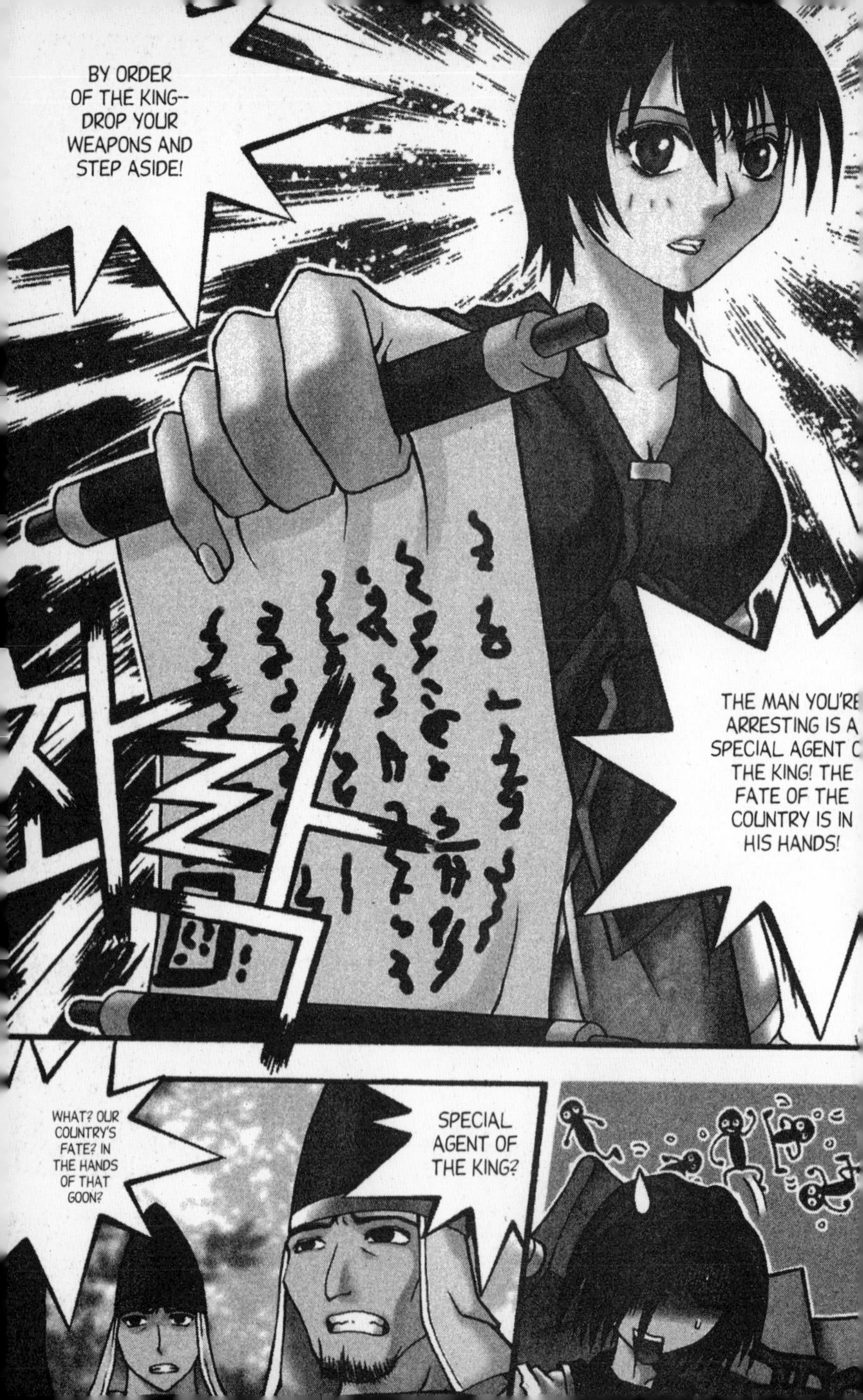
BY ORDER OF THE KING-- DROP YOUR WEAPONS AND STEP ASIDE!
THE MAN YOU'RE ARRESTING IS A SPECIAL AGENT O THE KING! THE FATE OF THE COUNTRY IS IN HIS HANDS!
WHAT? OUR COUNTRY'S FATE? IN THE HANDS OF THAT GOON?
SPECIAL AGENT OF THE KING?

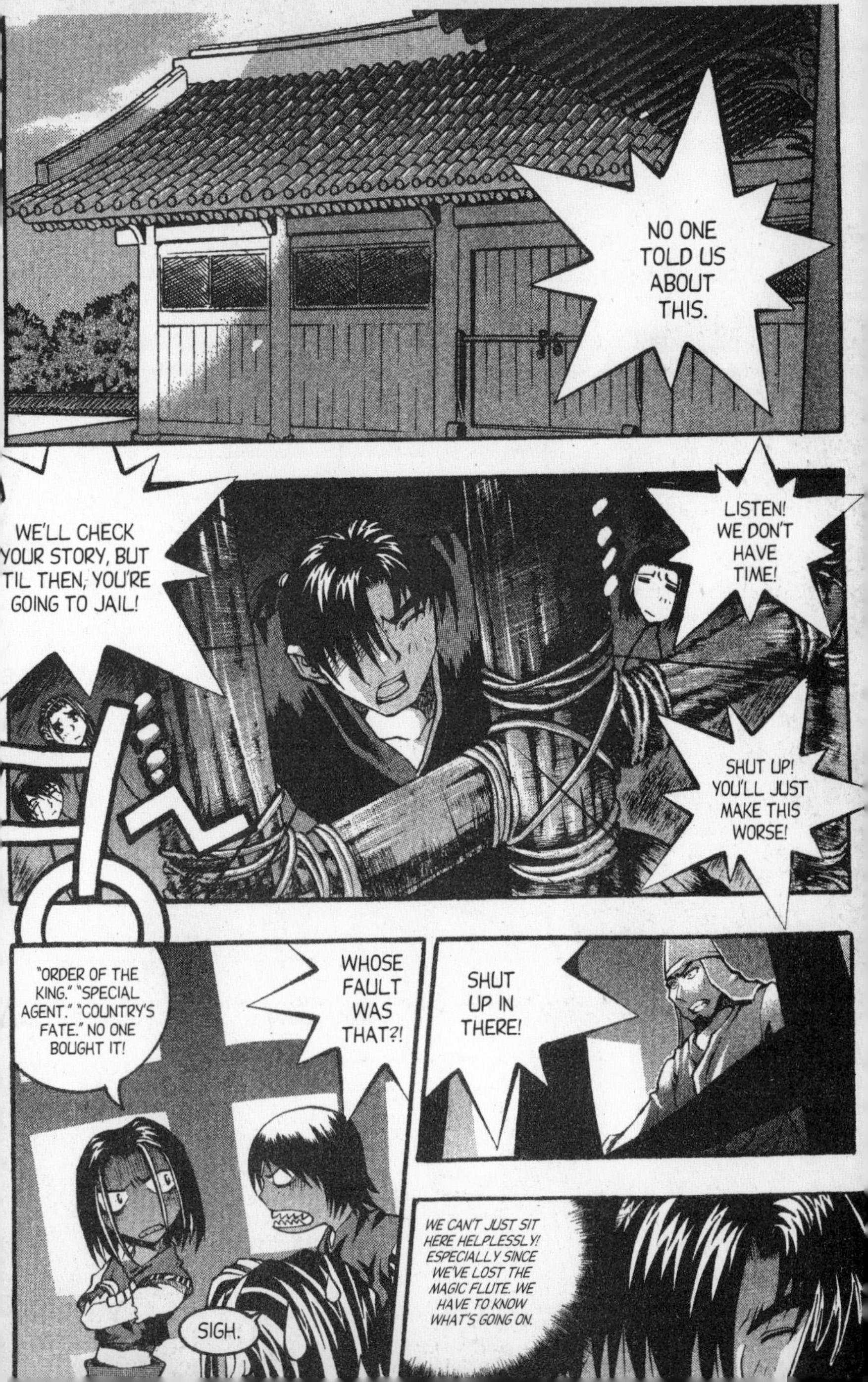
NO ONE TOLD US ABOUT THIS.
WE'LL CHECK YOUR STORY, BUT TIL THEN, YOU'RE GOING TO JAIL!
LISTEN! WE DON'T HAVE TIME!
SHUT UP! YOU'LL JUST MAKE THIS WORSE!
"ORDER OF THE KING." "SPECIAL AGENT." "COUNTRY'S FATE." NO ONE BOUGHT IT!
WHOSE FAULT WAS THAT?!
SIGH.
SHUT UP IN THERE!
WE CAN'T JUST SIT HERE HELPLESSLY! ESPECIALLY SINCE WE'VE LOST THE MAGIC FLUTE. WE HAVE TO KNOW WHAT'S GOING ON.

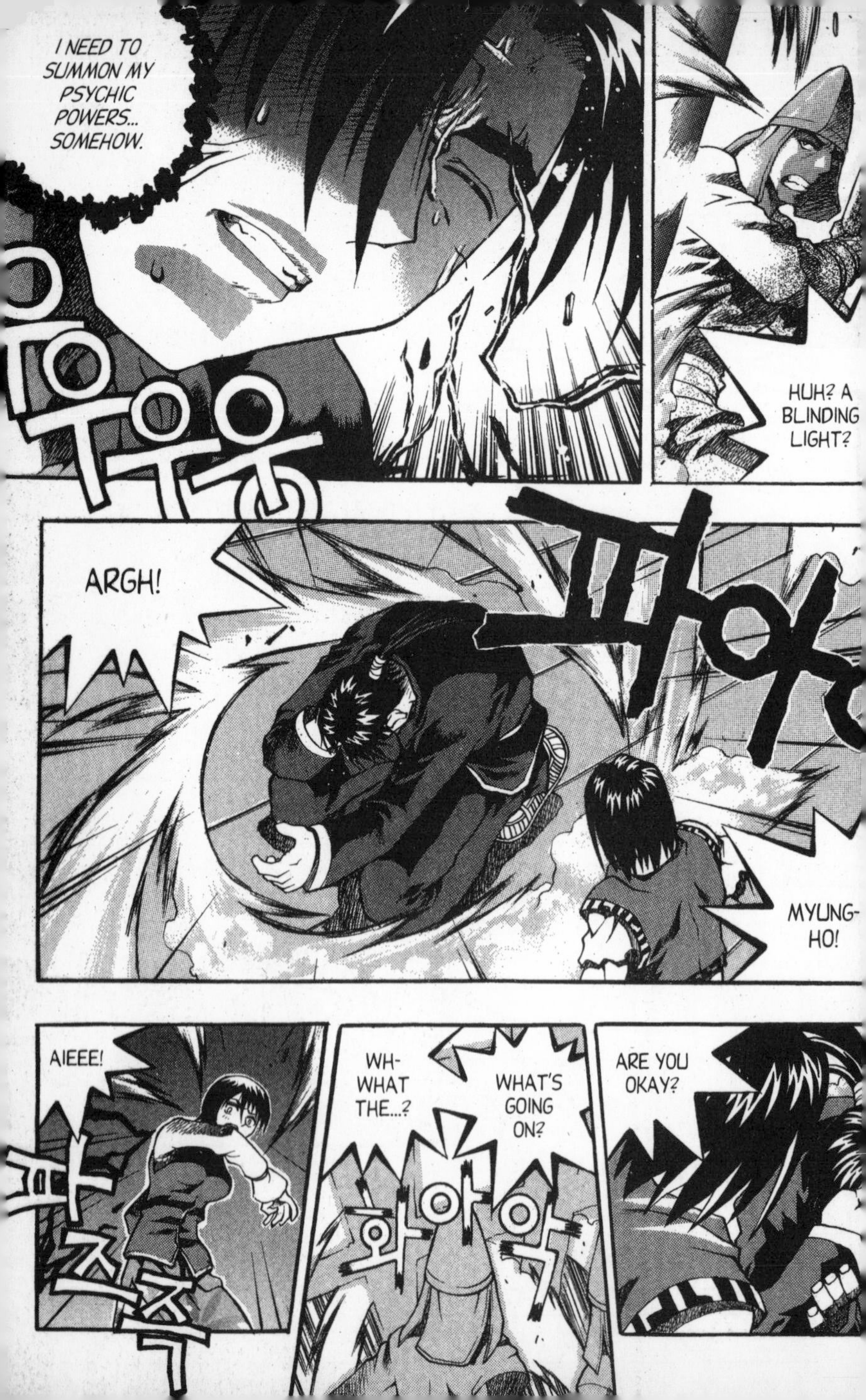
I NEED TO SUMMON MY PSYCHIC POWERS... SOMEHOW.
HUH? A BLINDING LIGHT?
ARGH!
MYUNG-HO!
AIEEE!
WH-WHAT THE...?
WHAT'S GOING ON?
화아악
ARE YOU OKAY?

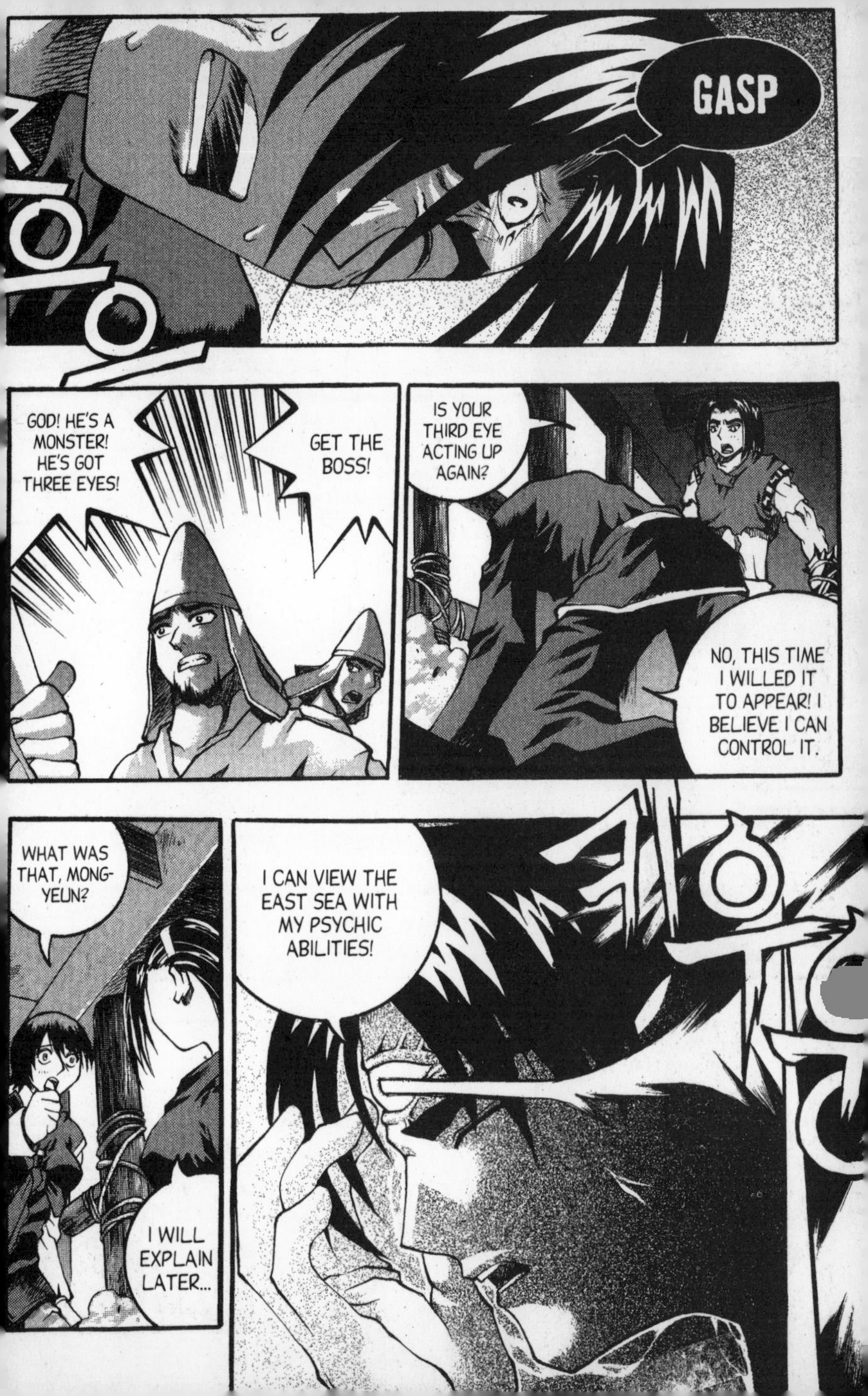
GASP
GOD! HE'S A MONSTER! HE'S GOT THREE EYES!
GET THE BOSS!
IS YOUR THIRD EYE ACTING UP AGAIN?
NO, THIS TIME I WILLED IT TO APPEAR! I BELIEVE I CAN CONTROL IT.
WHAT WAS THAT, MONG-YEUN?
I WILL EXPLAIN LATER...
I CAN VIEW THE EAST SEA WITH MY PSYCHIC ABILITIES!

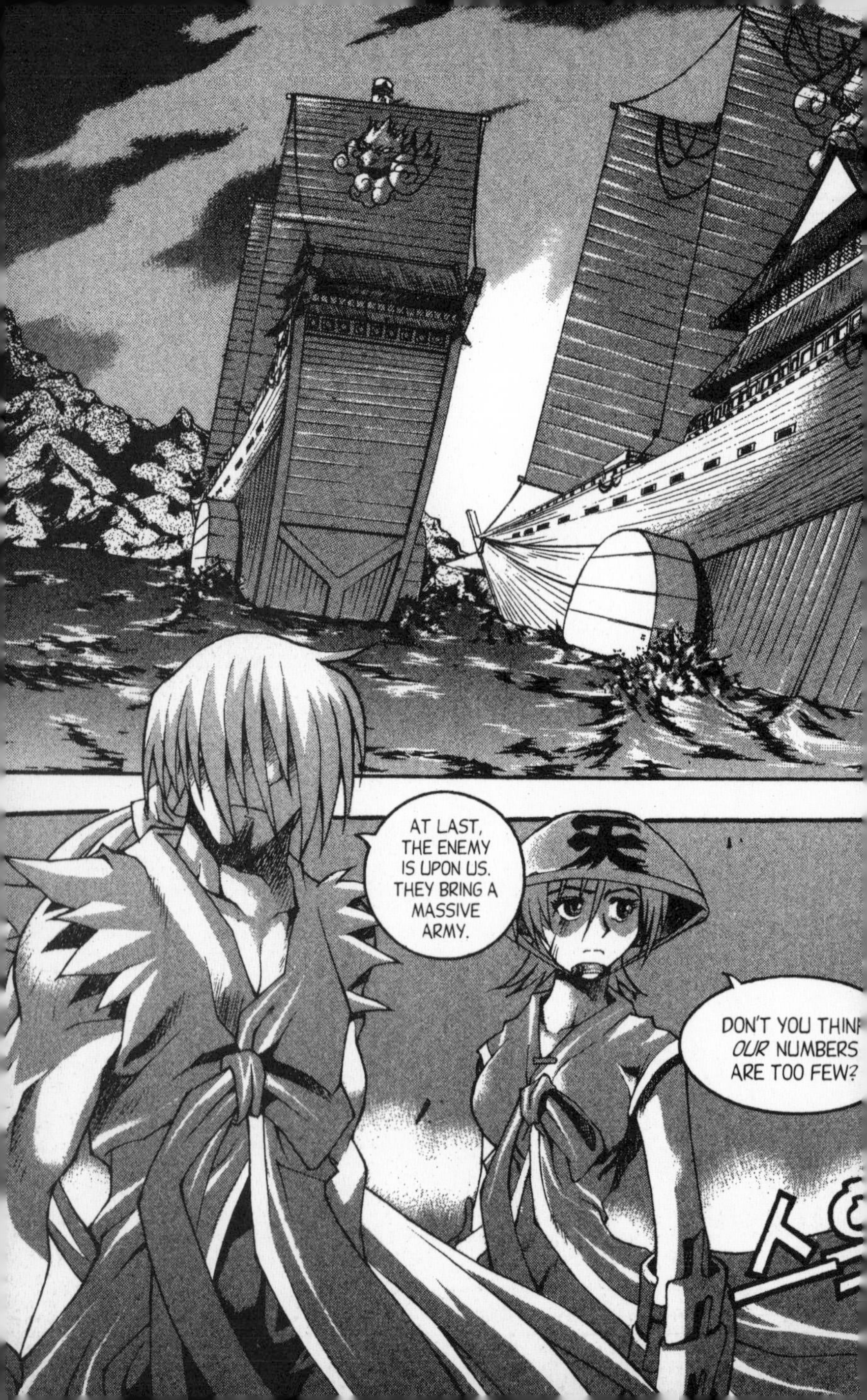
AT LAST, THE ENEMY IS UPON US. THEY BRING A MASSIVE ARMY.
DON'T YOU THINK *OUR* NUMBERS ARE TOO FEW?

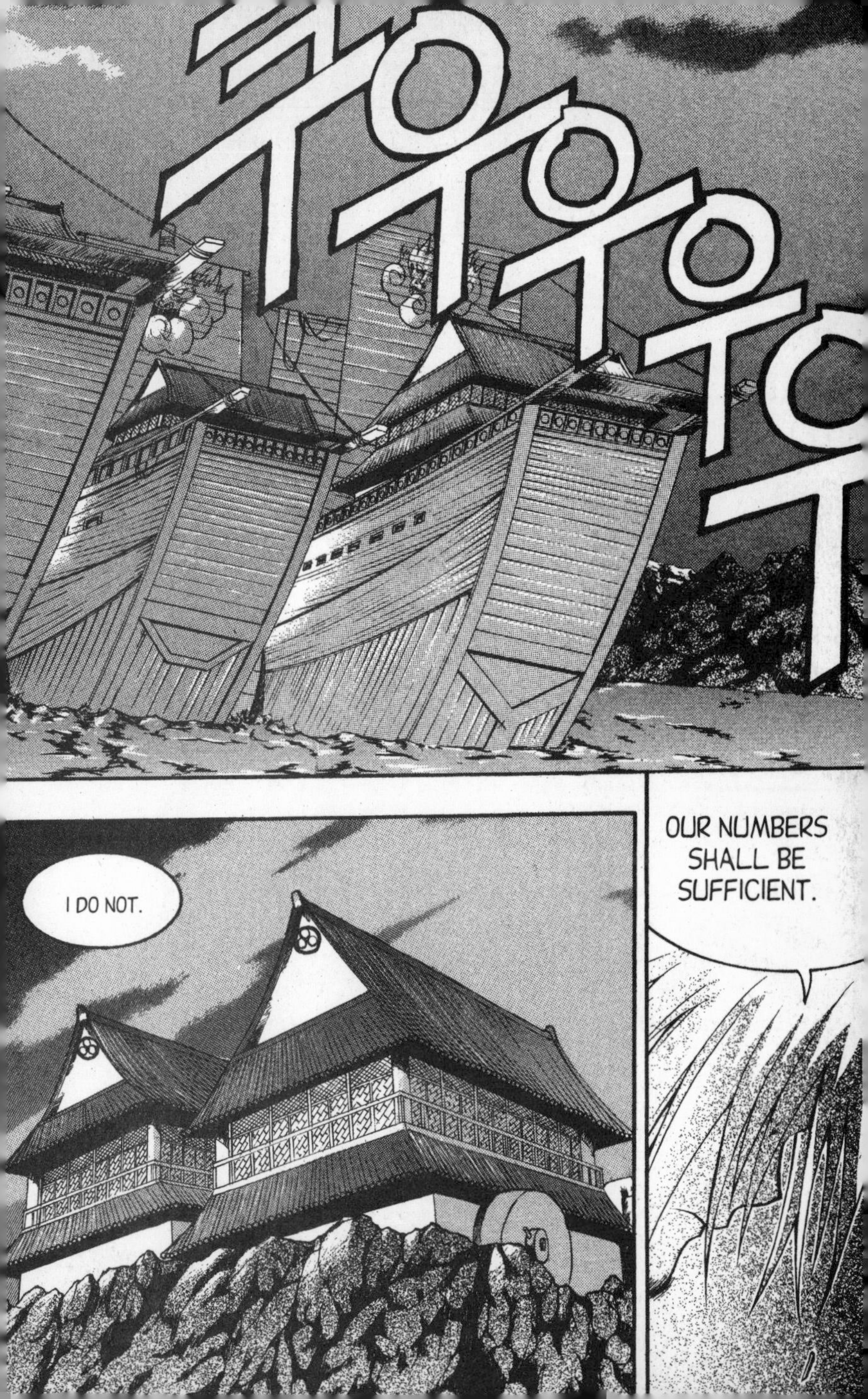
TOTOTOTOT
I DO NOT.
OUR NUMBERS SHALL BE SUFFICIENT.

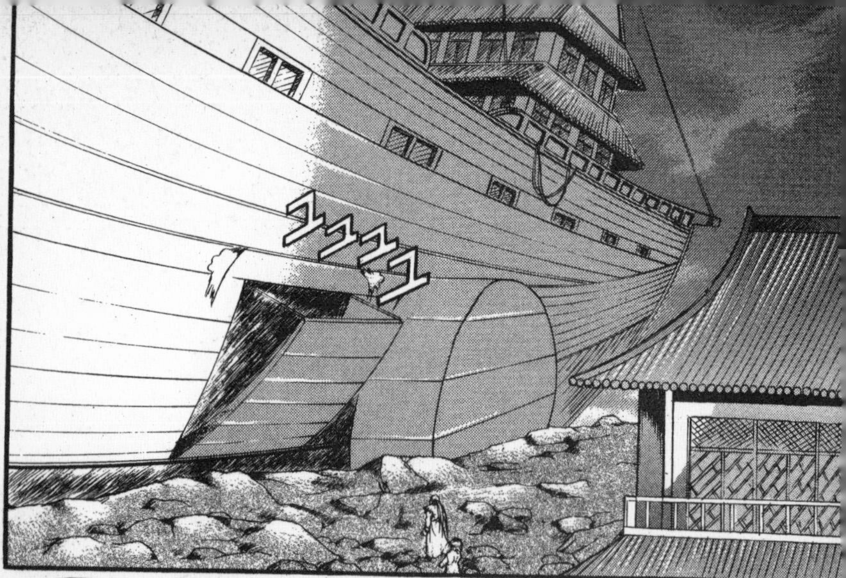

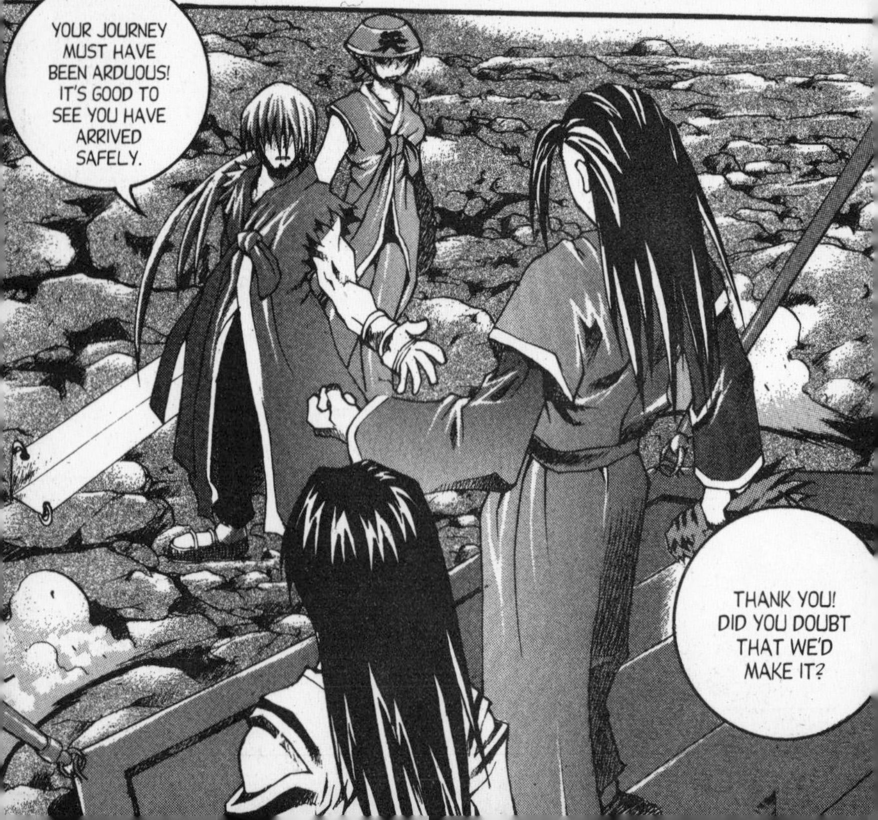
YOUR JOURNEY MUST HAVE BEEN ARDUOUS! IT'S GOOD TO SEE YOU HAVE ARRIVED SAFELY.
THANK YOU! DID YOU DOUBT THAT WE'D MAKE IT?

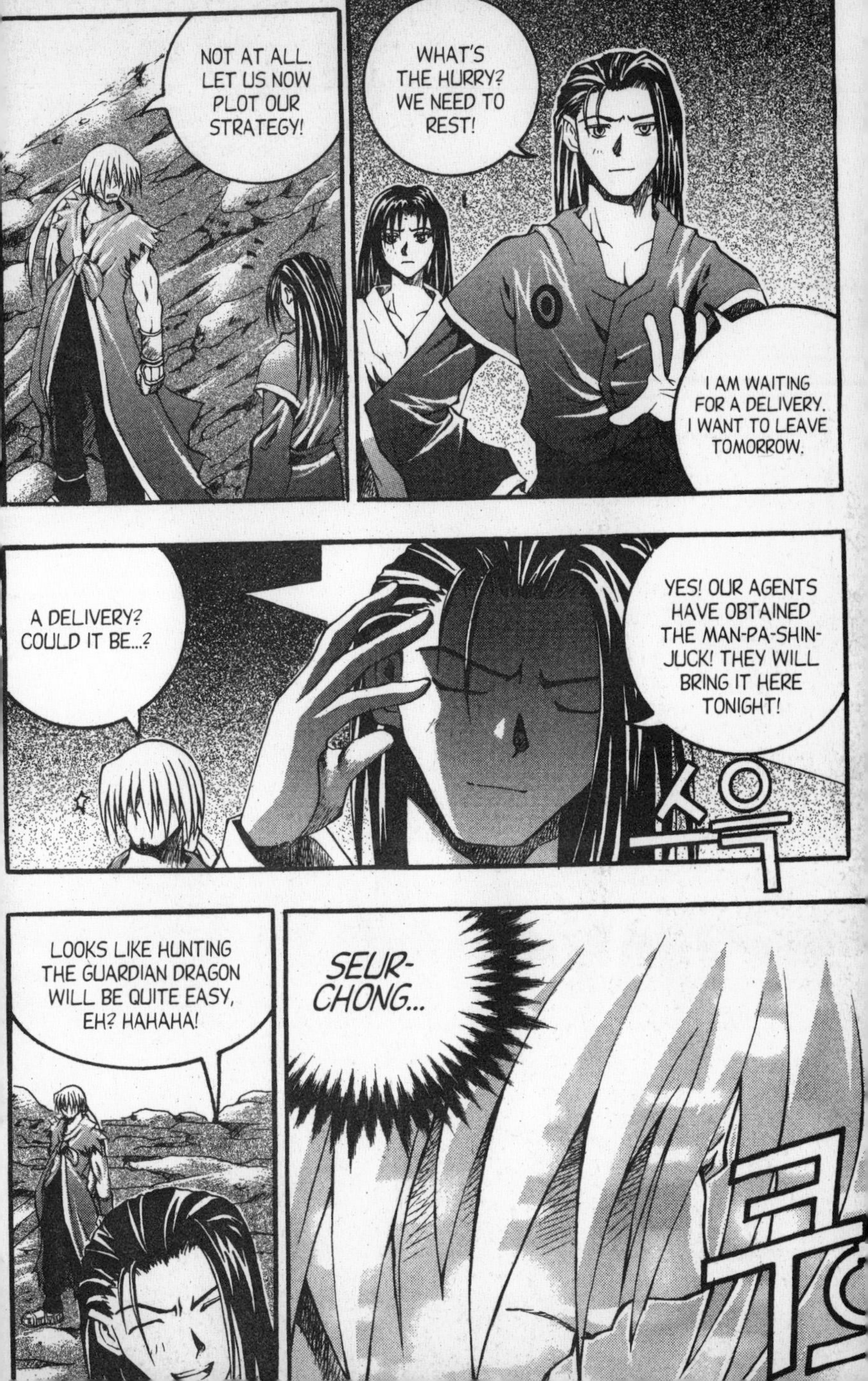
NOT AT ALL. LET US NOW PLOT OUR STRATEGY!
WHAT'S THE HURRY? WE NEED TO REST!
I AM WAITING FOR A DELIVERY. I WANT TO LEAVE TOMORROW.
A DELIVERY? COULD IT BE...?
YES! OUR AGENTS HAVE OBTAINED THE MAN-PA-SHIN-JUCK! THEY WILL BRING IT HERE TONIGHT!
LOOKS LIKE HUNTING THE GUARDIAN DRAGON WILL BE QUITE EASY, EH? HAHAHA!
SEUR-CHONG...

PANT

PANT

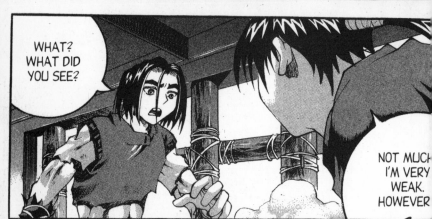

WHAT?
WHAT DID
YOU SEE?

NOT MUCH
I'M VERY
WEAK.
HOWEVER

...IT LOOKS LIKE THE
JAPANESE ARMY HAS
ARRIVED ON THE
SHORES OF THE EAST
SEA! IT APPEARS THAT
THEY ARE WORKING
FOR THE CHUNJOO
DAECHANG!

WHAT?!

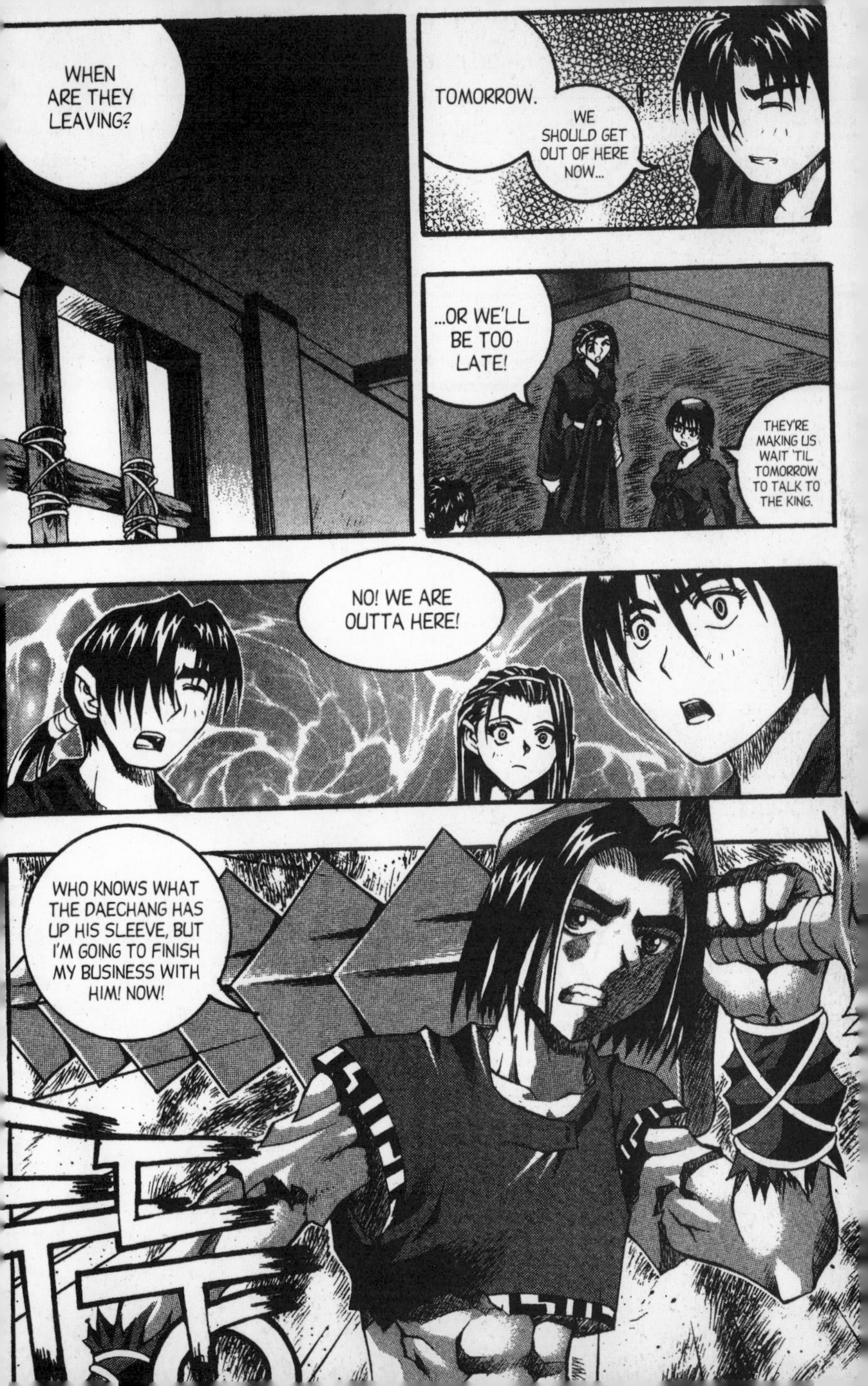
WHEN ARE THEY LEAVING?
TOMORROW.
WE SHOULD GET OUT OF HERE NOW...
...OR WE'LL BE TOO LATE!
THEY'RE MAKING US WAIT 'TIL TOMORROW TO TALK TO THE KING.
NO! WE ARE OUTTA HERE!
WHO KNOWS WHAT THE DAECHANG HAS UP HIS SLEEVE, BUT I'M GOING TO FINISH MY BUSINESS WITH HIM! NOW!

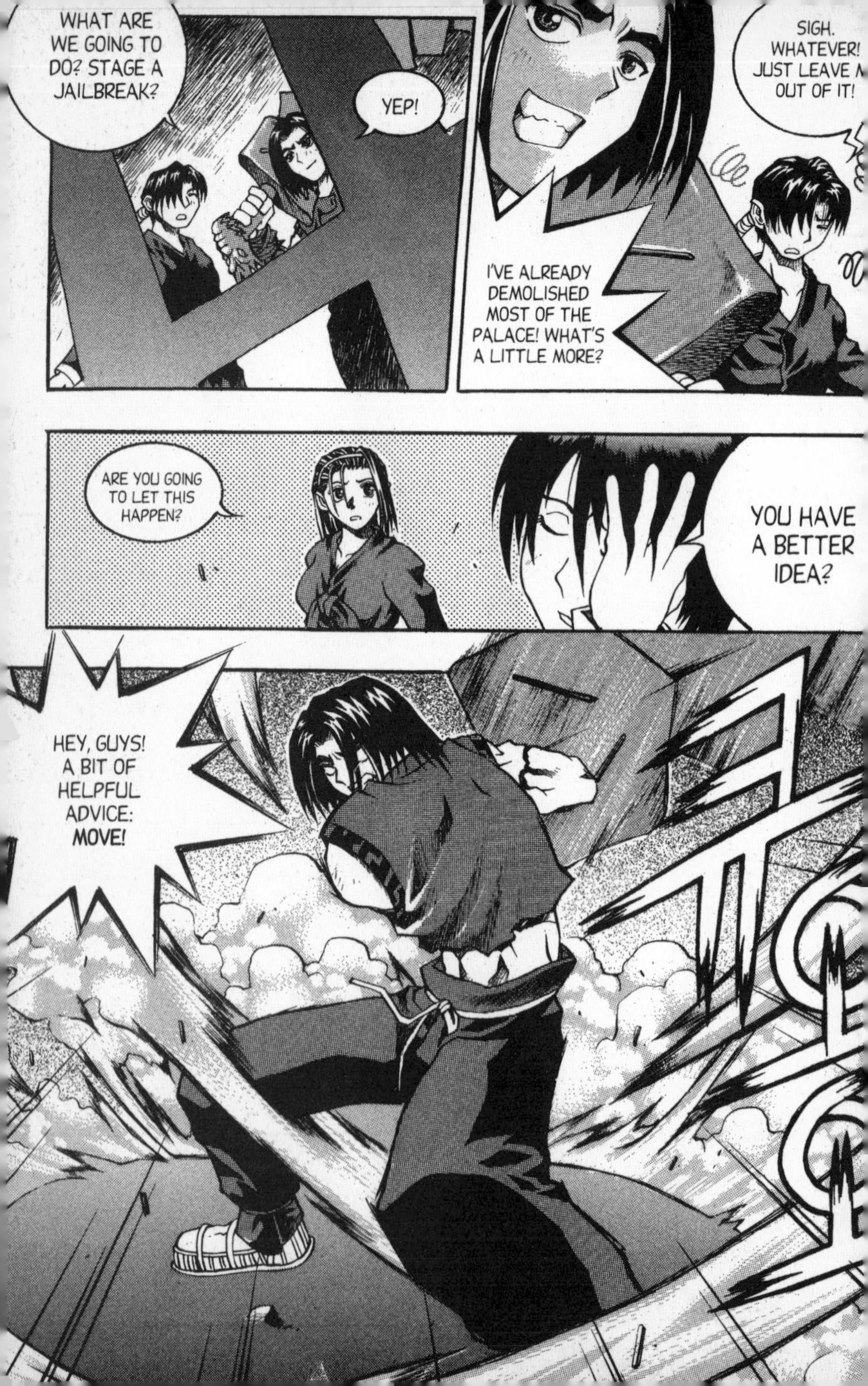
WHAT ARE WE GOING TO DO? STAGE A JAILBREAK?
YEP!
I'VE ALREADY DEMOLISHED MOST OF THE PALACE! WHAT'S A LITTLE MORE?
SIGH. WHATEVER! JUST LEAVE M OUT OF IT!
ARE YOU GOING TO LET THIS HAPPEN?
YOU HAVE A BETTER IDEA?
HEY, GUYS! A BIT OF HELPFUL ADVICE: **MOVE!**

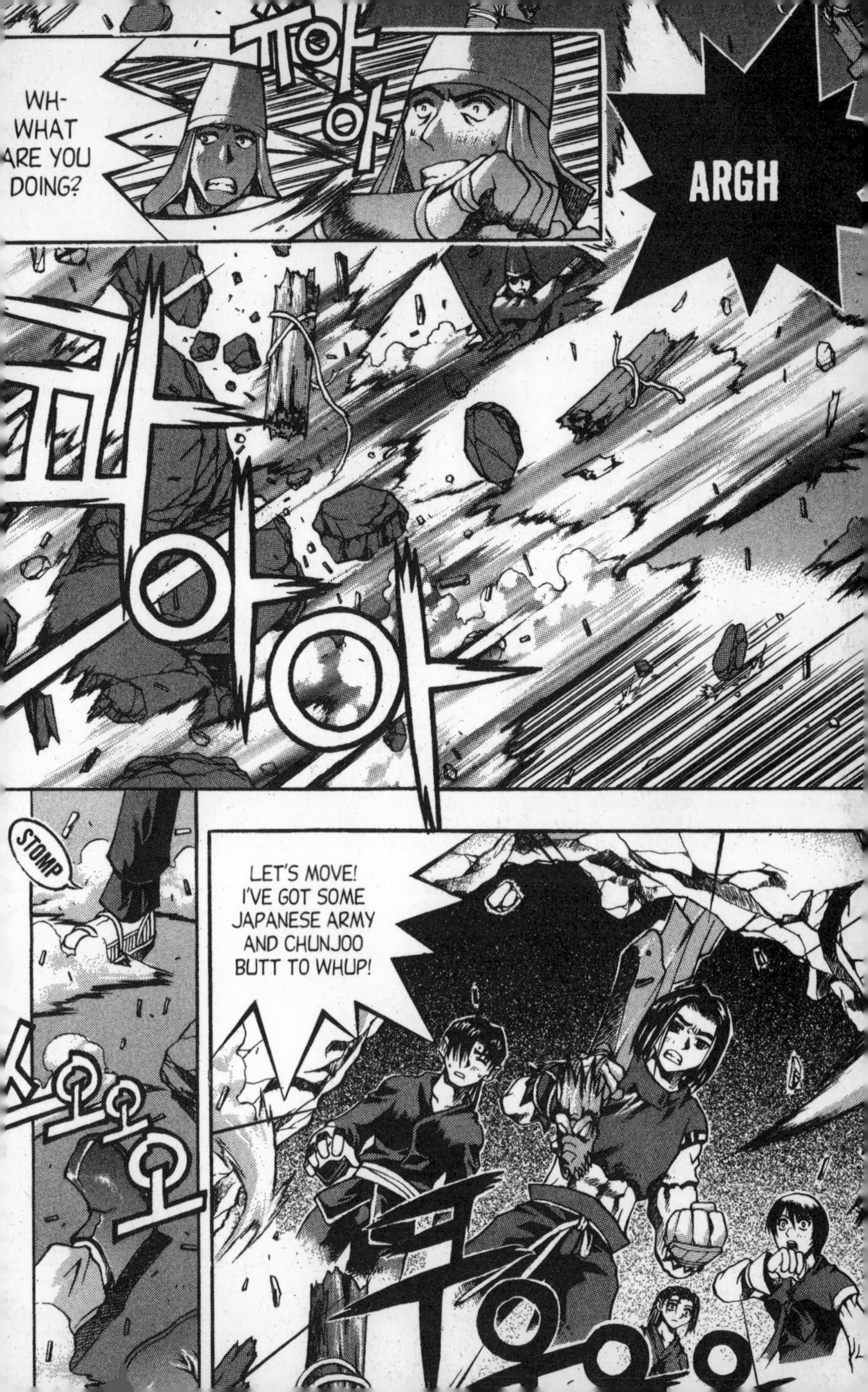
WH- WHAT ARE YOU DOING?
ARGH
STOMP
LET'S MOVE! I'VE GOT SOME JAPANESE ARMY AND CHUNJOO BUTT TO WHUP!

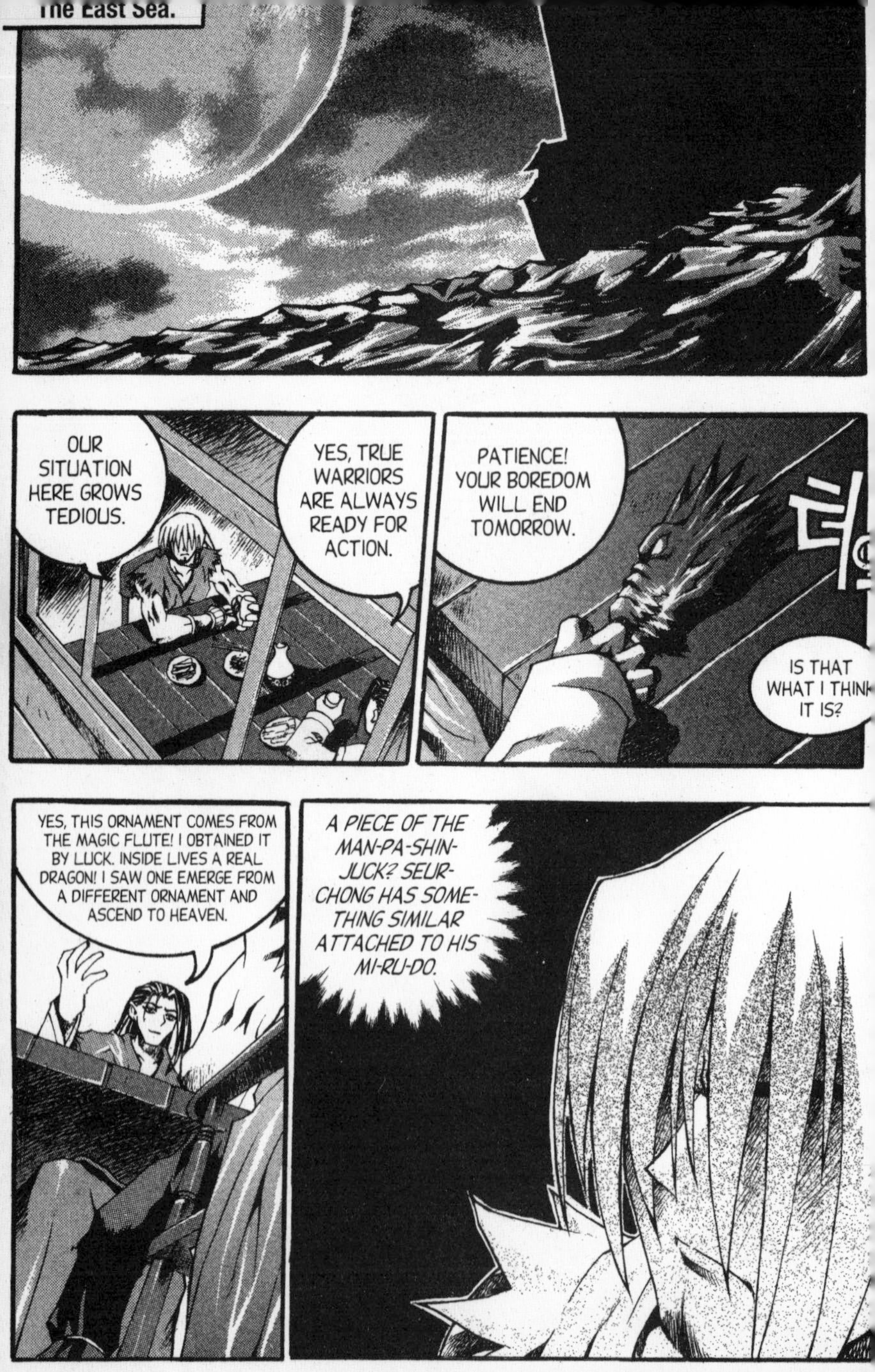
The East Sea.
OUR SITUATION HERE GROWS TEDIOUS.
YES, TRUE WARRIORS ARE ALWAYS READY FOR ACTION.
PATIENCE! YOUR BOREDOM WILL END TOMORROW.
IS THAT WHAT I THINK IT IS?
YES, THIS ORNAMENT COMES FROM THE MAGIC FLUTE! I OBTAINED IT BY LUCK. INSIDE LIVES A REAL DRAGON! I SAW ONE EMERGE FROM A DIFFERENT ORNAMENT AND ASCEND TO HEAVEN.
A PIECE OF THE MAN-PA-SHIN-JUCK? SEUR-CHONG HAS SOME-THING SIMILAR ATTACHED TO HIS MI-RU-DO.

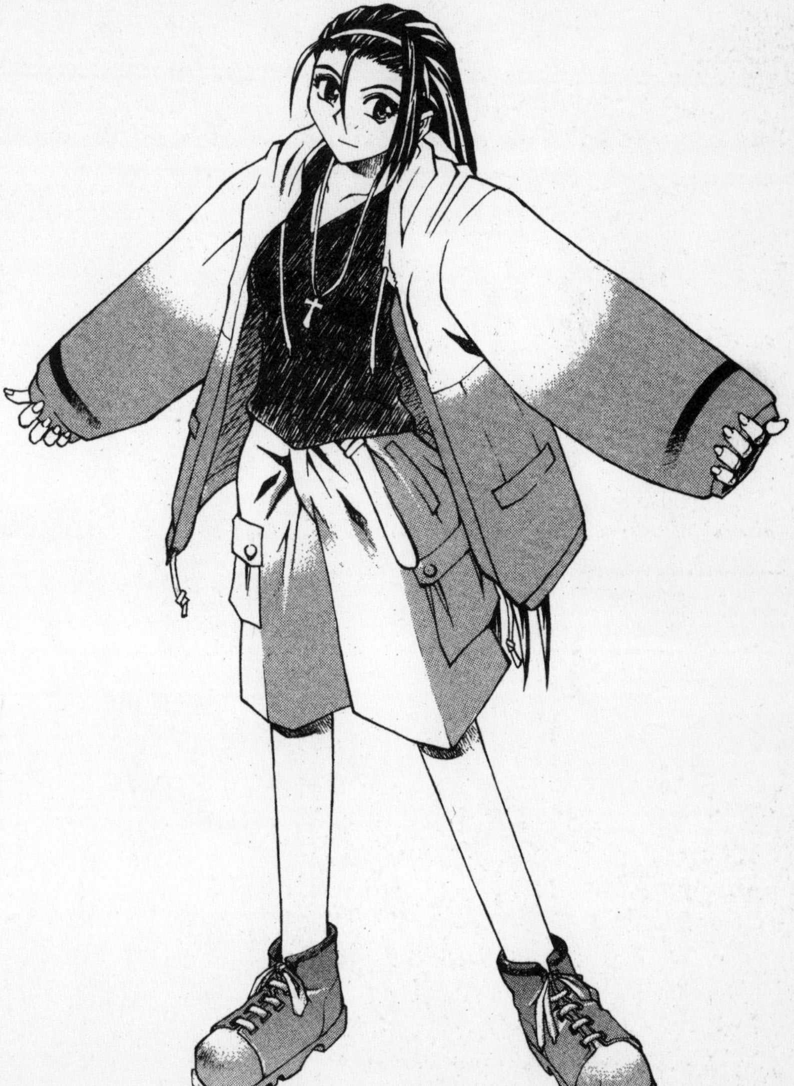

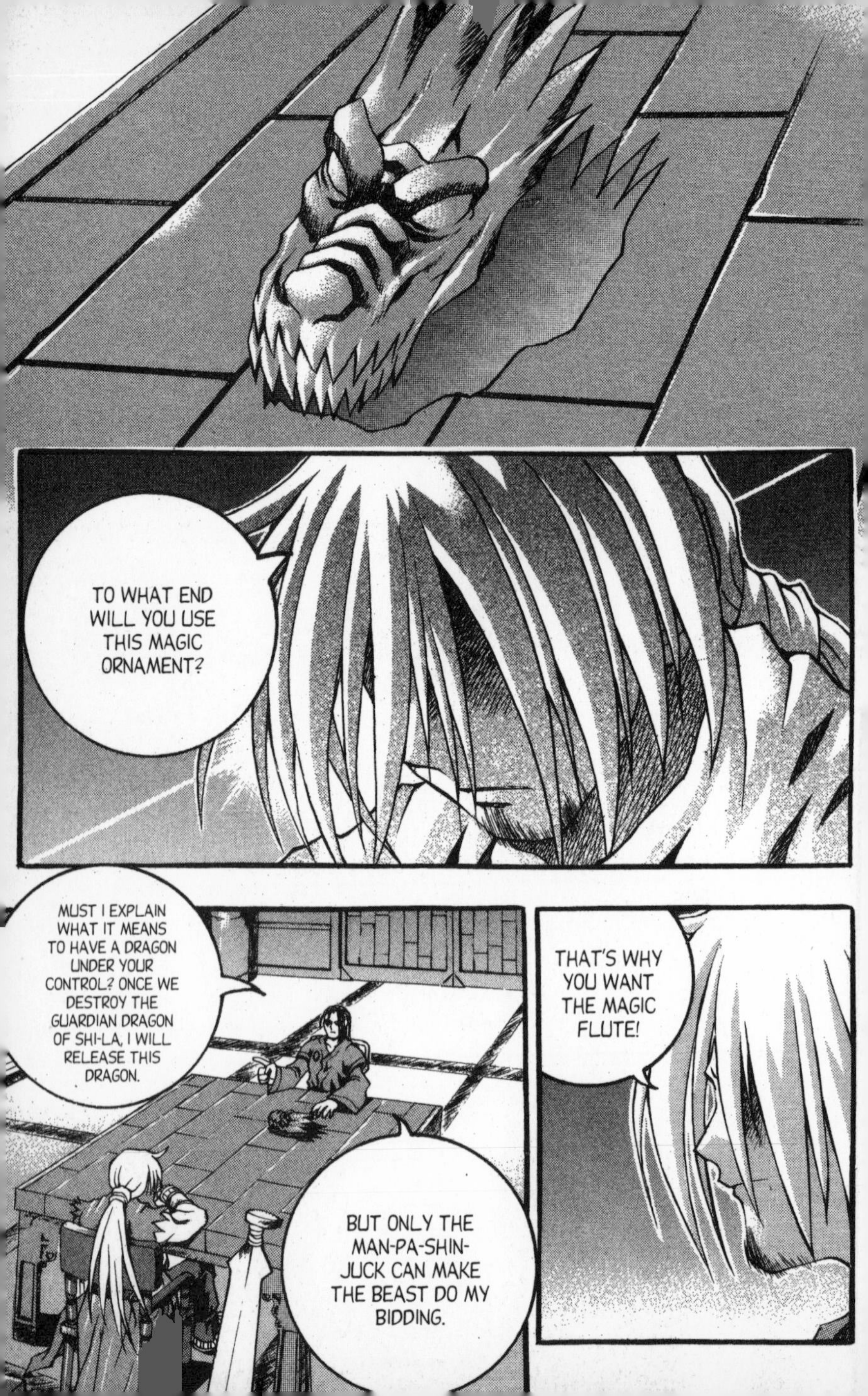
TO WHAT END WILL YOU USE THIS MAGIC ORNAMENT?
MUST I EXPLAIN WHAT IT MEANS TO HAVE A DRAGON UNDER YOUR CONTROL? ONCE WE DESTROY THE GUARDIAN DRAGON OF SHI-LA, I WILL RELEASE THIS DRAGON.
BUT ONLY THE MAN-PA-SHIN-JUCK CAN MAKE THE BEAST DO MY BIDDING.
THAT'S WHY YOU WANT THE MAGIC FLUTE!

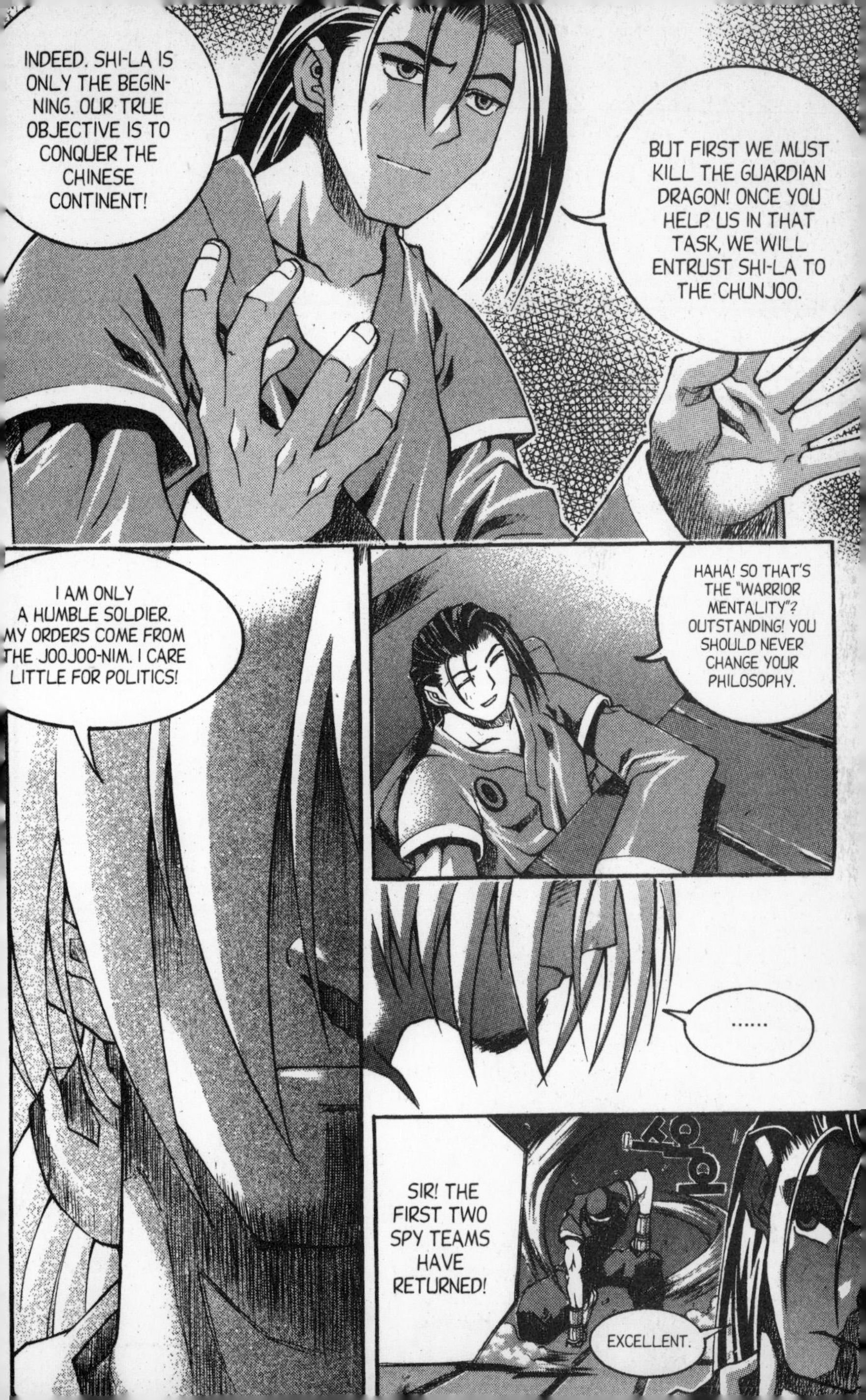
INDEED. SHI-LA IS ONLY THE BEGIN-NING. OUR TRUE OBJECTIVE IS TO CONQUER THE CHINESE CONTINENT!
BUT FIRST WE MUST KILL THE GUARDIAN DRAGON! ONCE YOU HELP US IN THAT TASK, WE WILL ENTRUST SHI-LA TO THE CHUNJOO.
I AM ONLY A HUMBLE SOLDIER. MY ORDERS COME FROM THE JOOJOO-NIM. I CARE LITTLE FOR POLITICS!
HAHA! SO THAT'S THE "WARRIOR MENTALITY"? OUTSTANDING! YOU SHOULD NEVER CHANGE YOUR PHILOSOPHY.
......
SIR! THE FIRST TWO SPY TEAMS HAVE RETURNED!
EXCELLENT.

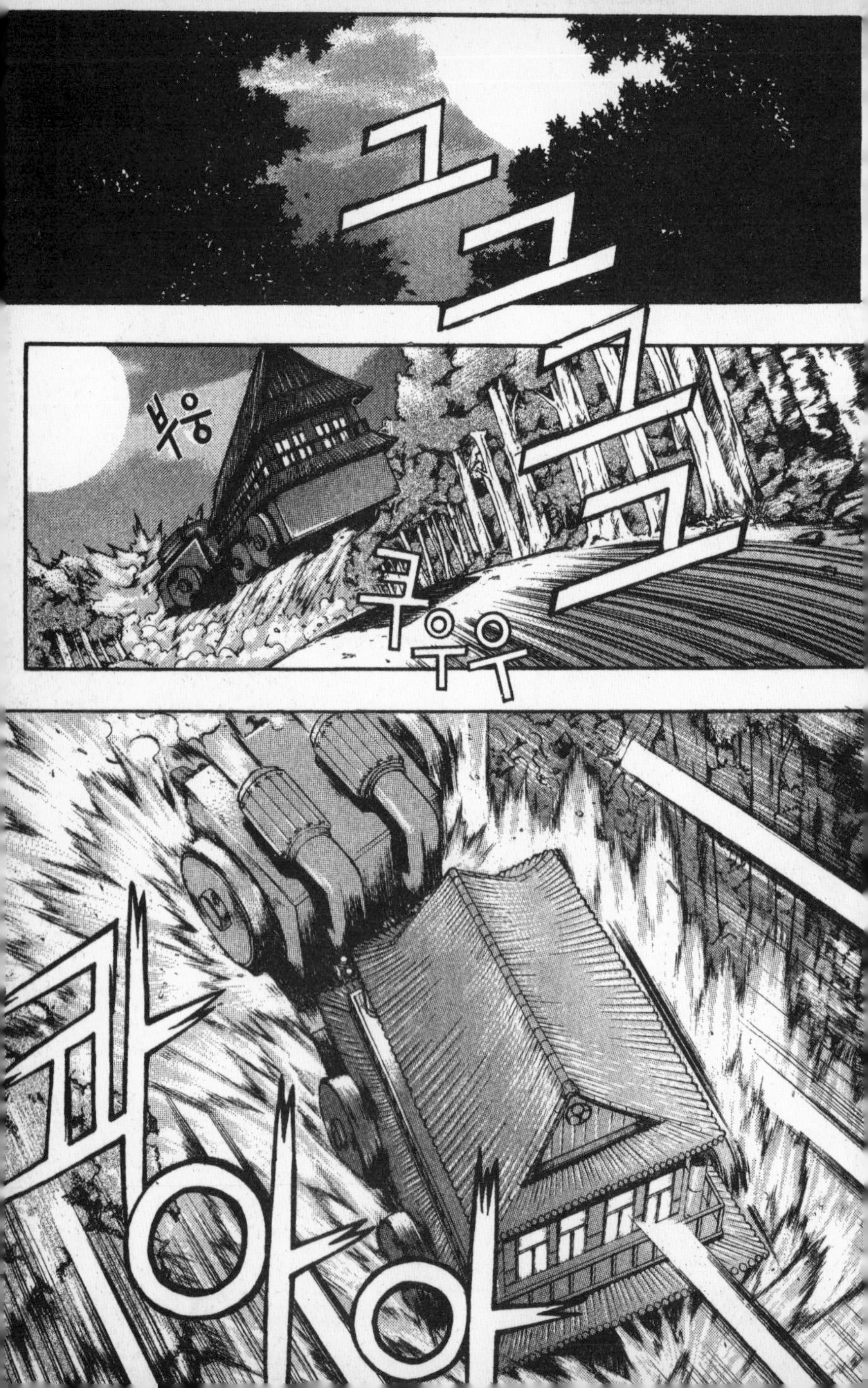

그그그그
부웅
쿠우우
콰아아

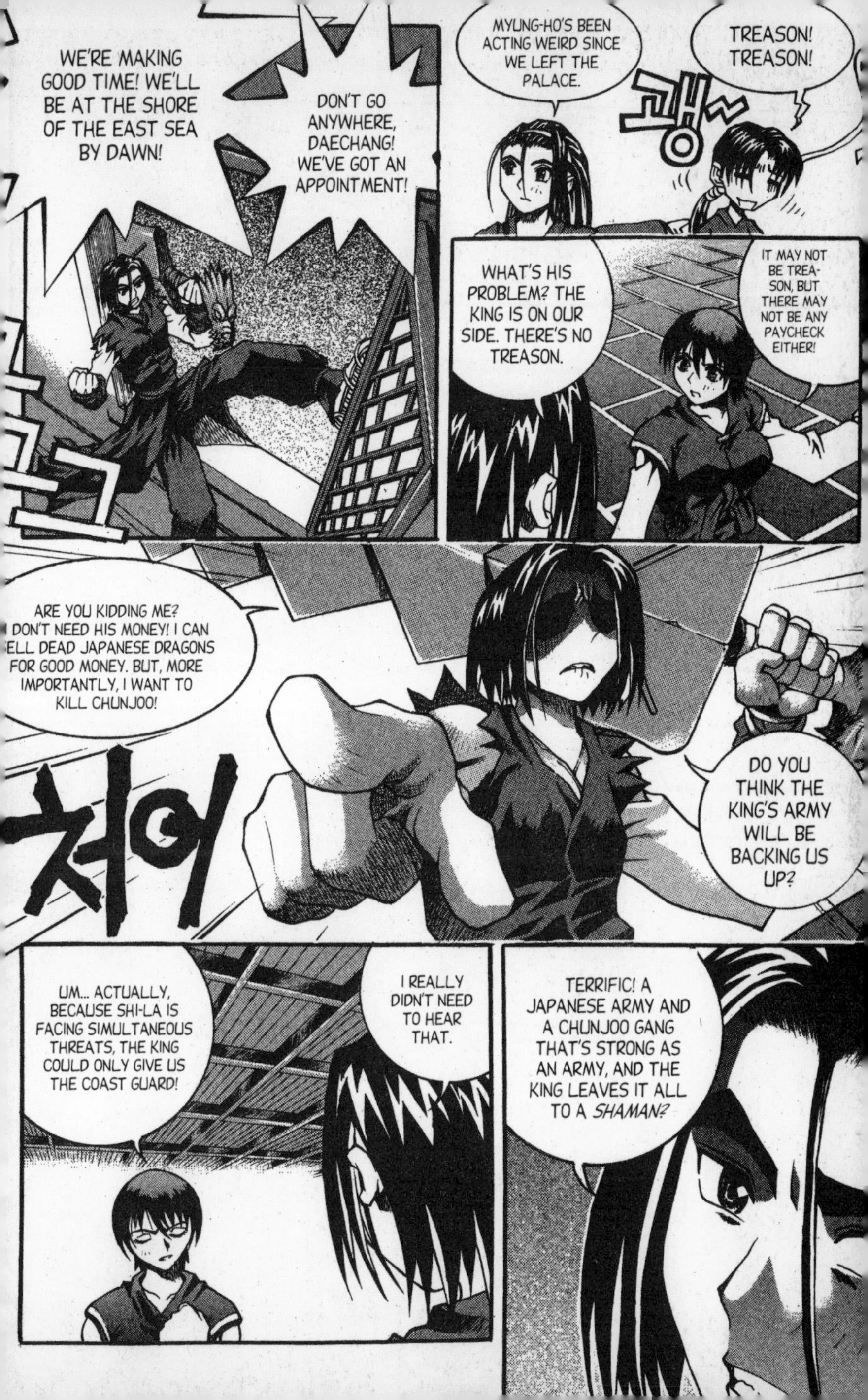
WE'RE MAKING GOOD TIME! WE'LL BE AT THE SHORE OF THE EAST SEA BY DAWN!
DON'T GO ANYWHERE, DAECHANG! WE'VE GOT AN APPOINTMENT!
MYUNG-HO'S BEEN ACTING WEIRD SINCE WE LEFT THE PALACE.
TREASON! TREASON!
괭
WHAT'S HIS PROBLEM? THE KING IS ON OUR SIDE. THERE'S NO TREASON.
IT MAY NOT BE TREA-SON, BUT THERE MAY NOT BE ANY PAYCHECK EITHER!
ARE YOU KIDDING ME? DON'T NEED HIS MONEY! I CAN ELL DEAD JAPANESE DRAGONS FOR GOOD MONEY. BUT, MORE IMPORTANTLY, I WANT TO KILL CHUNJOO!
DO YOU THINK THE KING'S ARMY WILL BE BACKING US UP?
UM... ACTUALLY, BECAUSE SHI-LA IS FACING SIMULTANEOUS THREATS, THE KING COULD ONLY GIVE US THE COAST GUARD!
I REALLY DIDN'T NEED TO HEAR THAT.
TERRIFIC! A JAPANESE ARMY AND A CHUNJOO GANG THAT'S STRONG AS AN ARMY, AND THE KING LEAVES IT ALL TO A SHAMAN?

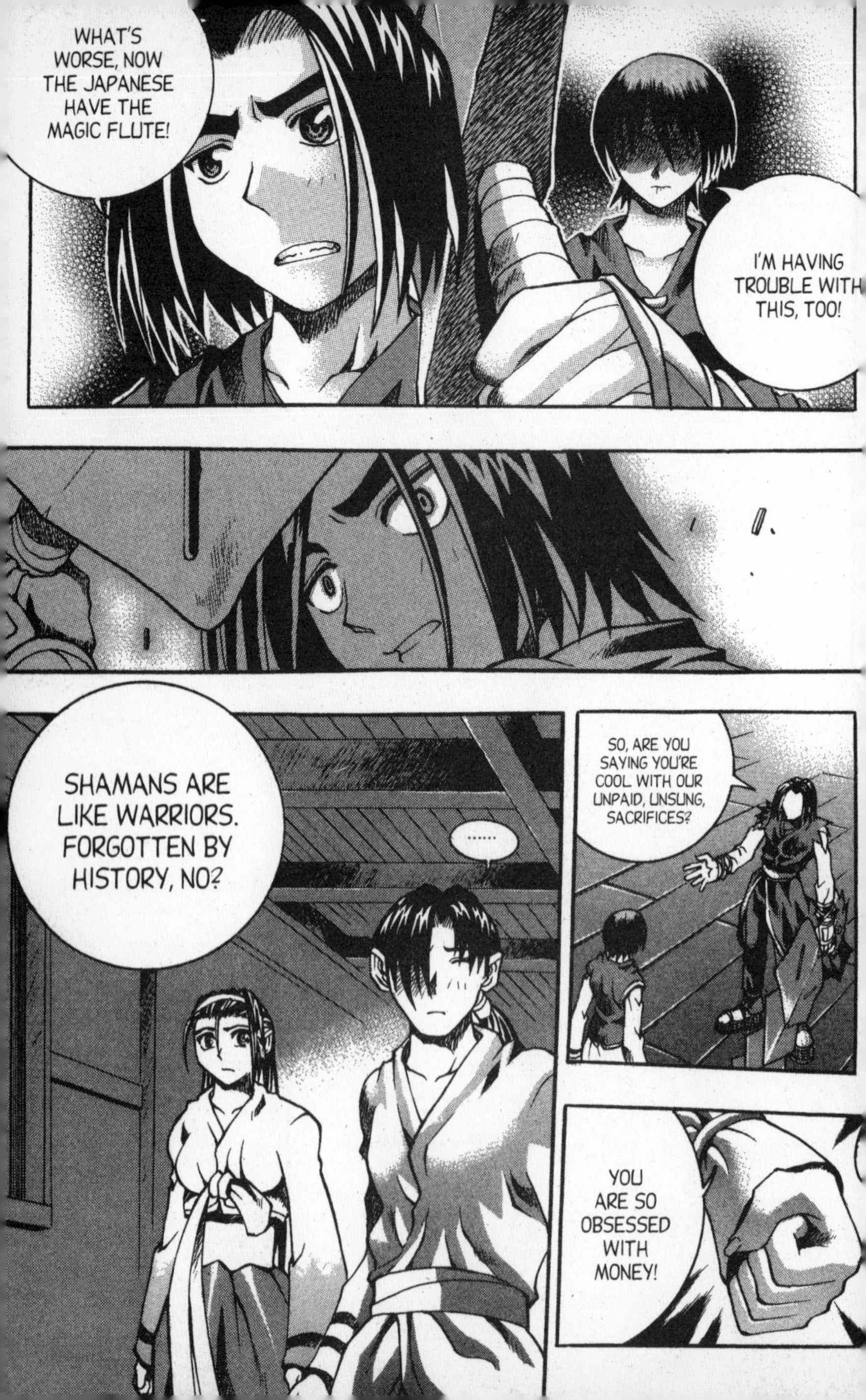
WHAT'S WORSE, NOW THE JAPANESE HAVE THE MAGIC FLUTE!
I'M HAVING TROUBLE WITH THIS, TOO!
SHAMANS ARE LIKE WARRIORS. FORGOTTEN BY HISTORY, NO?
......
SO, ARE YOU SAYING YOU'RE COOL WITH OUR UNPAID, UNSUNG, SACRIFICES?
YOU ARE SO OBSESSED WITH MONEY!

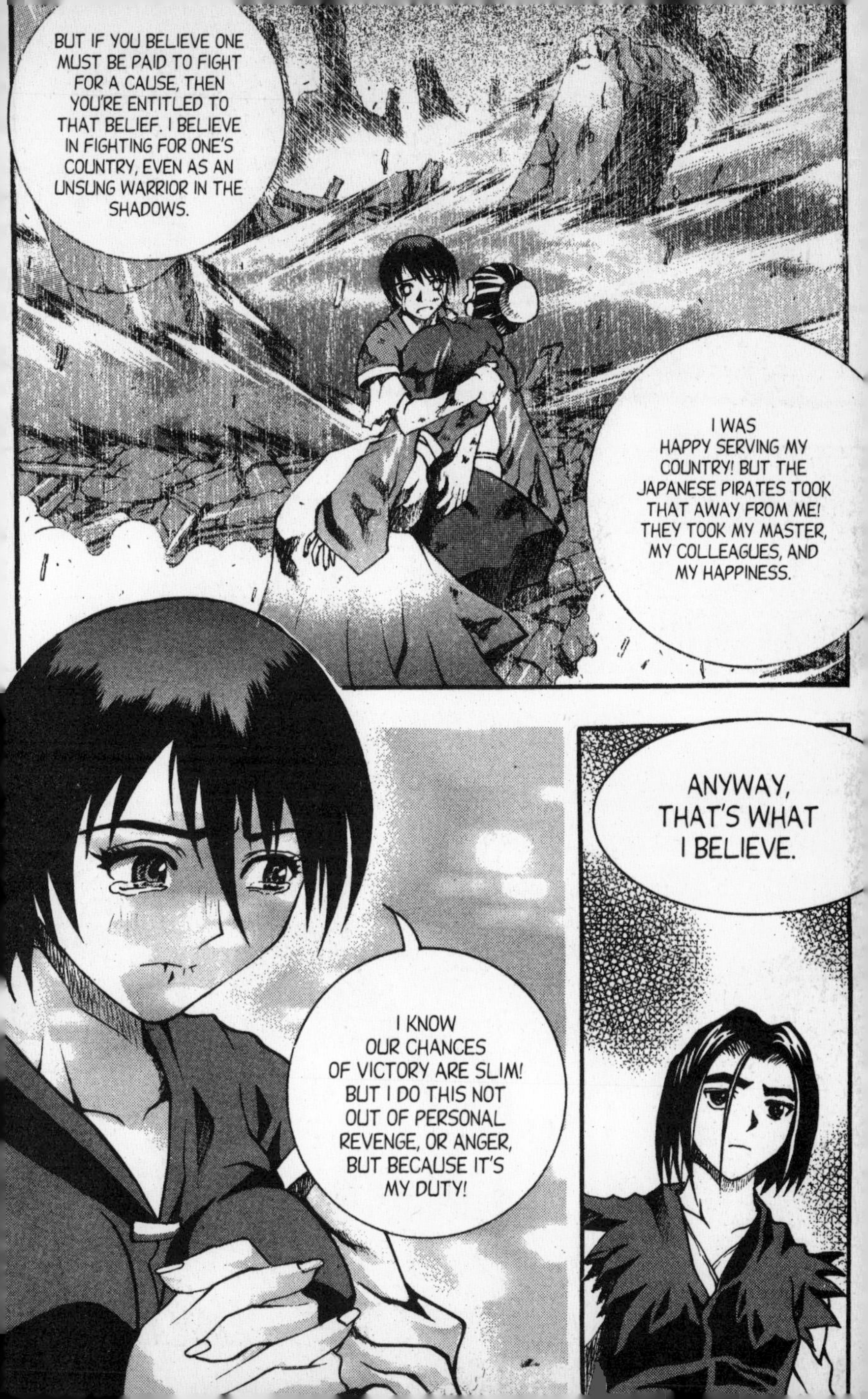
BUT IF YOU BELIEVE ONE MUST BE PAID TO FIGHT FOR A CAUSE, THEN YOU'RE ENTITLED TO THAT BELIEF. I BELIEVE IN FIGHTING FOR ONE'S COUNTRY, EVEN AS AN UNSUNG WARRIOR IN THE SHADOWS.
I WAS HAPPY SERVING MY COUNTRY! BUT THE JAPANESE PIRATES TOOK THAT AWAY FROM ME! THEY TOOK MY MASTER, MY COLLEAGUES, AND MY HAPPINESS.
I KNOW OUR CHANCES OF VICTORY ARE SLIM! BUT I DO THIS NOT OUT OF PERSONAL REVENGE, OR ANGER, BUT BECAUSE IT'S MY DUTY!
ANYWAY, THAT'S WHAT I BELIEVE.

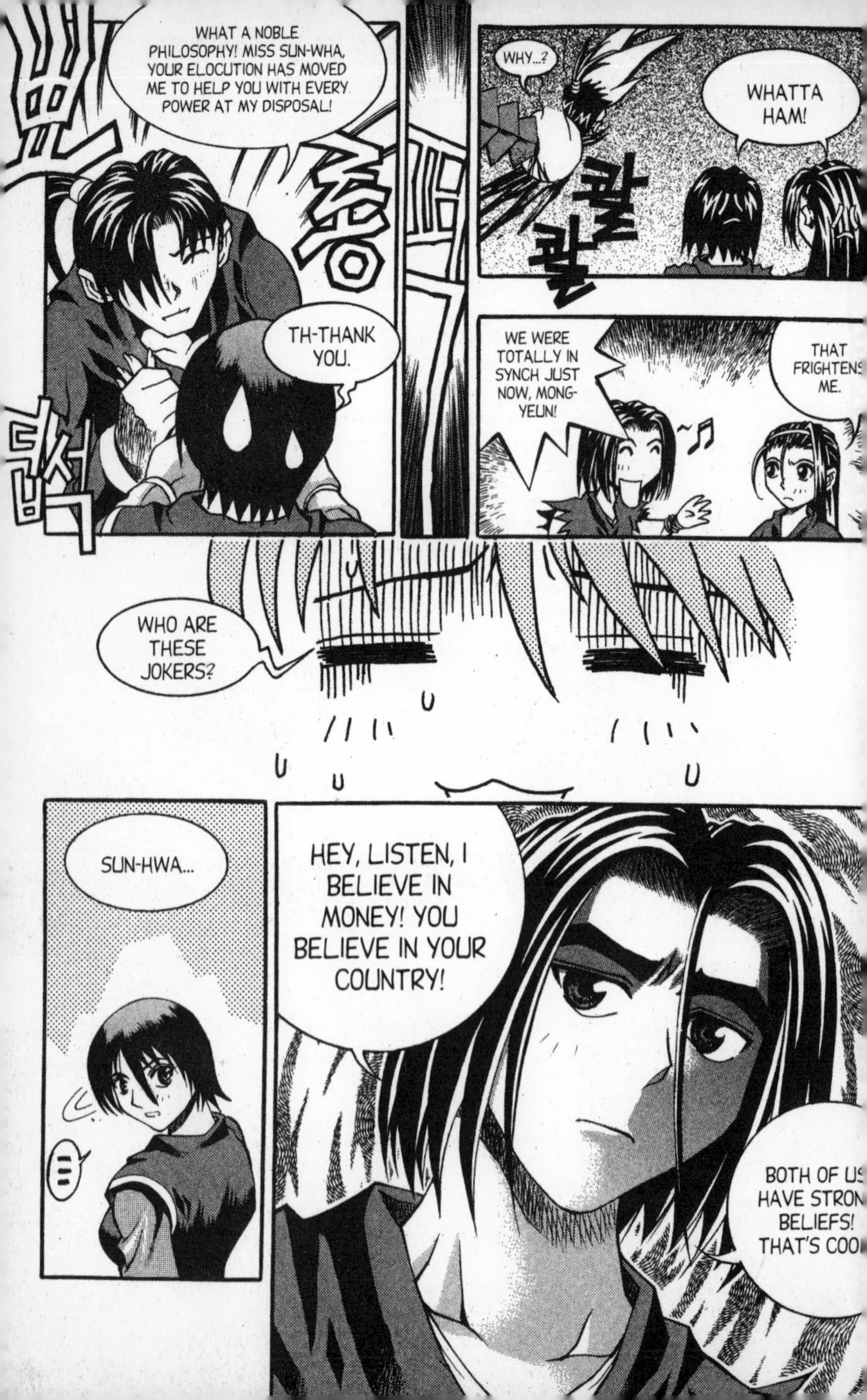
WHAT A NOBLE PHILOSOPHY! MISS SUN-WHA, YOUR ELOCUTION HAS MOVED ME TO HELP YOU WITH EVERY POWER AT MY DISPOSAL!
TH-THANK YOU.
WHY...?
WHATTA HAM!
WE WERE TOTALLY IN SYNCH JUST NOW, MONG-YEUN!
THAT FRIGHTENS ME.
WHO ARE THESE JOKERS?
SUN-HWA...
HEY, LISTEN, I BELIEVE IN MONEY! YOU BELIEVE IN YOUR COUNTRY!
BOTH OF US HAVE STRON BELIEFS! THAT'S COO

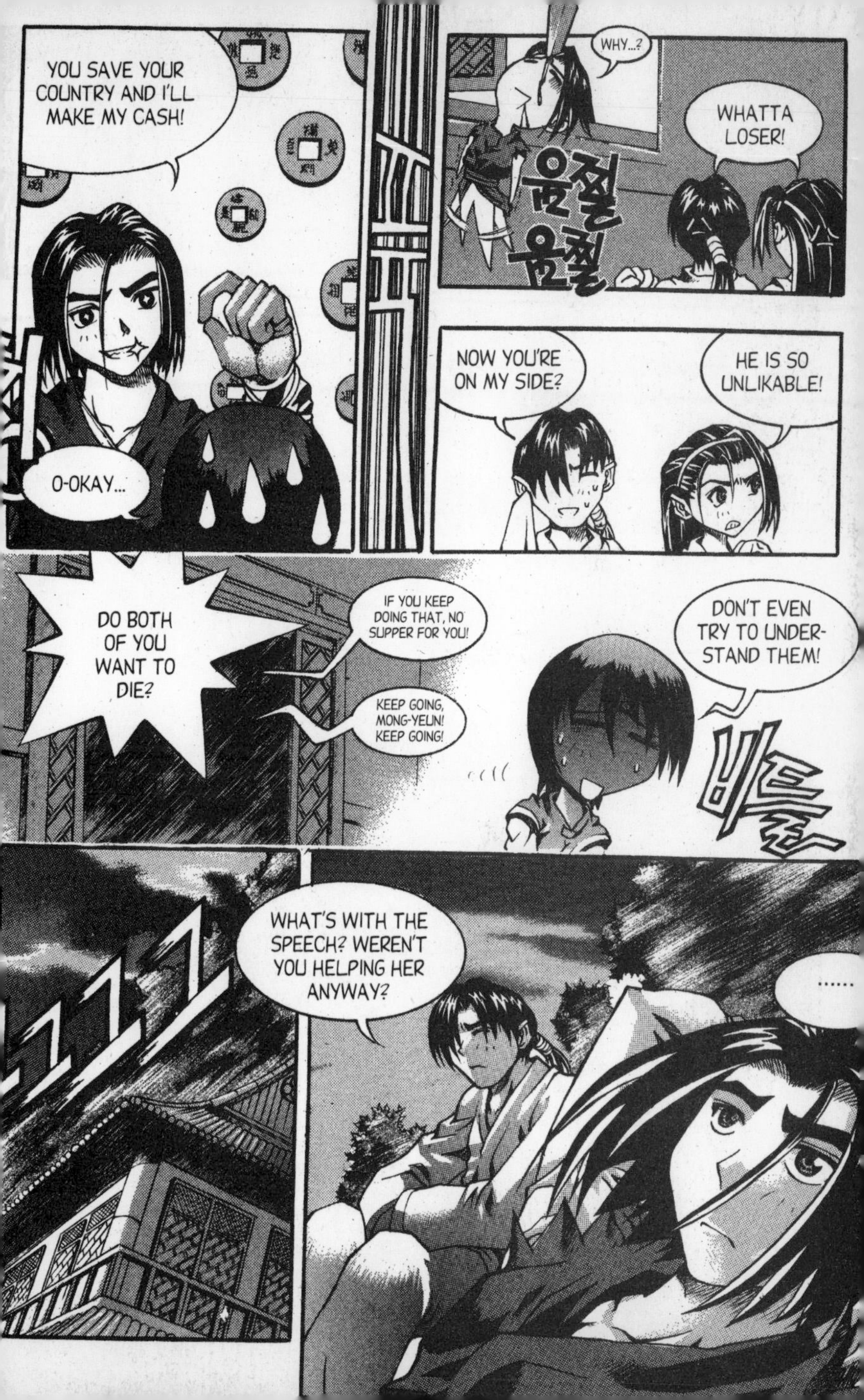
YOU SAVE YOUR COUNTRY AND I'LL MAKE MY CASH!
O-OKAY...
WHY...?
WHATTA LOSER!
움찔
움찔
NOW YOU'RE ON MY SIDE?
HE IS SO UNLIKABLE!
DO BOTH OF YOU WANT TO DIE?
IF YOU KEEP DOING THAT, NO SUPPER FOR YOU!
KEEP GOING, MONG-YEUN! KEEP GOING!
DON'T EVEN TRY TO UNDER-STAND THEM!
WHAT'S WITH THE SPEECH? WEREN'T YOU HELPING HER ANYWAY?
......

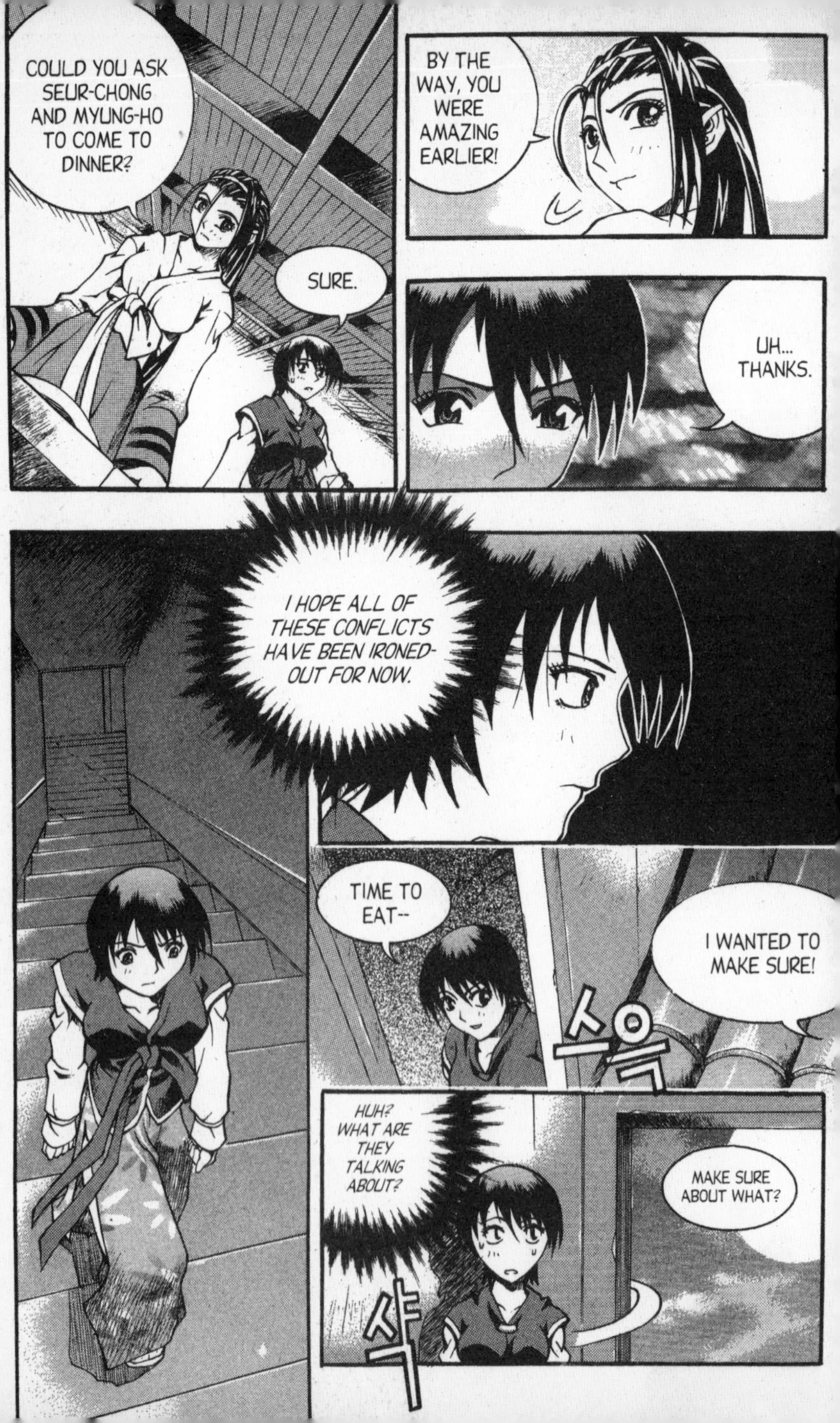

COULD YOU ASK SEUR-CHONG AND MYUNG-HO TO COME TO DINNER?
SURE.
BY THE WAY, YOU WERE AMAZING EARLIER!
UH... THANKS.
I HOPE ALL OF THESE CONFLICTS HAVE BEEN IRONED-OUT FOR NOW.
TIME TO EAT--
I WANTED TO MAKE SURE!
스윽
HUH? WHAT ARE THEY TALKING ABOUT?
MAKE SURE ABOUT WHAT?
샥

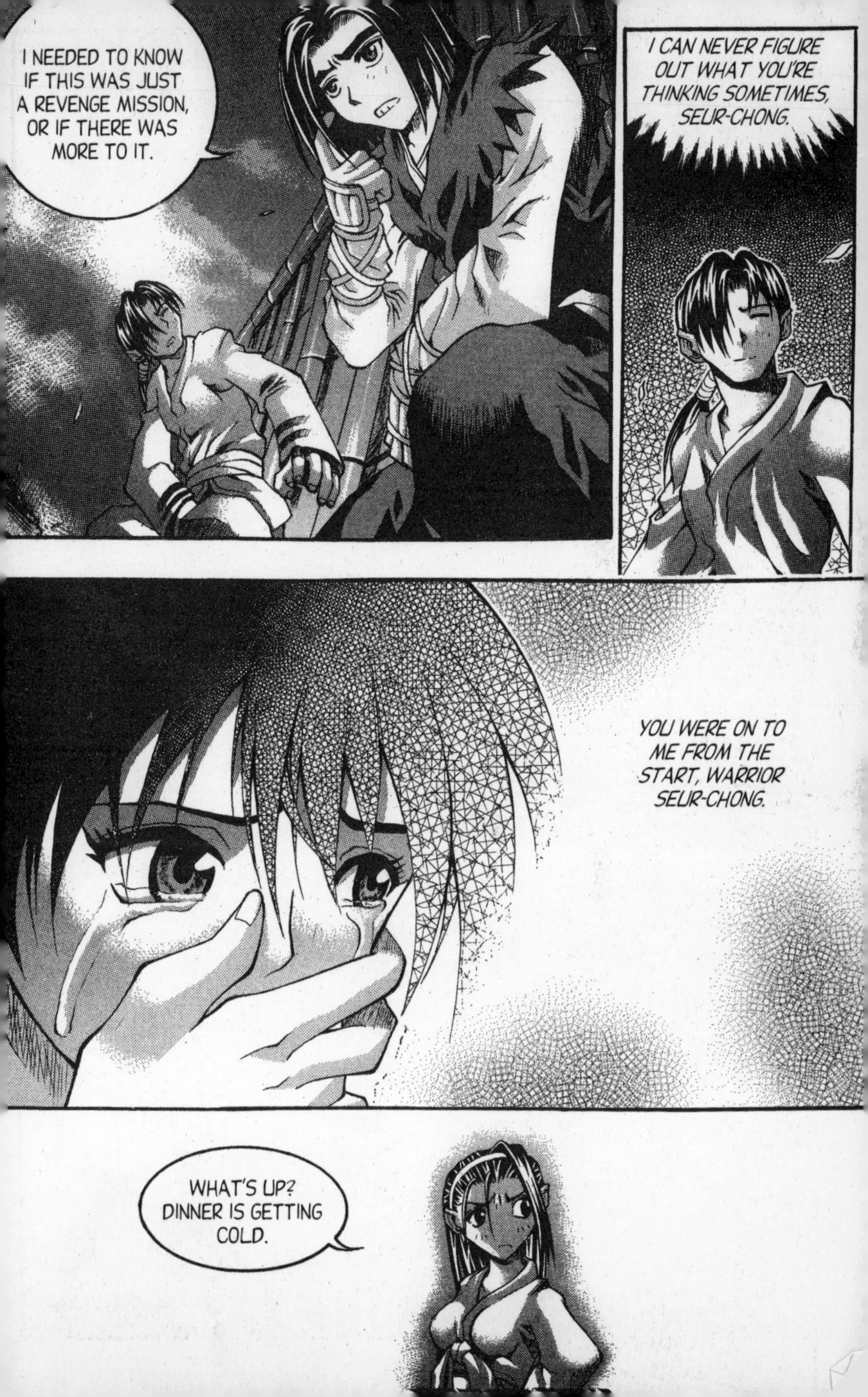
I NEEDED TO KNOW IF THIS WAS JUST A REVENGE MISSION, OR IF THERE WAS MORE TO IT.
I CAN NEVER FIGURE OUT WHAT YOU'RE THINKING SOMETIMES, SEUR-CHONG.
YOU WERE ON TO ME FROM THE START, WARRIOR SEUR-CHONG.
WHAT'S UP? DINNER IS GETTING COLD.

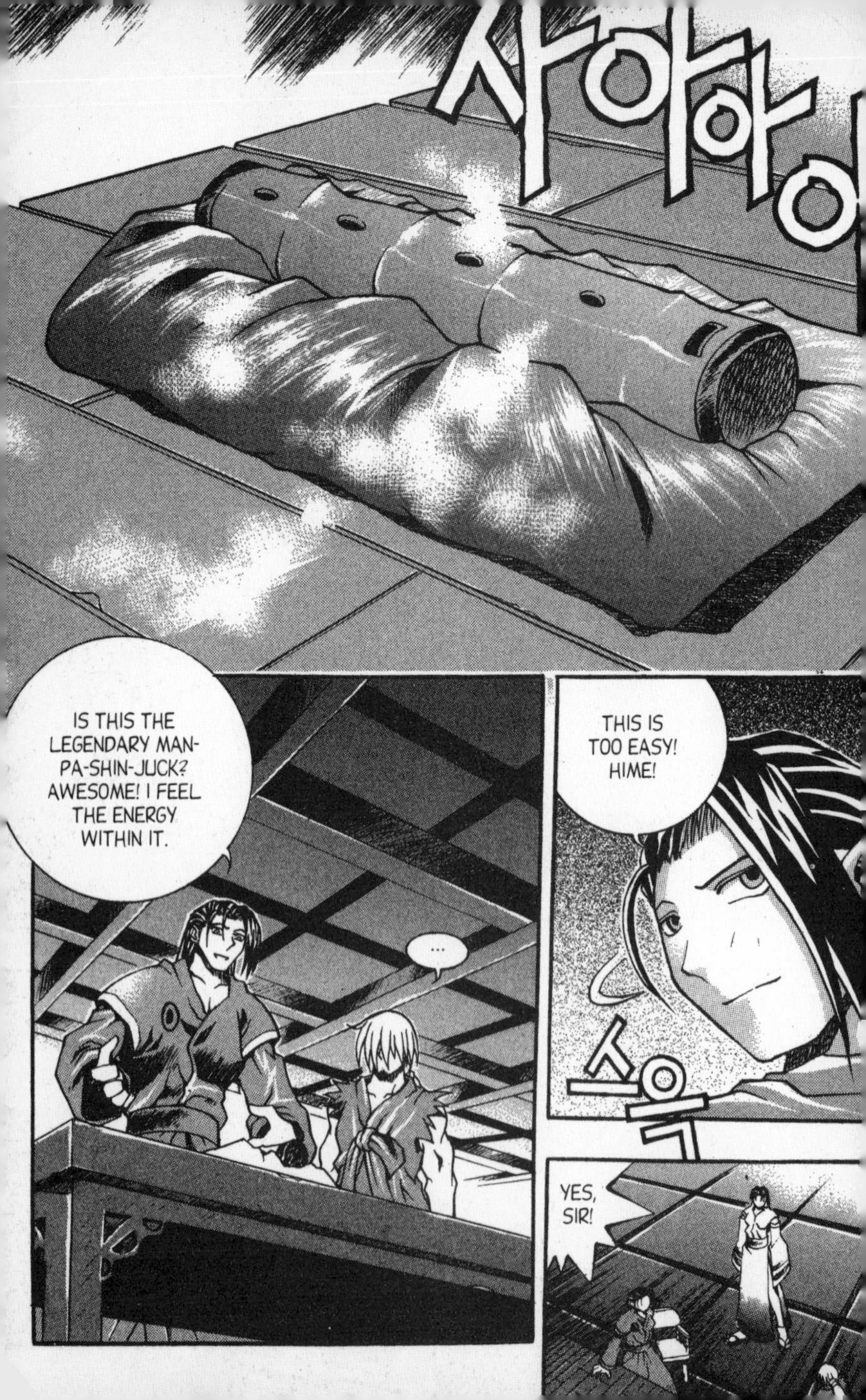
샤아아아
IS THIS THE LEGENDARY MAN-PA-SHIN-JUCK? AWESOME! I FEEL THE ENERGY WITHIN IT.
...
THIS IS TOO EASY! HIME!
스윽
YES, SIR!

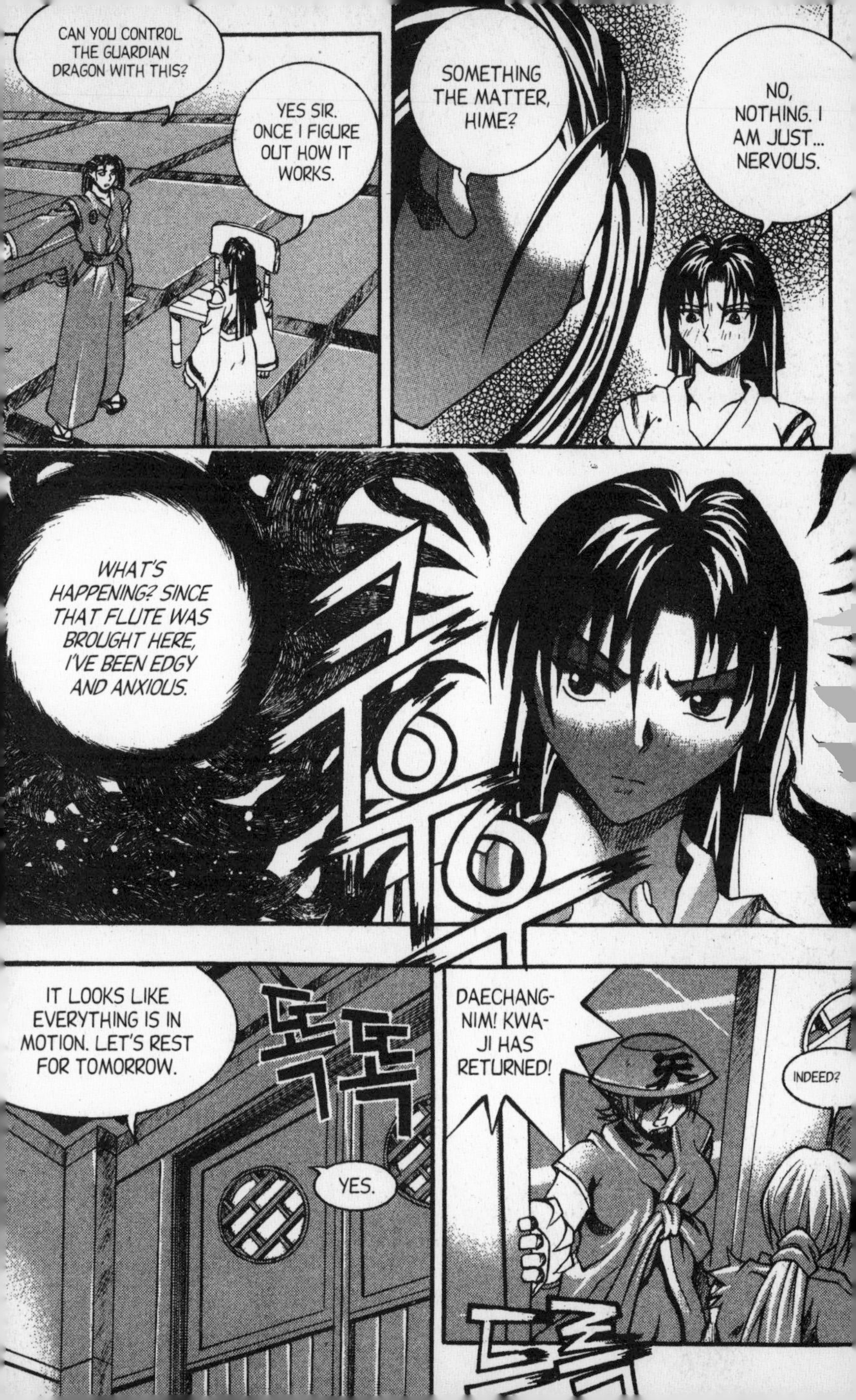

CAN YOU CONTROL THE GUARDIAN DRAGON WITH THIS?
YES SIR. ONCE I FIGURE OUT HOW IT WORKS.
SOMETHING THE MATTER, HIME?
NO, NOTHING. I AM JUST... NERVOUS.
WHAT'S HAPPENING? SINCE THAT FLUTE WAS BROUGHT HERE, I'VE BEEN EDGY AND ANXIOUS.
IT LOOKS LIKE EVERYTHING IS IN MOTION. LET'S REST FOR TOMORROW.
똑 똑
YES.
DAECHANG-NIM! KWA-JI HAS RETURNED!
INDEED?

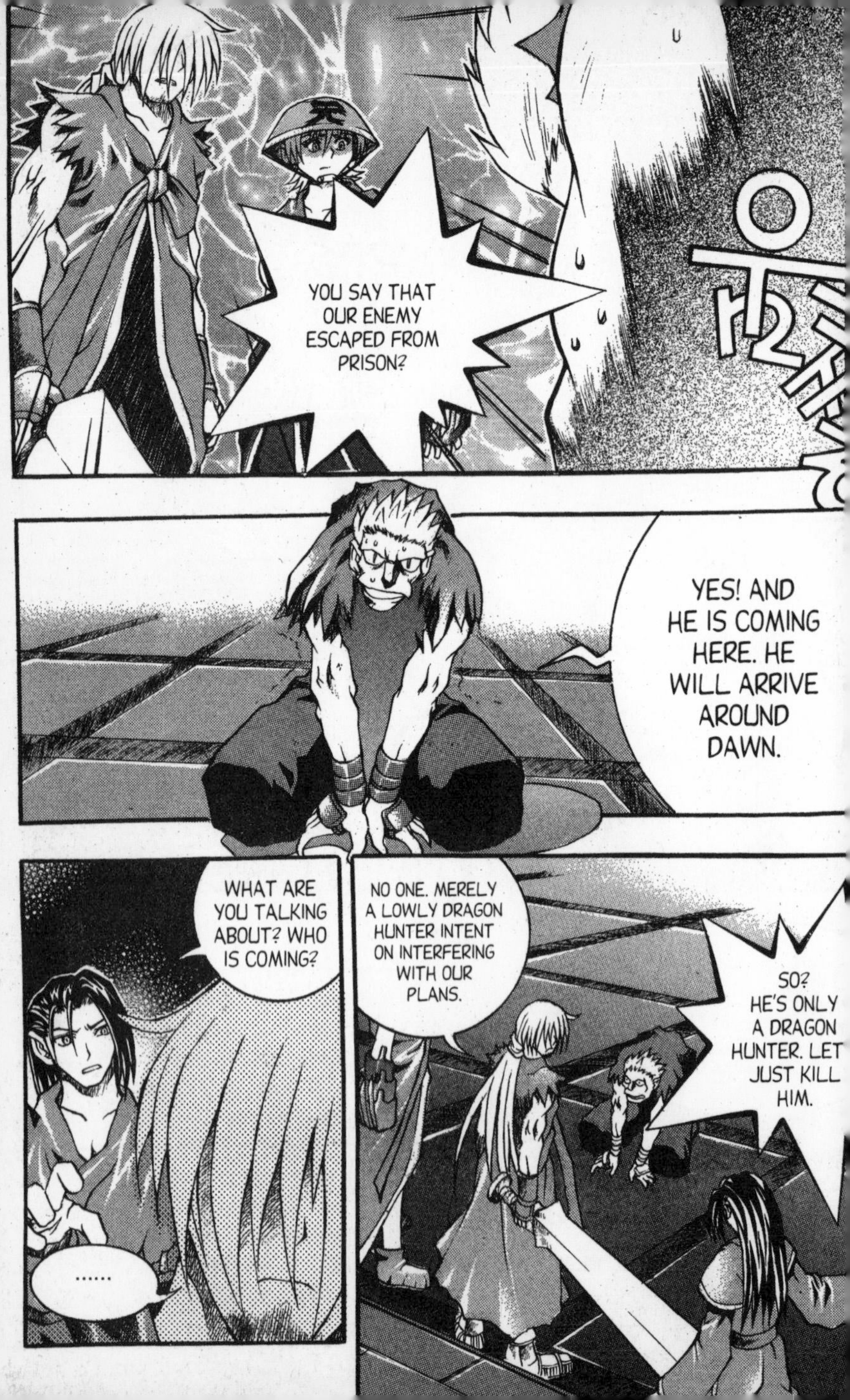
YOU SAY THAT OUR ENEMY ESCAPED FROM PRISON?
YES! AND HE IS COMING HERE. HE WILL ARRIVE AROUND DAWN.
WHAT ARE YOU TALKING ABOUT? WHO IS COMING?
......
NO ONE. MERELY A LOWLY DRAGON HUNTER INTENT ON INTERFERING WITH OUR PLANS.
SO? HE'S ONLY A DRAGON HUNTER. LET JUST KILL HIM.

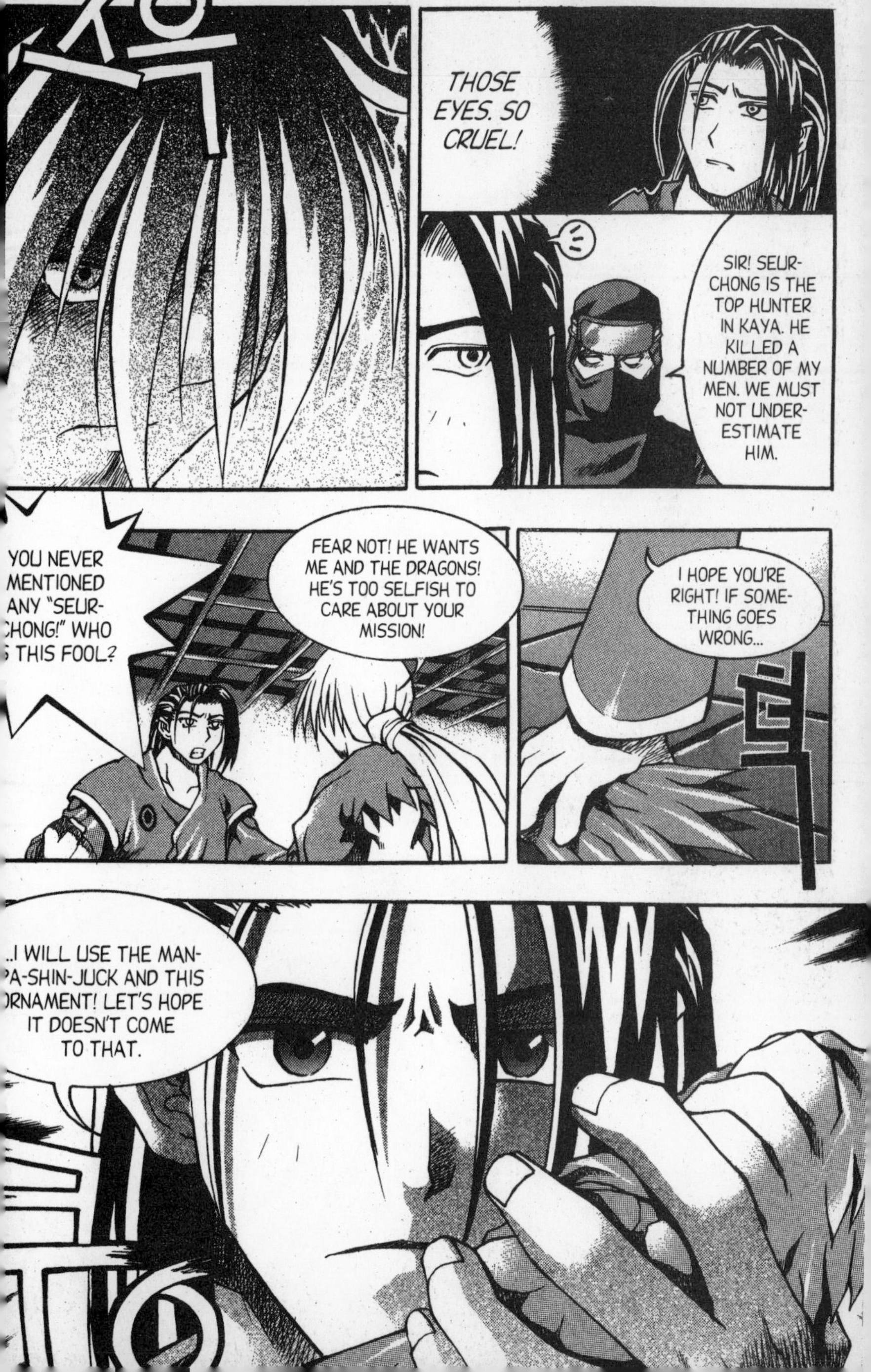
THOSE EYES. SO CRUEL!
SIR! SEUR-CHONG IS THE TOP HUNTER IN KAYA. HE KILLED A NUMBER OF MY MEN. WE MUST NOT UNDER-ESTIMATE HIM.
YOU NEVER MENTIONED ANY "SEUR-CHONG!" WHO IS THIS FOOL?
FEAR NOT! HE WANTS ME AND THE DRAGONS! HE'S TOO SELFISH TO CARE ABOUT YOUR MISSION!
I HOPE YOU'RE RIGHT! IF SOME-THING GOES WRONG...
...I WILL USE THE MAN-PA-SHIN-JUCK AND THIS ORNAMENT! LET'S HOPE IT DOESN'T COME TO THAT.

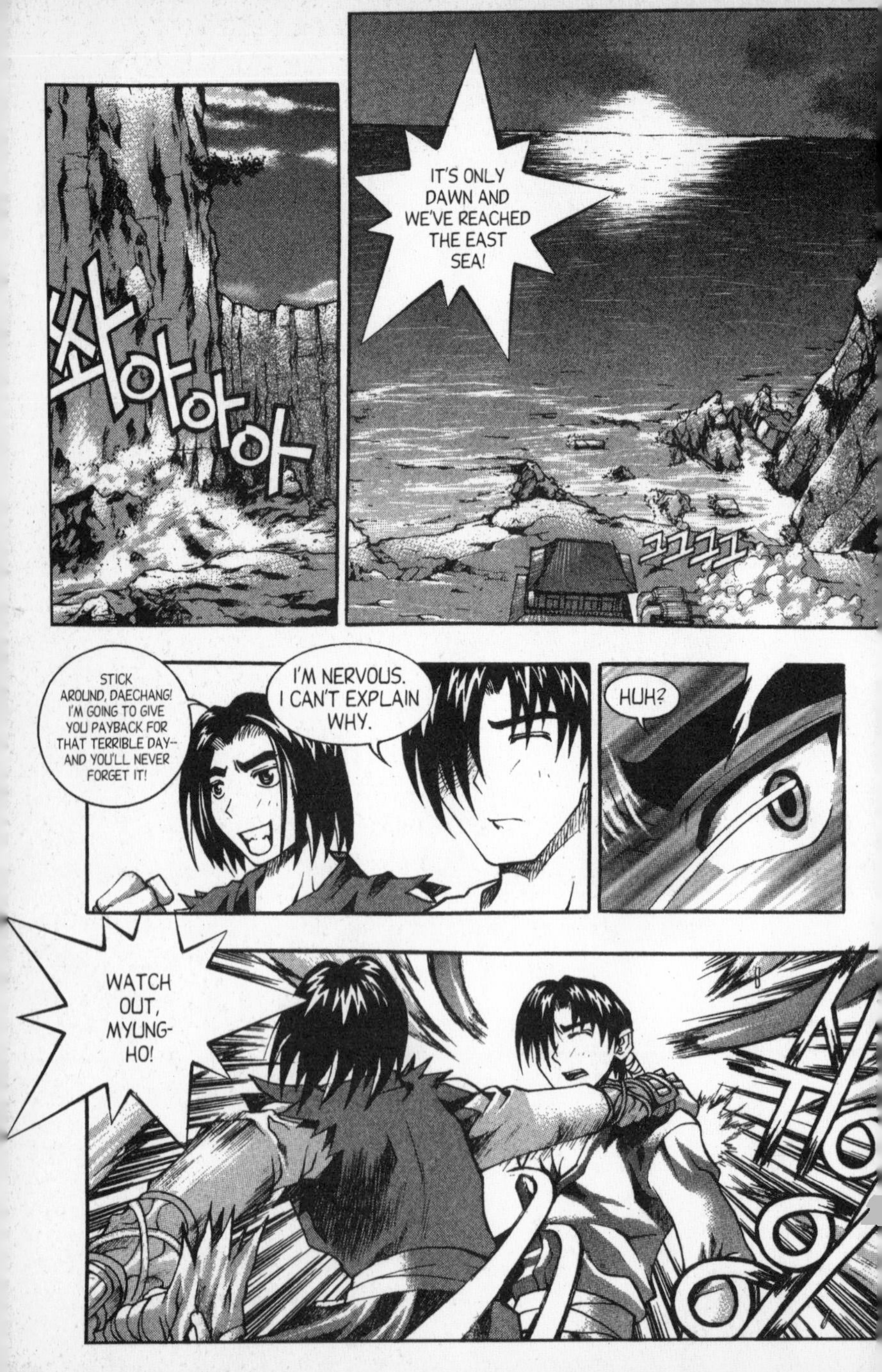
IT'S ONLY DAWN AND WE'VE REACHED THE EAST SEA!
STICK AROUND, DAECHANG! I'M GOING TO GIVE YOU PAYBACK FOR THAT TERRIBLE DAY--AND YOU'LL NEVER FORGET IT!
I'M NERVOUS. I CAN'T EXPLAIN WHY.
HUH?
WATCH OUT, MYUNG-HO!

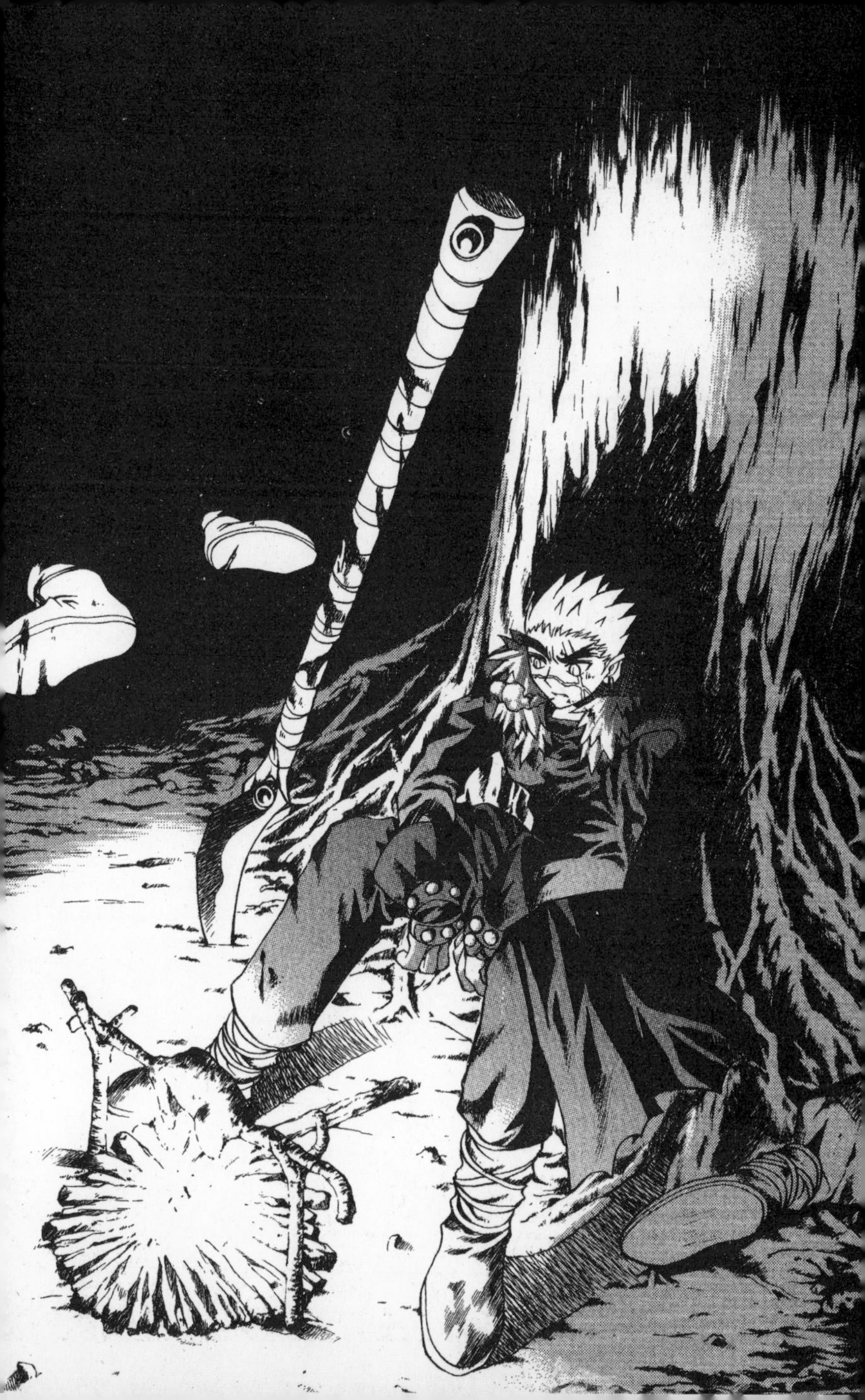

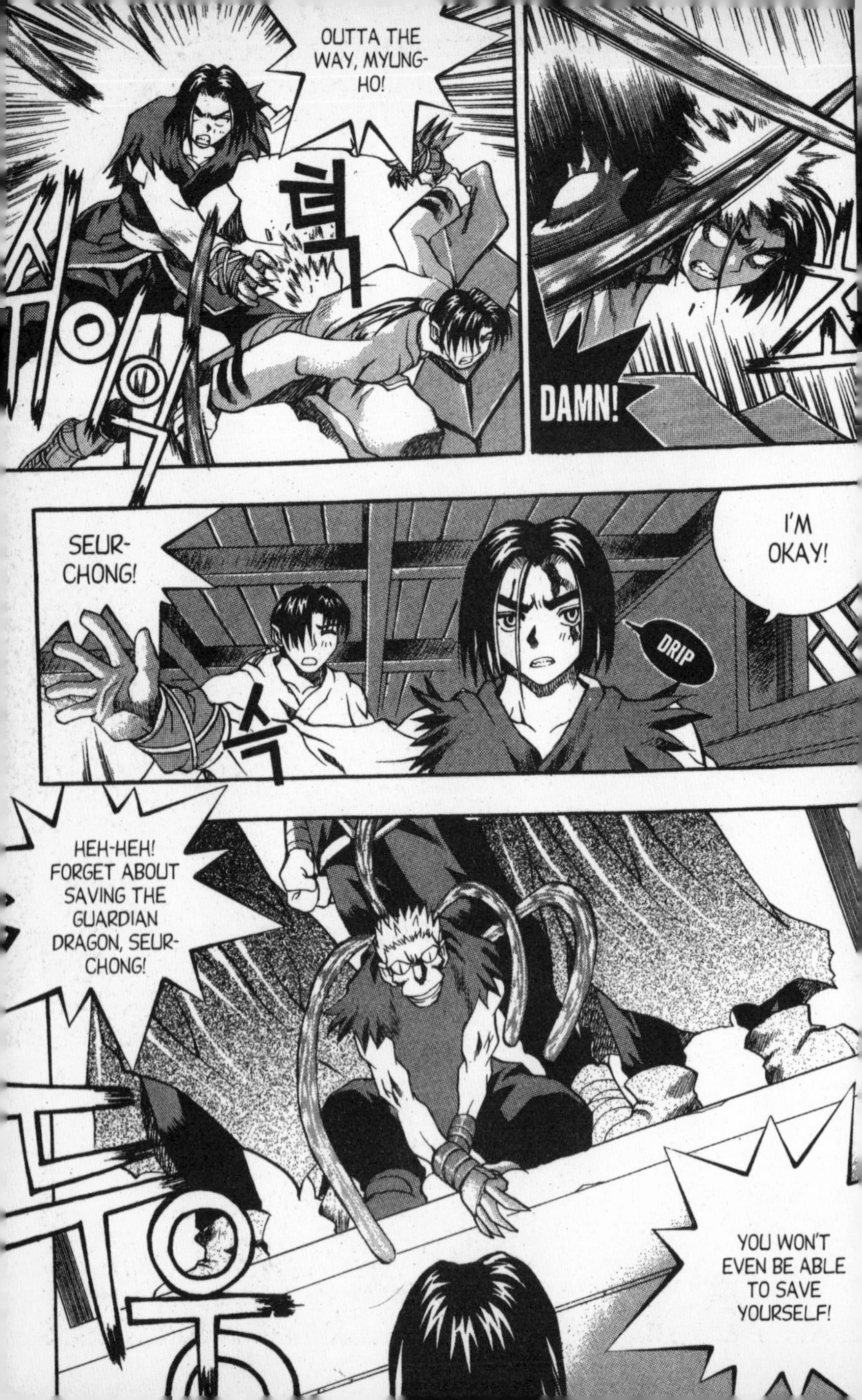
OUTTA THE WAY, MYUNG-HO!
DAMN!
SEUR-CHONG!
I'M OKAY!
DRIP
HEH-HEH! FORGET ABOUT SAVING THE GUARDIAN DRAGON, SEUR-CHONG!
YOU WON'T EVEN BE ABLE TO SAVE YOURSELF!

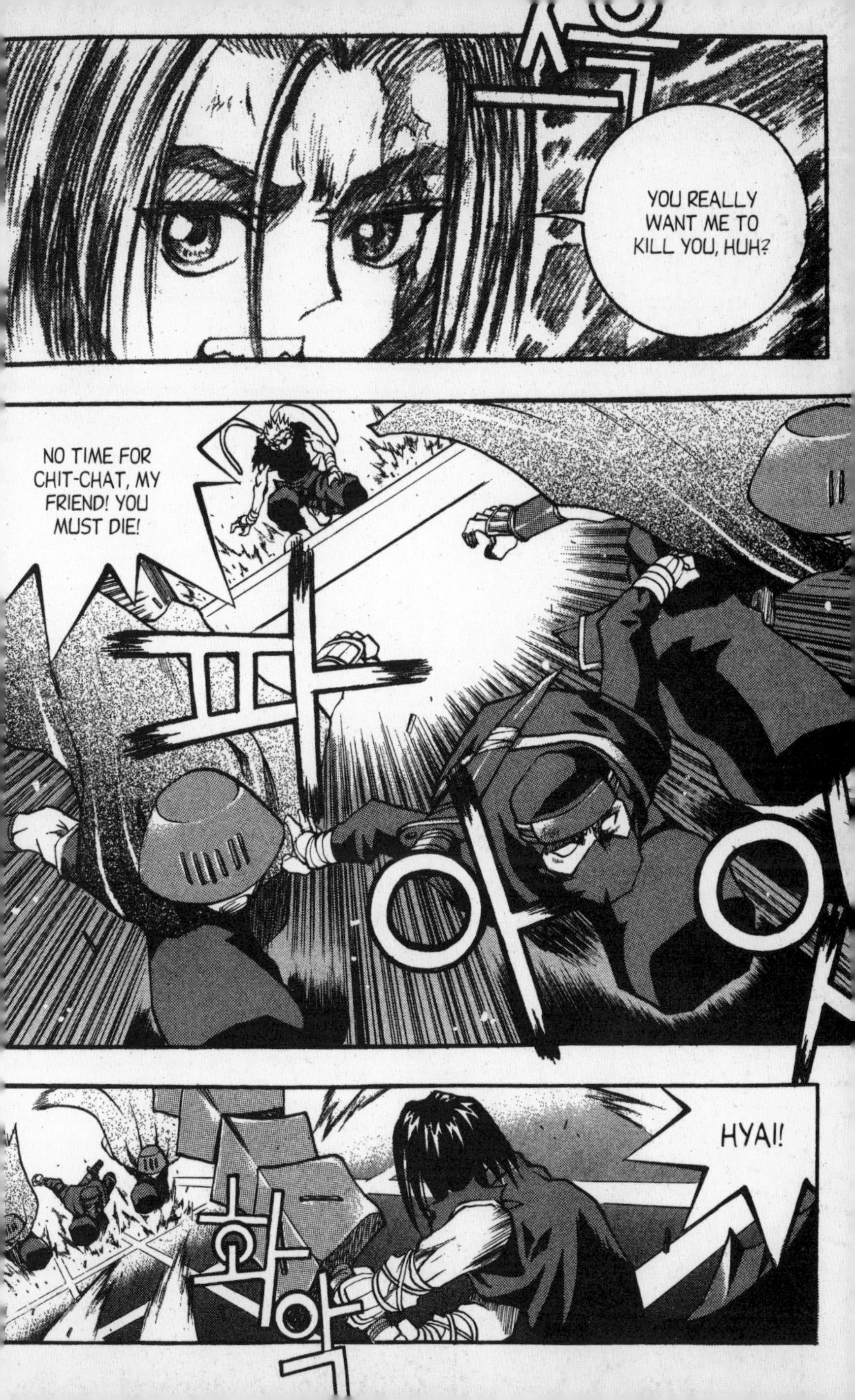
YOU REALLY WANT ME TO KILL YOU, HUH?
NO TIME FOR CHIT-CHAT, MY FRIEND! YOU MUST DIE!
HYAI!

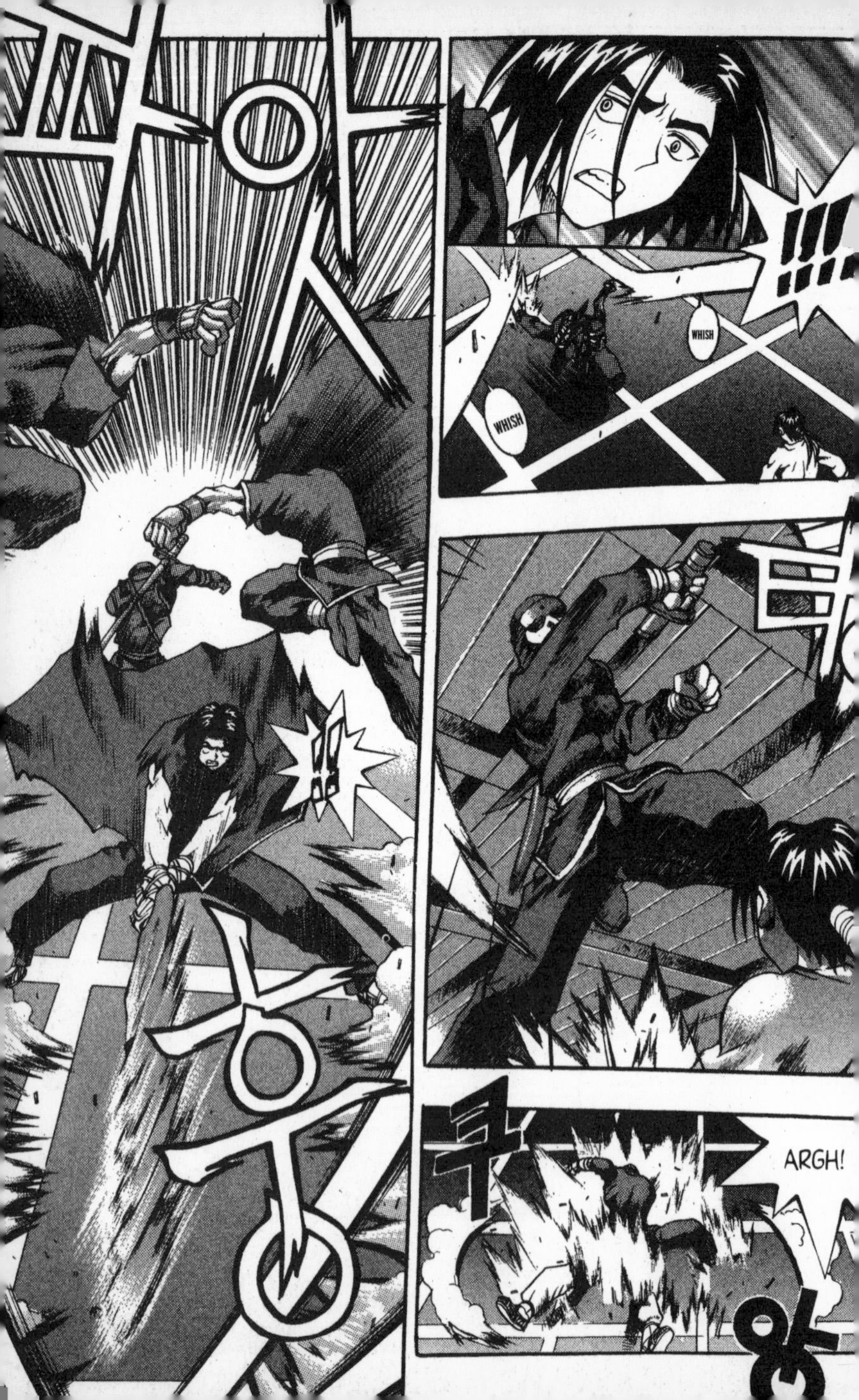

!!!
WHISH
WHISH
!!
ARGH!

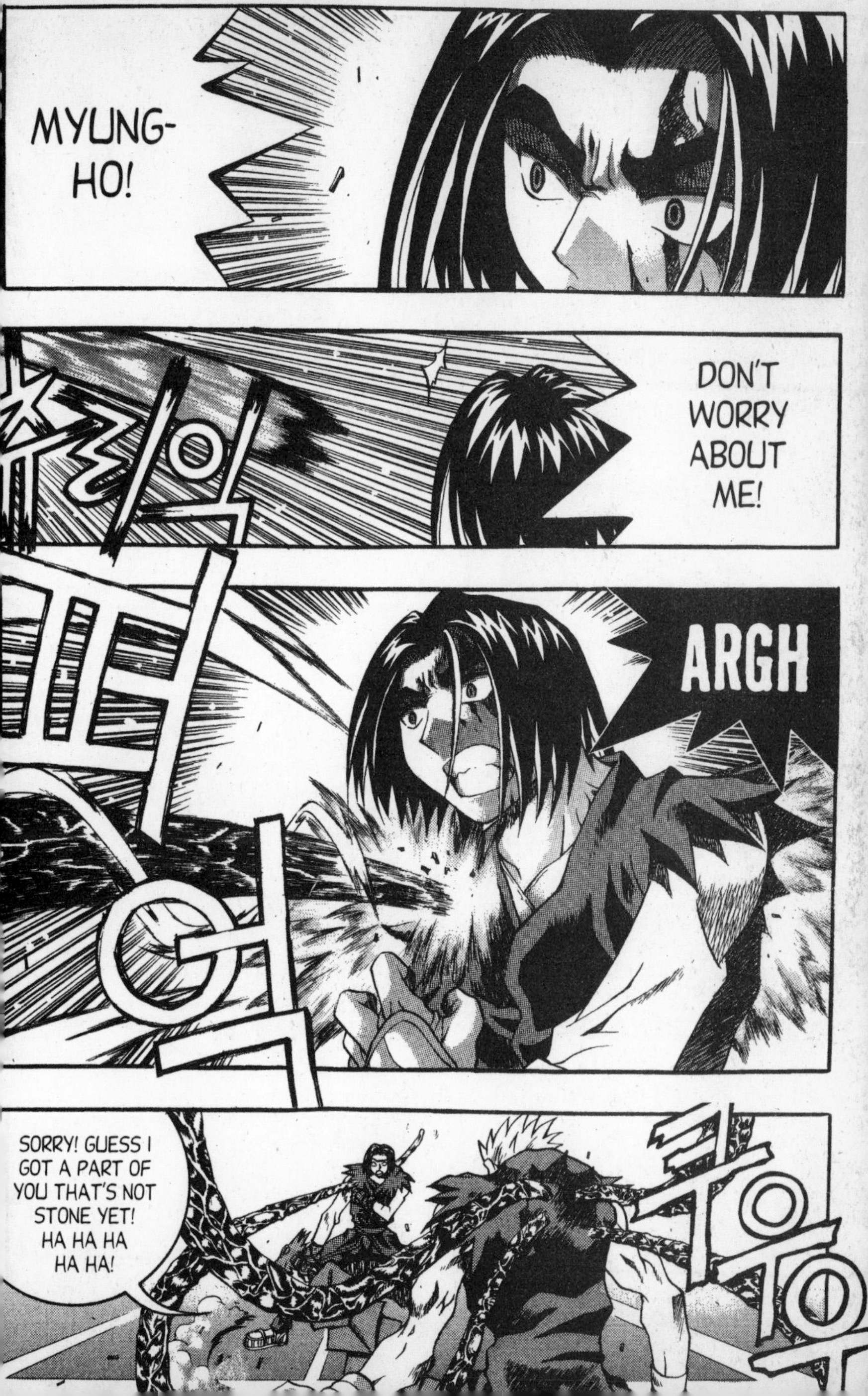
MYUNG-HO!
DON'T WORRY ABOUT ME!
ARGH
SORRY! GUESS I GOT A PART OF YOU THAT'S NOT STONE YET! HA HA HA HA HA!

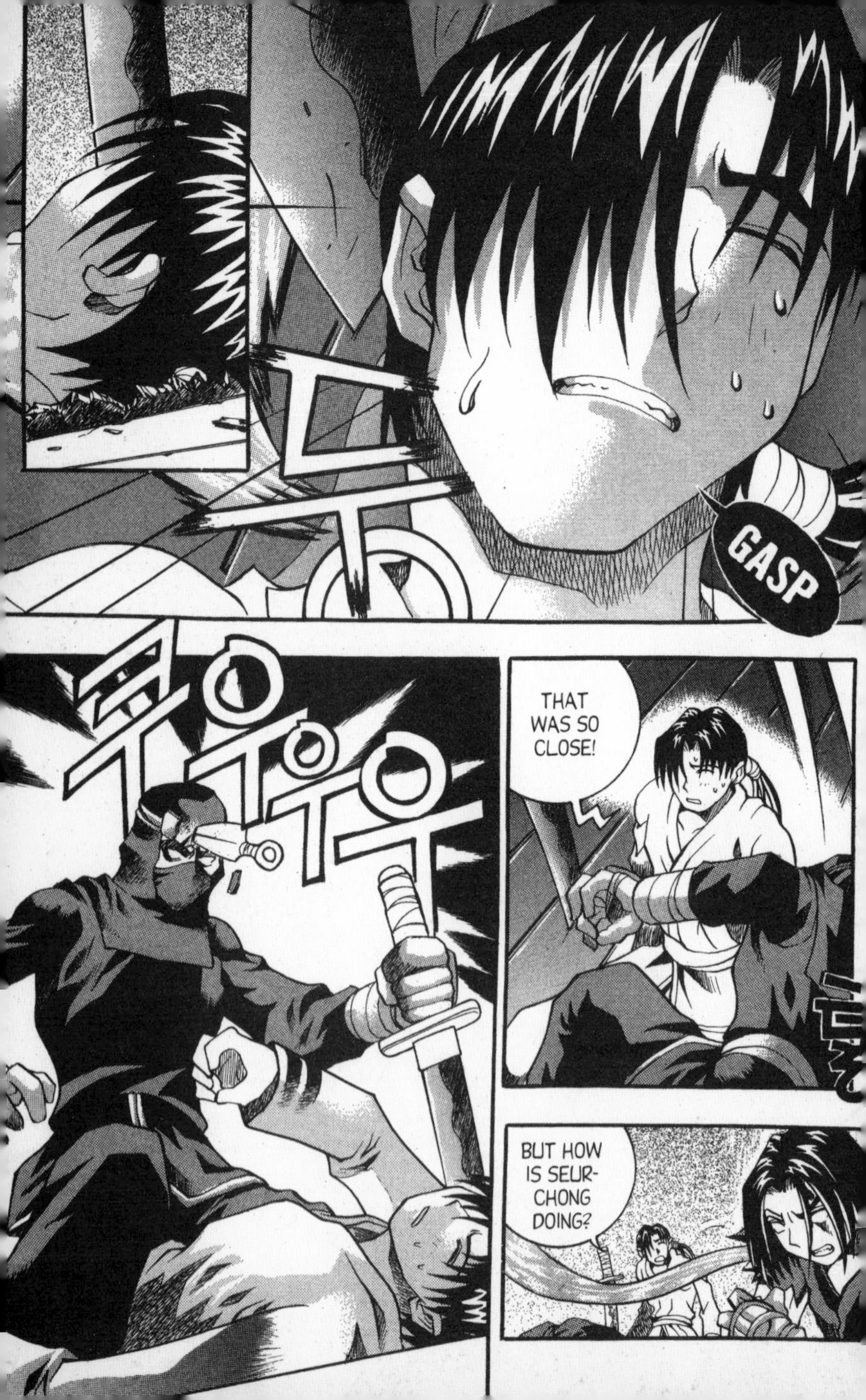
GASP
THAT WAS SO CLOSE!
BUT HOW IS SEUR-CHONG DOING?

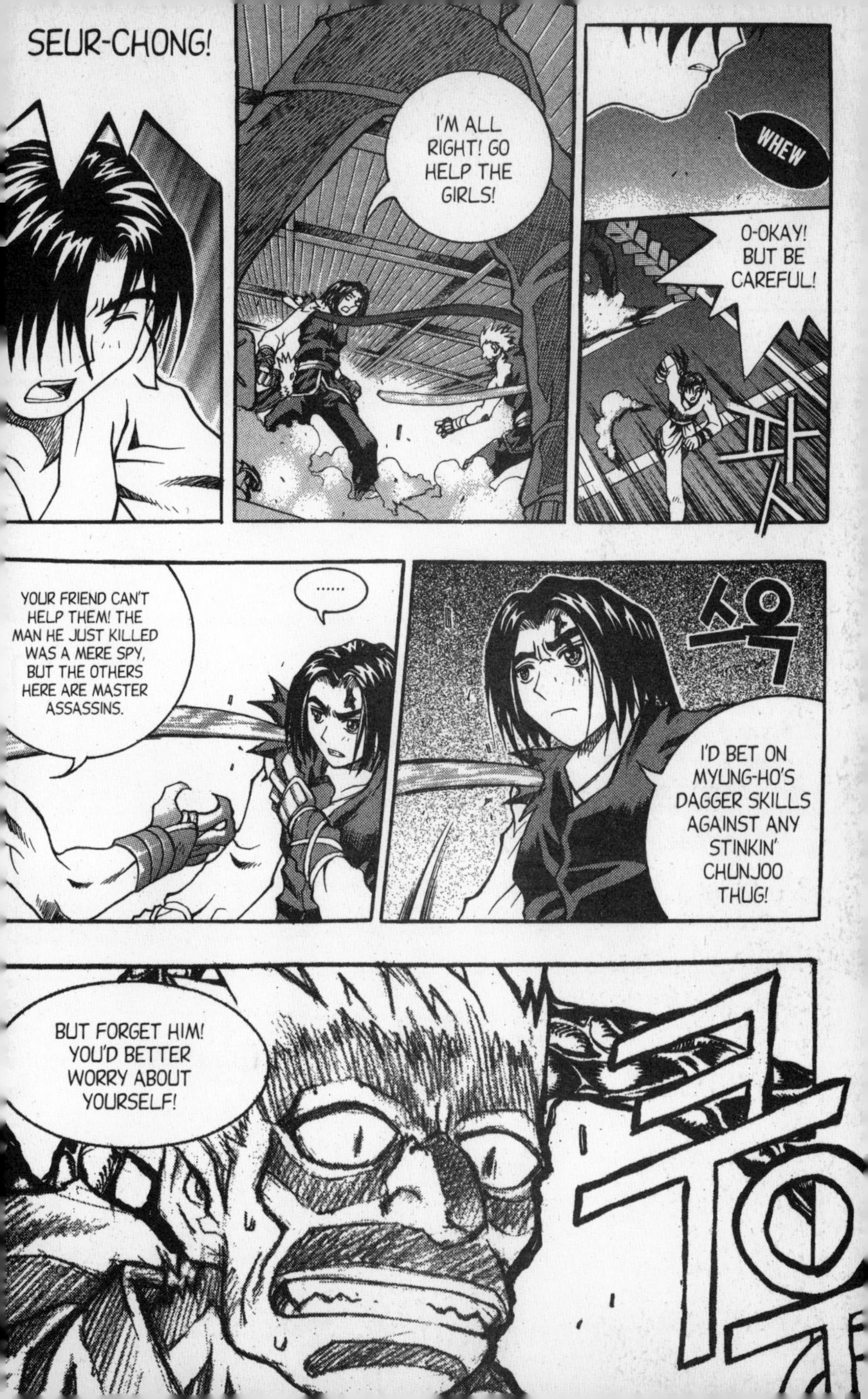
SEUR-CHONG!
I'M ALL RIGHT! GO HELP THE GIRLS!
WHEW
O-OKAY! BUT BE CAREFUL!
YOUR FRIEND CAN'T HELP THEM! THE MAN HE JUST KILLED WAS A MERE SPY, BUT THE OTHERS HERE ARE MASTER ASSASSINS.
....
I'D BET ON MYUNG-HO'S DAGGER SKILLS AGAINST ANY STINKIN' CHUNJOO THUG!
BUT FORGET HIM! YOU'D BETTER WORRY ABOUT YOURSELF!

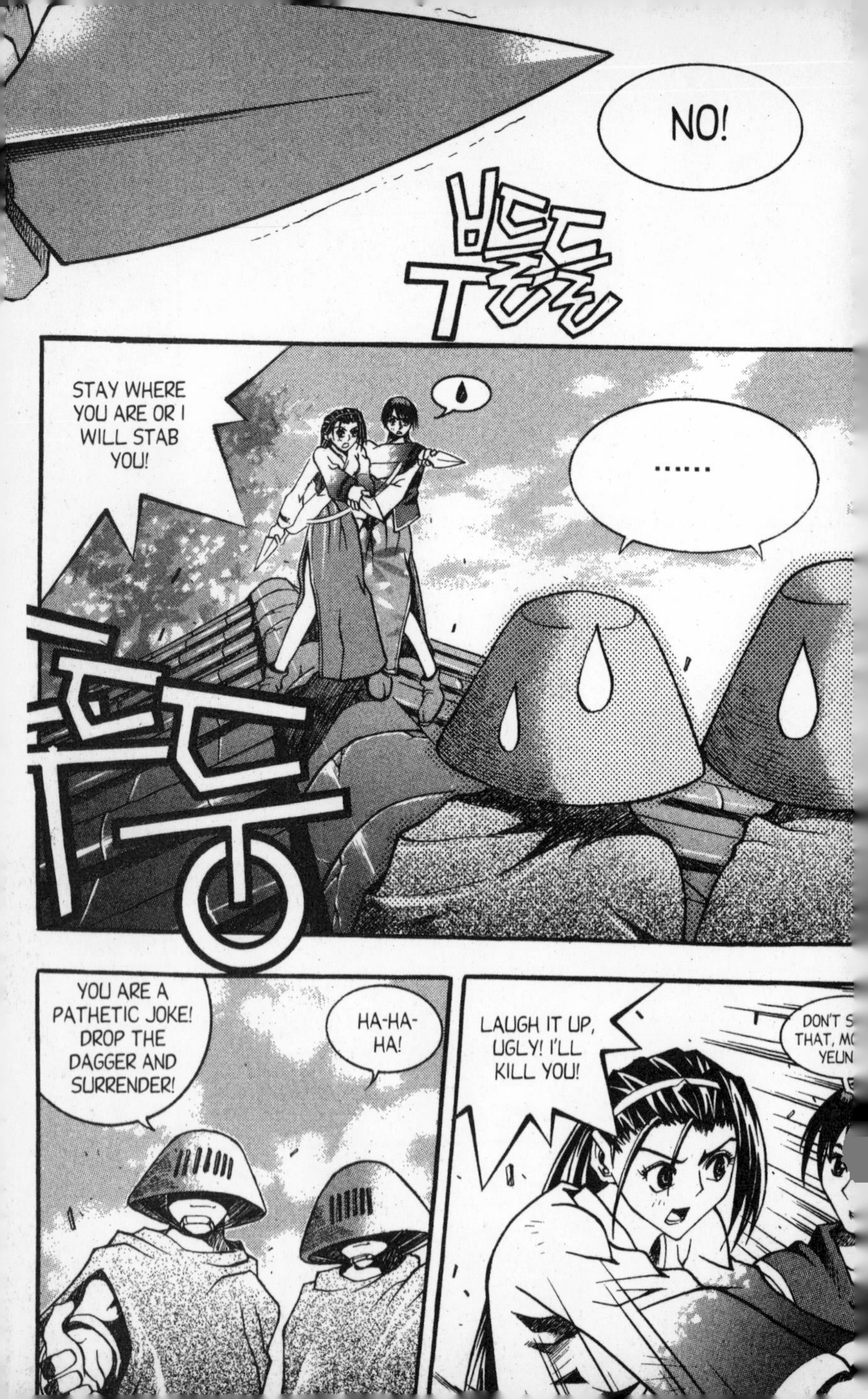
NO!
STAY WHERE YOU ARE OR I WILL STAB YOU!
......
YOU ARE A PATHETIC JOKE! DROP THE DAGGER AND SURRENDER!
HA-HA-HA!
LAUGH IT UP, UGLY! I'LL KILL YOU!
DON'T S THAT, MO YEUN

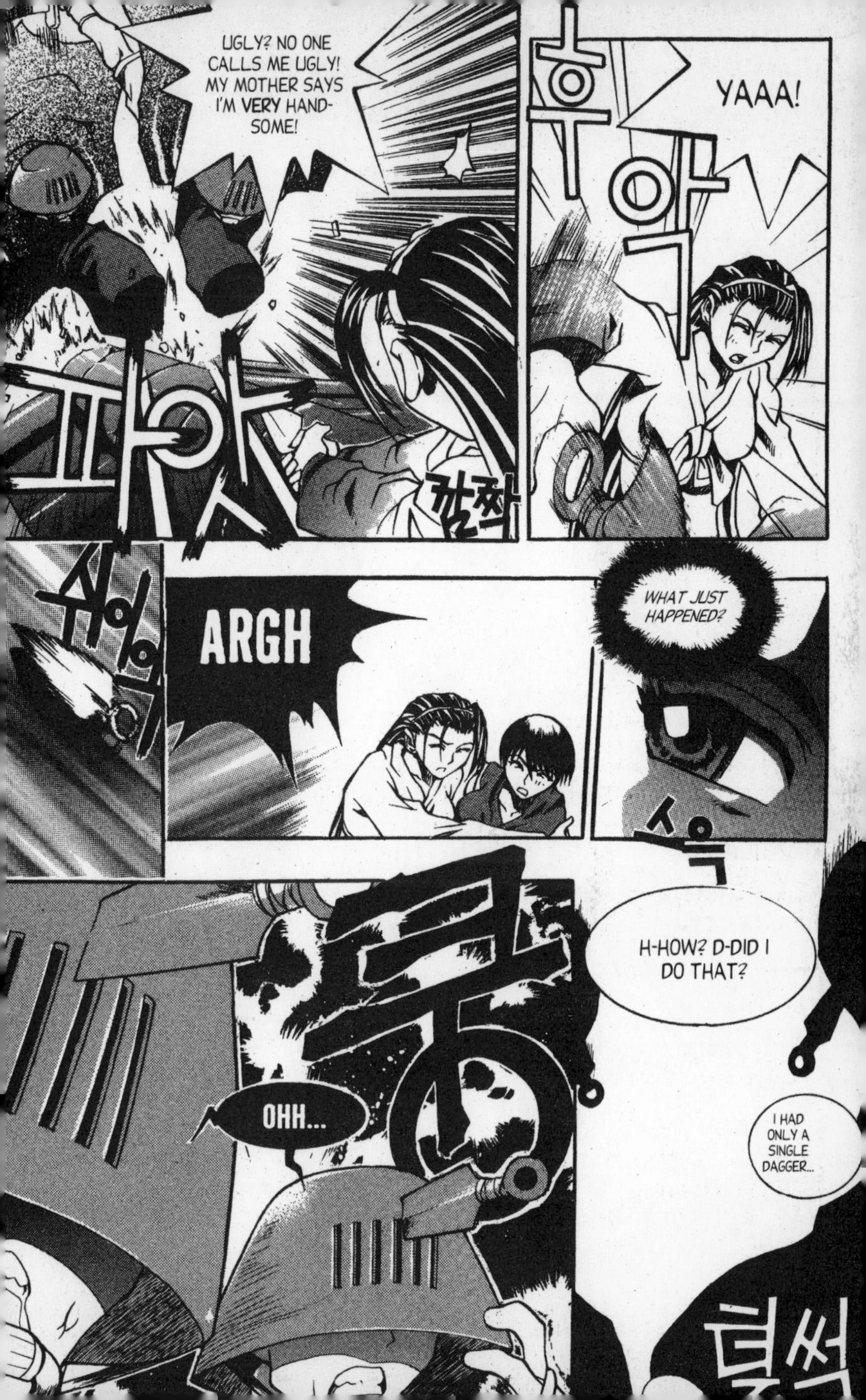

UGLY? NO ONE CALLS ME UGLY! MY MOTHER SAYS I'M **VERY** HAND-SOME!
YAAA!
ARGH
WHAT JUST HAPPENED?
OHH...
쿵
H-HOW? D-DID I DO THAT?
I HAD ONLY A SINGLE DAGGER...
털썩

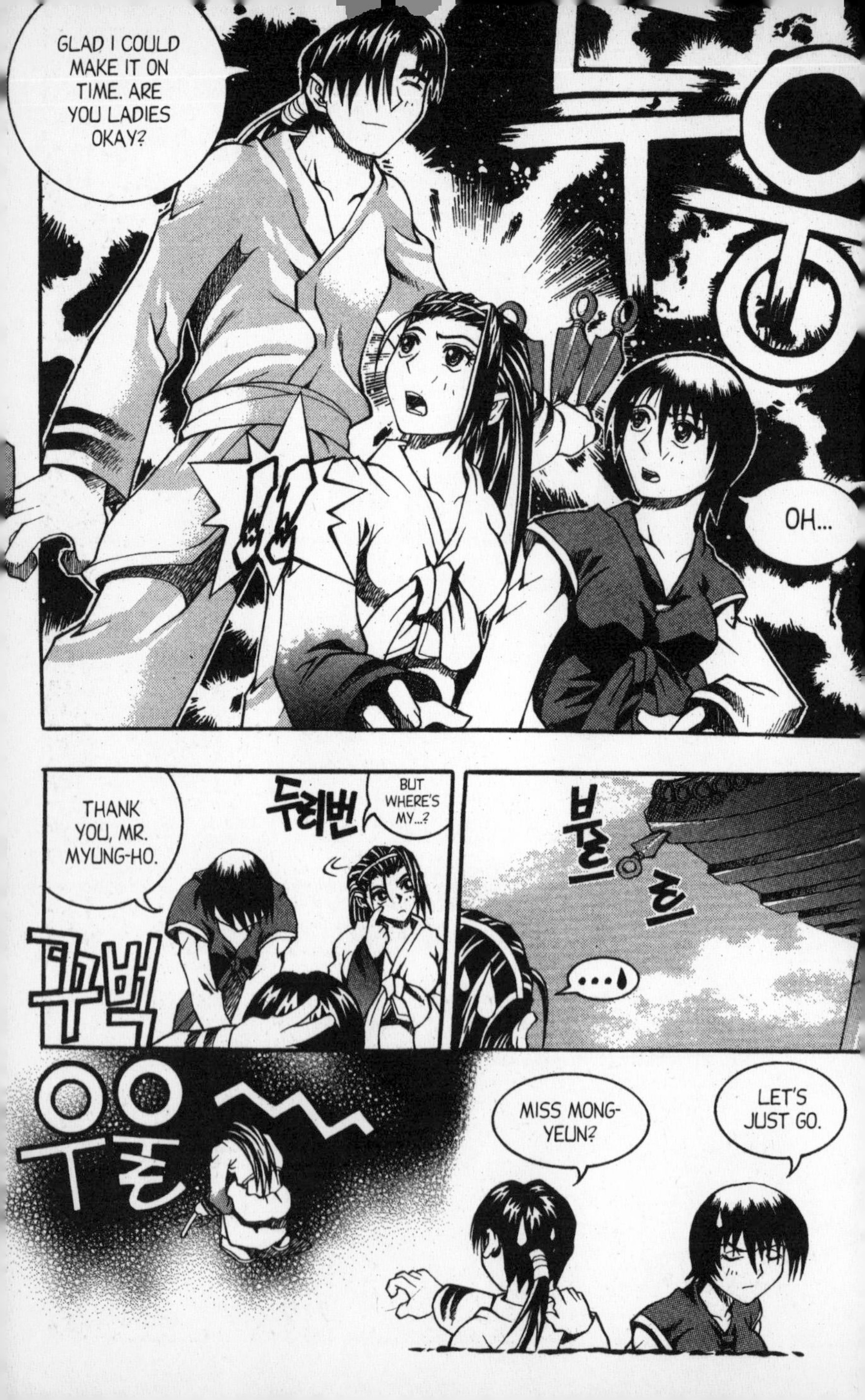
GLAD I COULD MAKE IT ON TIME. ARE YOU LADIES OKAY?
OH...
THANK YOU, MR. MYUNG-HO.
두리번
BUT WHERE'S MY...?
...!
MISS MONG-YEUN?
LET'S JUST GO.

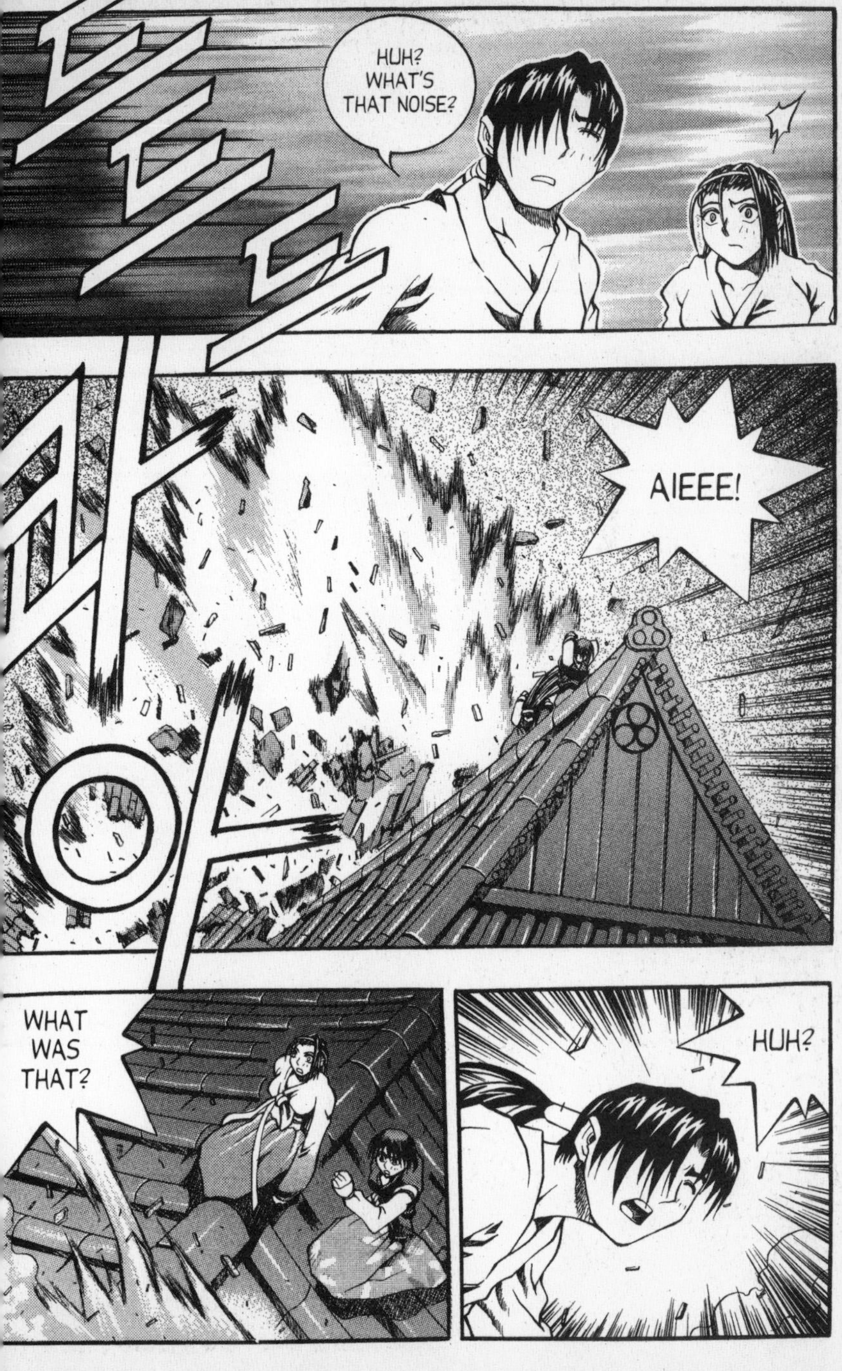
HUH? WHAT'S THAT NOISE?
AIEEE!
WHAT WAS THAT?
HUH?

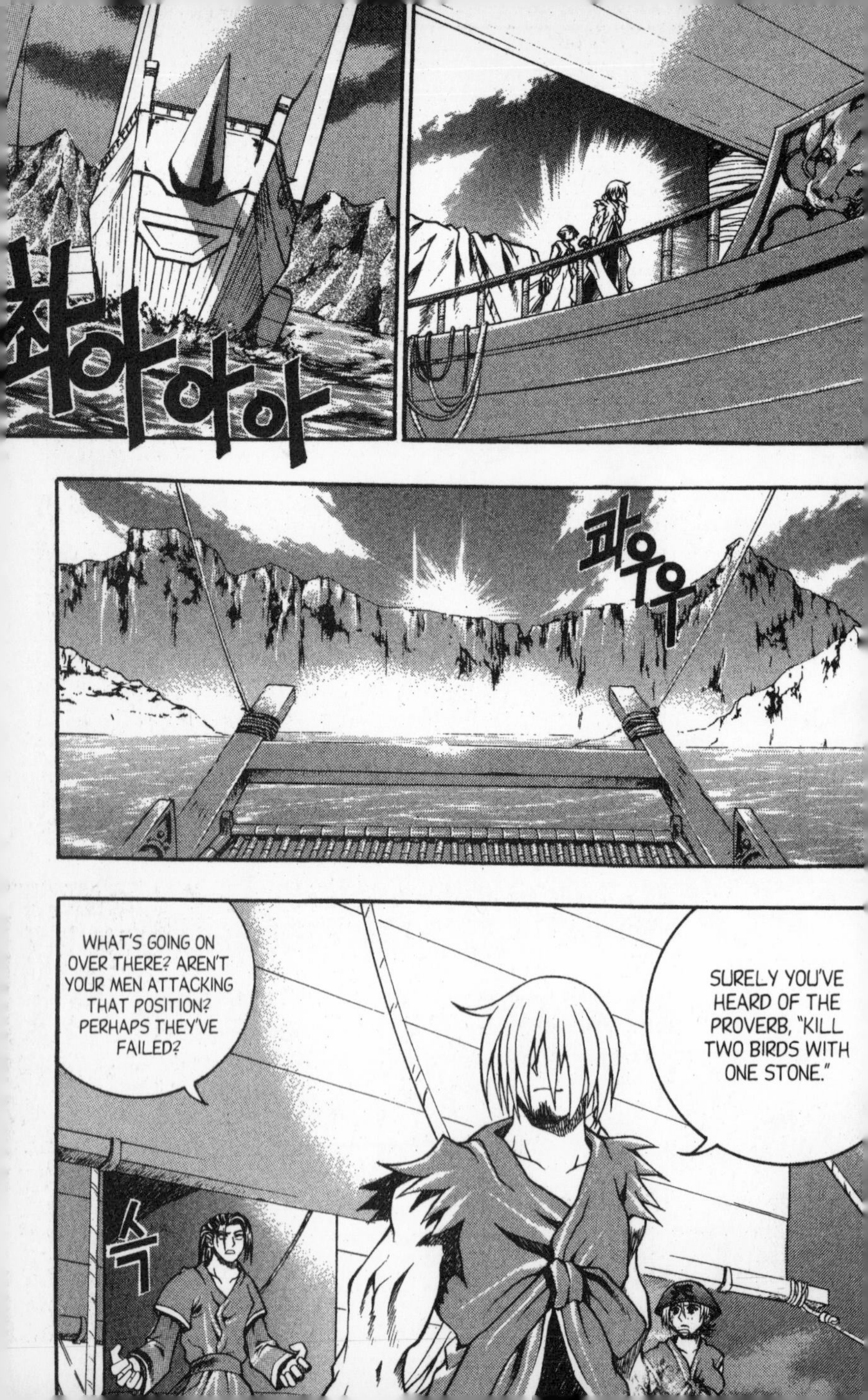
쏴아아아
콰우우
WHAT'S GOING ON OVER THERE? AREN'T YOUR MEN ATTACKING THAT POSITION? PERHAPS THEY'VE FAILED?
SURELY YOU'VE HEARD OF THE PROVERB, "KILL TWO BIRDS WITH ONE STONE."
슥

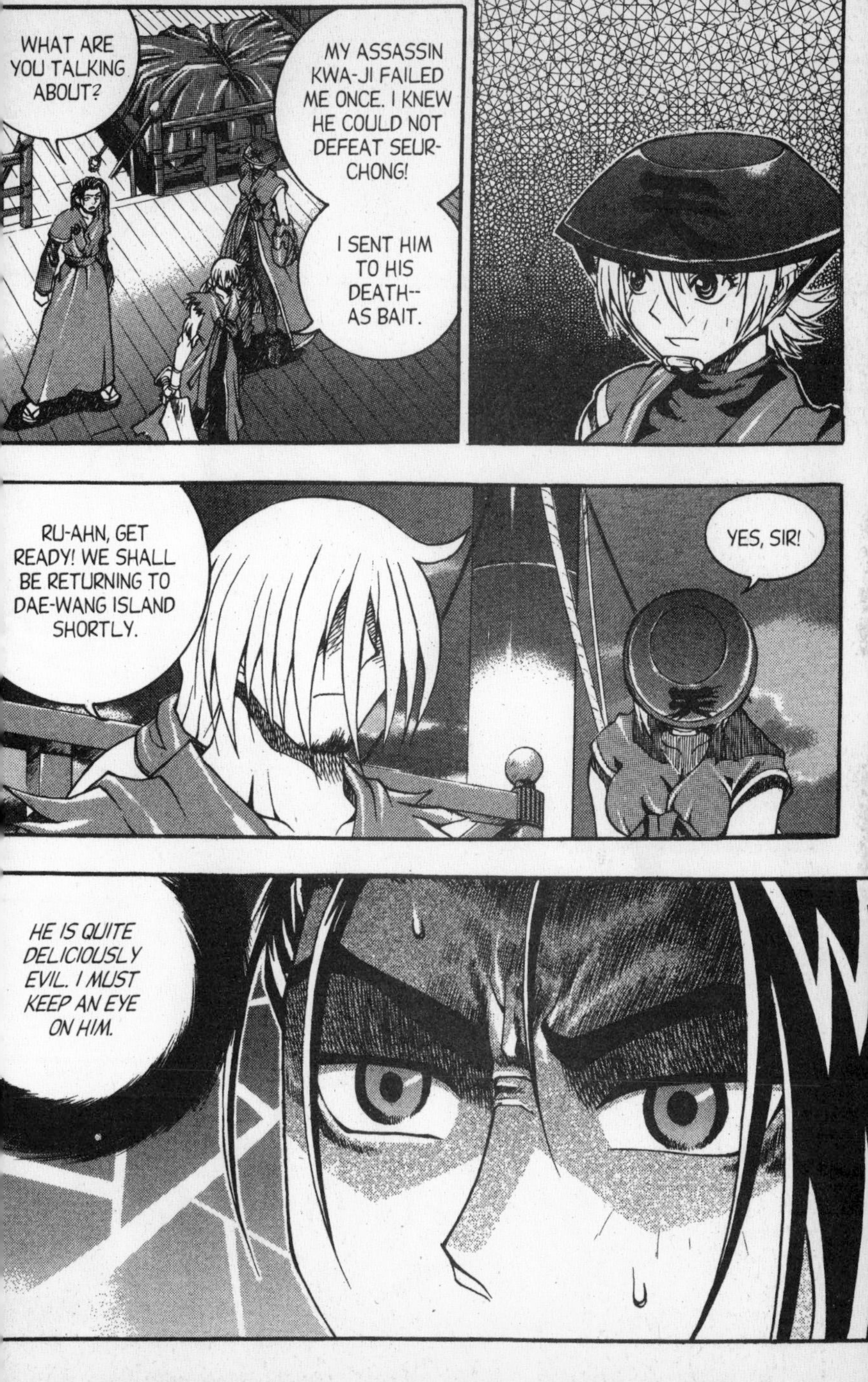
WHAT ARE YOU TALKING ABOUT?
MY ASSASSIN KWA-JI FAILED ME ONCE. I KNEW HE COULD NOT DEFEAT SEUR-CHONG!
I SENT HIM TO HIS DEATH-- AS BAIT.
RU-AHN, GET READY! WE SHALL BE RETURNING TO DAE-WANG ISLAND SHORTLY.
YES, SIR!
HE IS QUITE DELICIOUSLY EVIL. I MUST KEEP AN EYE ON HIM.

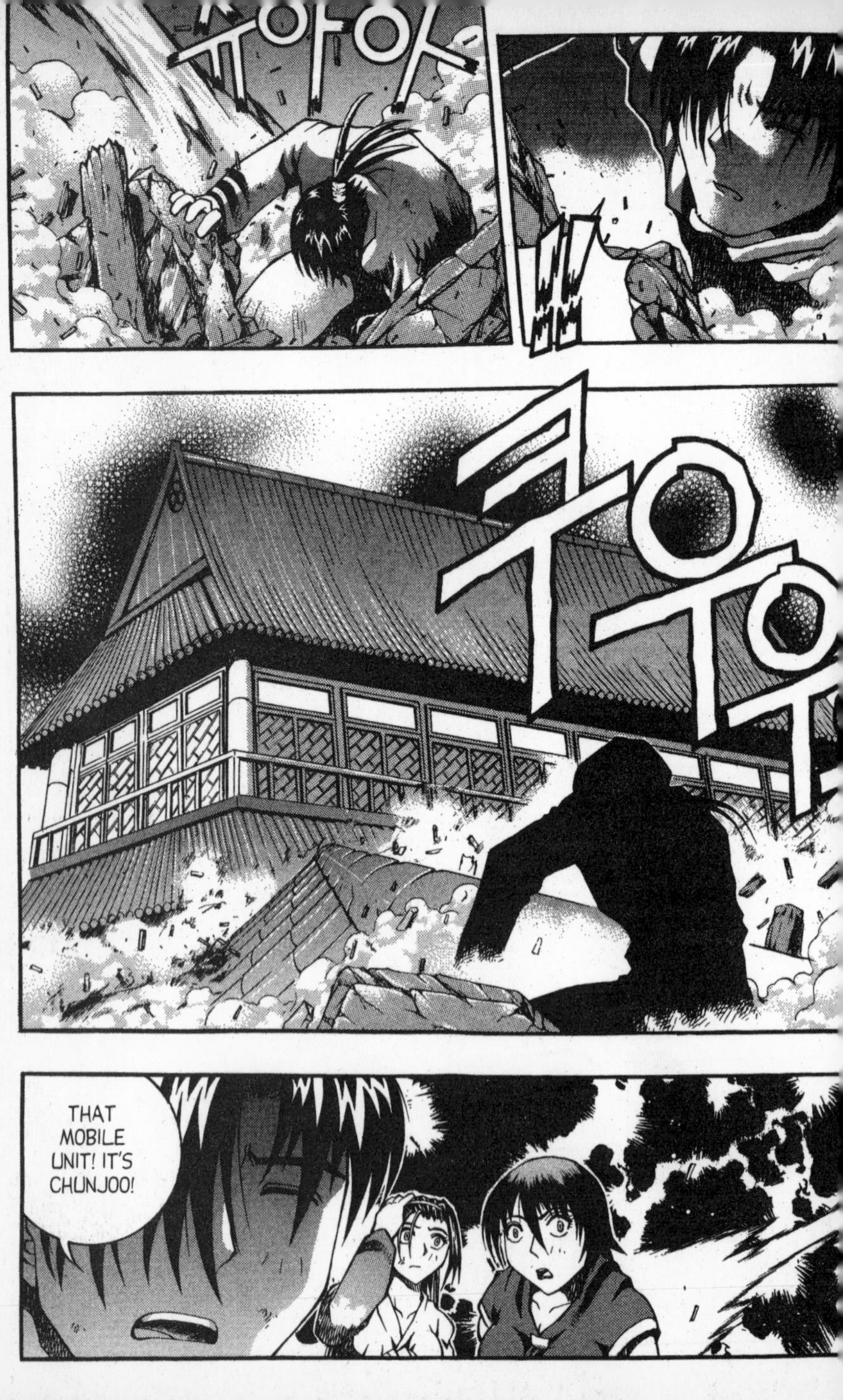
THAT MOBILE UNIT! IT'S CHUNJOO!

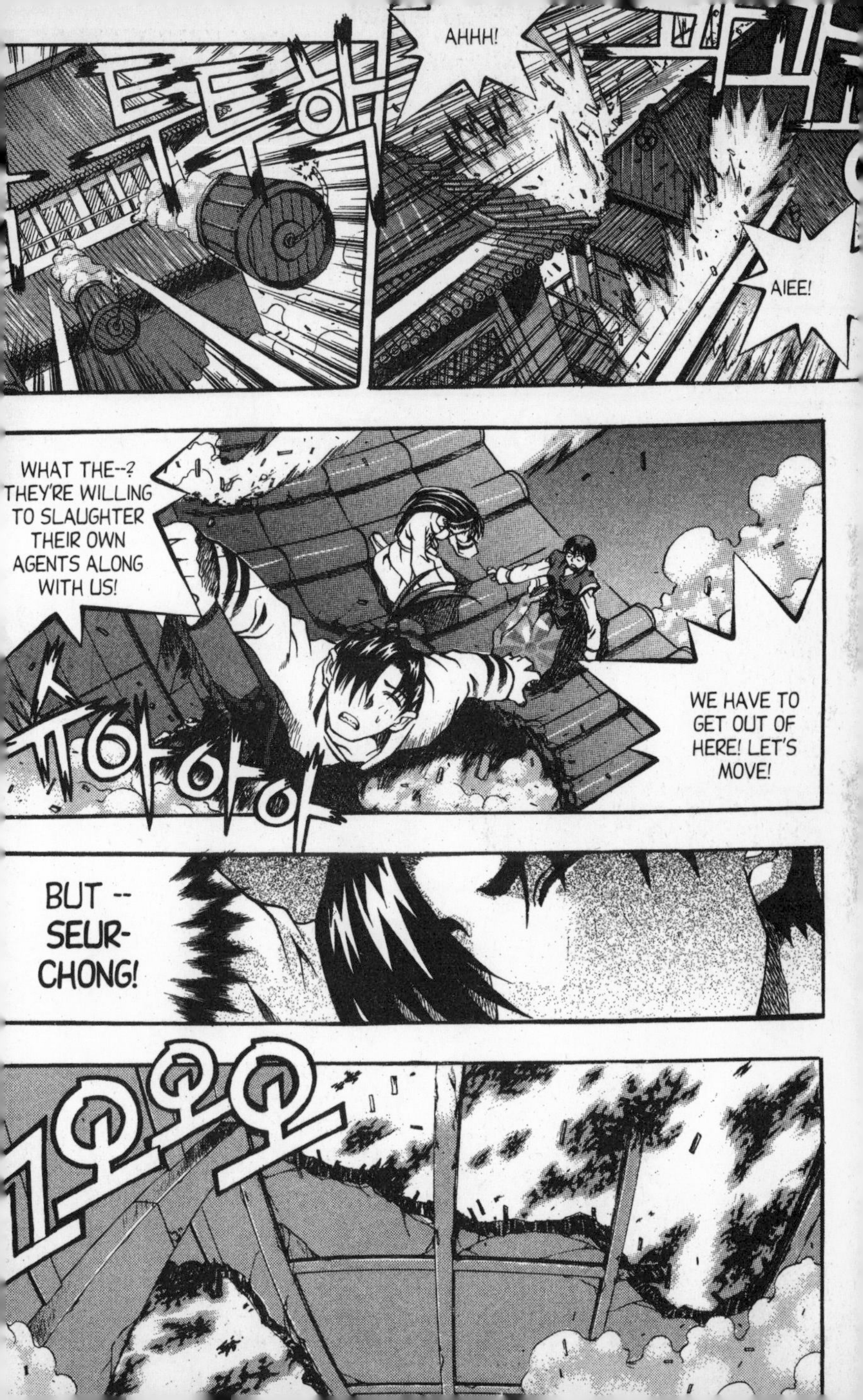
AHHH!
AIEE!
WHAT THE--? THEY'RE WILLING TO SLAUGHTER THEIR OWN AGENTS ALONG WITH US!
WE HAVE TO GET OUT OF HERE! LET'S MOVE!
BUT -- SEUR-CHONG!

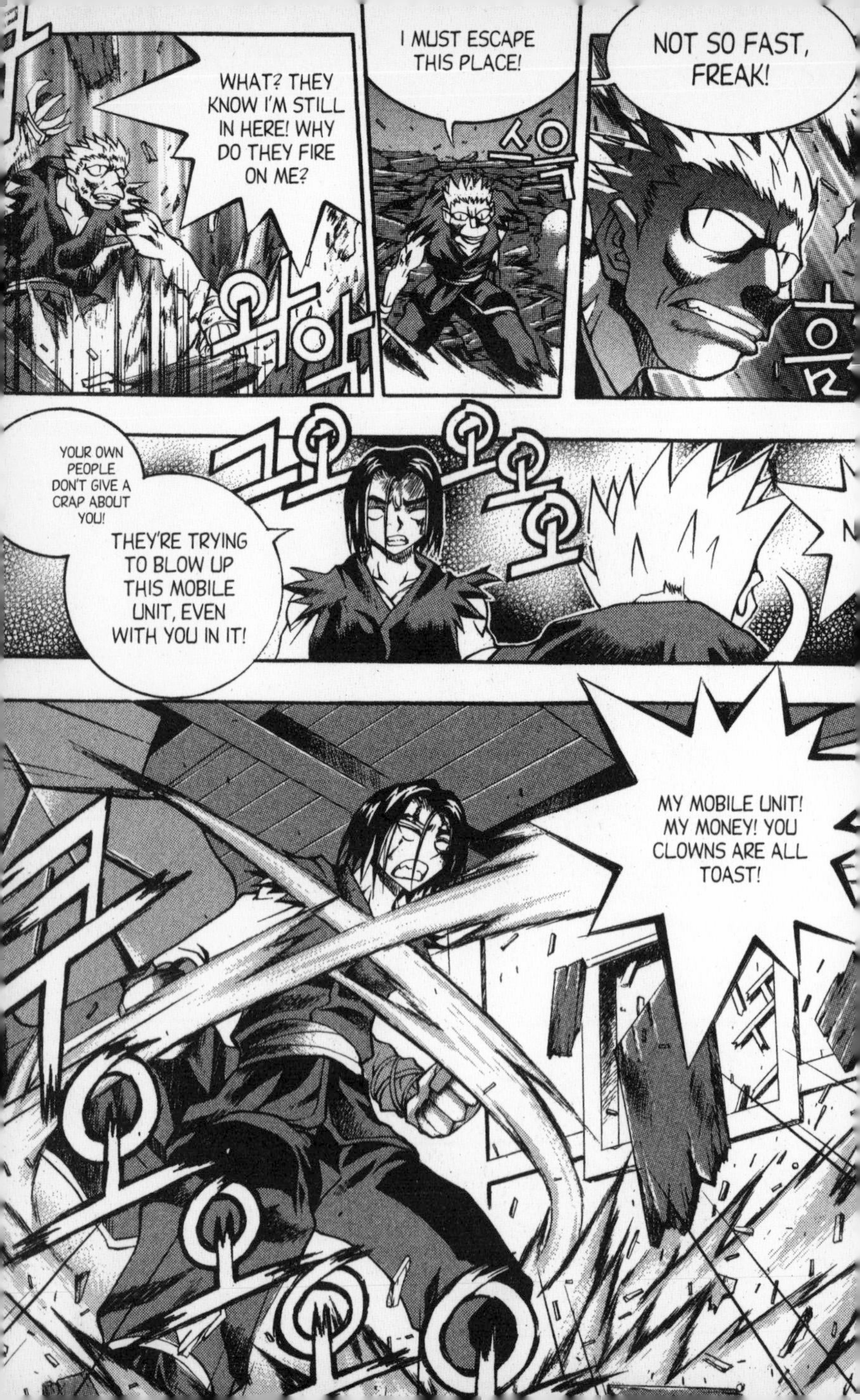
WHAT? THEY KNOW I'M STILL IN HERE! WHY DO THEY FIRE ON ME?
I MUST ESCAPE THIS PLACE!
NOT SO FAST, FREAK!
YOUR OWN PEOPLE DON'T GIVE A CRAP ABOUT YOU!
THEY'RE TRYING TO BLOW UP THIS MOBILE UNIT, EVEN WITH YOU IN IT!
MY MOBILE UNIT! MY MONEY! YOU CLOWNS ARE ALL TOAST!

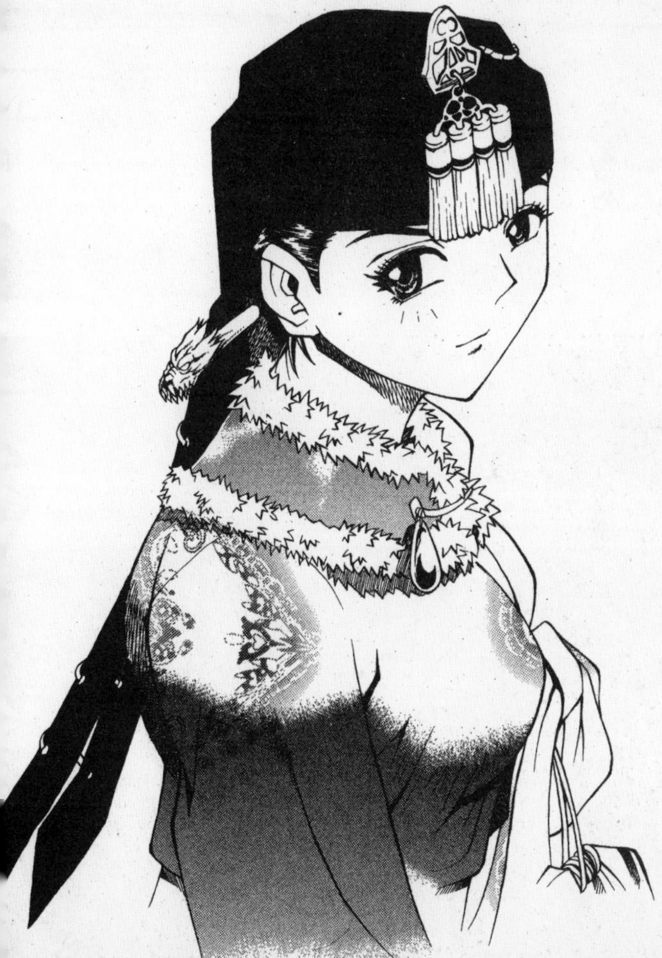

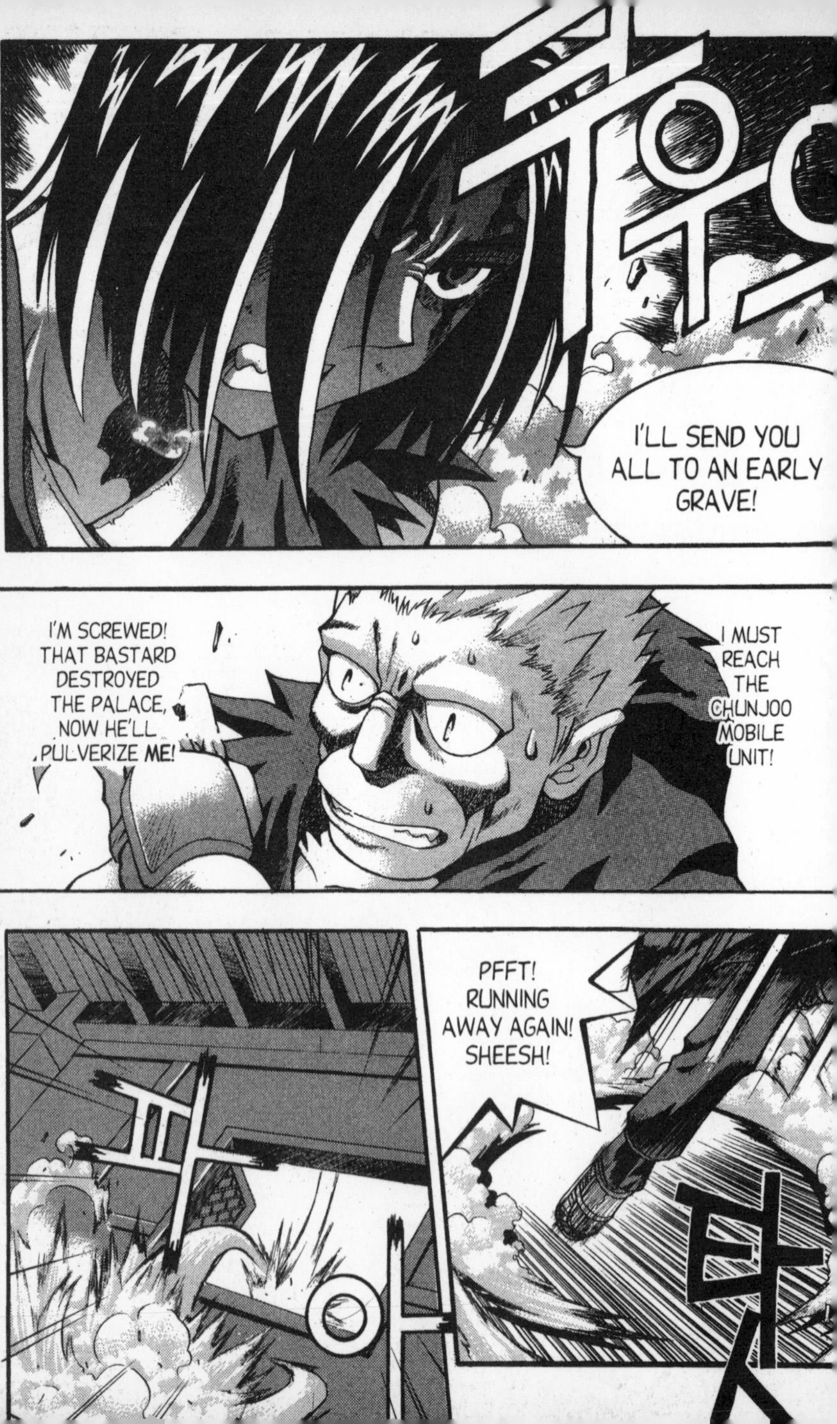
I'LL SEND YOU ALL TO AN EARLY GRAVE!
I'M SCREWED! THAT BASTARD DESTROYED THE PALACE, NOW HE'LL PULVERIZE ME!
I MUST REACH THE CHUNJOO MOBILE UNIT!
PFFT! RUNNING AWAY AGAIN! SHEESH!

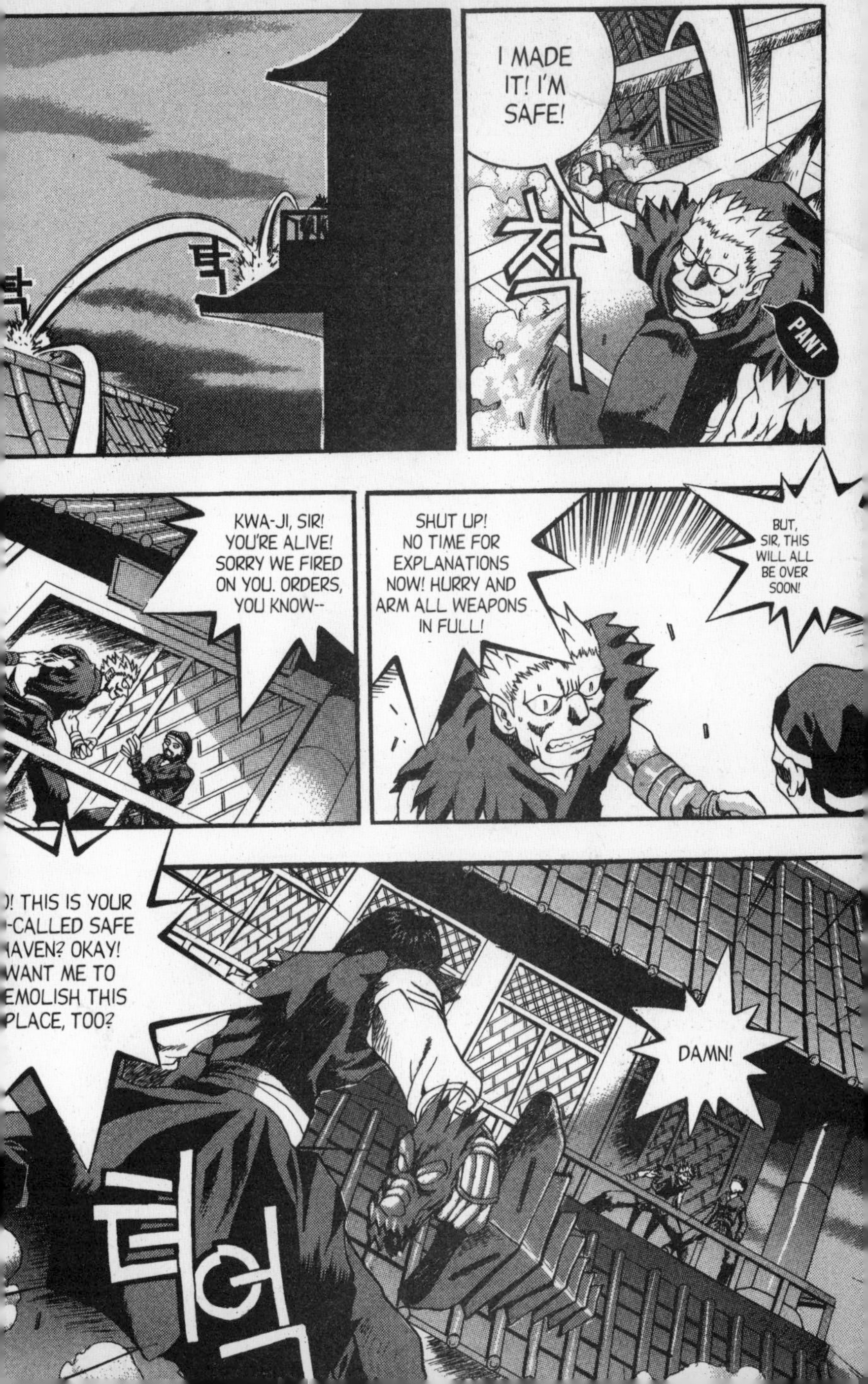
I MADE IT! I'M SAFE!
PANT
KWA-JI, SIR! YOU'RE ALIVE! SORRY WE FIRED ON YOU. ORDERS, YOU KNOW--
SHUT UP! NO TIME FOR EXPLANATIONS NOW! HURRY AND ARM ALL WEAPONS IN FULL!
BUT, SIR, THIS WILL ALL BE OVER SOON!
)! THIS IS YOUR -CALLED SAFE HAVEN? OKAY! WANT ME TO EMOLISH THIS PLACE, TOO?
DAMN!

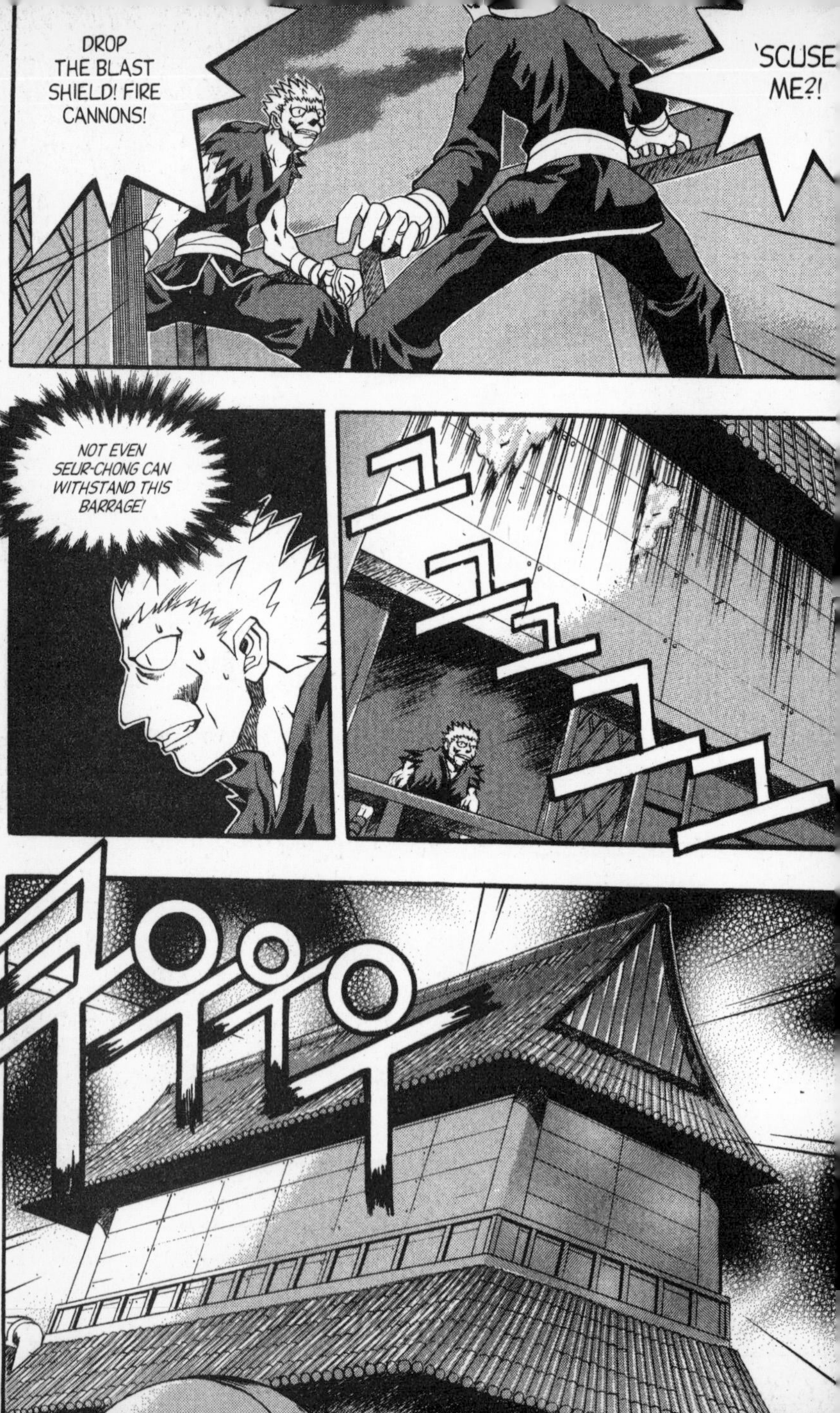
DROP THE BLAST SHIELD! FIRE CANNONS!
'SCUSE ME?!
NOT EVEN SEUR-CHONG CAN WITHSTAND THIS BARRAGE!

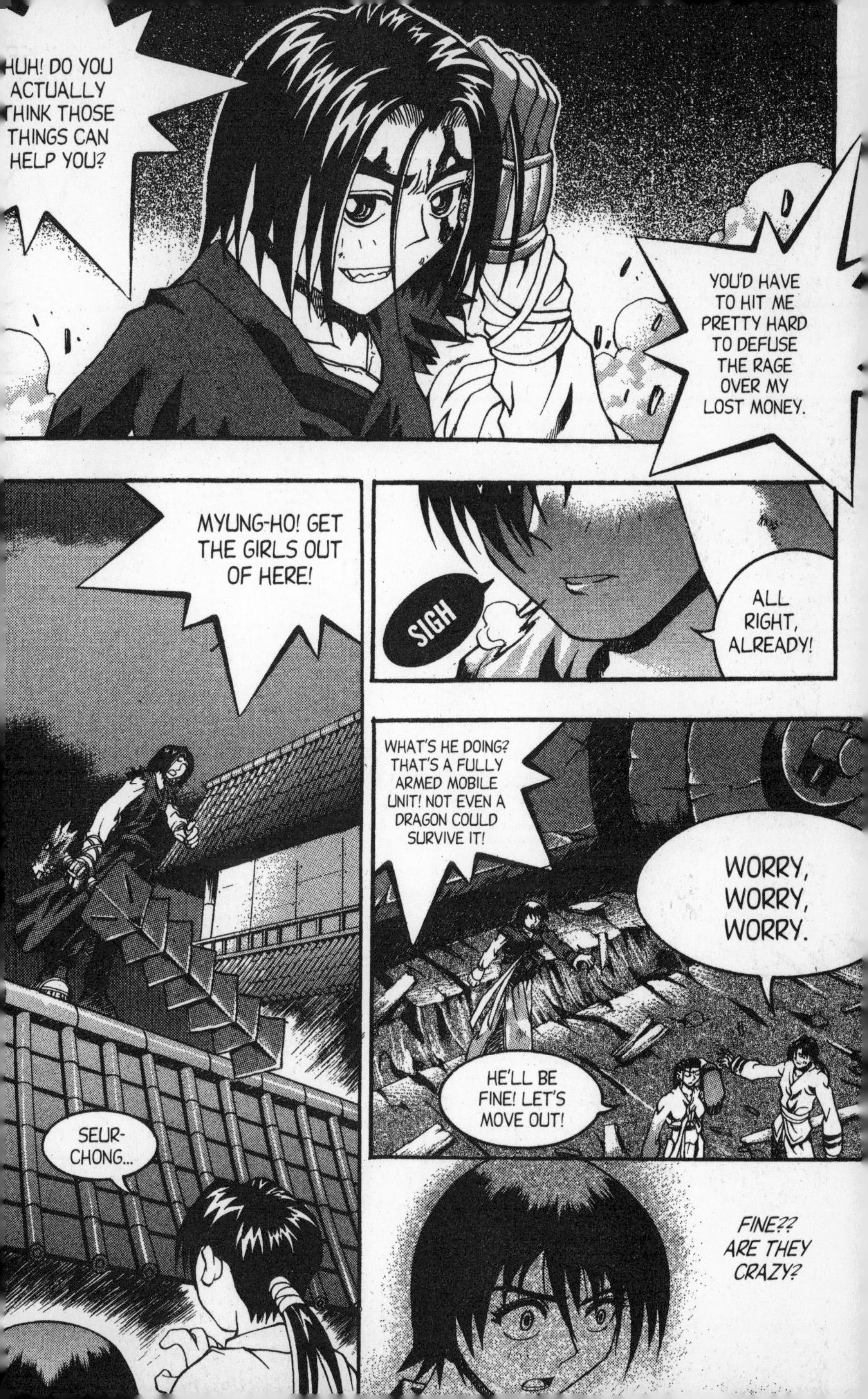
HUH! DO YOU ACTUALLY THINK THOSE THINGS CAN HELP YOU?
YOU'D HAVE TO HIT ME PRETTY HARD TO DEFUSE THE RAGE OVER MY LOST MONEY.
MYUNG-HO! GET THE GIRLS OUT OF HERE!
SEUR-CHONG...
SIGH
ALL RIGHT, ALREADY!
WHAT'S HE DOING? THAT'S A FULLY ARMED MOBILE UNIT! NOT EVEN A DRAGON COULD SURVIVE IT!
WORRY, WORRY, WORRY.
HE'LL BE FINE! LET'S MOVE OUT!
FINE?? ARE THEY CRAZY?

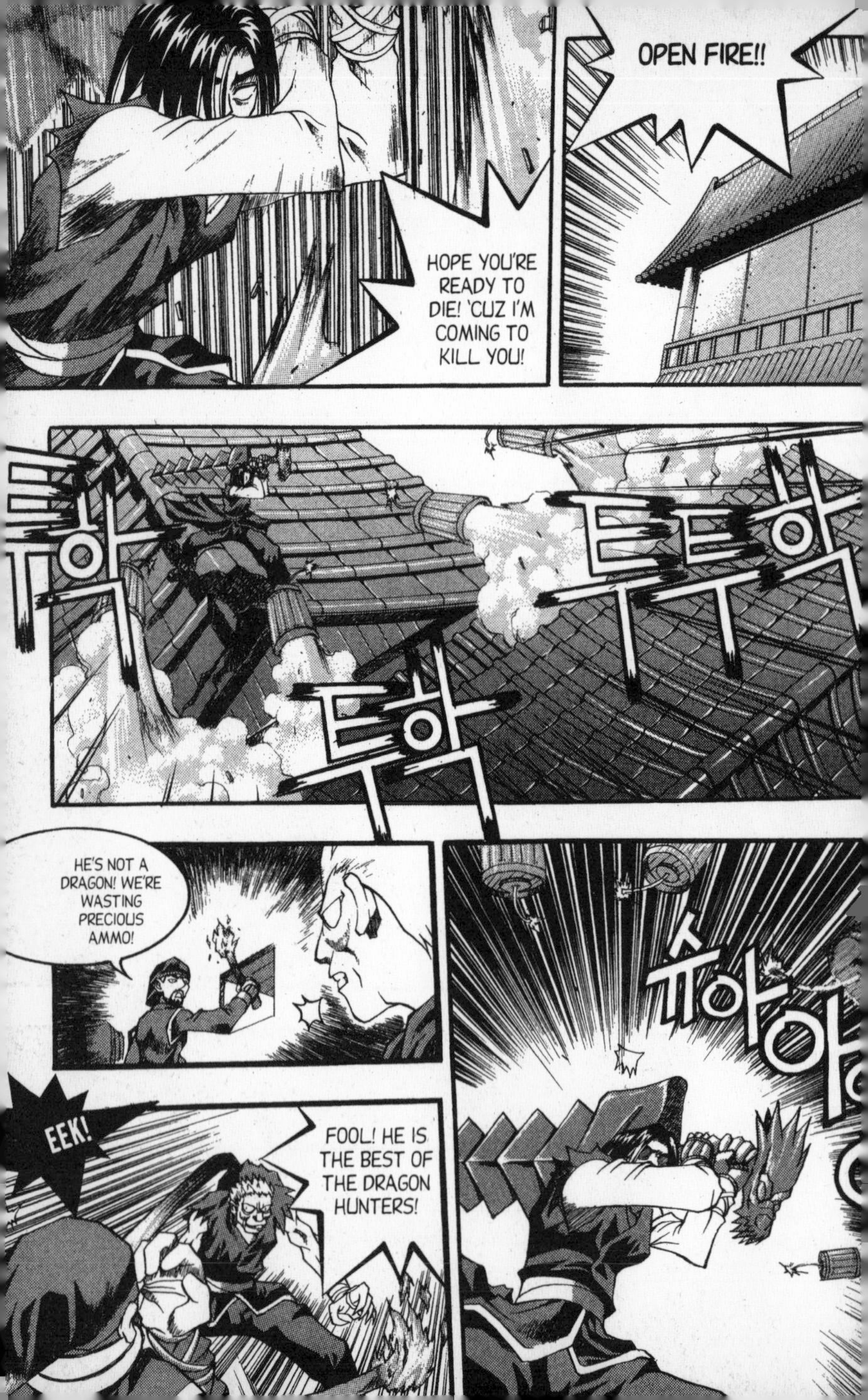
HOPE YOU'RE READY TO DIE! 'CUZ I'M COMING TO KILL YOU!
OPEN FIRE!!
HE'S NOT A DRAGON! WE'RE WASTING PRECIOUS AMMO!
EEK!
FOOL! HE IS THE BEST OF THE DRAGON HUNTERS!

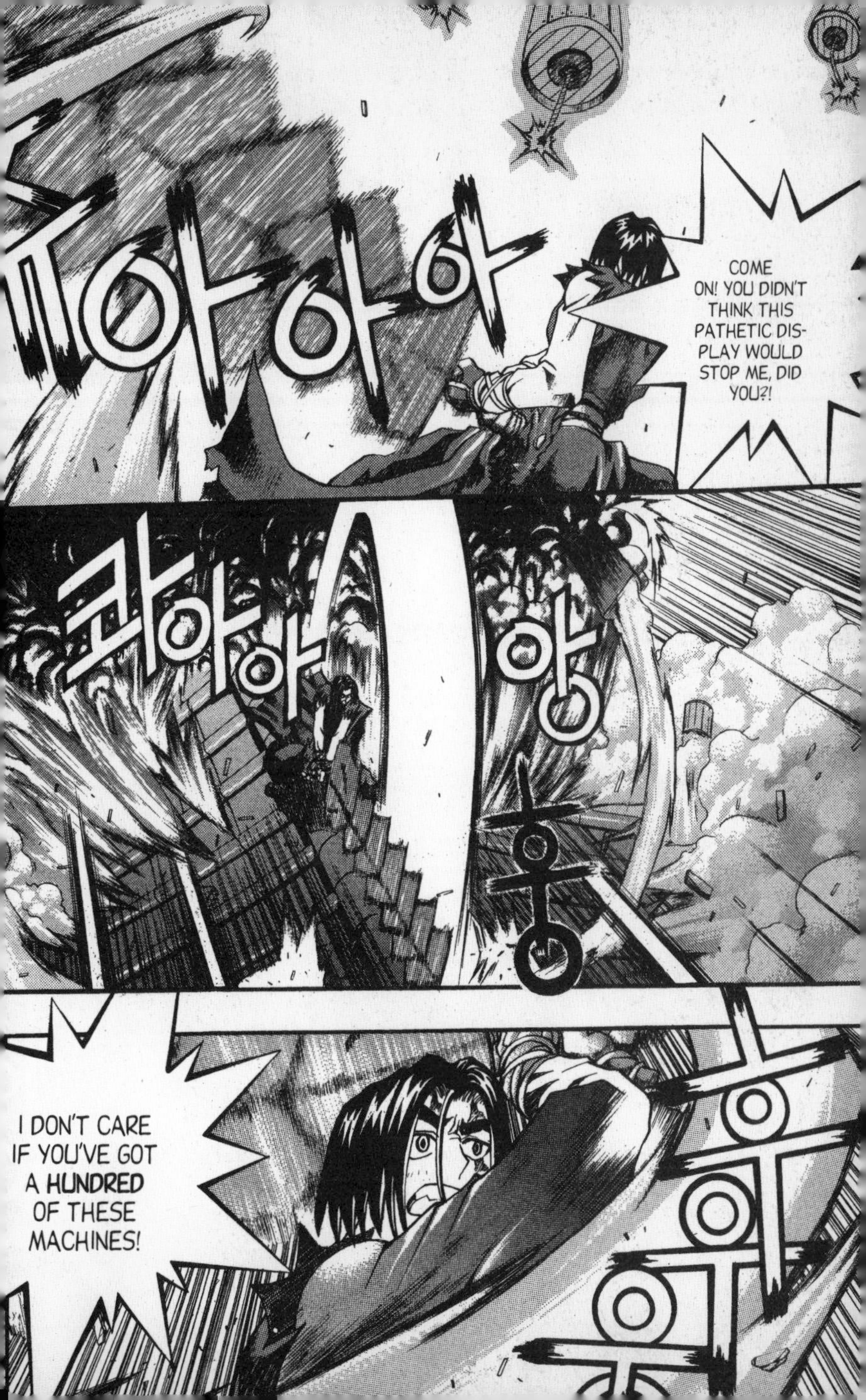
COME ON! YOU DIDN'T THINK THIS PATHETIC DIS-PLAY WOULD STOP ME, DID YOU?!
I DON'T CARE IF YOU'VE GOT A **HUNDRED** OF THESE MACHINES!

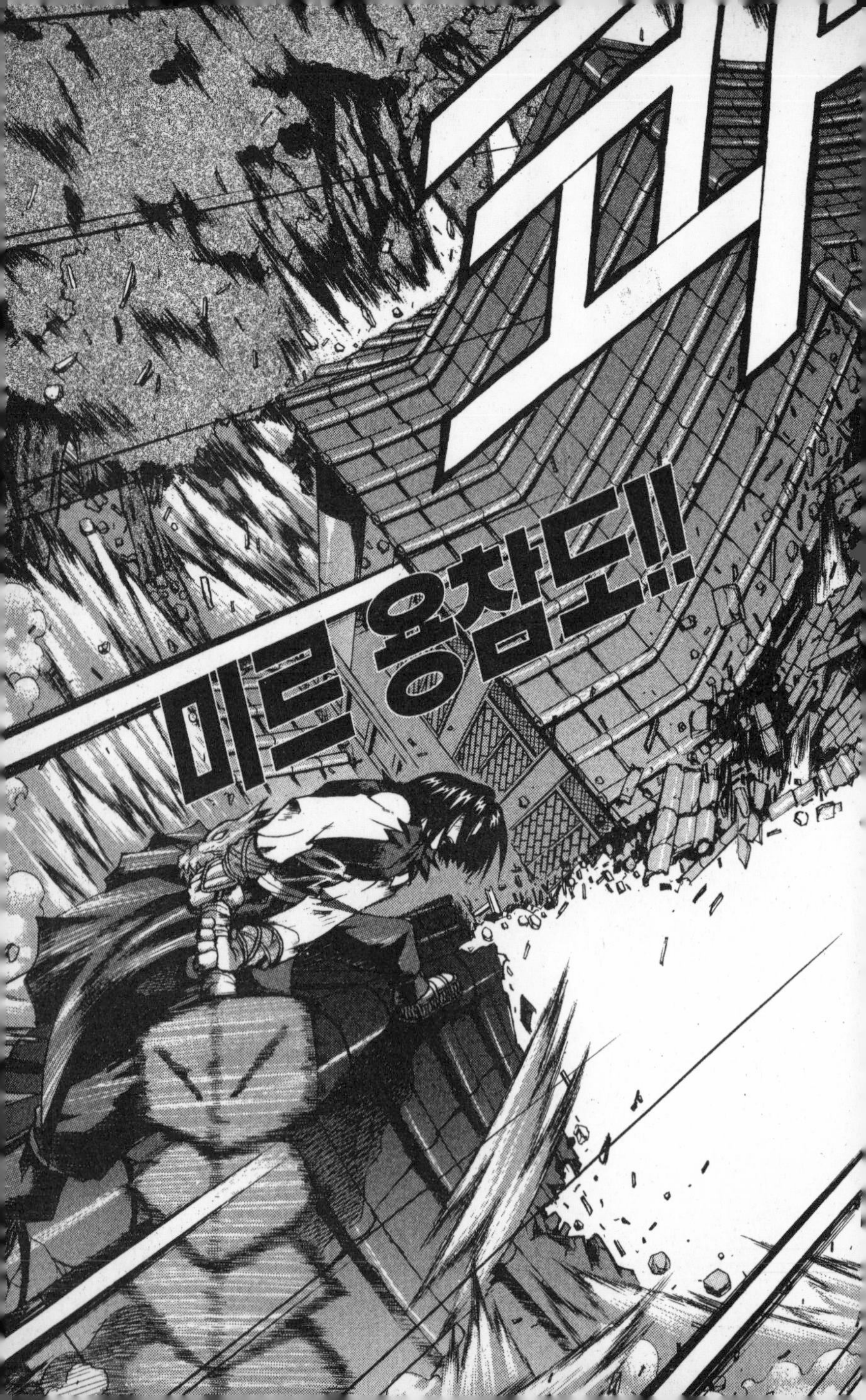
미르 용참도!!

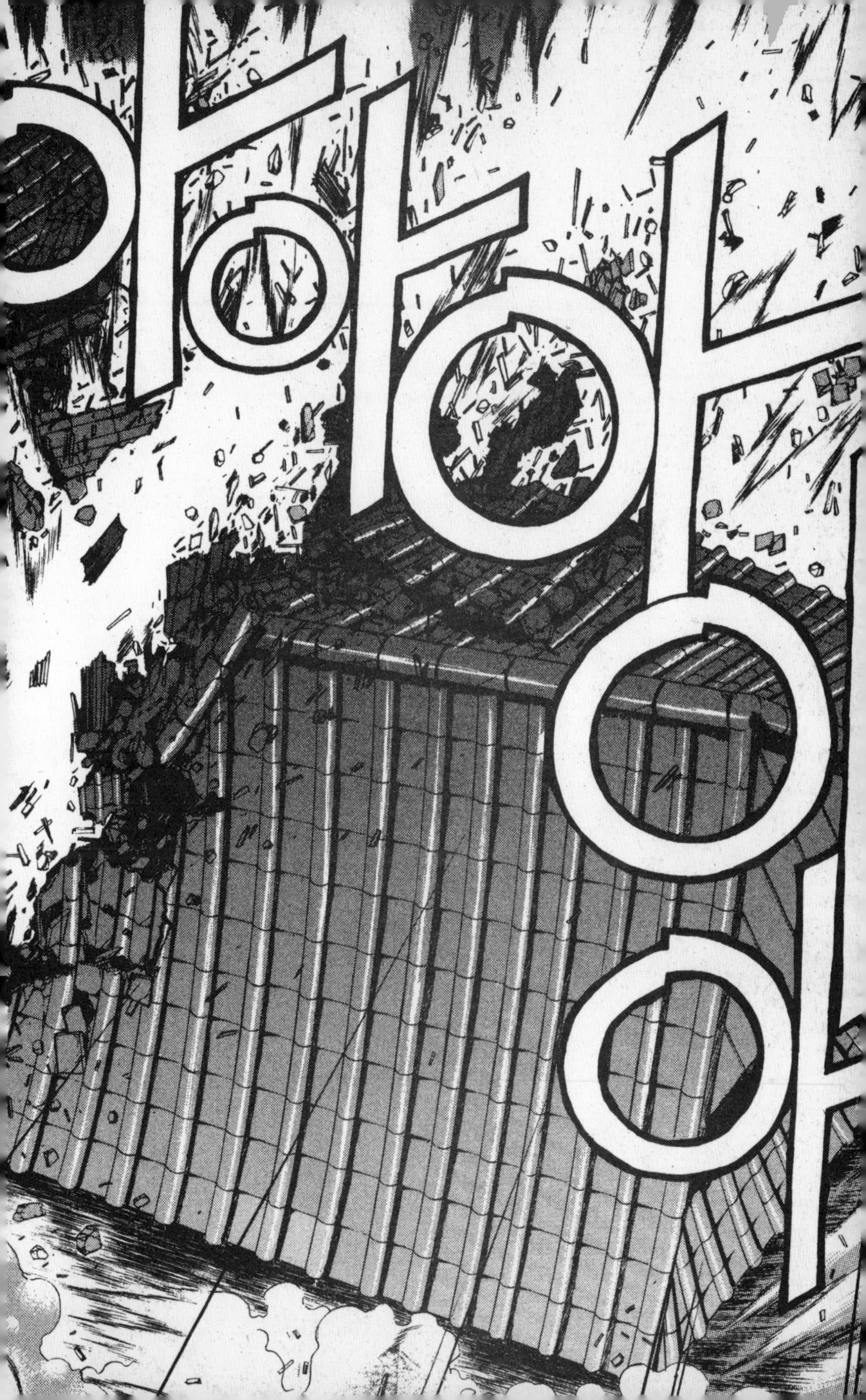

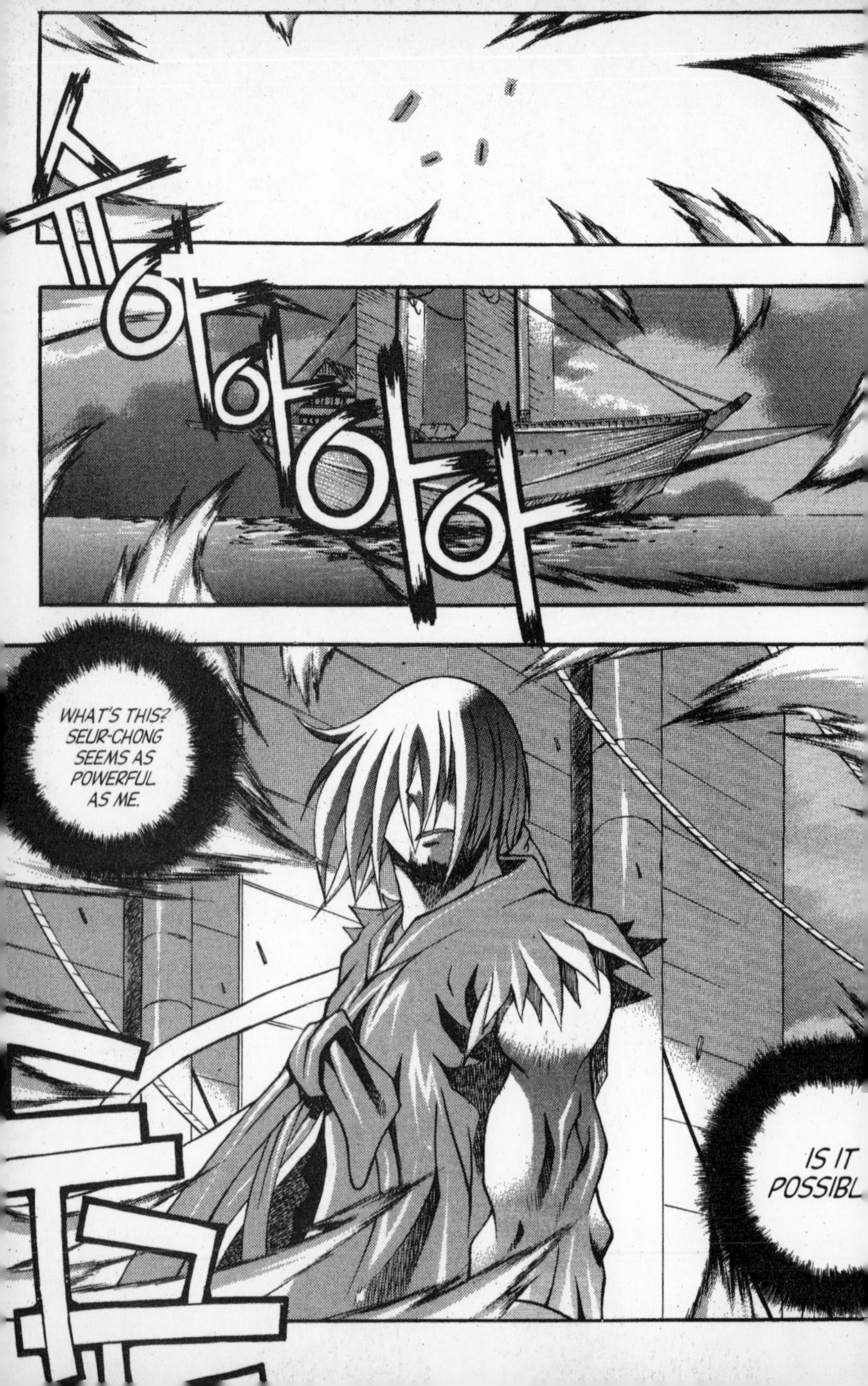
WHAT'S THIS? SEUR-CHONG SEEMS AS POWERFUL AS ME.
IS IT POSSIBL

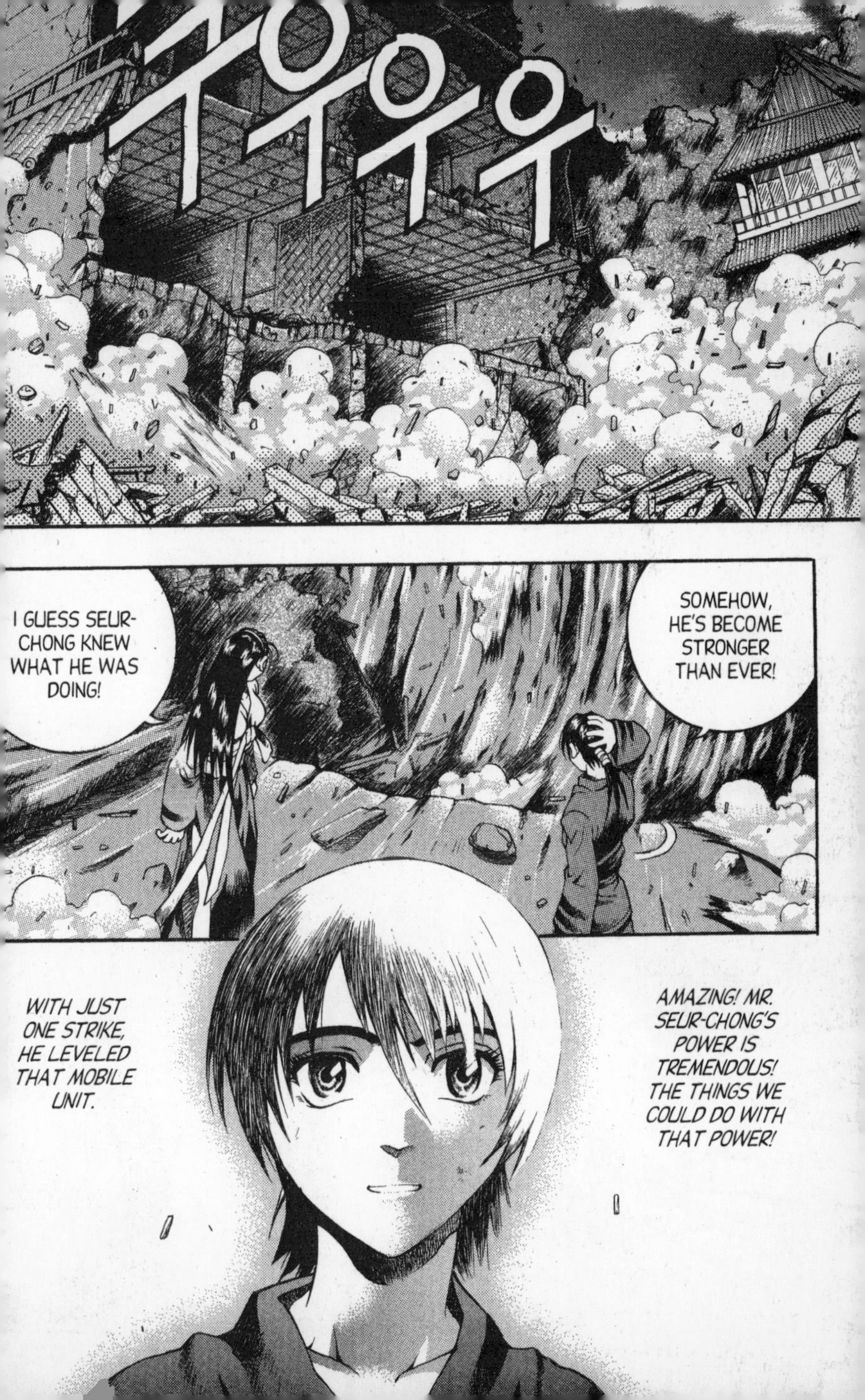
I GUESS SEUR-CHONG KNEW WHAT HE WAS DOING!
SOMEHOW, HE'S BECOME STRONGER THAN EVER!
WITH JUST ONE STRIKE, HE LEVELED THAT MOBILE UNIT.
AMAZING! MR. SEUR-CHONG'S POWER IS TREMENDOUS! THE THINGS WE COULD DO WITH THAT POWER!

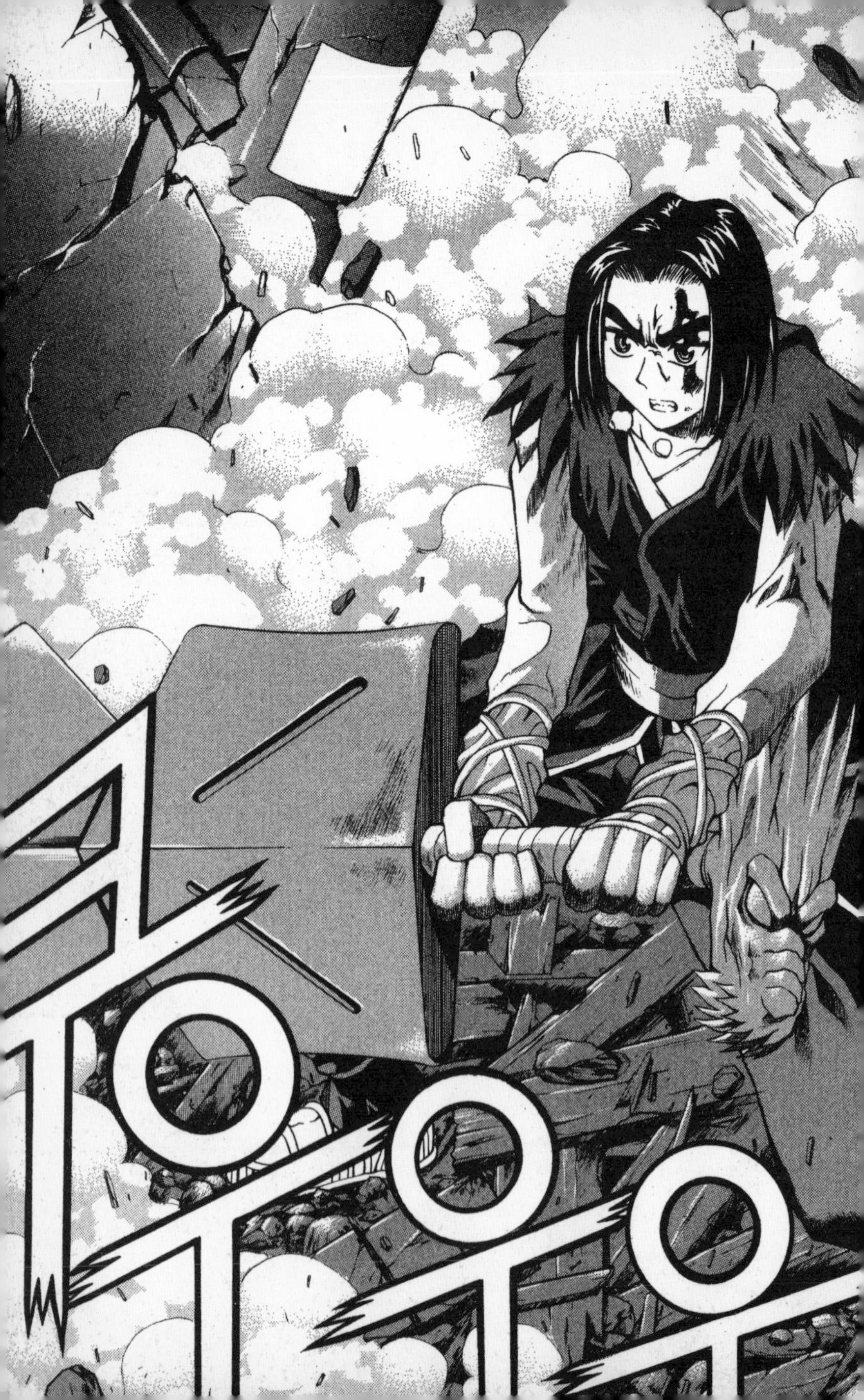

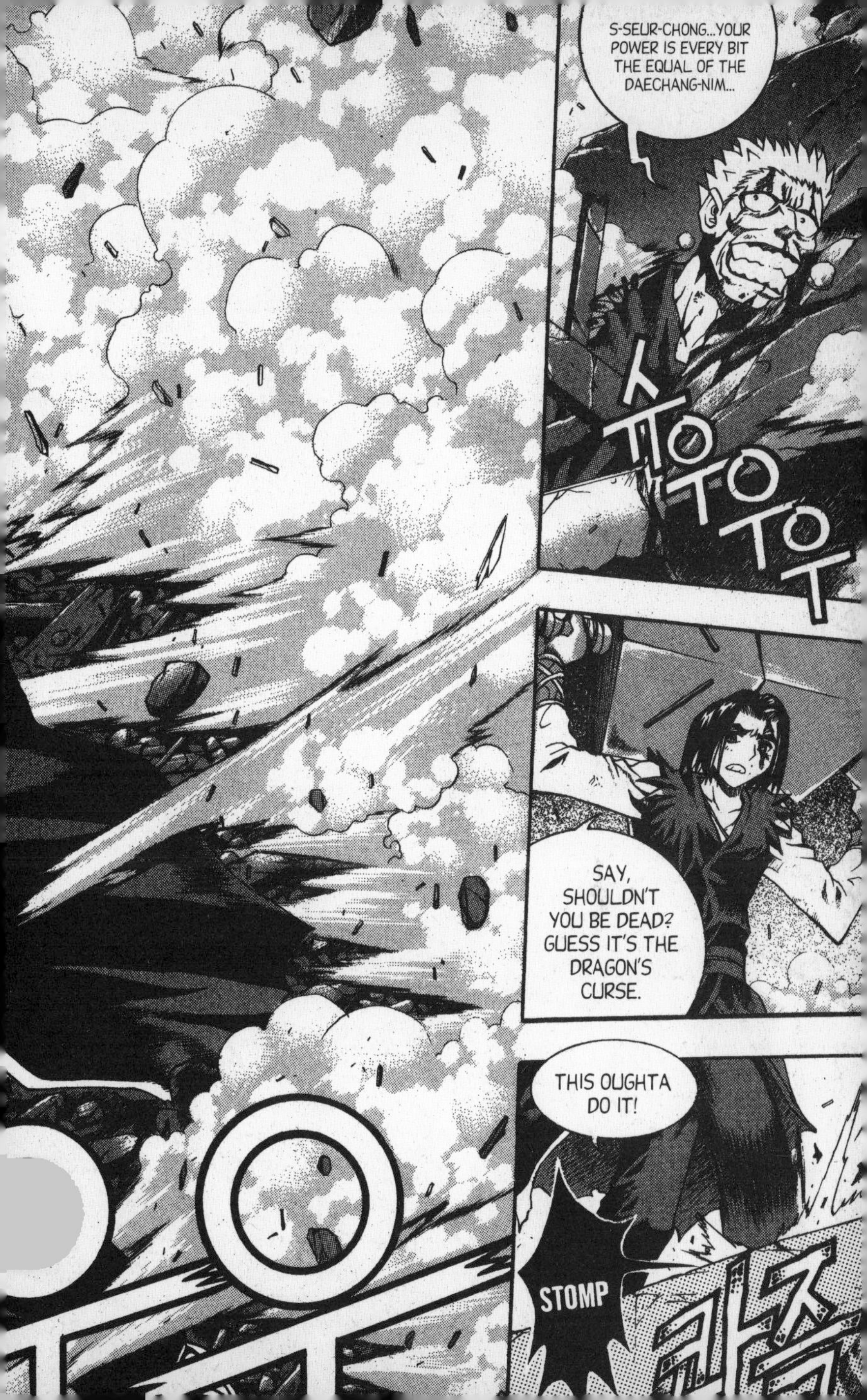
S-SEUR-CHONG...YOUR POWER IS EVERY BIT THE EQUAL OF THE DAECHANG-NIM...
SAY, SHOULDN'T YOU BE DEAD? GUESS IT'S THE DRAGON'S CURSE.
THIS OUGHTA DO IT!
STOMP

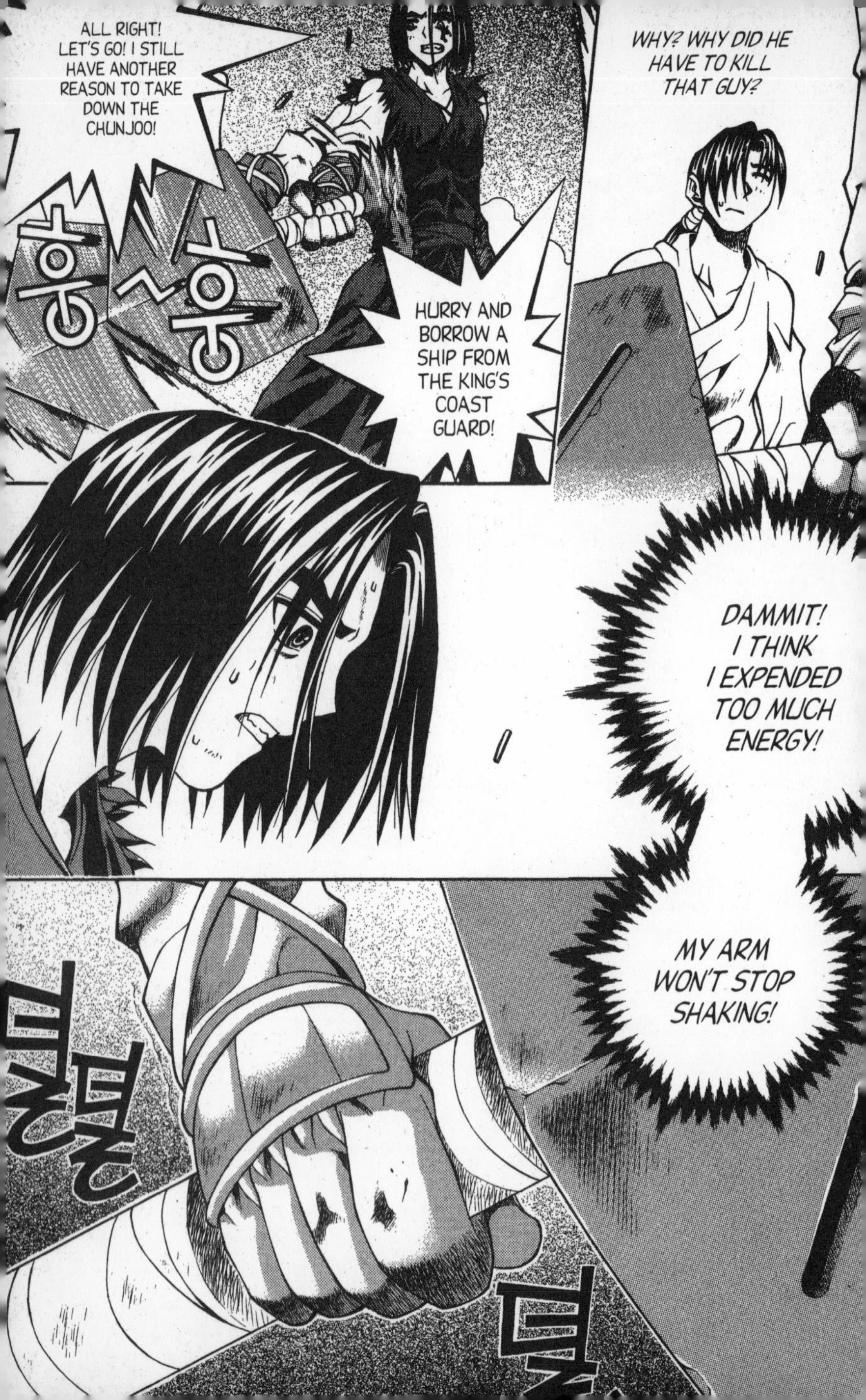
ALL RIGHT! LET'S GO! I STILL HAVE ANOTHER REASON TO TAKE DOWN THE CHUNJOO!
HURRY AND BORROW A SHIP FROM THE KING'S COAST GUARD!
WHY? WHY DID HE HAVE TO KILL THAT GUY?
DAMMIT! I THINK I EXPENDED TOO MUCH ENERGY!
MY ARM WON'T STOP SHAKING!

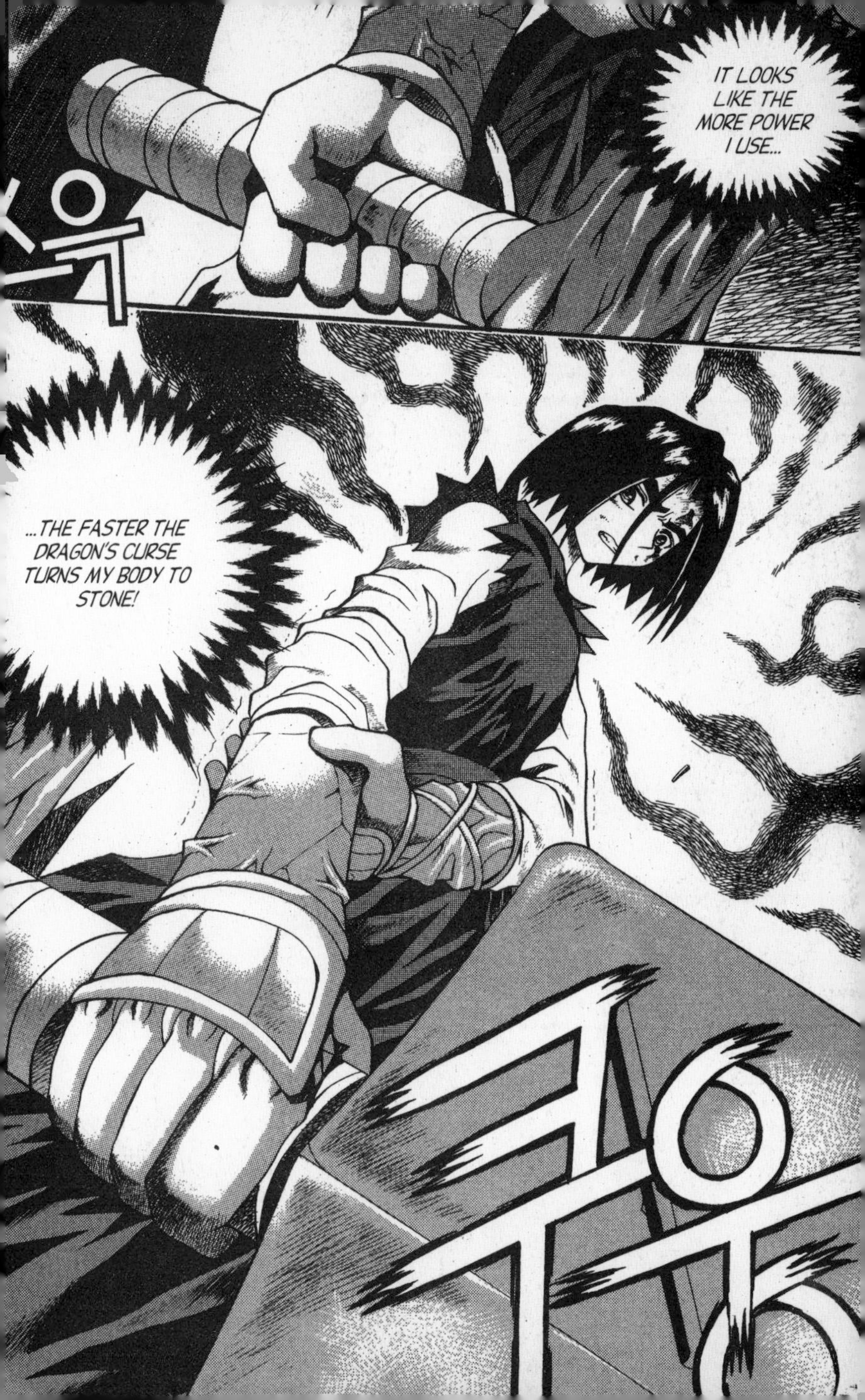
IT LOOKS LIKE THE MORE POWER I USE...
...THE FASTER THE DRAGON'S CURSE TURNS MY BODY TO STONE!

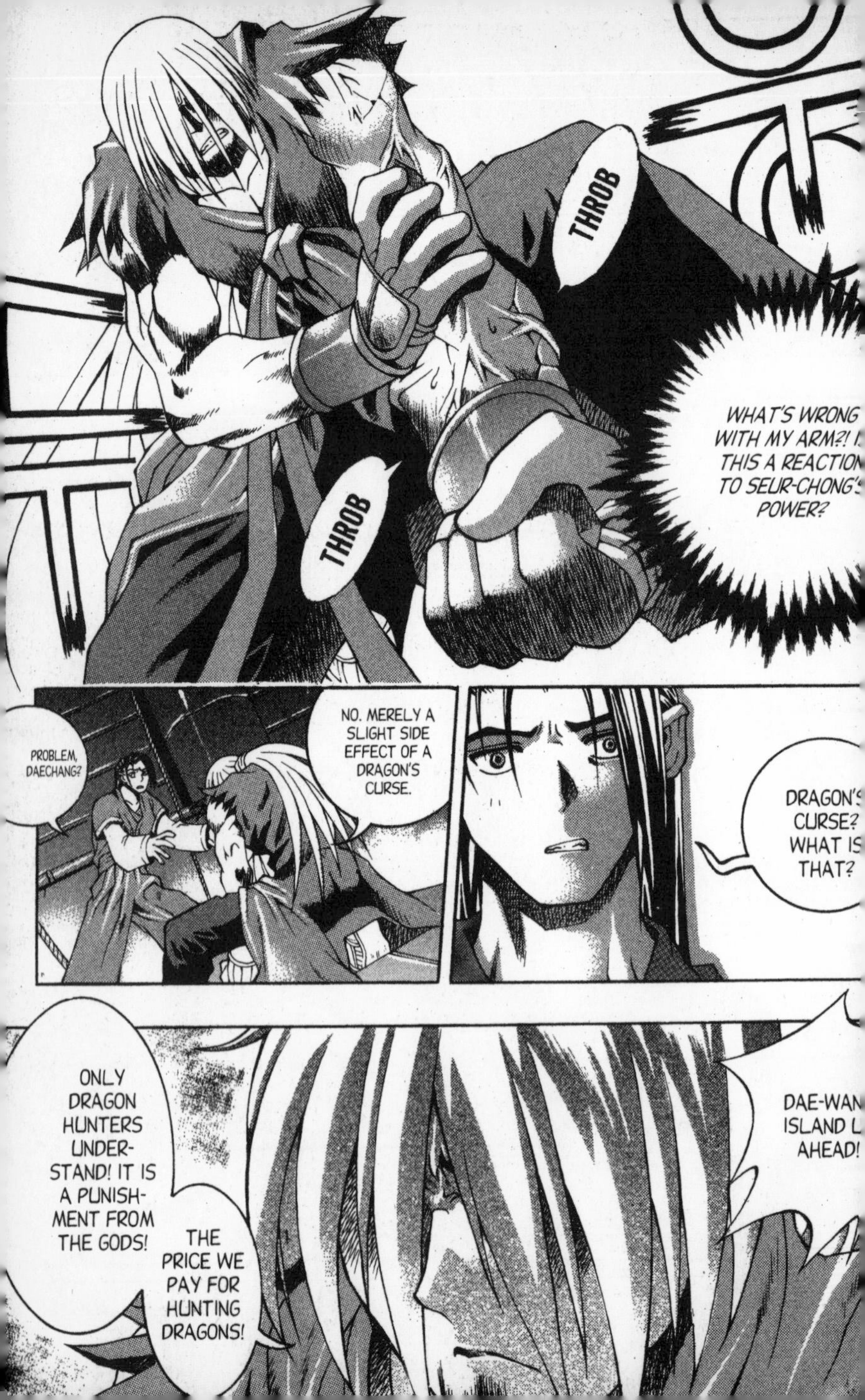
THROB
WHAT'S WRONG WITH MY ARM?! I THIS A REACTION TO SEUR-CHONG'S POWER?
THROB
PROBLEM, DAECHANG?
NO. MERELY A SLIGHT SIDE EFFECT OF A DRAGON'S CURSE.
DRAGON'S CURSE? WHAT IS THAT?
ONLY DRAGON HUNTERS UNDER-STAND! IT IS A PUNISH-MENT FROM THE GODS!
THE PRICE WE PAY FOR HUNTING DRAGONS!
DAE-WAN ISLAND L AHEAD!

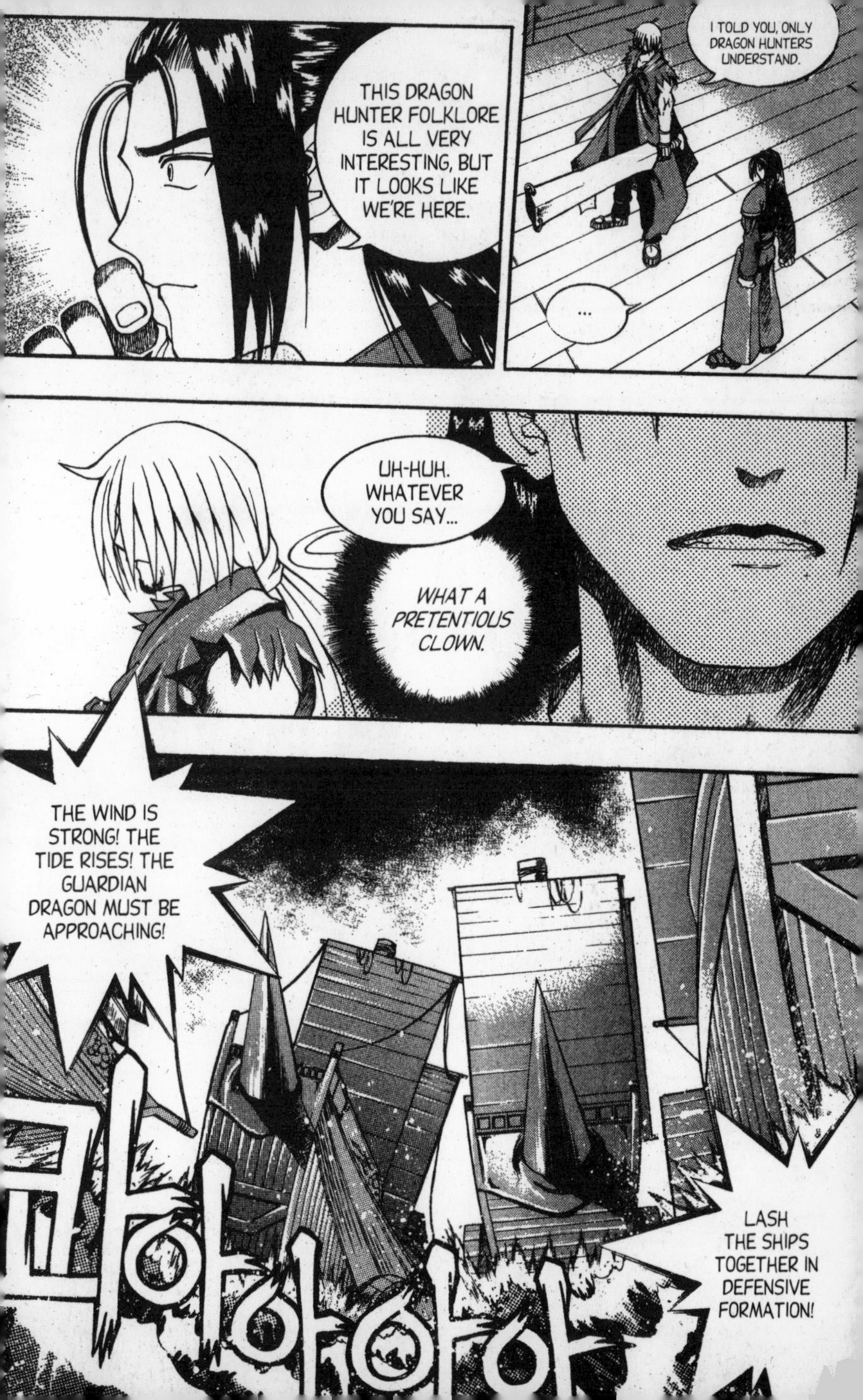
THIS DRAGON HUNTER FOLKLORE IS ALL VERY INTERESTING, BUT IT LOOKS LIKE WE'RE HERE.
I TOLD YOU, ONLY DRAGON HUNTERS UNDERSTAND.
...
UH-HUH. WHATEVER YOU SAY...
WHAT A PRETENTIOUS CLOWN.
THE WIND IS STRONG! THE TIDE RISES! THE GUARDIAN DRAGON MUST BE APPROACHING!
LASH THE SHIPS TOGETHER IN DEFENSIVE FORMATION!

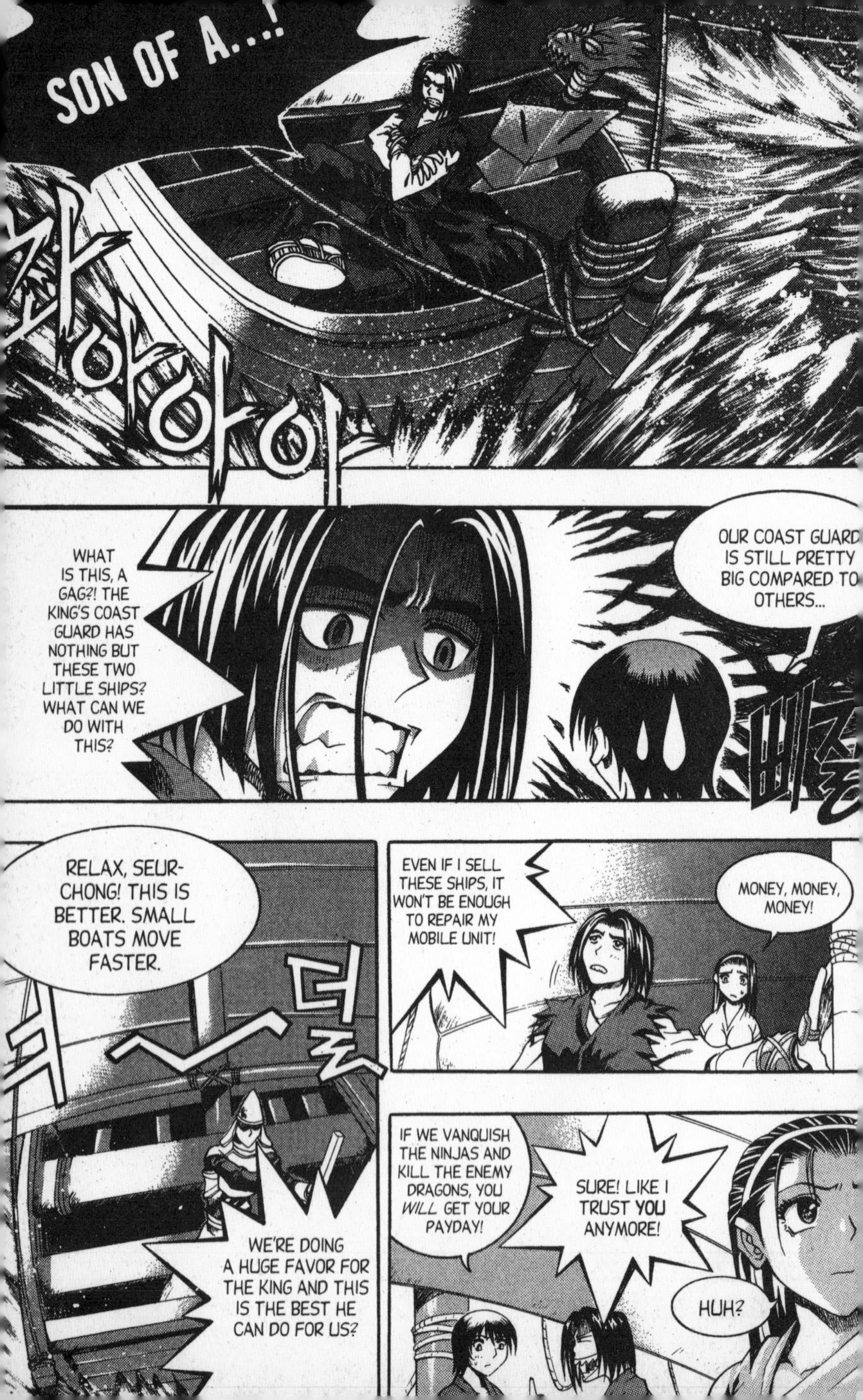
SON OF A...!
WHAT IS THIS, A GAG?! THE KING'S COAST GUARD HAS NOTHING BUT THESE TWO LITTLE SHIPS? WHAT CAN WE DO WITH THIS?
OUR COAST GUARD IS STILL PRETTY BIG COMPARED TO OTHERS...
RELAX, SEUR-CHONG! THIS IS BETTER. SMALL BOATS MOVE FASTER.
WE'RE DOING A HUGE FAVOR FOR THE KING AND THIS IS THE BEST HE CAN DO FOR US?
EVEN IF I SELL THESE SHIPS, IT WON'T BE ENOUGH TO REPAIR MY MOBILE UNIT!
MONEY, MONEY, MONEY!
IF WE VANQUISH THE NINJAS AND KILL THE ENEMY DRAGONS, YOU *WILL* GET YOUR PAYDAY!
SURE! LIKE I TRUST **YOU** ANYMORE!
HUH?

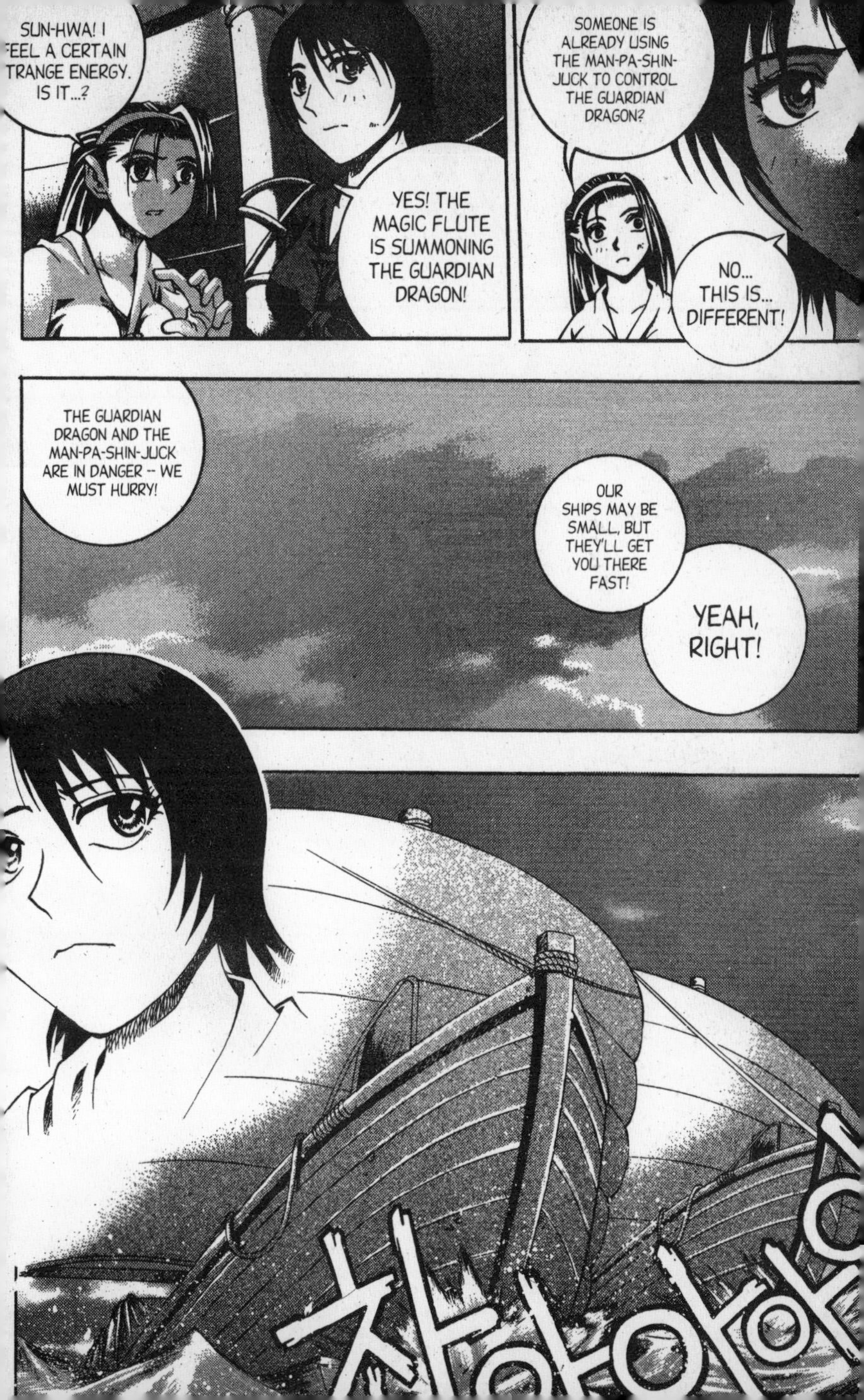
SUN-HWA! I FEEL A CERTAIN TRANGE ENERGY. IS IT...?
YES! THE MAGIC FLUTE IS SUMMONING THE GUARDIAN DRAGON!
SOMEONE IS ALREADY USING THE MAN-PA-SHIN-JUCK TO CONTROL THE GUARDIAN DRAGON?
NO... THIS IS... DIFFERENT!
THE GUARDIAN DRAGON AND THE MAN-PA-SHIN-JUCK ARE IN DANGER -- WE MUST HURRY!
OUR SHIPS MAY BE SMALL, BUT THEY'LL GET YOU THERE FAST!
YEAH, RIGHT!
샤아아아아

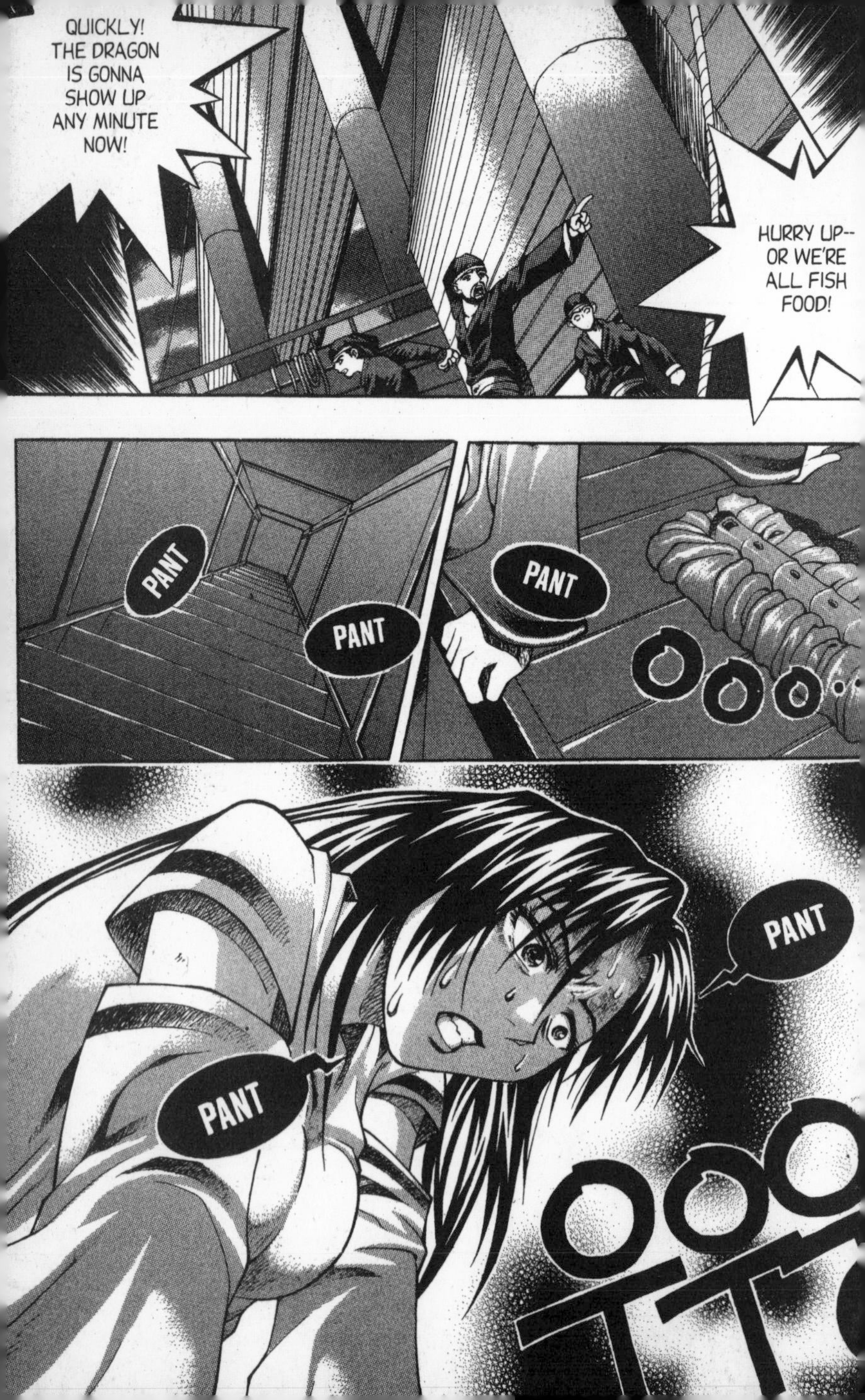
QUICKLY! THE DRAGON IS GONNA SHOW UP ANY MINUTE NOW!
HURRY UP-- OR WE'RE ALL FISH FOOD!
PANT
PANT
PANT
OOO...
PANT
PANT
OOOTTO

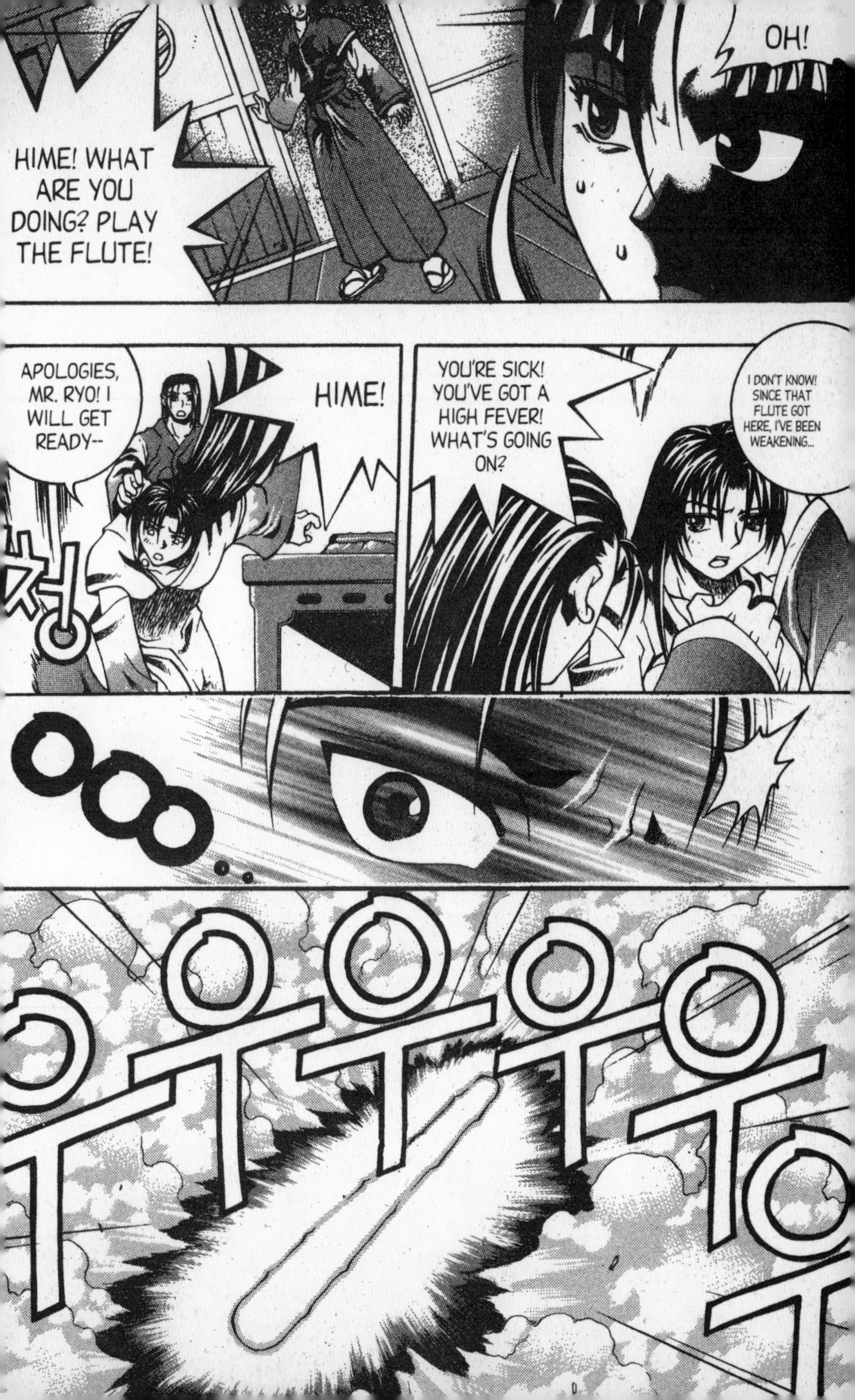
HIME! WHAT ARE YOU DOING? PLAY THE FLUTE!
OH!
APOLOGIES, MR. RYO! I WILL GET READY--
HIME!
YOU'RE SICK! YOU'VE GOT A HIGH FEVER! WHAT'S GOING ON?
I DON'T KNOW! SINCE THAT FLUTE GOT HERE, I'VE BEEN WEAKENING...
OOO...

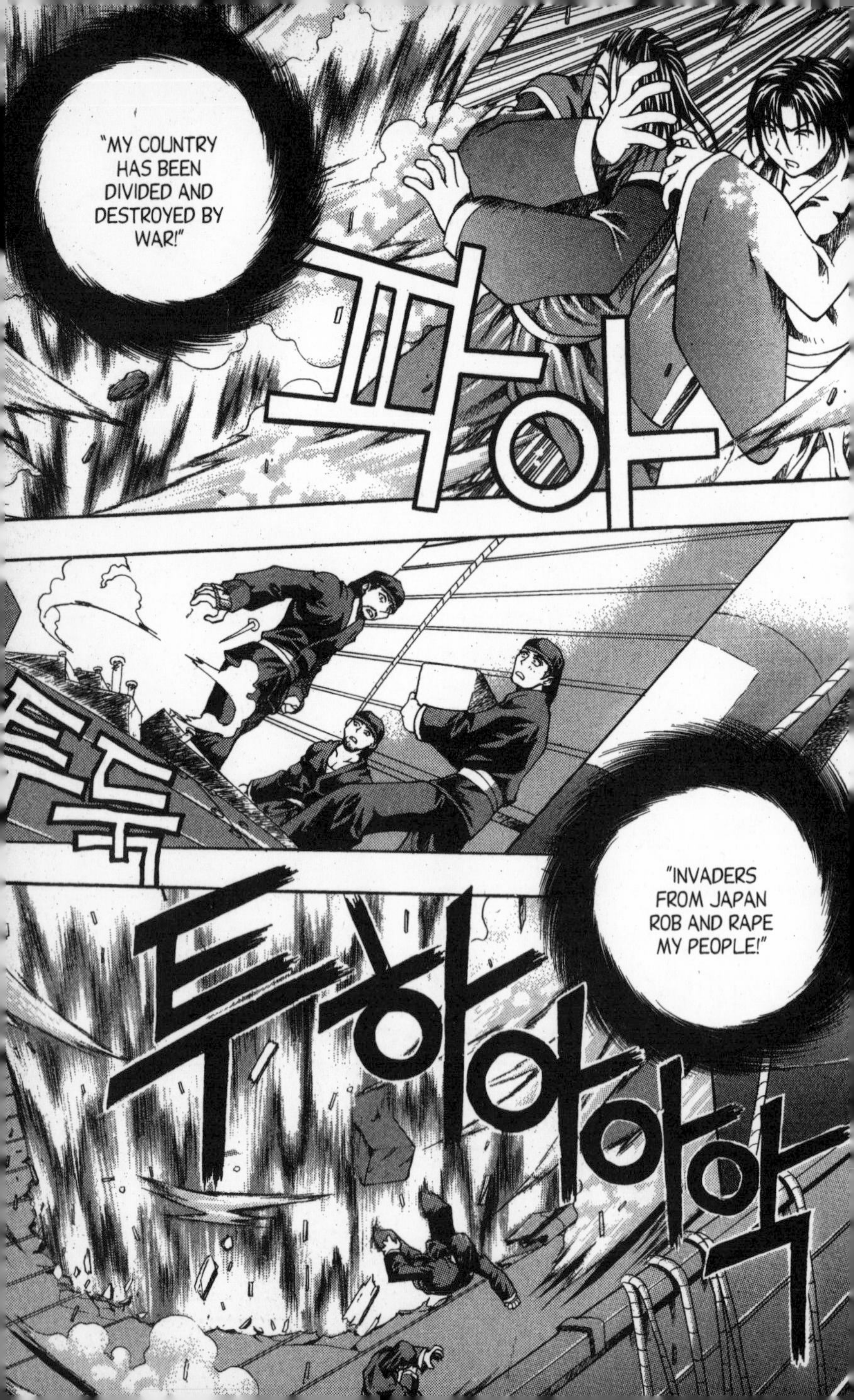
"MY COUNTRY HAS BEEN DIVIDED AND DESTROYED BY WAR!"
"INVADERS FROM JAPAN ROB AND RAPE MY PEOPLE!"

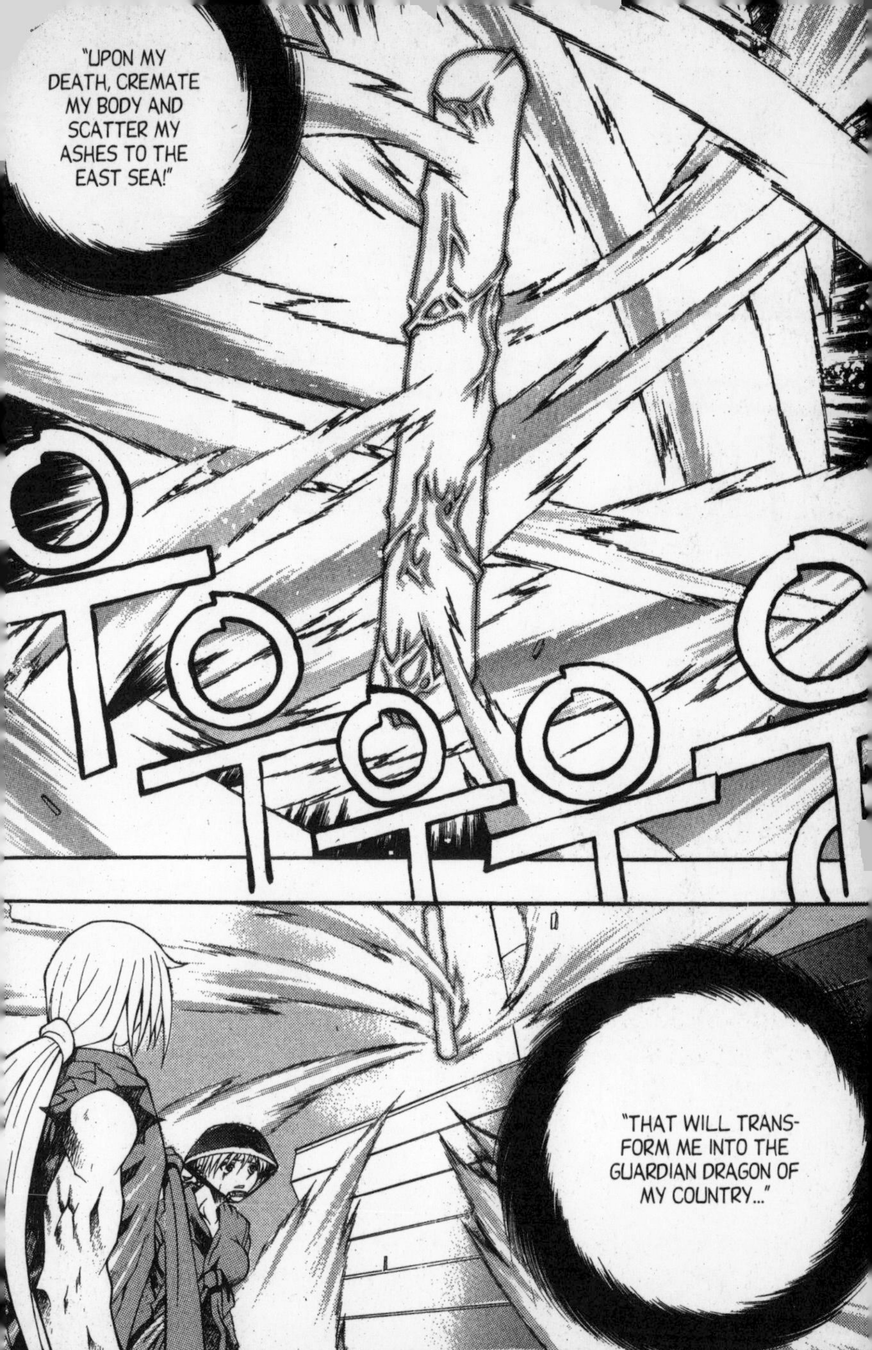
"UPON MY DEATH, CREMATE MY BODY AND SCATTER MY ASHES TO THE EAST SEA!"
"THAT WILL TRANS-FORM ME INTO THE GUARDIAN DRAGON OF MY COUNTRY..."

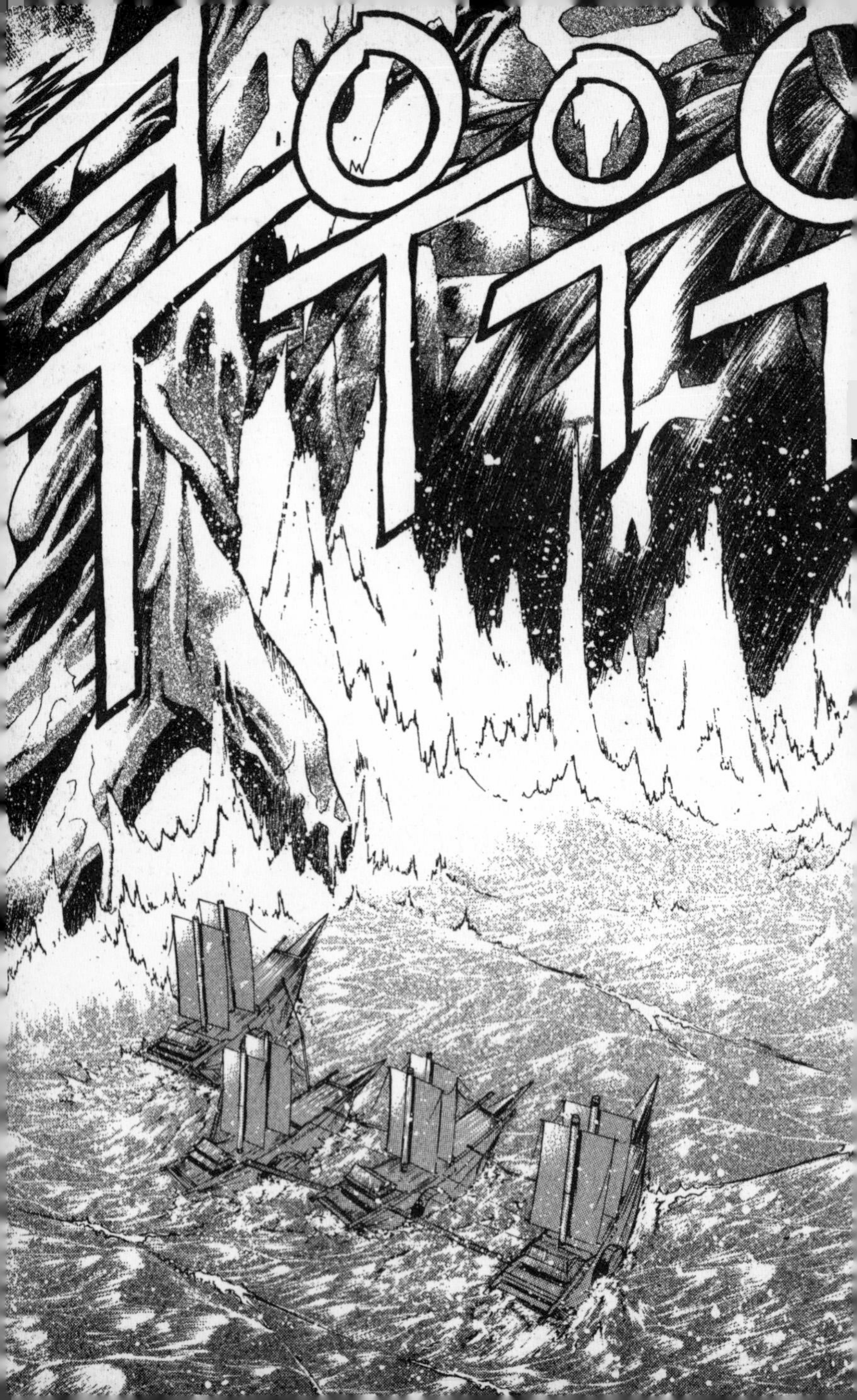

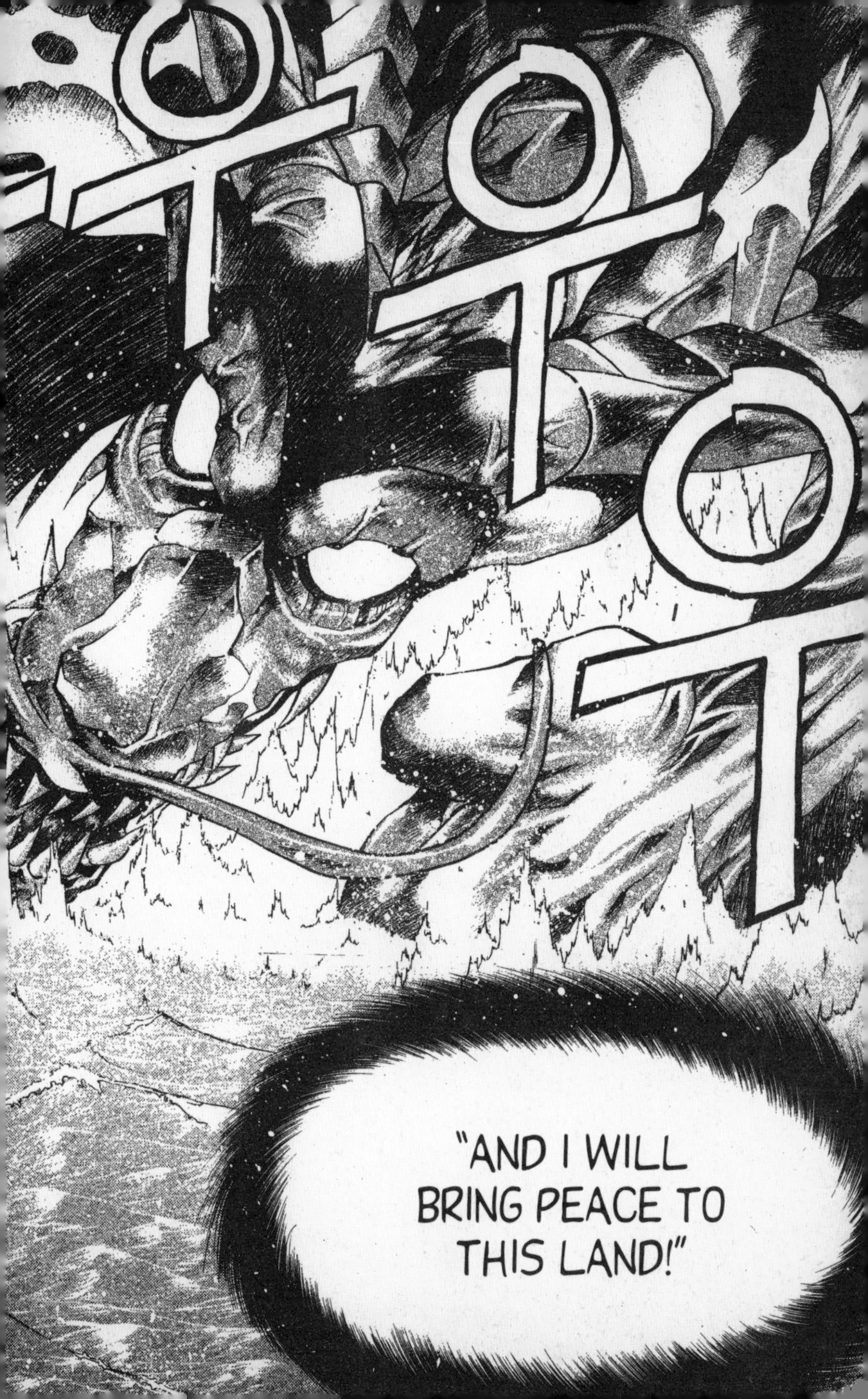
"AND I WILL BRING PEACE TO THIS LAND!"

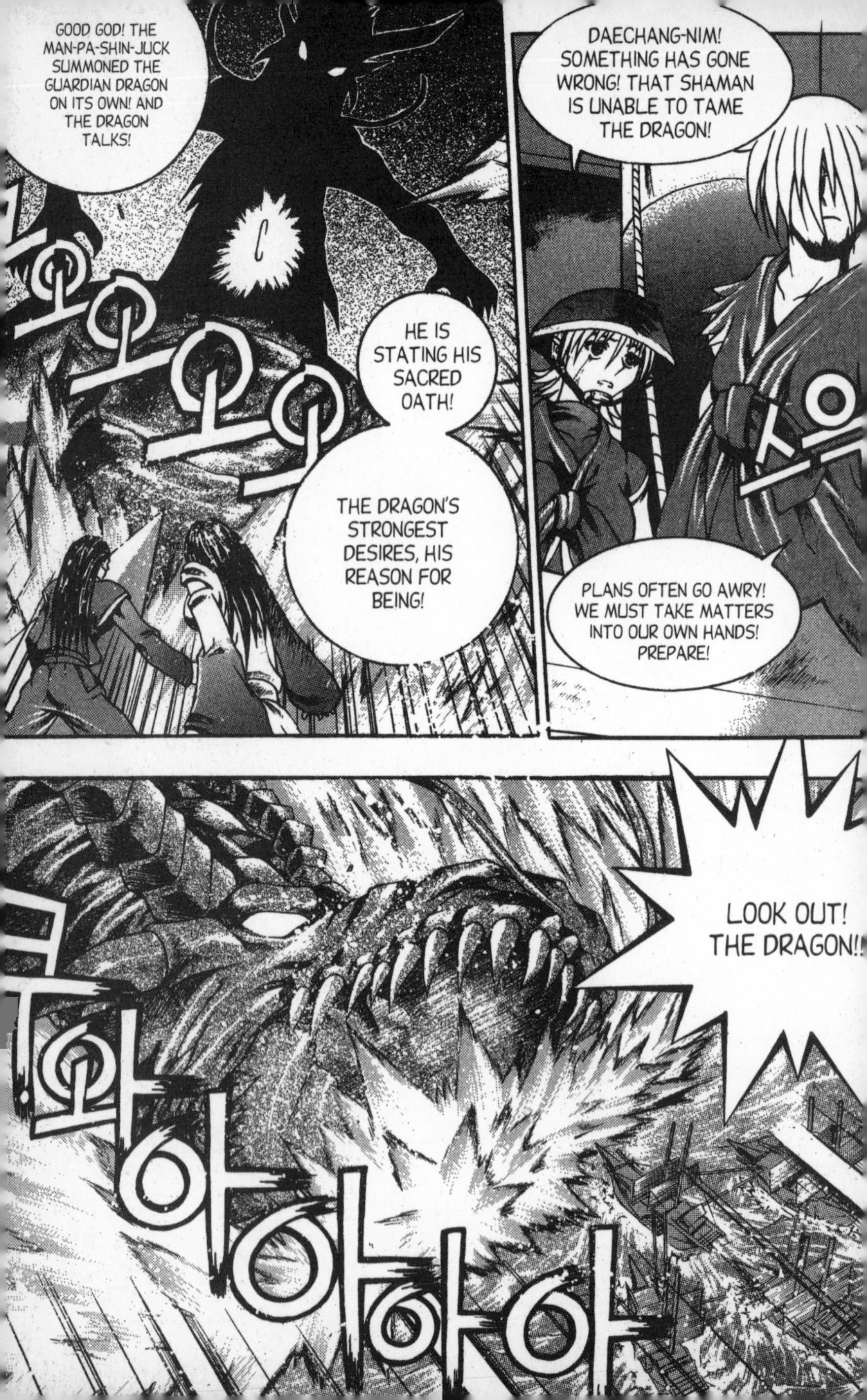
GOOD GOD! THE MAN-PA-SHIN-JUCK SUMMONED THE GUARDIAN DRAGON ON ITS OWN! AND THE DRAGON TALKS!
HE IS STATING HIS SACRED OATH!
THE DRAGON'S STRONGEST DESIRES, HIS REASON FOR BEING!
DAECHANG-NIM! SOMETHING HAS GONE WRONG! THAT SHAMAN IS UNABLE TO TAME THE DRAGON!
PLANS OFTEN GO AWRY! WE MUST TAKE MATTERS INTO OUR OWN HANDS! PREPARE!
LOOK OUT! THE DRAGON!!

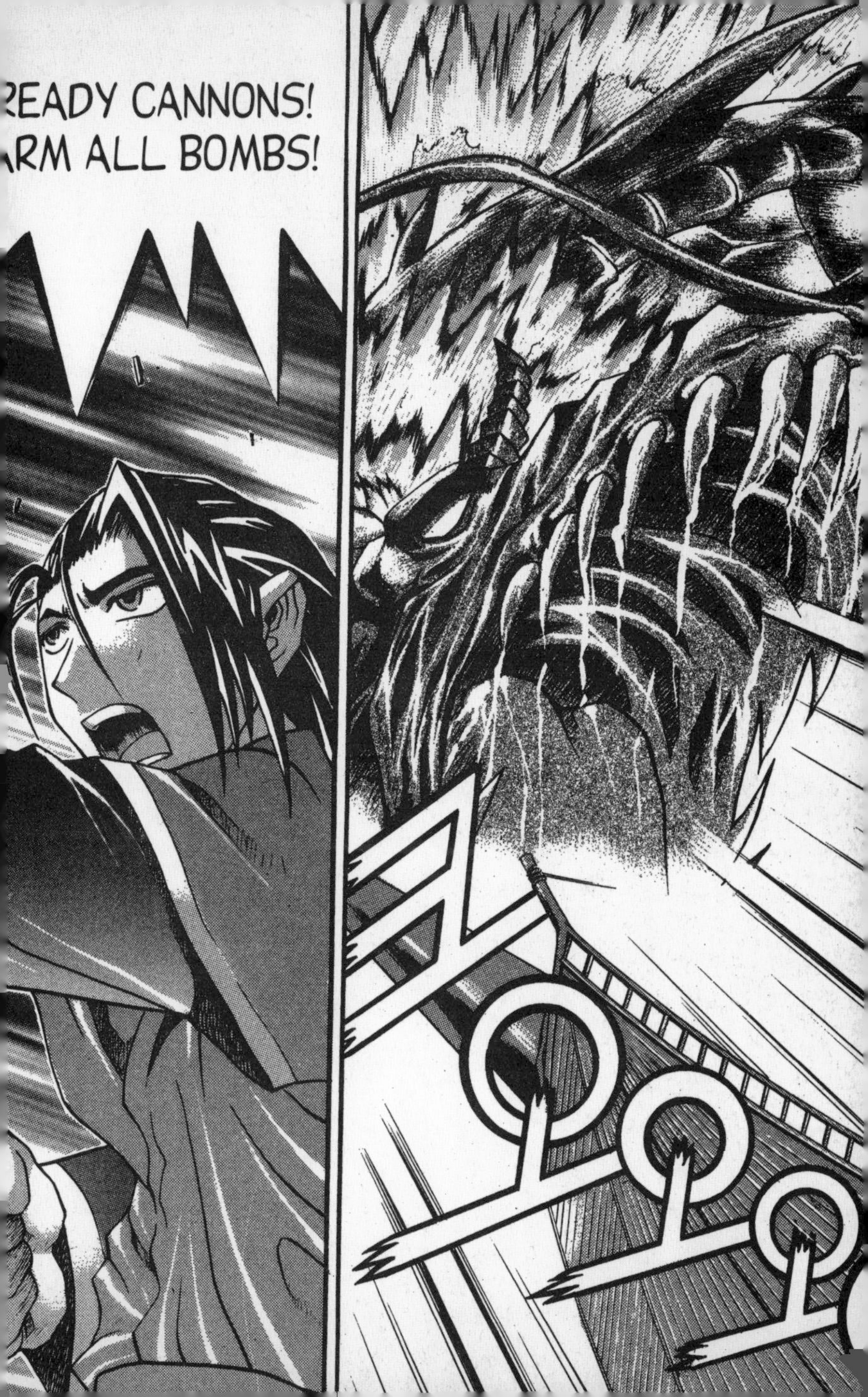
READY CANNONS! ARM ALL BOMBS!

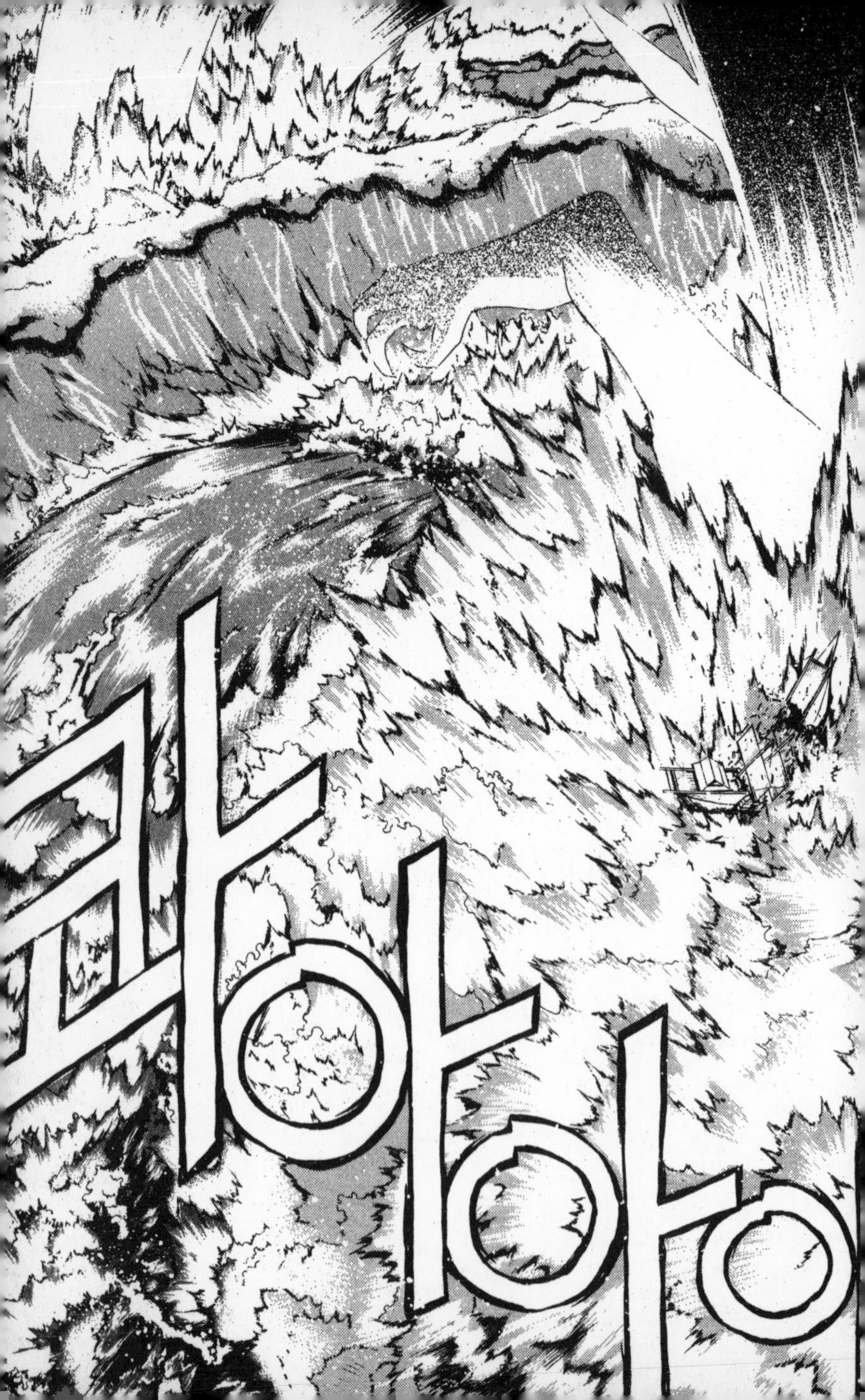

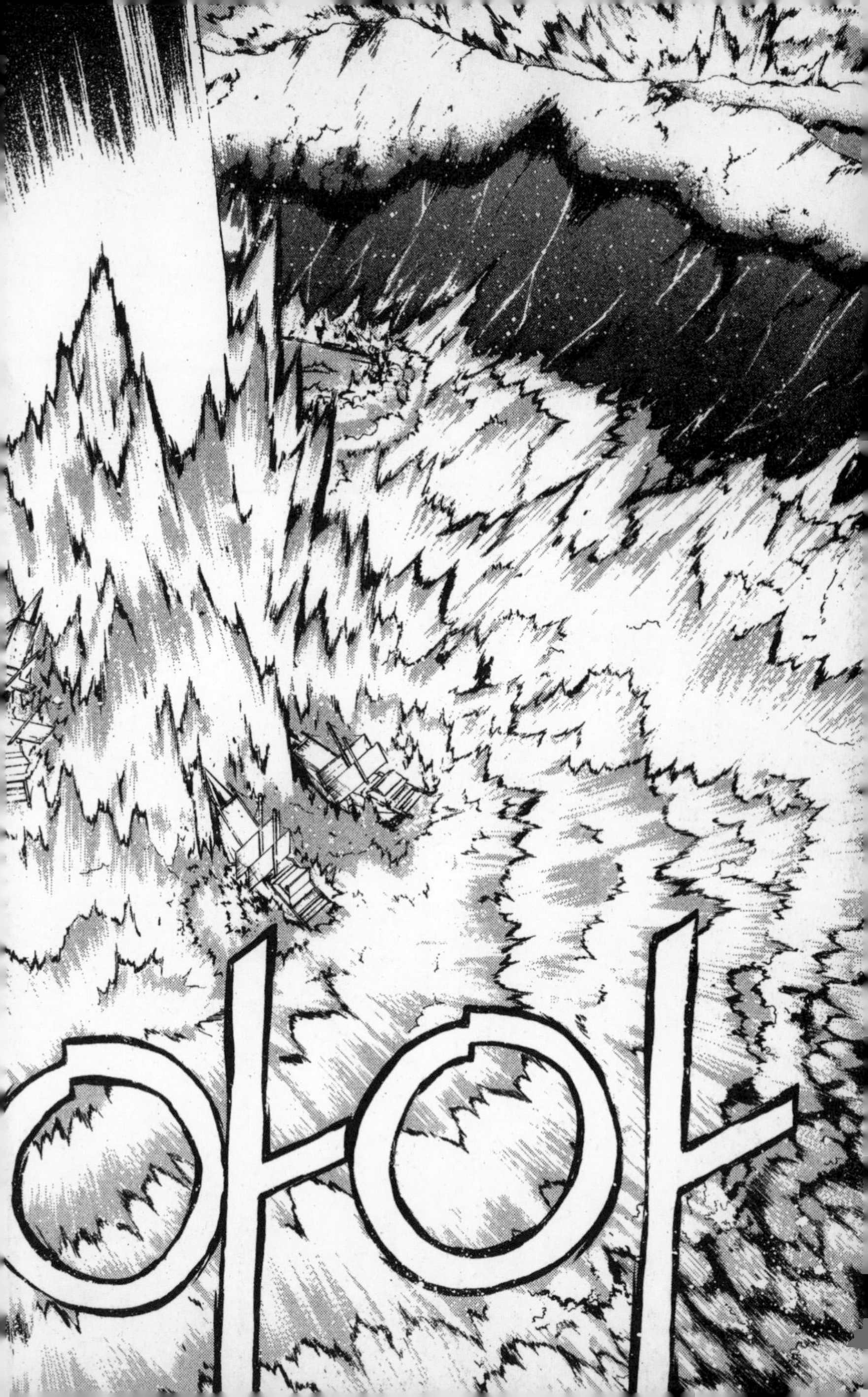
아아

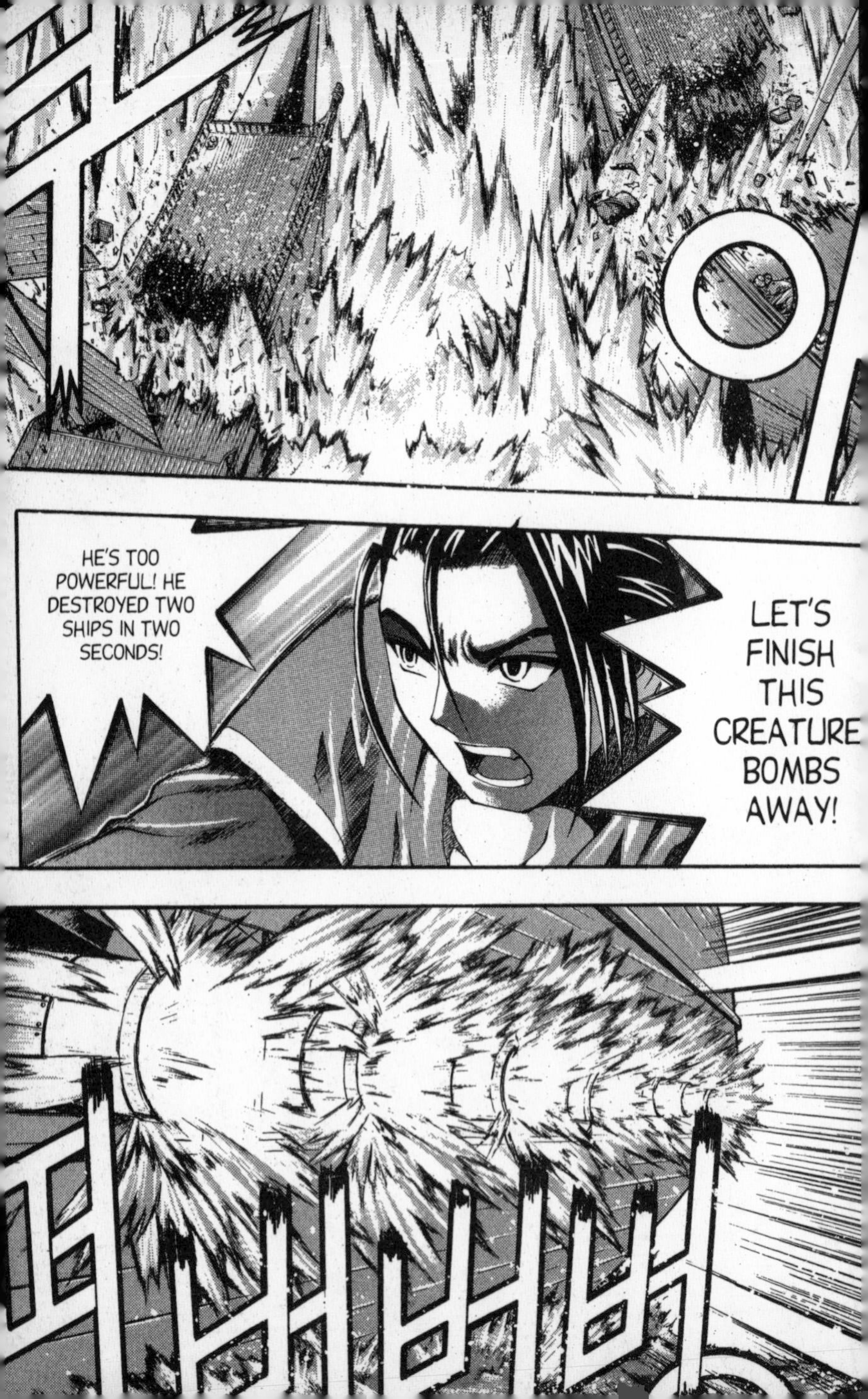
HE'S TOO POWERFUL! HE DESTROYED TWO SHIPS IN TWO SECONDS!
LET'S FINISH THIS CREATURE BOMBS AWAY!

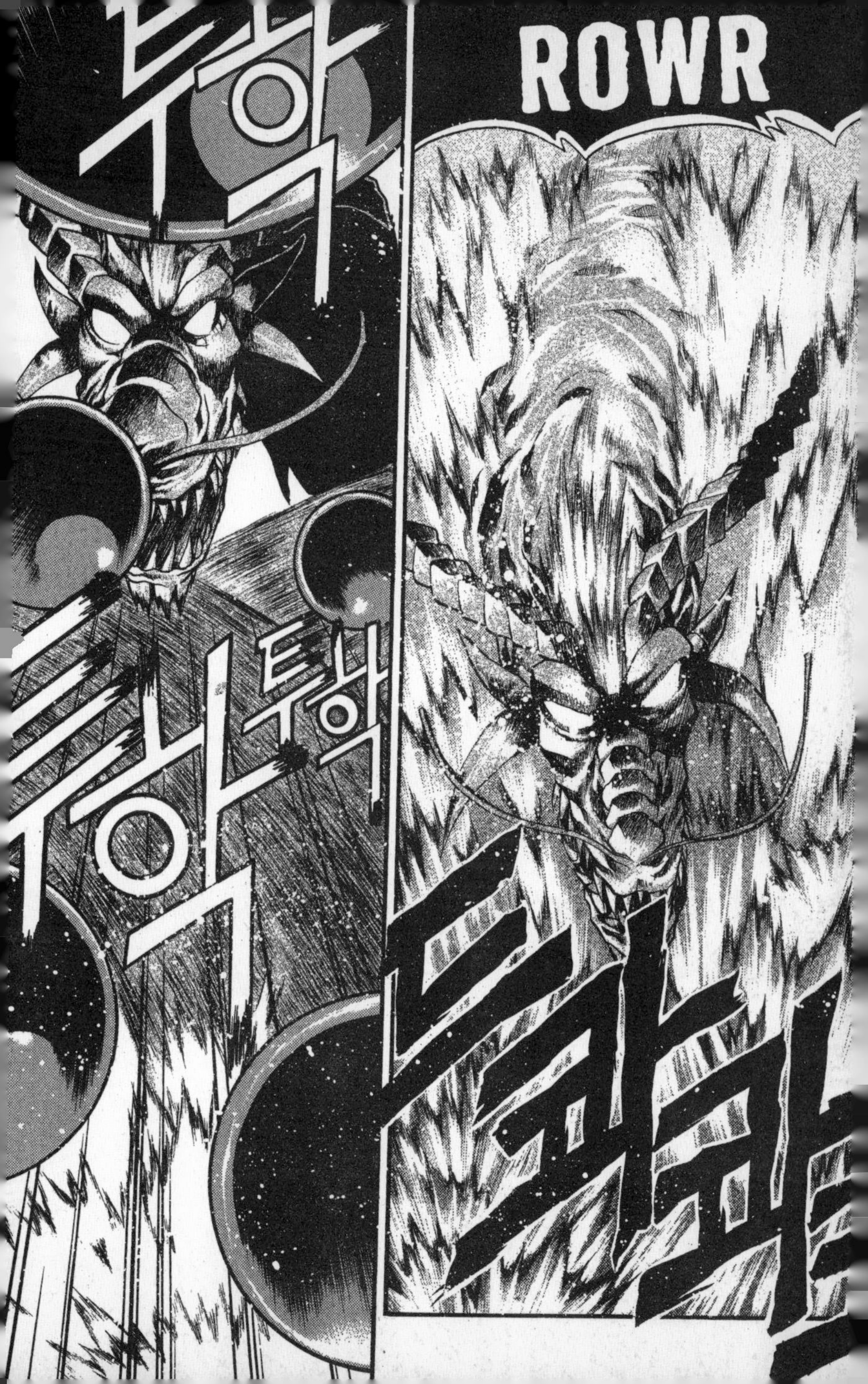
ROWR

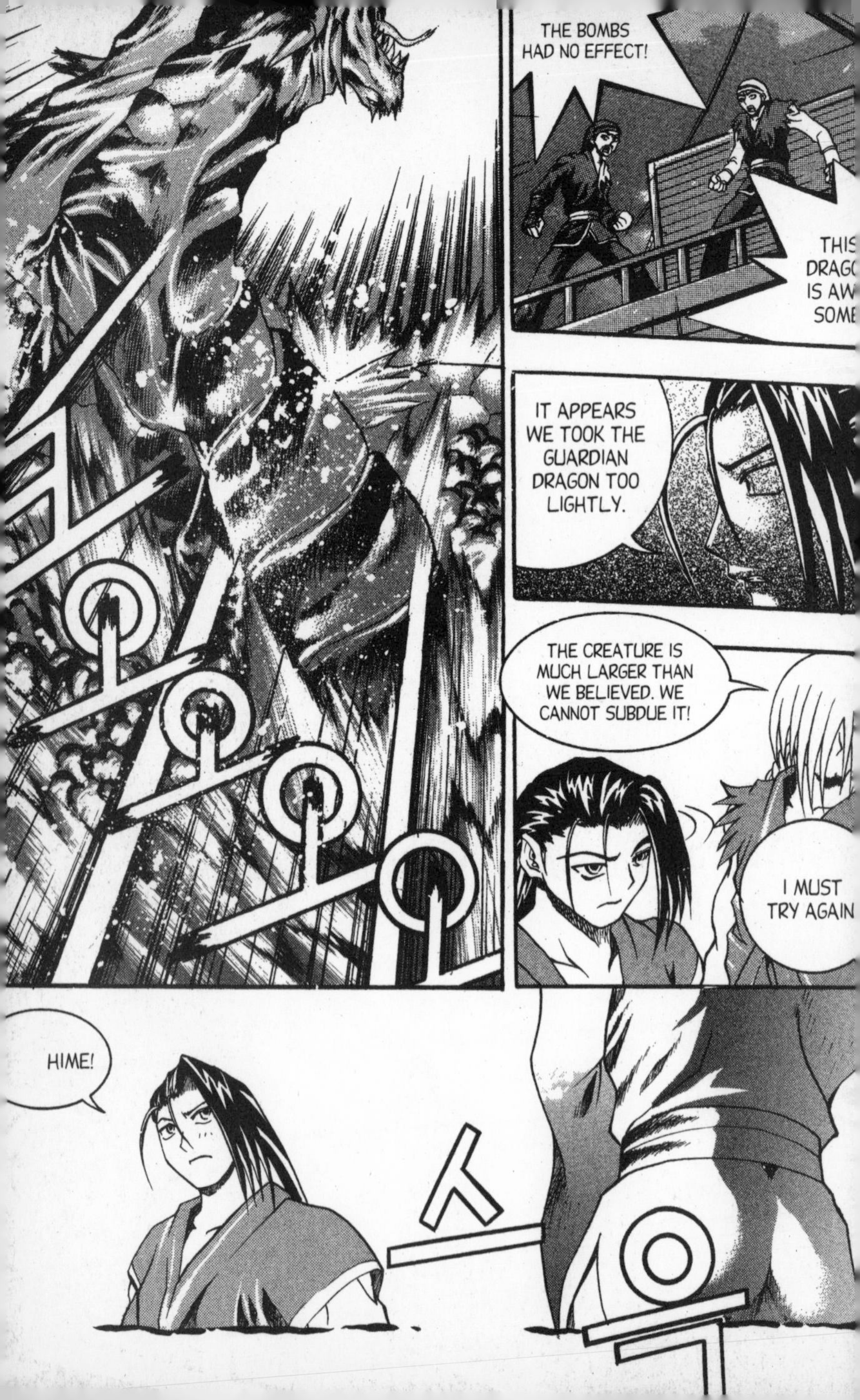
THE BOMBS HAD NO EFFECT!
THIS DRAG IS AW SOME
IT APPEARS WE TOOK THE GUARDIAN DRAGON TOO LIGHTLY.
THE CREATURE IS MUCH LARGER THAN WE BELIEVED. WE CANNOT SUBDUE IT!
I MUST TRY AGAIN
HIME!

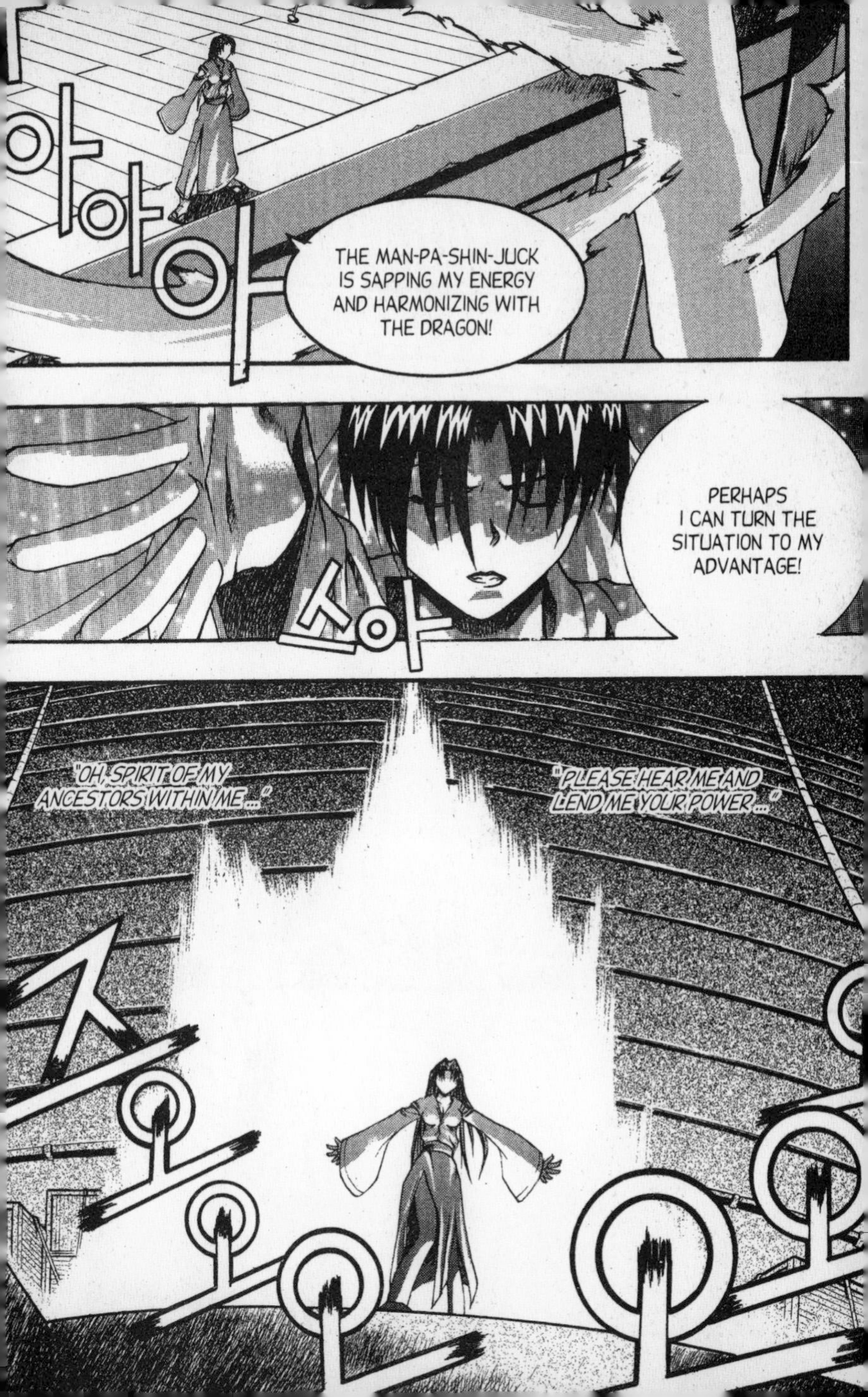
THE MAN-PA-SHIN-JUCK IS SAPPING MY ENERGY AND HARMONIZING WITH THE DRAGON!
PERHAPS I CAN TURN THE SITUATION TO MY ADVANTAGE!
"OH, SPIRIT OF MY ANCESTORS WITHIN ME..."
"PLEASE HEAR ME AND LEND ME YOUR POWER..."

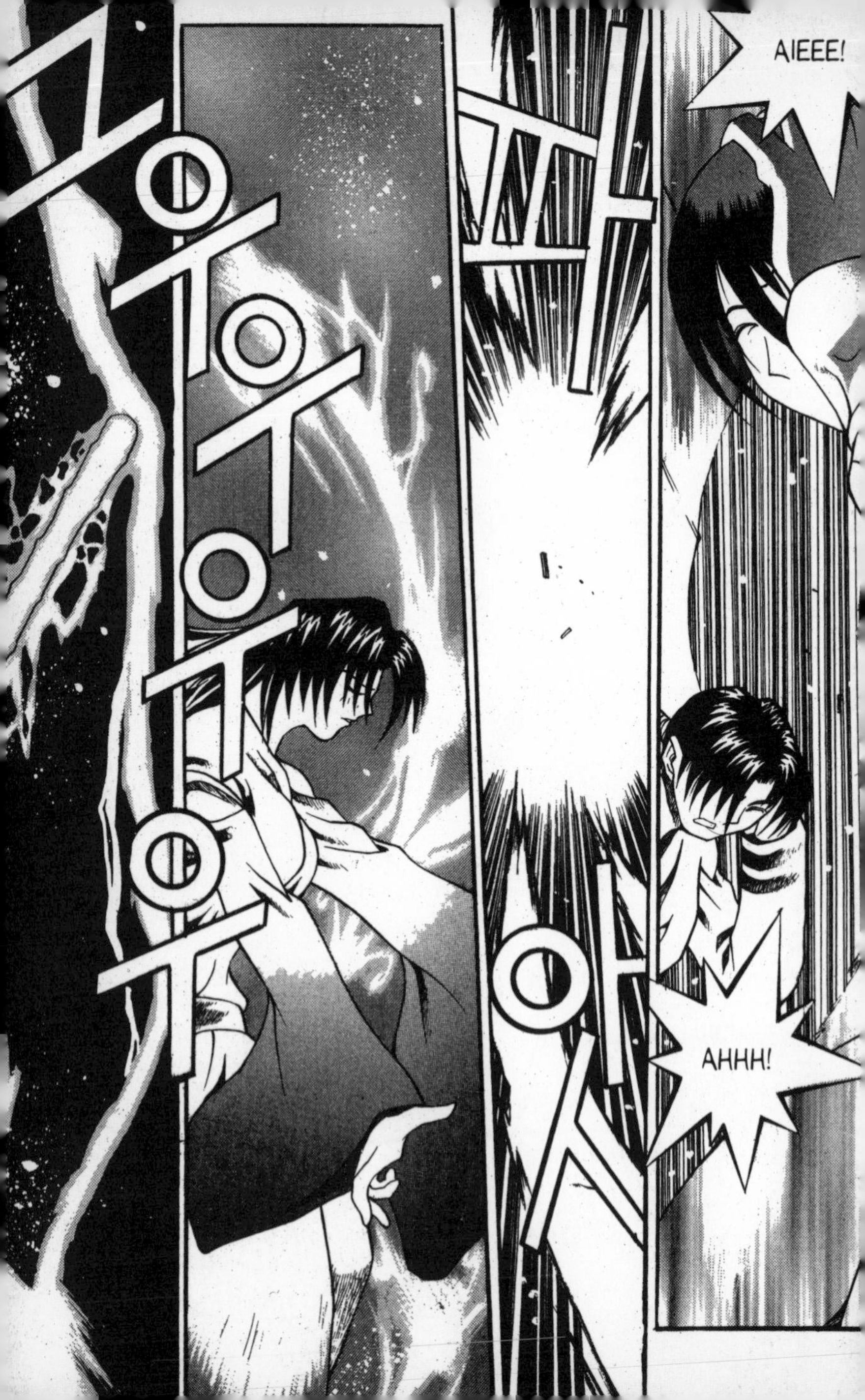
AIEEE!
AHHH!

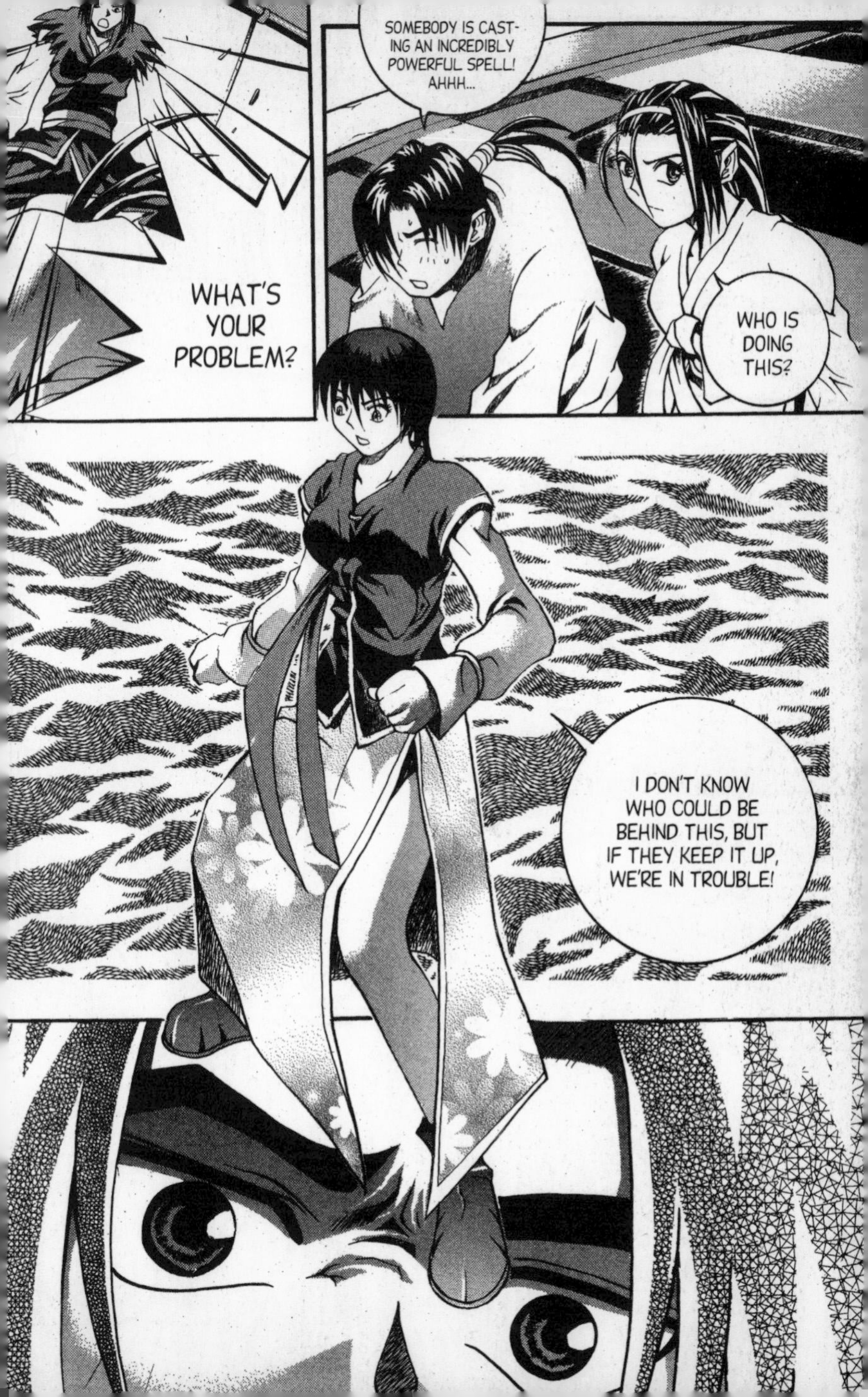
WHAT'S YOUR PROBLEM?
SOMEBODY IS CAST-ING AN INCREDIBLY POWERFUL SPELL! AHHH...
WHO IS DOING THIS?
I DON'T KNOW WHO COULD BE BEHIND THIS, BUT IF THEY KEEP IT UP, WE'RE IN TROUBLE!

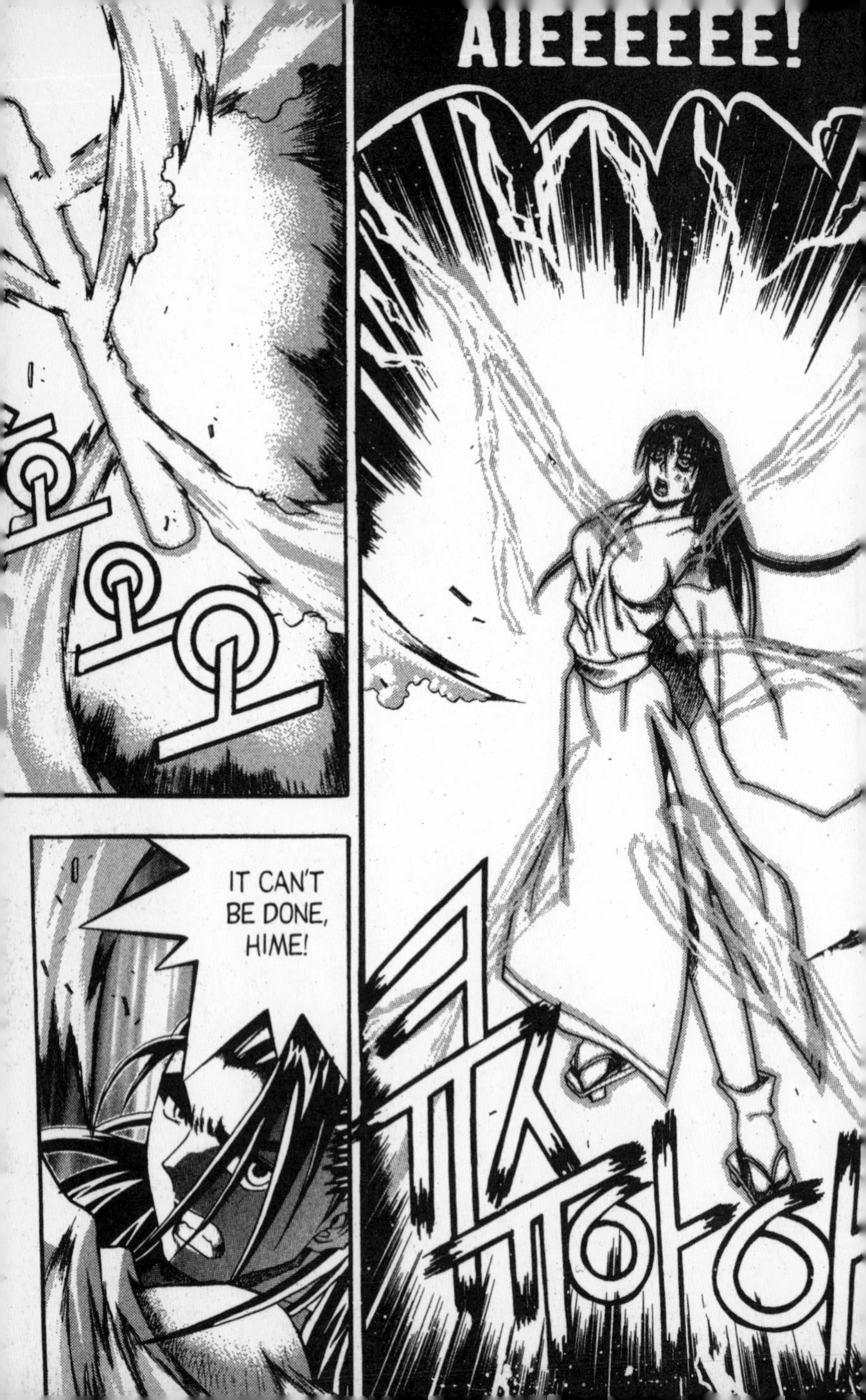
IT CAN'T BE DONE, HIME!
AIEEEEEEE!

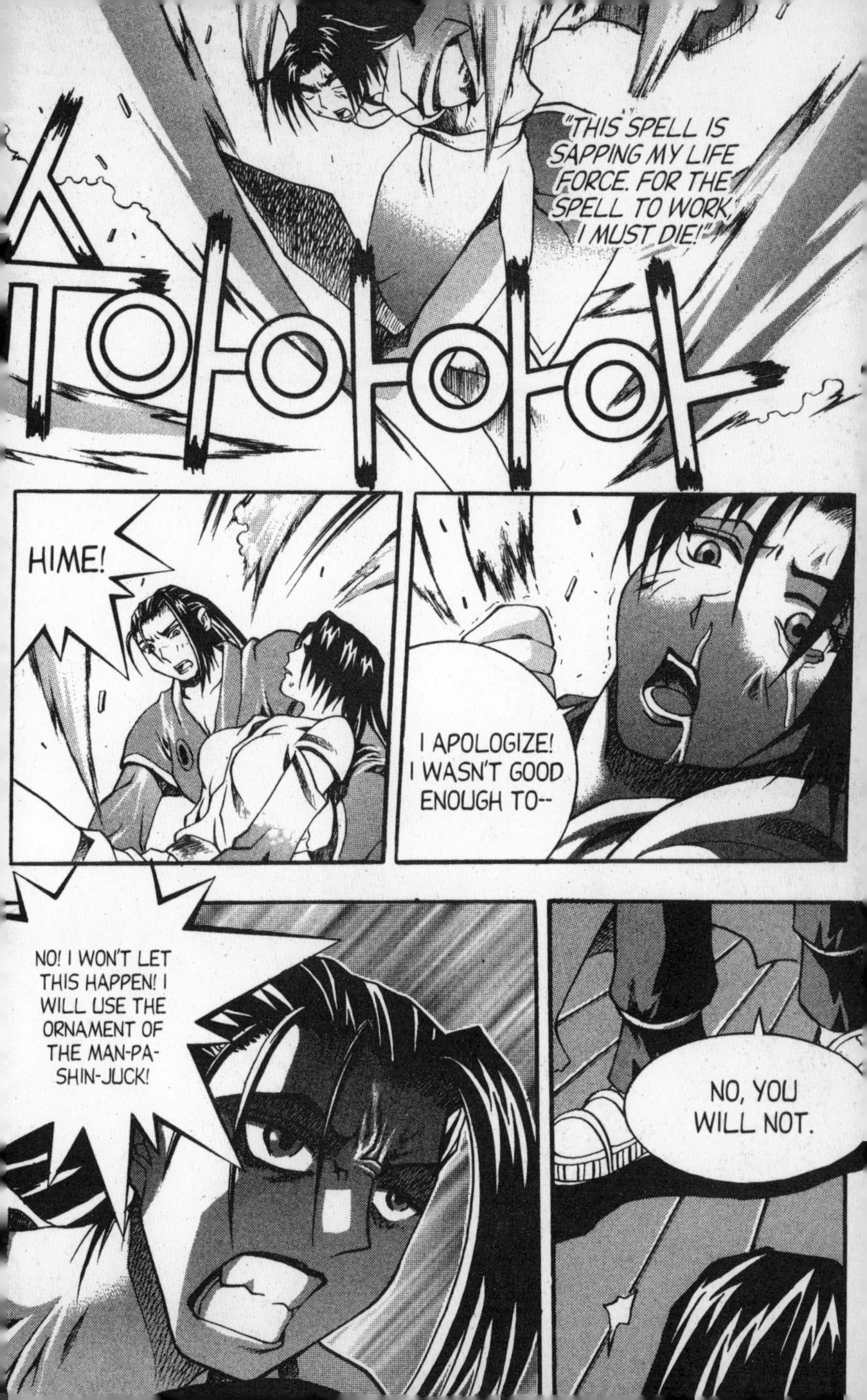
"THIS SPELL IS SAPPING MY LIFE FORCE. FOR THE SPELL TO WORK, I MUST DIE!"
HIME!
I APOLOGIZE! I WASN'T GOOD ENOUGH TO--
NO! I WON'T LET THIS HAPPEN! I WILL USE THE ORNAMENT OF THE MAN-PA-SHIN-JUCK!
NO, YOU WILL NOT.

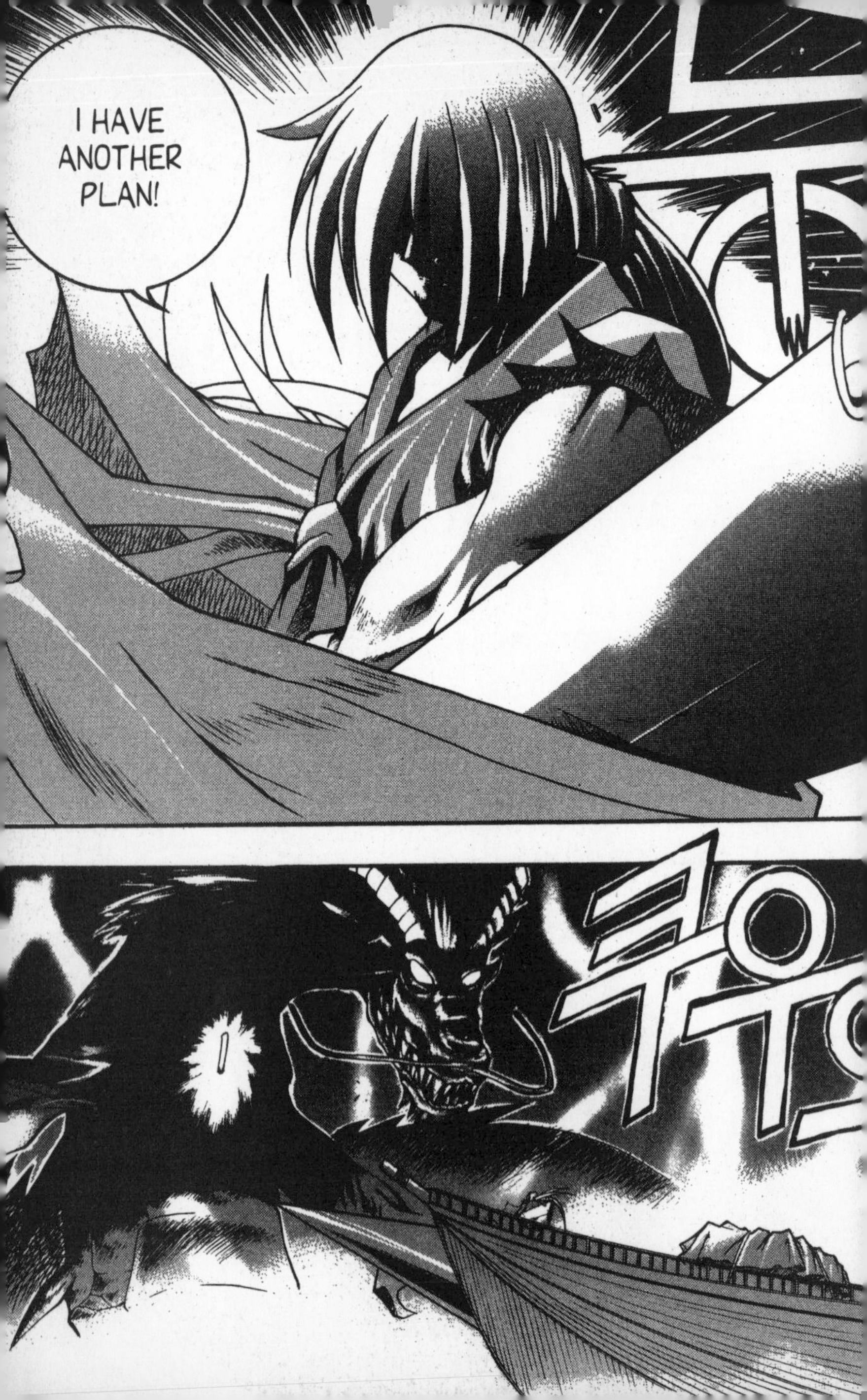
I HAVE ANOTHER PLAN!

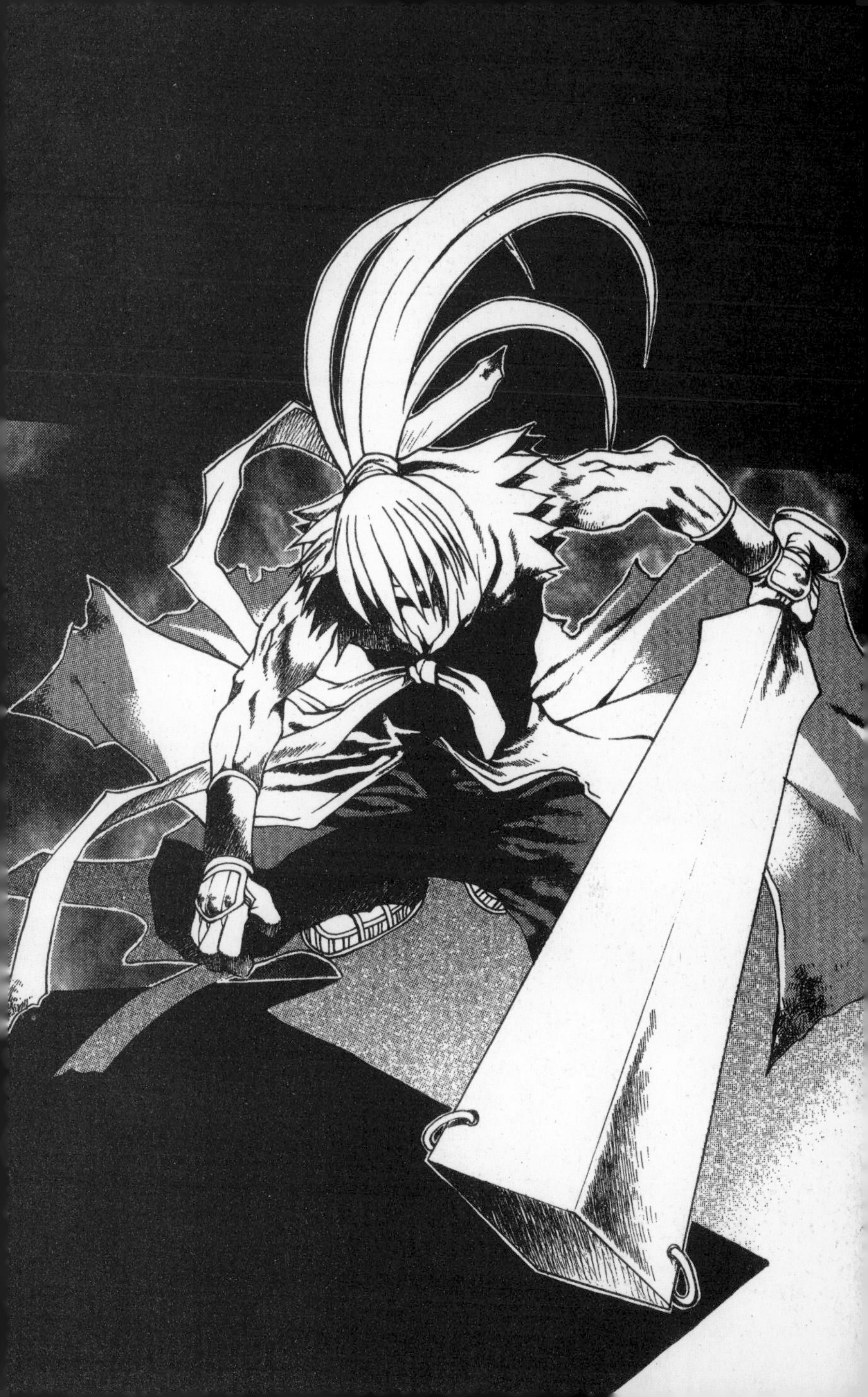

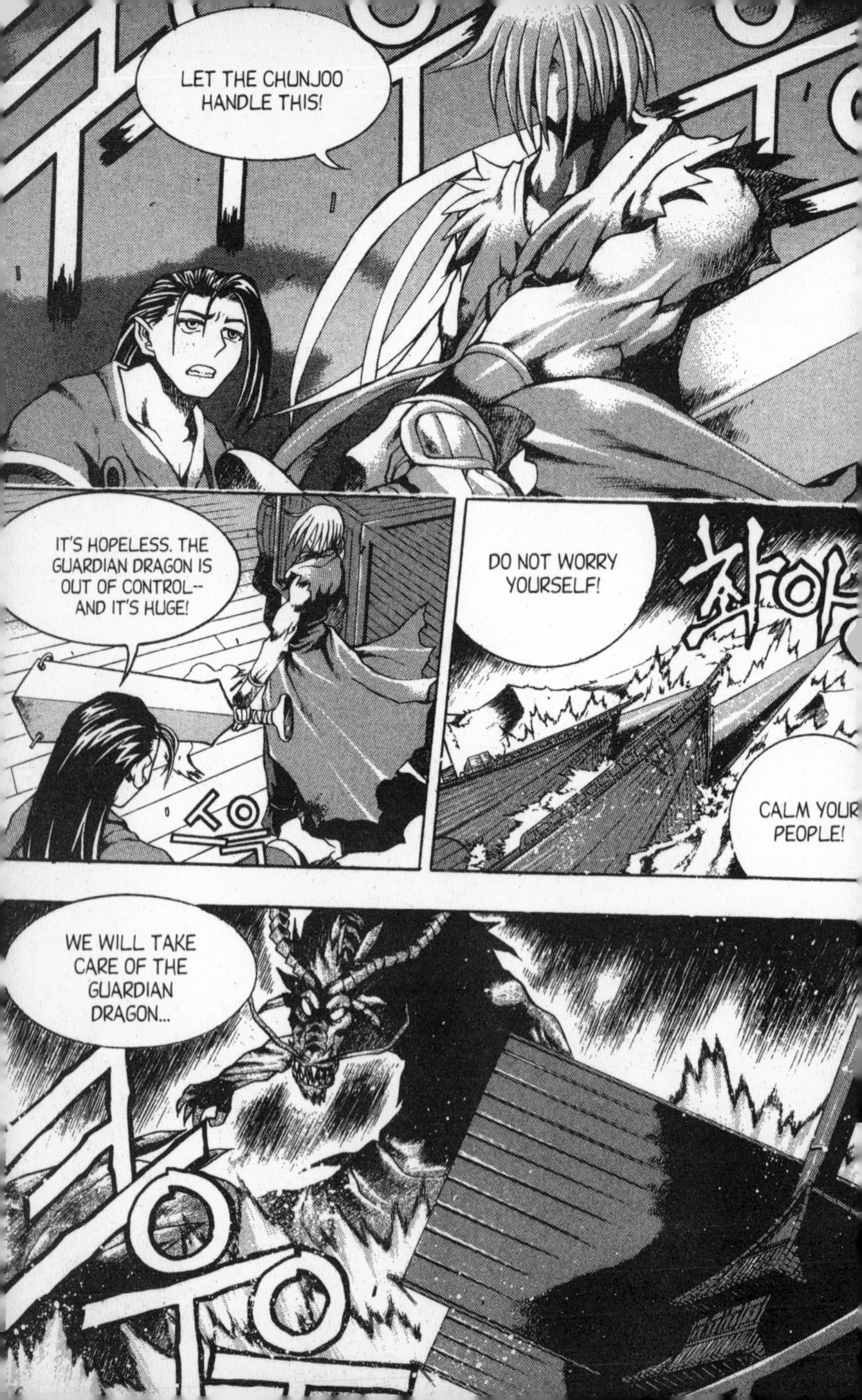
LET THE CHUNJOO HANDLE THIS!
IT'S HOPELESS. THE GUARDIAN DRAGON IS OUT OF CONTROL-- AND IT'S HUGE!
DO NOT WORRY YOURSELF!
CALM YOUR PEOPLE!
WE WILL TAKE CARE OF THE GUARDIAN DRAGON...

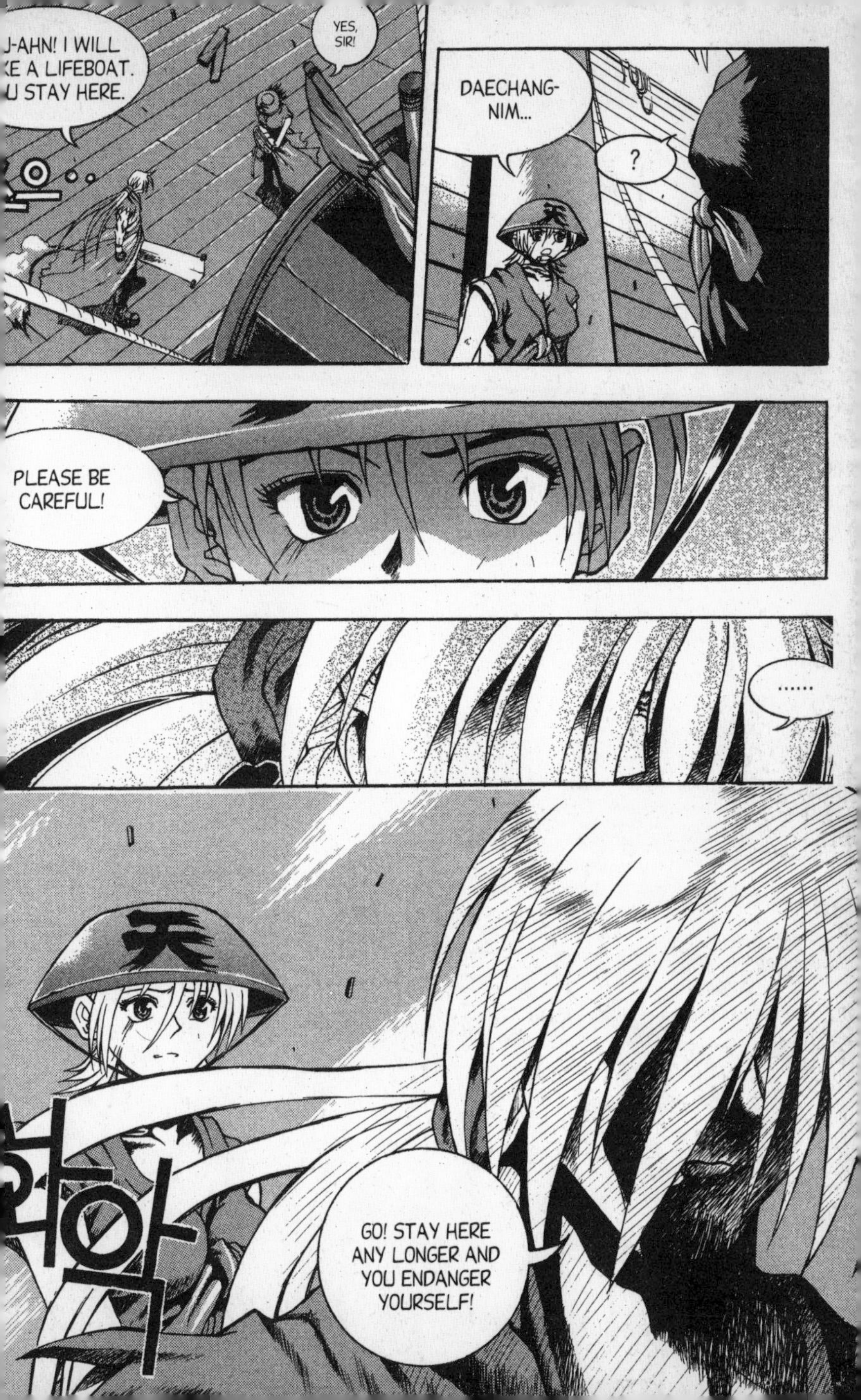

-AHN! I WILL
E A LIFEBOAT.
U STAY HERE.
YES, SIR!
DAECHANG-NIM...
?
PLEASE BE CAREFUL!
......
GO! STAY HERE ANY LONGER AND YOU ENDANGER YOURSELF!

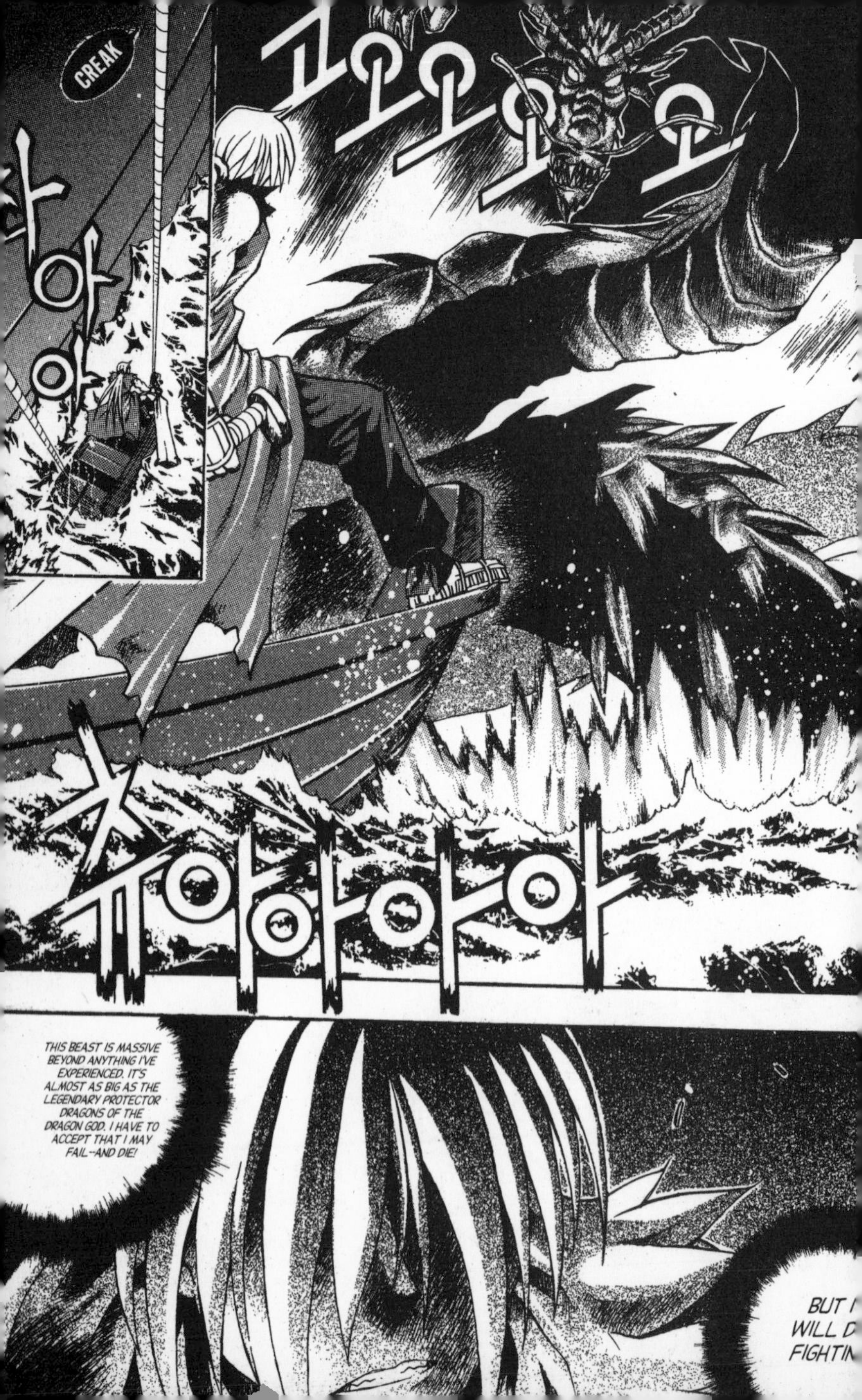
CREAK
THIS BEAST IS MASSIVE BEYOND ANYTHING I'VE EXPERIENCED. IT'S ALMOST AS BIG AS THE LEGENDARY PROTECTOR DRAGONS OF THE DRAGON GOD. I HAVE TO ACCEPT THAT I MAY FAIL--AND DIE!
BUT I WILL D FIGHTIN

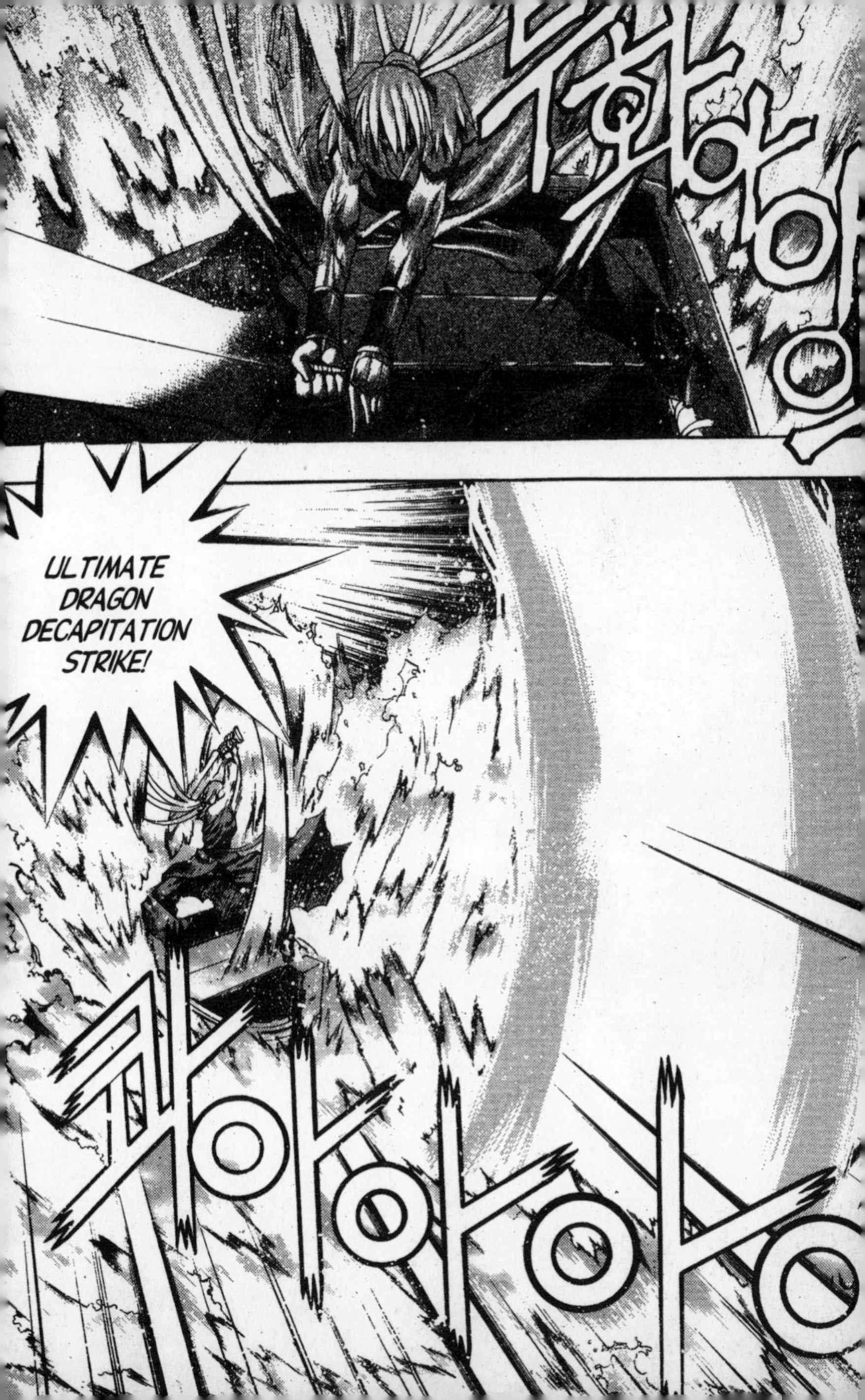
ULTIMATE DRAGON DECAPITATION STRIKE!

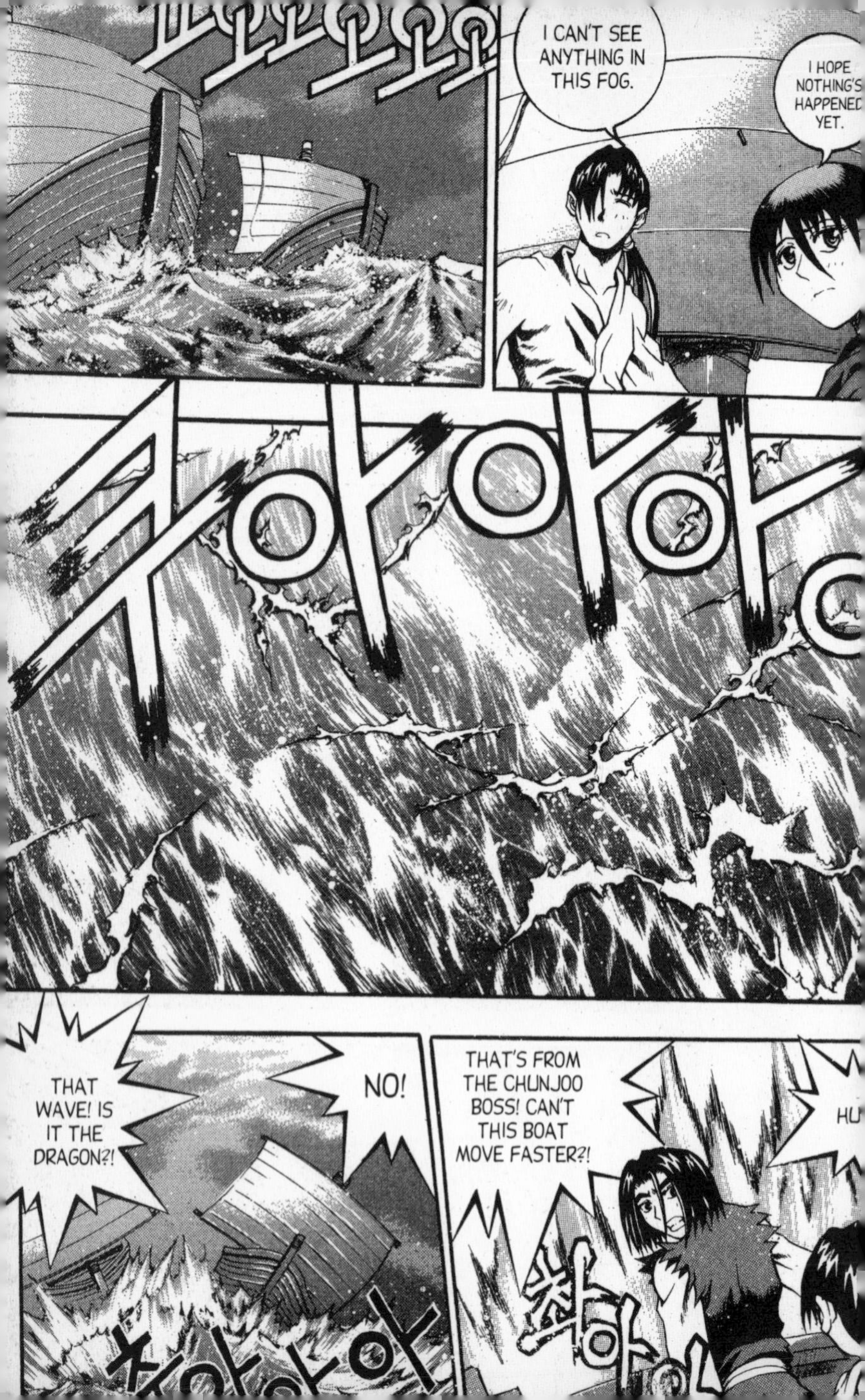
I CAN'T SEE ANYTHING IN THIS FOG.
I HOPE NOTHING'S HAPPENED YET.
THAT WAVE! IS IT THE DRAGON?!
NO!
THAT'S FROM THE CHUNJOO BOSS! CAN'T THIS BOAT MOVE FASTER?!

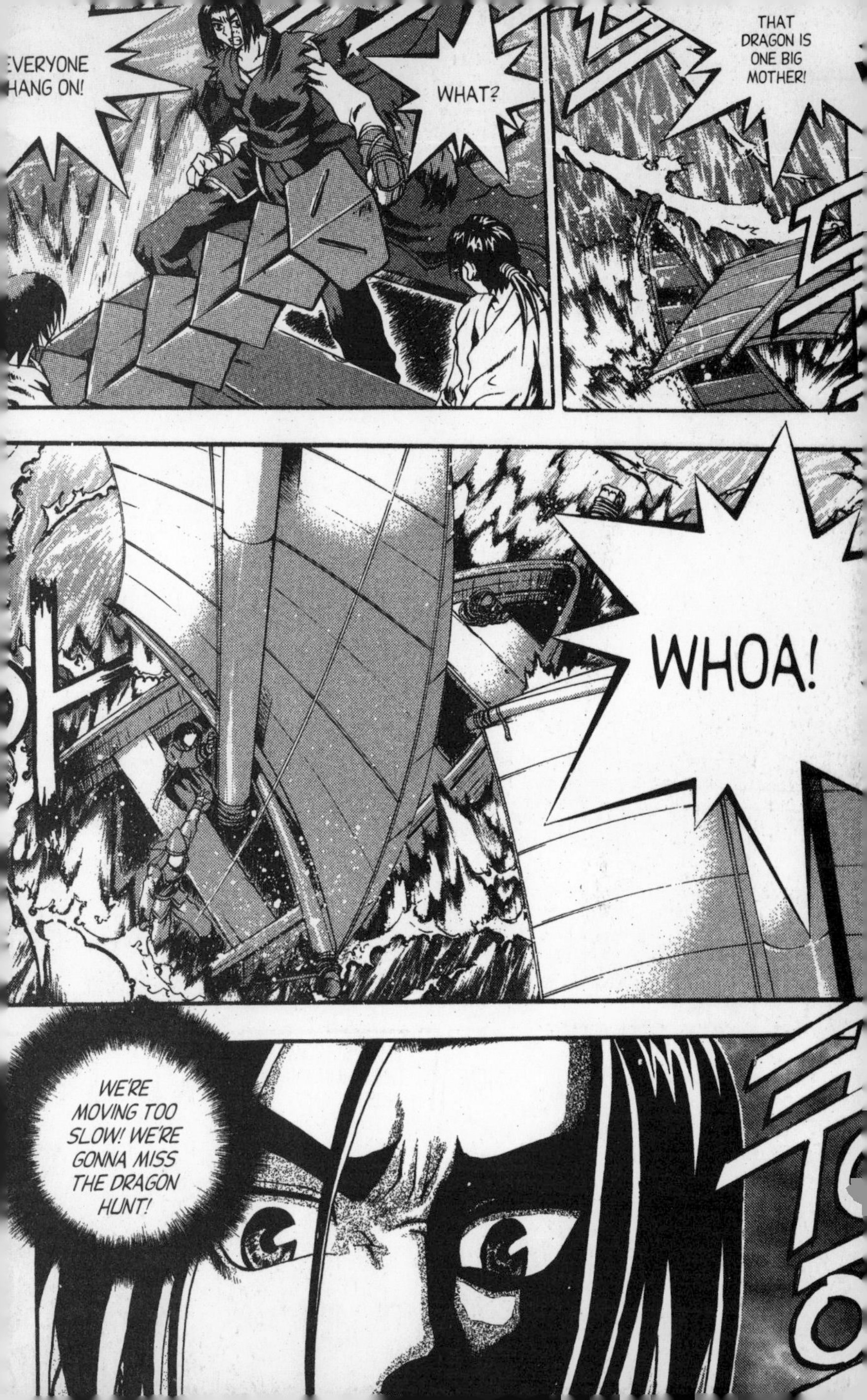
EVERYONE HANG ON!
WHAT?
THAT DRAGON IS ONE BIG MOTHER!
WHOA!
WE'RE MOVING TOO SLOW! WE'RE GONNA MISS THE DRAGON HUNT!

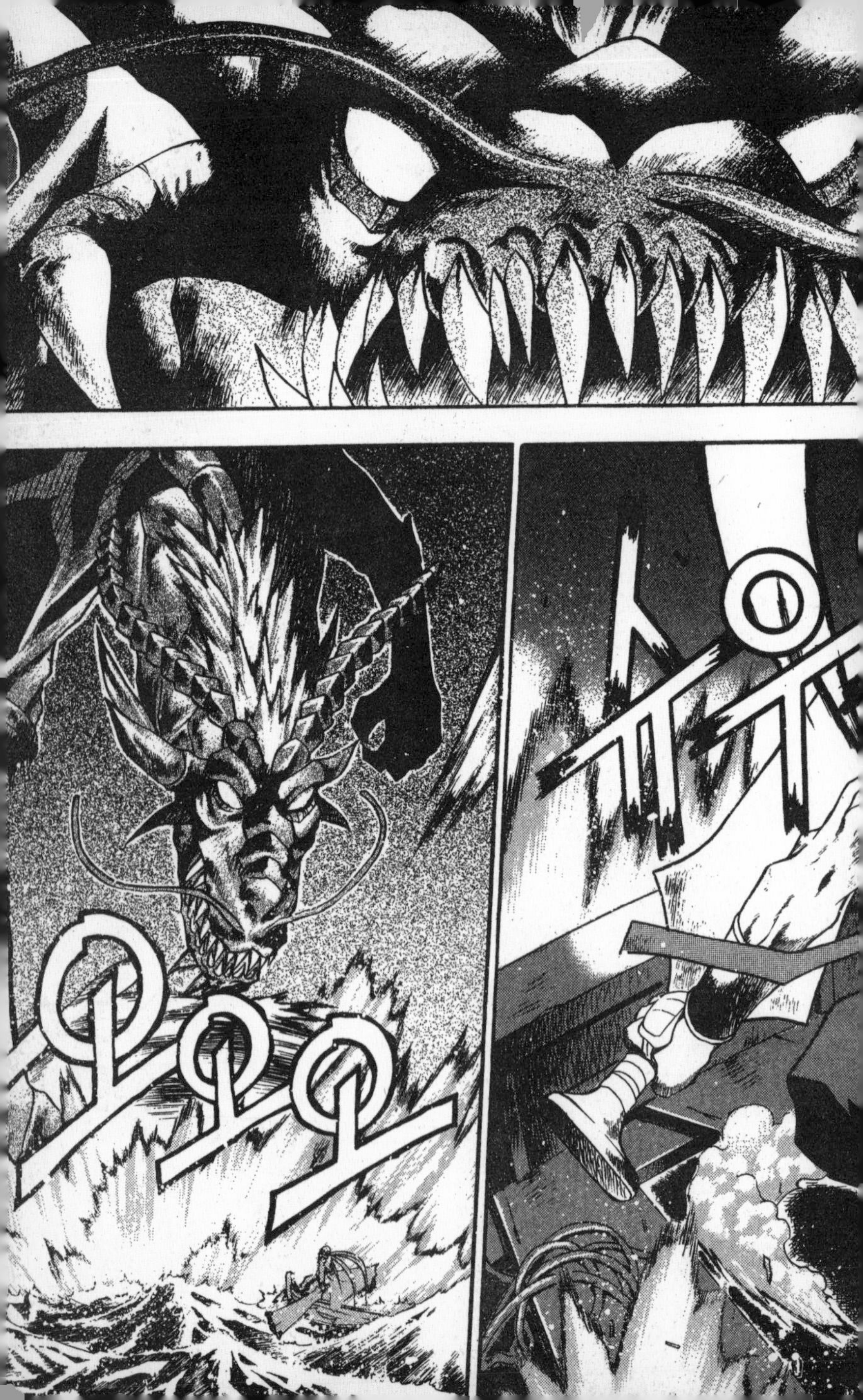

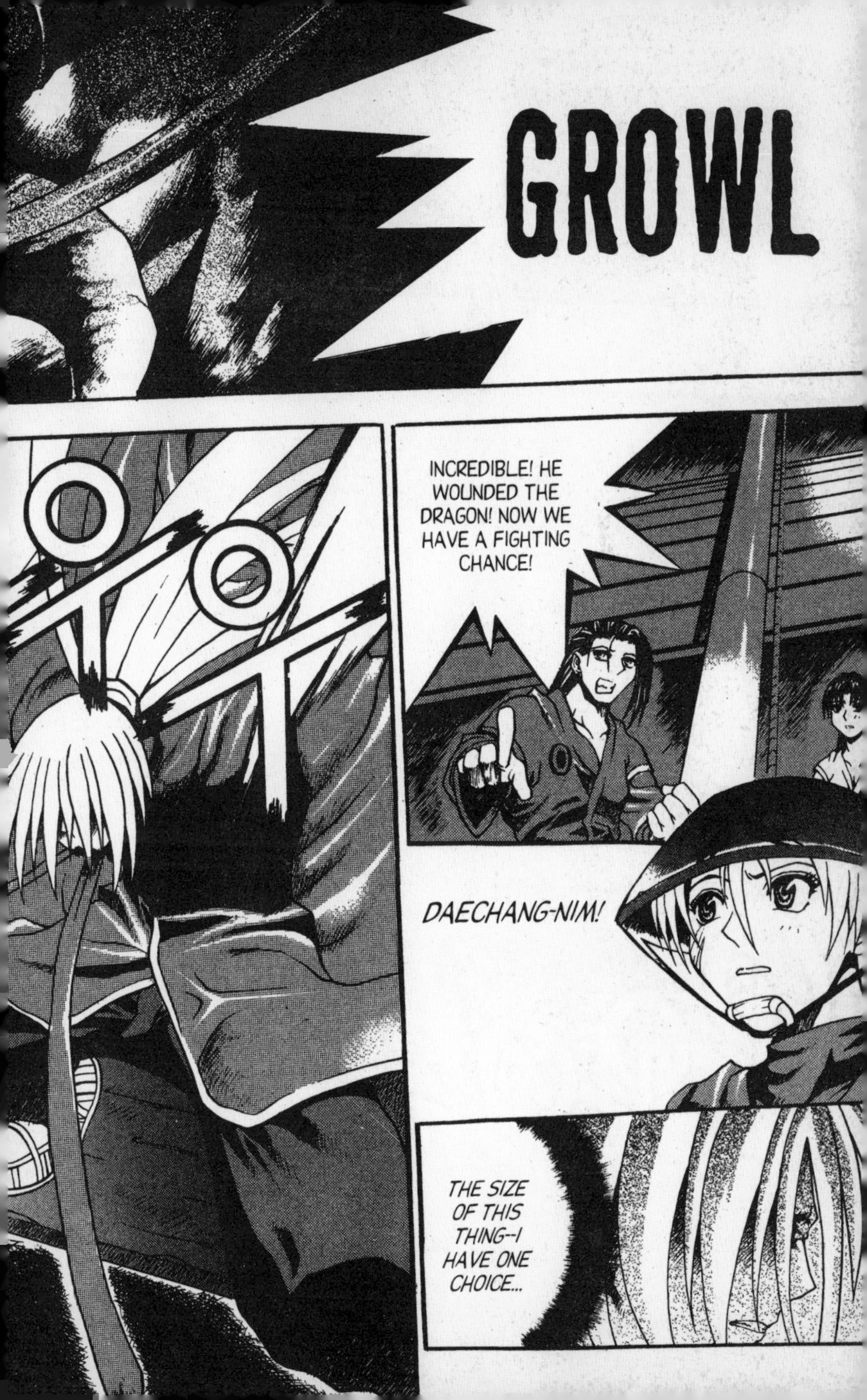
GROWL
INCREDIBLE! HE WOUNDED THE DRAGON! NOW WE HAVE A FIGHTING CHANCE!
DAECHANG-NIM!
THE SIZE OF THIS THING--I HAVE ONE CHOICE...

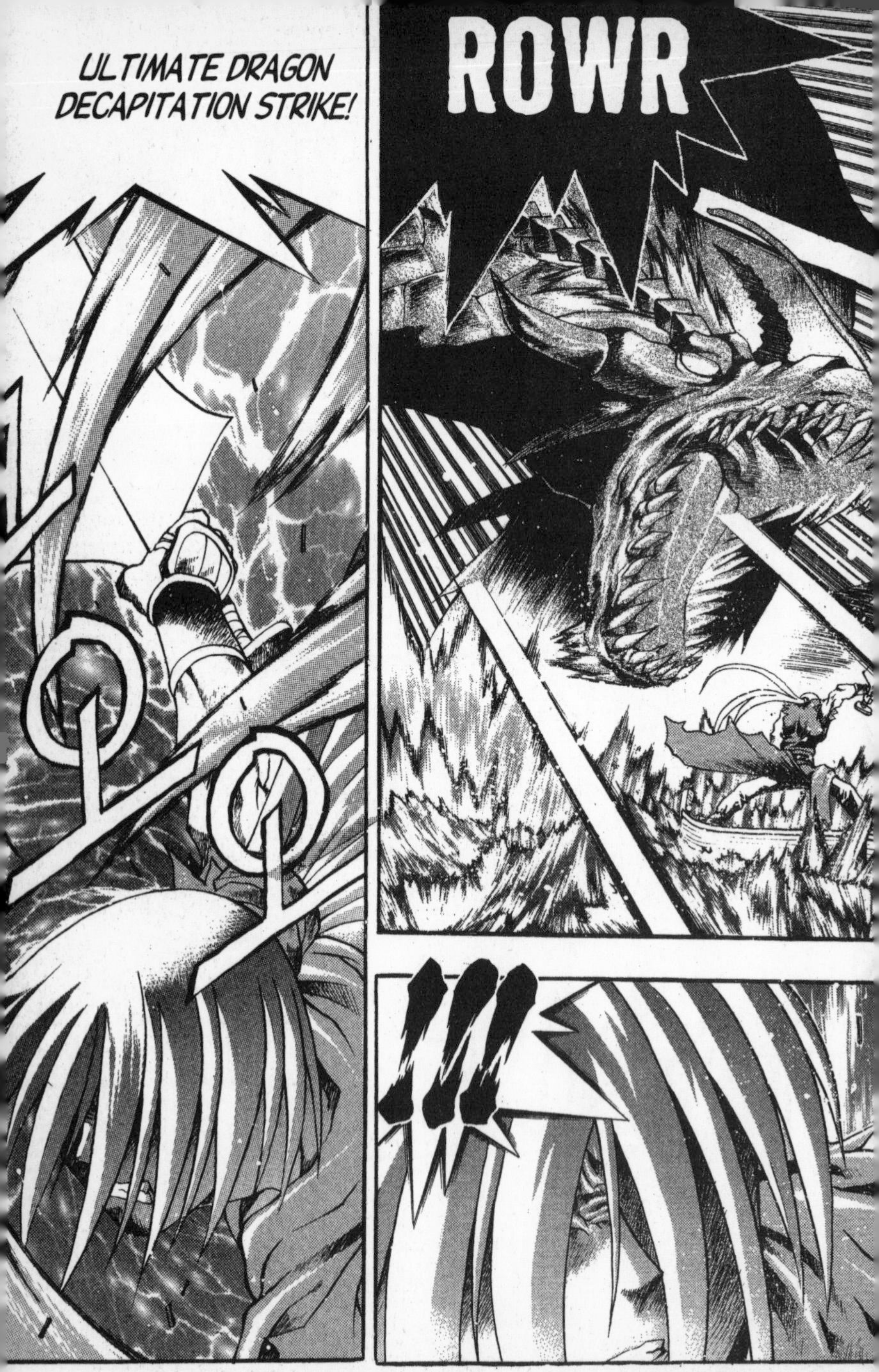
ULTIMATE DRAGON DECAPITATION STRIKE!
ROWR
!!!

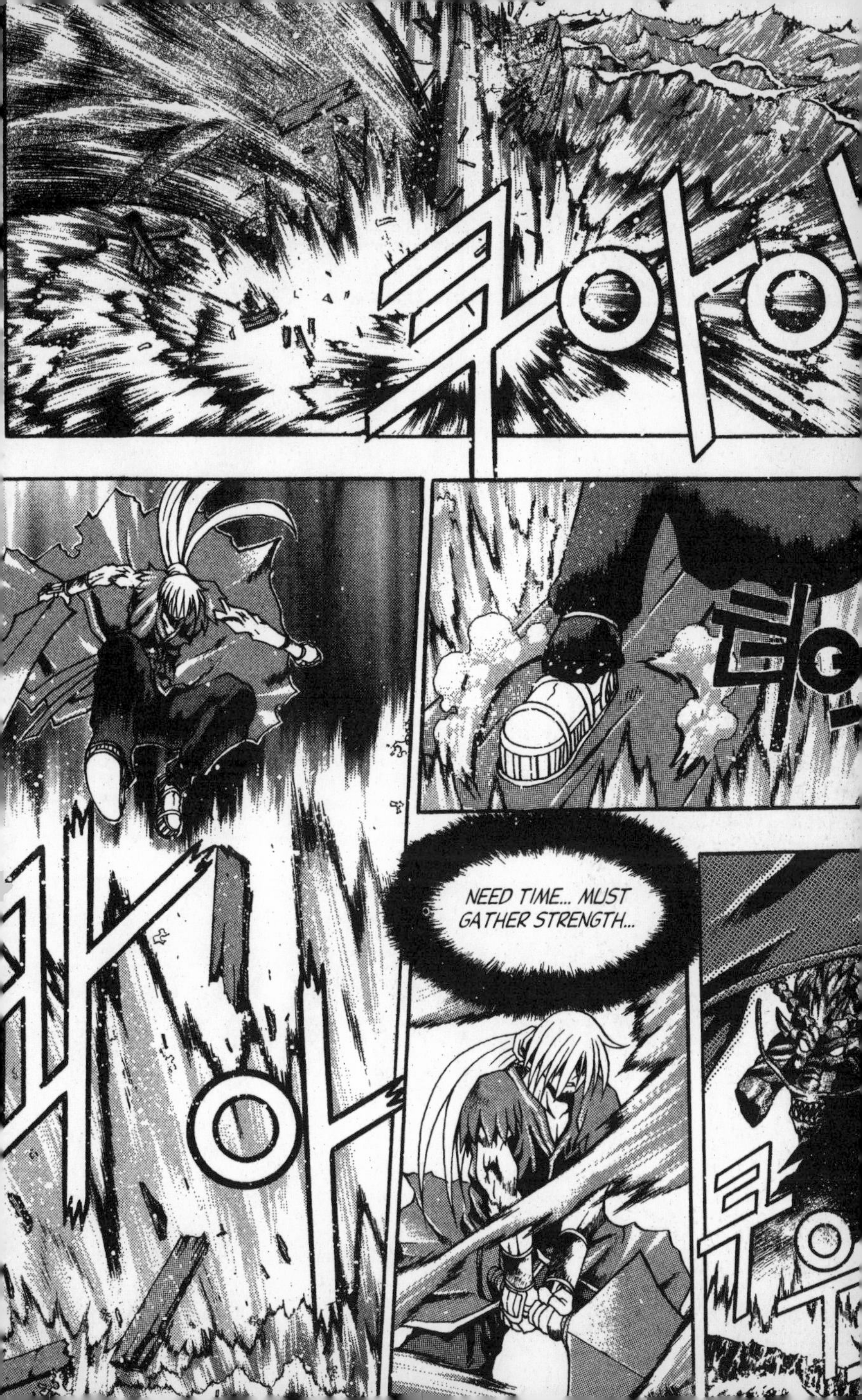
NEED TIME... MUST GATHER STRENGTH...

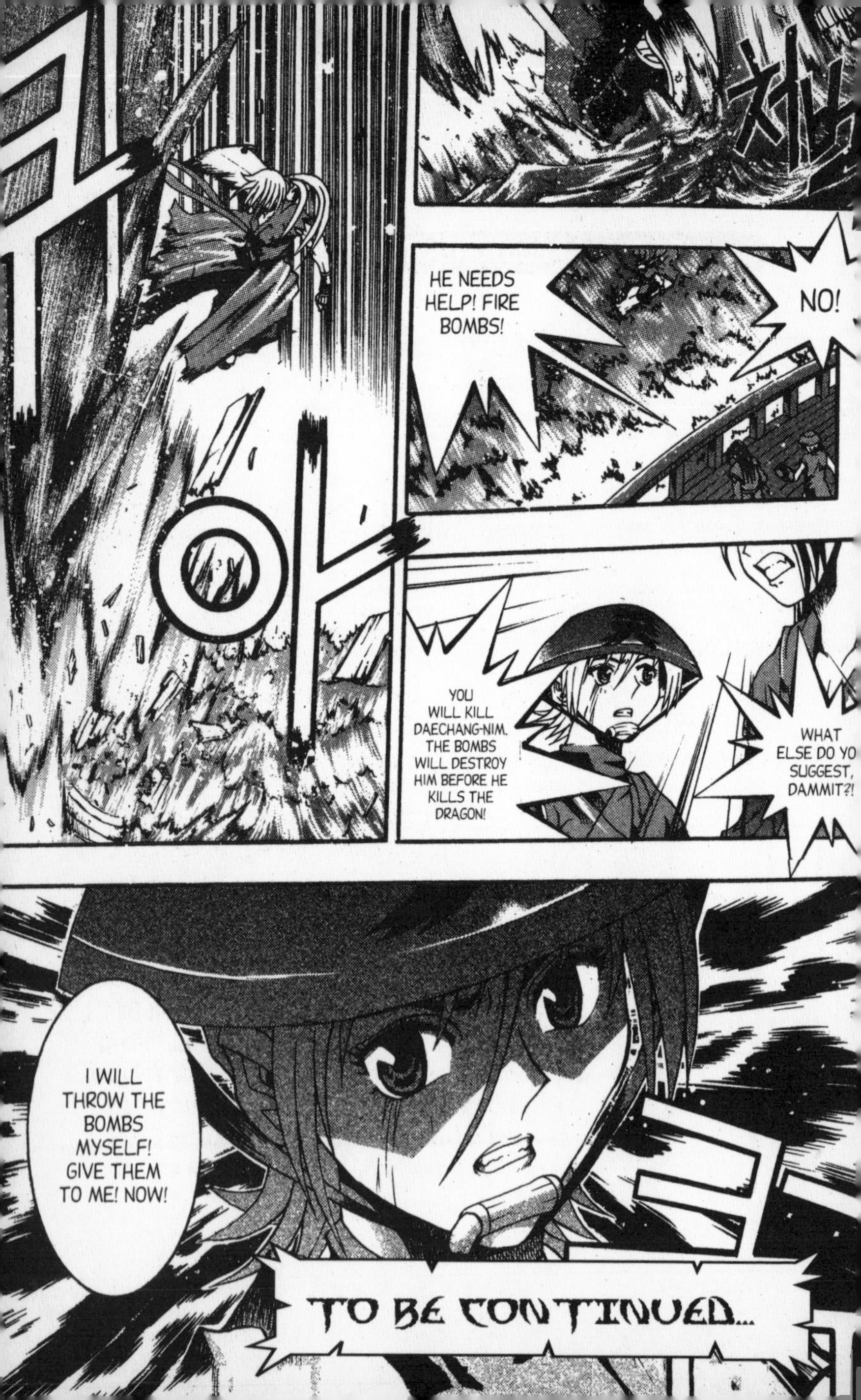
HE NEEDS HELP! FIRE BOMBS!
NO!
YOU WILL KILL DAECHANG-NIM. THE BOMBS WILL DESTROY HIM BEFORE HE KILLS THE DRAGON!
WHAT ELSE DO YO SUGGEST, DAMMIT?!
I WILL THROW THE BOMBS MYSELF! GIVE THEM TO ME! NOW!
TO BE CONTINUED...

THE STUDIO REDSTONE STORY (CHAPTER 4)

Greetings! I hope you enjoyed the intriguing developments in Volume 4 of Dragon Hunter! As for me, things have been rather eventful since last issue. Really!

As I told you last time, I got married! My wife works in comics too! I'm a lot happier now than when I was a single guy.

And guess what? I have a new studio. After I got married, I had to find a new place to work. But I have a great commute--the new place is right in my neighborhood. I can walk there in the time it takes me to drink one cup of coffee.

And here's the best thing: the studio staff has switched from all boys to all girls. The studio doesn't look so messy anymore, and I don't have to stock as much food. But these girls are a noisy bunch! Anyway, I hope they do a good job.

Finally, here's funny news! As I was writing this, I got a phone call from my editor. She said, "Hong Seock, we have almost enough pages for Volume 5. Finish that next chapter in a damn hurry!" I guess I'm quicker than I thought! Volume 5 will be out in two months! Until then, take it easy!

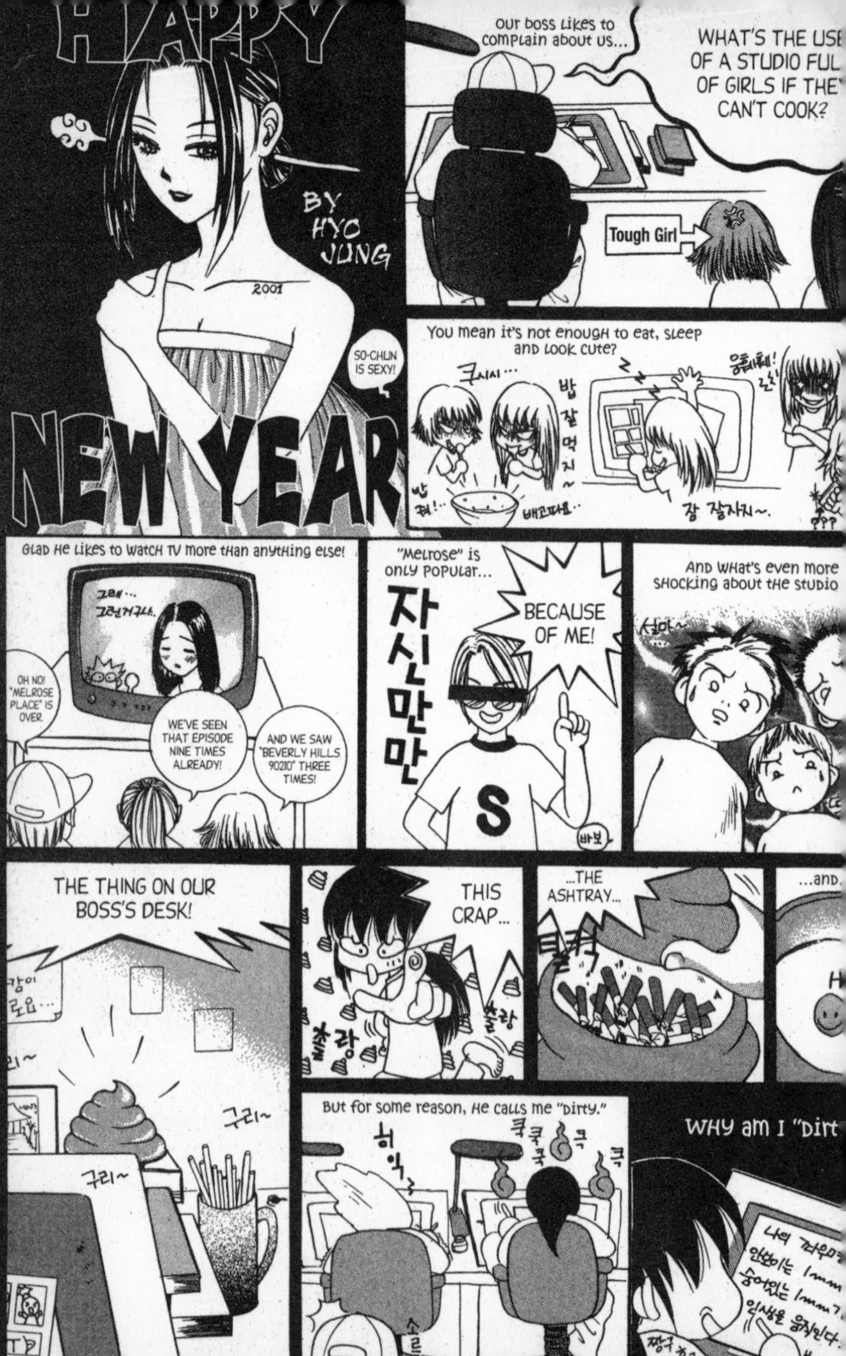

HAPPY
BY HYO JUNG
2001
SO-CHUN IS SEXY!
NEW YEAR
Our boss likes to complain about us...
WHAT'S THE USE OF A STUDIO FULL OF GIRLS IF THEY CAN'T COOK?
Tough Girl
You mean it's not enough to eat, sleep and look cute?
밥 잘 먹지~
배고파요..
잠 잘자지~.
???
Glad he likes to watch TV more than anything else!
그래... 그런거구나.
OH NO! "MELROSE PLACE" IS OVER.
WE'VE SEEN THAT EPISODE NINE TIMES ALREADY!
AND WE SAW "BEVERLY HILLS 90210" THREE TIMES!
"Melrose" is only popular...
자신만만
BECAUSE OF ME!
S
바보
And what's even more shocking about the studio
설마~
THE THING ON OUR BOSS'S DESK!
구리~
구리~
구리~
THIS CRAP...
...THE ASHTRAY...
...and...
But for some reason, he calls me "dirty."
쿡쿡 쿡 쿡
WHY am I "Dirt

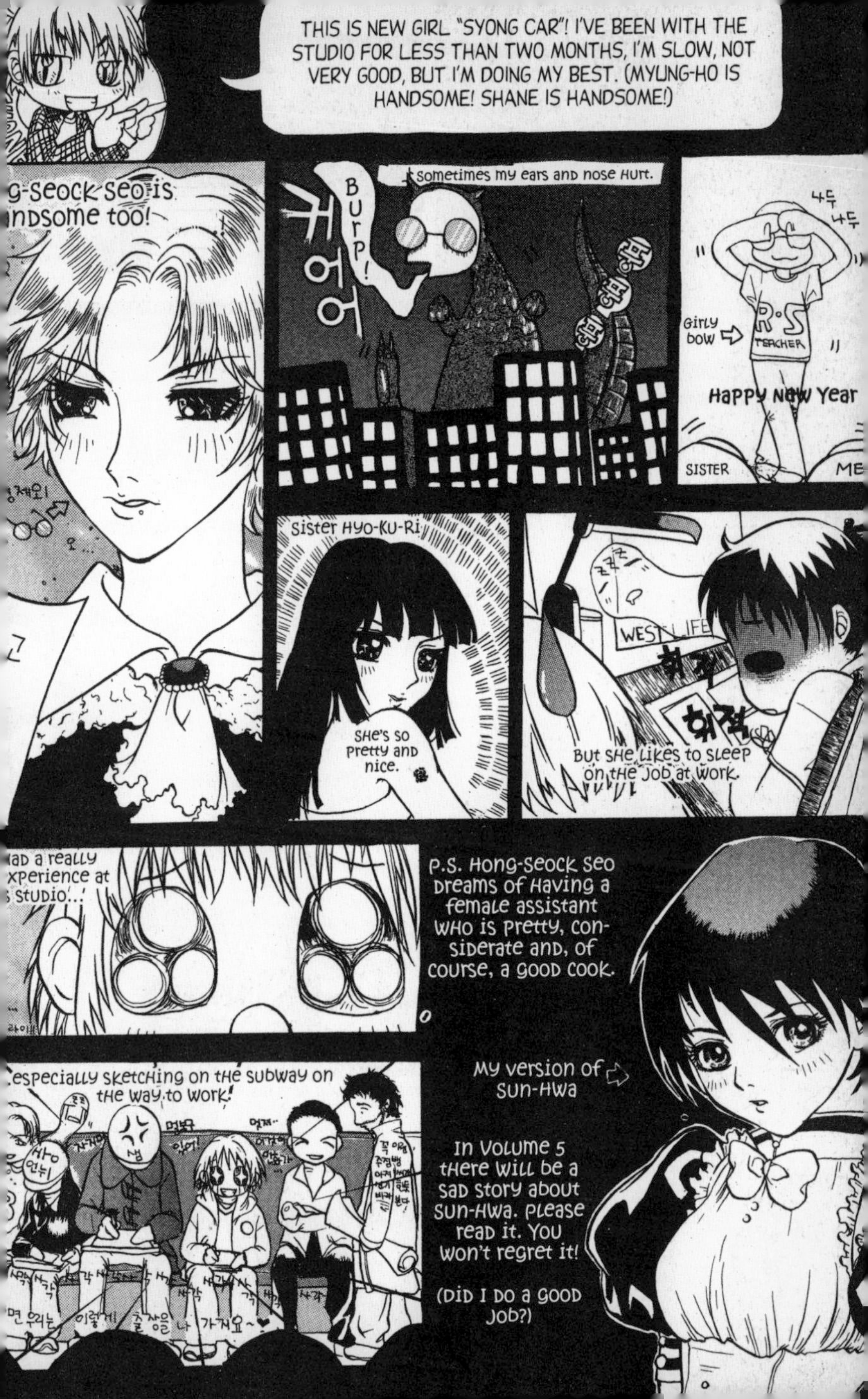

THIS IS NEW GIRL "SYONG CAR"! I'VE BEEN WITH THE STUDIO FOR LESS THAN TWO MONTHS, I'M SLOW, NOT VERY GOOD, BUT I'M DOING MY BEST. (MYUNG-HO IS HANDSOME! SHANE IS HANDSOME!)
g-seock seo is
ndsome too!
Sometimes my ears and nose hurt.
Burp!
Girly bow
R·S
TEACHER
Happy New Year
SISTER
ME
Sister Hyo-Ku-Ri
She's so pretty and nice.
WEST LIFE
But she likes to sleep on the job at work.
ad a really
xperience at
s studio...!
P.S. Hong-seock seo dreams of having a female assistant who is pretty, considerate and, of course, a good cook.
especially sketching on the subway on the way to work!
My version of Sun-Hwa
In Volume 5 there will be a sad story about Sun-Hwa. Please read it. You won't regret it!
(Did I do a good job?)

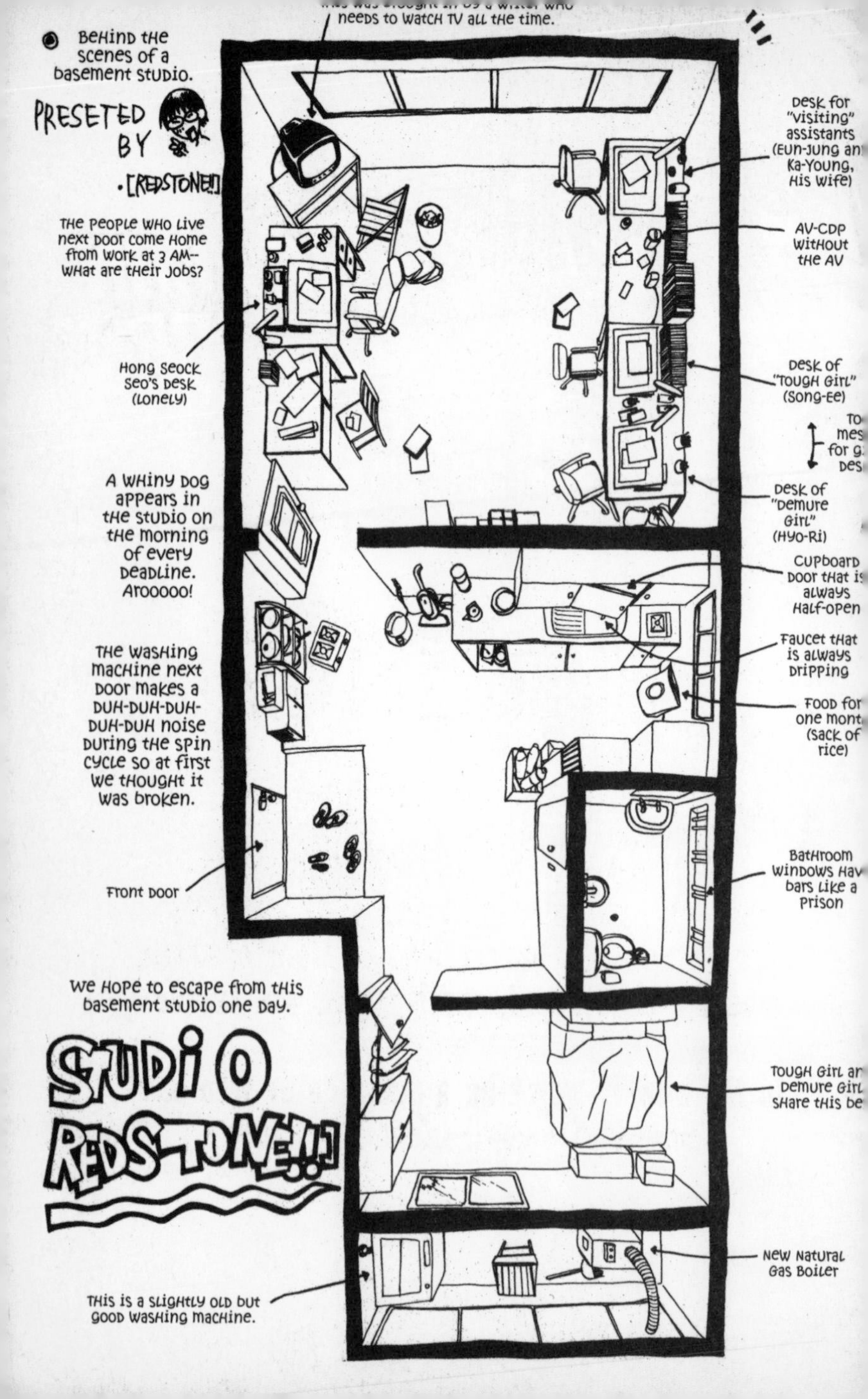

needs to watch TV all the time.
Behind the scenes of a basement studio.
PRESETED BY
·[REDSTONE!!]
The people who live next door come home from work at 3 AM-- what are their jobs?
Hong Seock Seo's desk (lonely)
A whiny dog appears in the studio on the morning of every deadline. Arooooo!
The washing machine next door makes a DUH-DUH-DUH-DUH-DUH noise during the spin cycle so at first we thought it was broken.
Front door
We hope to escape from this basement studio one day.
STUDIO REDSTONE!!]
This is a slightly old but good washing machine.
Desk for "visiting" assistants (Eun-Jung an Ka-Young, his wife)
AV-CDP without the AV
Desk of "Tough Girl" (Song-Ee)
Desk of "Demure Girl" (Hyo-Ri)
Cupboard door that is always half-open
Faucet that is always dripping
Food for one mont (sack of rice)
Bathroom windows hav bars like a prison
Tough Girl an Demure Girl share this be
New Natural Gas Boiler

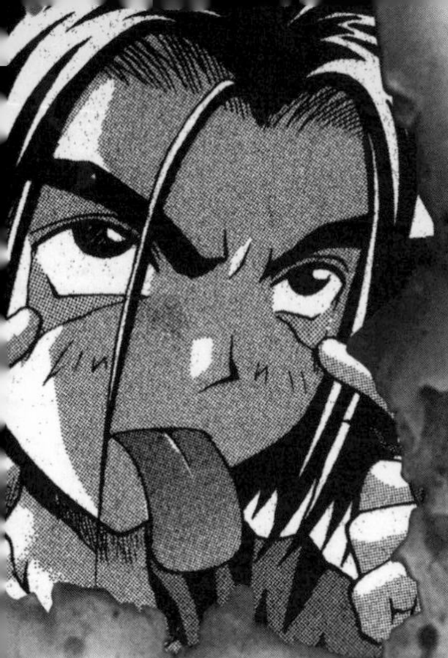

DRAGON HUNTER

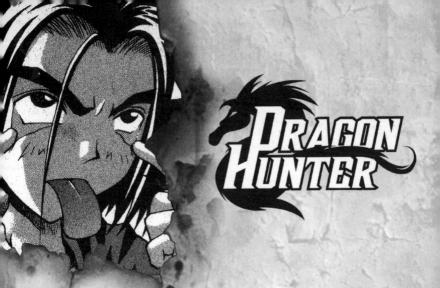

IN THE NEXT VOLUME OF DRAGON HUNTER

• • • • • •

The fight for the Man-Pa-Shin-Juck reaches new heights of chaos. In the midst of a devastating battle, alliances are changed, trusts are betrayed, and loyalties are tested.

In the end, it won't be a question of who has won...but who has lost the most!

MANGA

.HACK//LEGEND OF THE TWILIGHT
@LARGE
A.I. LOVE YOU February 2004
AI YORI AOSHI January 2004
ANGELIC LAYER
BABY BIRTH
BATTLE ROYALE
BATTLE VIXENS April 2004
BIRTH May 2004
BRAIN POWERED
BRIGADOON
B'TX January 2004
CARDCAPTOR SAKURA
CARDCAPTOR SAKURA: MASTER OF THE CLOW
CARDCAPTOR SAKURA: BOXED SET COLLECTION 1
CARDCAPTOR SAKURA: BOXED SET COLLECTION 2
   March 2004
CHOBITS
CHRONICLES OF THE CURSED SWORD
CLAMP SCHOOL DETECTIVES
CLOVER
COMIC PARTY June 2004
CONFIDENTIAL CONFESSIONS
CORRECTOR YUI
COWBOY BEBOP: BOXED SET THE COMPLETE
   COLLECTION
CRESCENT MOON May 2004
CREST OF THE STARS June 2004
CYBORG 009
DEMON DIARY
DIGIMON
DIGIMON SERIES 3 April 2004
DIGIMON ZERO TWO February 2004
DNANGEL April 2004
DOLL May 2004
DRAGON HUNTER
DRAGON KNIGHTS
DUKLYON: CLAMP SCHOOL DEFENDERS
DV June 2004
ERICA SAKURAZAWA
FAERIES' LANDING January 2004
FAKE
FLCL
FORBIDDEN DANCE
FRUITS BASKET February 2004
G GUNDAM
GATEKEEPERS
GETBACKERS February 2004
GHOST! March 2004
GIRL GOT GAME January 2004
GRAVITATION
GTO

GUNDAM WING
GUNDAM WING: BATTLEFIELD OF PACIFISTS
GUNDAM WING: ENDLESS WALTZ
GUNDAM WING: THE LAST OUTPOST
HAPPY MANIA
HARLEM BEAT
I.N.V.U.
INITIAL D
ISLAND
JING: KING OF BANDITS
JULINE
JUROR 13 March 2004
KARE KANO
KILL ME, KISS ME February 2004
KINDAICHI CASE FILES, THE
KING OF HELL
KODOCHA: SANA'S STAGE
LAMENT OF THE LAMB May 2004
LES BIJOUX February 2004
LIZZIE MCGUIRE
LOVE HINA
LUPIN III
LUPIN III SERIES 2
MAGIC KNIGHT RAYEARTH I
MAGIC KNIGHT RAYEARTH II February 2004
MAHOROMATIC: AUTOMATIC MAIDEN May 2004
MAN OF MANY FACES
MARMALADE BOY
MARS
METEOR METHUSELA June 2004
METROID June 2004
MINK April 2004
MIRACLE GIRLS
MIYUKI-CHAN IN WONDERLAND
MODEL May 2004
NELLY MUSIC MANGA April 2004
ONE April 2004
PARADISE KISS
PARASYTE
PEACH GIRL
PEACH GIRL CHANGE OF HEART
PEACH GIRL RELAUNCH BOX SET
PET SHOP OF HORRORS
PITA-TEN January 2004
PLANET LADDER February 2004
PLANETES
PRIEST
PRINCESS AI April 2004
PSYCHIC ACADEMY March 2004
RAGNAROK
RAGNAROK: BOXED SET COLLECTION 1
RAVE MASTER
RAVE MASTER: BOXED SET March 2004

10103

ALSO AVAILABLE FROM  TOKYOPOP®

REALITY CHECK
REBIRTH
REBOUND
REMOTE June 2004
RISING STARS OF MANGA December 2003
SABER MARIONETTE J
SAILOR MOON
SAINT TAIL
SAIYUKI
SAMURAI DEEPER KYO
SAMURAI GIRL REAL BOUT HIGH SCHOOL
SCRYED
SGT. FROG March 2004
SHAOLIN SISTERS
SHIRAHIME-SYO: SNOW GODDESS TALES December 2004
SHUTTERBOX
SNOW DROP January 2004
SOKORA REFUGEES May 2004
SORCEROR HUNTERS
SUIKODEN May 2004
SUKI February 2004
THE CANDIDATE FOR GODDESS April 2004
THE DEMON ORORON April 2004
THE LEGEND OF CHUN HYANG
THE SKULL MAN
THE VISION OF ESCAFLOWNE
TOKYO MEW MEW
TREASURE CHESS March 2004
UNDER THE GLASS MOON
VAMPIRE GAME
WILD ACT
WISH
WORLD OF HARTZ
X-DAY
ZODIAC P.I.

NOVELS

KARMA CLUB APRIL 2004
SAILOR MOON

ART BOOKS

CARDCAPTOR SAKURA
MAGIC KNIGHT RAYEARTH
PEACH GIRL ART BOOK April 2004

ANIME GUIDES

COWBOY BEBOP ANIME GUIDES
GUNDAM TECHNICAL MANUALS
SAILOR MOON SCOUT GUIDES

CINE-MANGA™

CARDCAPTORS
FAIRLY ODD PARENTS MARCH 2004
FINDING NEMO
G.I. JOE SPY TROOPS
JACKIE CHAN ADVENTURES
KIM POSSIBLE
LIZZIE MCGUIRE
POWER RANGERS: NINJA STORM
SPONGEBOB SQUAREPANTS
SPY KIDS
SPY KIDS 3-D March 2004
THE ADVENTURES OF JIMMY NEUTRON: BOY GENIUS
TRANSFORMERS: ARMADA
TRANSFORMERS: ENERGON May 2004

TOKYOPOP KIDS

STRAY SHEEP

For more
information visit
www.TOKYOPOP.com

10103

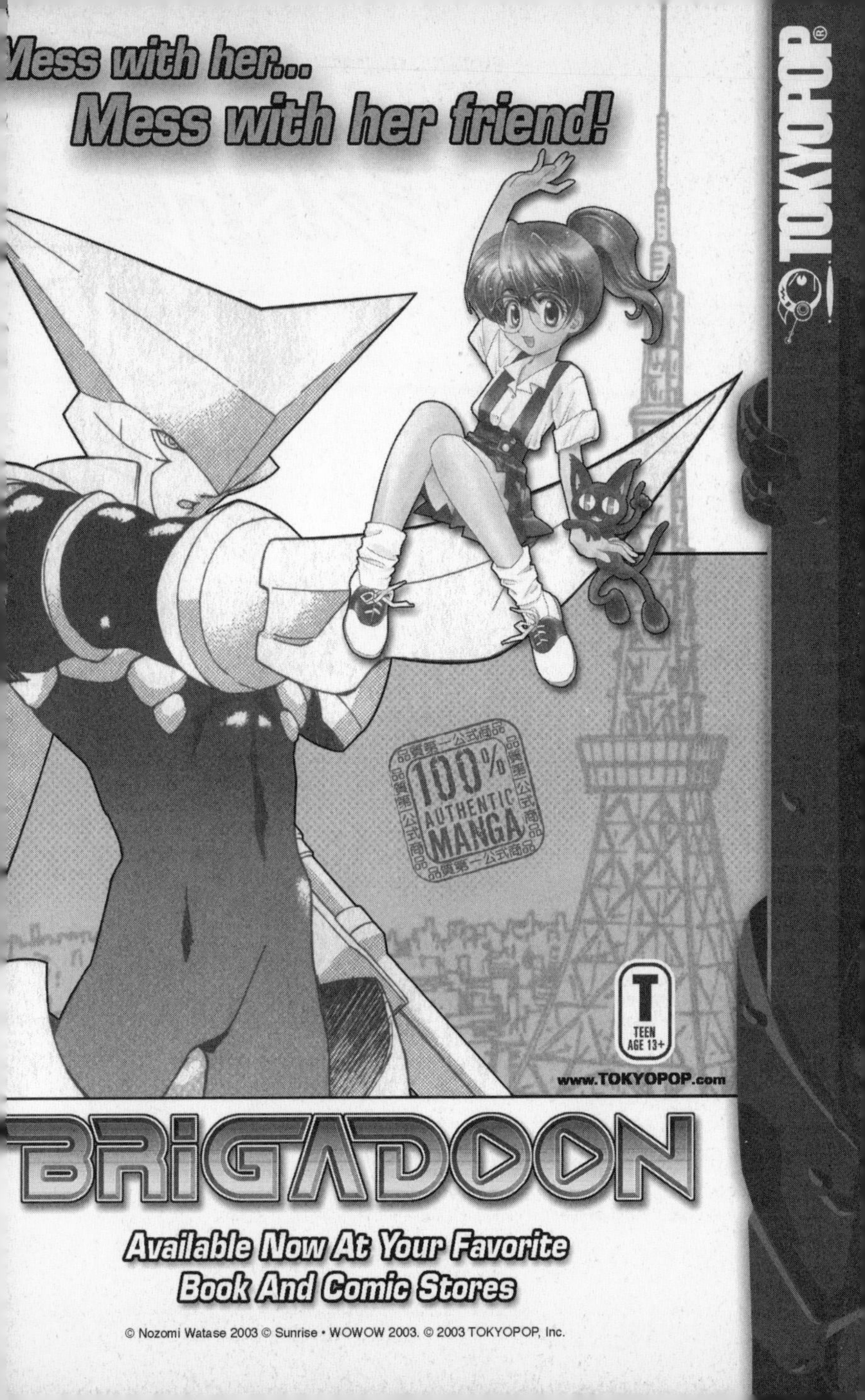
Mess with her...
Mess with her friend!
TOKYOPOP
100% AUTHENTIC MANGA
T
TEEN AGE 13+
www.TOKYOPOP.com
BRIGADOON
Available Now At Your Favorite
Book And Comic Stores
© Nozomi Watase 2003 © Sunrise • WOWOW 2003. © 2003 TOKYOPOP, Inc.